GENDER AND POLITICS IN AUSTRIAN FICTION

Edited by Ritchie Robertson and Edward Timms
AUSTRIAN STUDIES VII

GENDER AND POLITICS IN AUSTRIAN FICTION

Edited by Ritchie Robertson and Edward Timms

AUSTRIAN STUDIES VII

EDINBURGH UNIVERSITY PRESS

© Edinburgh University Press, 1996

Edinburgh University Press Ltd
22 George Square, Edinburgh

Typeset in Linotron Ehrhardt by
Koinonia Ltd, Bury, and
printed in Great Britain by
The University Press, Cambridge

A CIP record for this book is available
from the British Library

ISBN 0 7486 0838 9

Contents

Preface   ix

PART ONE

Jeffrey L. Sammons
An Austrian Jacksonian: Charles Sealsfield's Political Evolution,
1829–1833   3

Ritchie Robertson
German Idealists and American Rowdies: Ferdinand Kürnberger's
Novel *Der Amerika-Müde*   17

R. C. Ockenden
Unconscious Poesy?: Marie von Ebner-Eschenbach's *Die Poesie
des Unbewußten*   36

Ian Foster
Ferdinand von Saar's *Doktor Trojan*: Politics, Medicine and Myth   47

Jens Rieckmann
Knowing the Other: Leopold von Andrian's *Der Garten der Erkenntnis*
and the Homoerotic Discourse of the Fin de Siècle   61

Mark M. Anderson
Kafka, Homosexuality and the Aesthetics of 'Male Culture'   79

Andrew Barker
The First World War Fiction of Andreas Latzko   100

Martha Wörsching
Misogyny and the Myth of Masculinity in Joseph Roth's
Radetzkymarsch   118

Simon Tyler
Homage or Parody?: Elias Canetti and Otto Weininger   134

Stephanie Bird
'What matters who's speaking?': Identity, Experience, and Problems
with Feminism in Ingeborg Bachmann's *Malina*   150

Contents

Andrea Reiter
Austrophobia as it is: Charles Sealsfield, Thomas Bernhard and the
Art of Exaggeration   166

PART TWO: REVIEW ARTICLES

Duncan Large
Recent Studies of Musil   181

Ritchie Robertson
Keeping up with Kafka   187

PART THREE: REVIEWS

Charles Ingrao
John Stoye, *Marsigli's Europe*   192

T. J. Hochstrasser
Franz A. J. Szabo, *Kaunitz and Enlightened Absolutism 1753–1780*;
T. C. W. Blanning, *Joseph II*   193

W. E. Yates
Charles Sealsfield (Karl Postl), *Austria as it is*,
ed. Primus-Heinz Kucher   195

Raymond Lucas
Eva Wagner, *An Analysis of Franz Grillparzer's Dramas: Fate, Guilt
and Tragedy*   196

Peter Branscombe
Jeanne Benay, *Friedrich Kaiser (1814–1874) et le théâtre populaire
en Autriche au XIXᵉ siècle*   197

Patricia Howe
Ferrel V. Rose, *The Guises of Modesty: Marie von Ebner-Eschenbach's
Female Artists*   198

Jens Rieckmann
Stefan Scherer, *Richard Beer-Hofmann und die Wiener Moderne*;
Ulrike Peters, *Richard Beer-Hofmann*   199

Gilbert J. Carr
Jürgen Nautz and Richard Vahrenkamp (eds), *Die Wiener
Jahrhundertwende: Einflüsse, Umwelt, Wirkungen*   201

Brian Keith-Smith
Paul Stefanek, *Vom Ritual zum Theater*   205

Victoria Martin
Ulrike Lang, *Mordshetz und Pahöl: Austriazismen als Stilmittel bei
Karl Kraus*   206

Lothar Huber
Jennifer E. Michaels, *Franz Werfel and the Critics*   208

Contents

Joyce Crick
Darius Gray Ornston (ed.), *Translating Freud; The Complete Correspondence of Sigmund Freud and Ernest Jones, 1908–1939,* ed. R. Andrew Paskauskas   209

Karen Leeder
Allyson Fiddler, *Rewriting Reality: An Introduction to Elfriede Jelinek*   212

Andrew Barker
Joseph P. Strelka, *Zwischen Wirklichkeit und Traum: Das Wesen des Österreichischen in der Literatur*   213

Notes on Contributors   217

Austrian Studies   220

Preface

In commissioning a volume of essays on Austrian fiction, our main aim was to draw attention to a number of prose writers who have been unjustly neglected by scholars, critics and the general reader because they do not fit into a familiar canon of German literature. The canon we all know was formed particularly in the latter half of the nineteenth century. It singled out the 'Bildungsroman', the novel of individual development, as the supreme type of German novel, not least because this genre's concentration on the protagonist's inwardness tends to rule out any wide-ranging realistic and critical portrayal of society; and the canon also gives precedence to humorous, elegiac or historical Novellen by Keller, Storm or Meyer rather than the more urbane fiction of Saar or the socially conscious work of Ebner-Eschenbach. The strongly Protestant bias of this dominant consensus, formed partly in an Imperial Germany that undertook a 'Kulturkampf' against the political position of the Roman Catholic Church, helps to explain the undervaluation of consciously Catholic writers like Ebner-Eschenbach or Stifter.

The editors of this volume half expected to be offered papers dealing with that long-standing theme of Austrian literary scholarship, the specifically 'Austrian' character of Austrian as opposed to German literature. Instead, we found a different set of preoccupations, arguably more appropriate to a period in which Austria has joined other European nations in a European Union that is itself becoming a multi-cultural society. Our contributors turned out to be predominantly interested in the fictional treatment of politics and gender, the two principal – and sometimes intersecting – themes of this book.

The first two essays concern Austrian writers who wrote about the United States of America. 'Charles Sealsfield', the runaway monk who spent some ten years in America and wrote some of his books in English, resists classification and has remained outside any literary canon, but as a literary artist and an independent commentator on democratic politics he is of great interest. Here, Jeffrey L. Sammons tries to define Sealsfield's stance in relation to the populist politics associated with the Democrat Andrew Jackson, who was President from 1829 to 1837. The America depicted in *Der Amerika-Müde* by Ferdinand Kürnberger is a fictional construct derived from travel books and displayed for satiric effect; but, as Ritchie Robertson argues, Kürnberger's real purpose is to comment indirectly on European politics and express his doubts about the future development of the liberalism for which he had mounted the barricades in 1848.

There follow two close analyses of little-known Novellen by major literary artists. In examining Ebner-Eschenbach's *Die Poesie des Unbewußten*, a Novelle written almost entirely as a series of fictive postcards exchanged by the characters, R. C. Ockenden suggests that critics have been too ready to assume that the newly-wed heroine is naive and unconscious, and shows how Ebner-Eschenbach sketches marital problems that are more familiar from Fontane's *Effi Briest*. And in his reading of Saar's *Doktor Trojan*, Ian Foster goes beyond the preoccupation with mythic archetypes that has dominated discussion of this story and points out that it also engages such pressing political issues as relations between Czechs and Germans in late nineteenth-century Bohemia and the controversy over surgical methods at a time when the famous Vienna Medical School was responding to the discovery of antisepsis and anaesthesia.

Two further chapters break new ground in their discussion of male homosexuality in Central European literature. The diplomat Leopold von Andrian, mainly remembered as a friend and correspondent of Hofmannsthal and an object of Karl Kraus's satire, published a story called *Der Garten der Erkenntnis* which, as Jens Rieckmann shows with the aid of Andrian's extensive posthumous papers, can now be interpreted as a disguised expression of the author's homosexuality. A homosocial attraction to the male body and a revulsion from the female body is apparent from the passages in Kafka's diaries that have recently been published in full after being censored by Max Brod; Mark Anderson considers the significance of these passages in relation to some of Kafka's best-known works of fiction.

The Austro-Hungarian army is a frequent presence and an object of nostalgia in much Austrian fiction from Saar to Lernet-Holenia. Andrew Barker shows the other side of the coin in his study of Andreas Latzko, whose fiction concerning the First World War, especially *Menschen im Krieg*, is a protest against warfare as powerful as the better-known anti-war books written in Germany by E. M. Remarque and Arnold Zweig. Joseph Roth's *Radetzkymarsch* is for many readers an ironic celebration of a Habsburg Austria focused on the army; Martha Wörsching reads the novel against the grain and argues that it both illustrates and analyses the fragile construction of a masculinity which relies on male bonding, represses emotion, and assigns women a limited number of pejorative roles.

The construction of masculinity is also the subject of Simon Tyler's essay on Canetti. Grasping a nettle that most commentators have shunned, Tyler argues that Canetti draws extensively on Otto Weininger's notoriously misogynistic treatise *Geschlecht und Charakter* for his presentation of the central male and female characters in *Die Blendung* (known in English as *Auto da Fe*), and that while the pedantic protagonist is certainly satirised, some of the criteria by which he is mocked come directly from Weininger. Stephanie Bird then looks afresh at the important and challenging novel *Malina* by Ingeborg Bachmann, taking issue with readers who see in it a simple polarity of sensitive female vs. brutally rational male, and argues that Bachmann is interested rather in utopian moments where a male/female opposition is transcended by a productive interaction between 'male' and 'female' qualities.

Finally, Andrea Reiter returns to Charles Sealsfield, this time as the author of the scathing polemic *Austria as it is,* comparing him with the mid-twentieth-century novelist, Thomas Bernhard, whose satirical polemics against a decaying Austria still riddled with Nazism made him notorious from the publication of his first novel, *Frost,* in 1963 till his death in 1989. She points out that in each case the writer's apparent radicalism is undermined by his enjoyable rhetoric of exaggeration and by his shrewd awareness of the market value of polemic.

There follow two essay-reviews dealing with recent work on Musil and Kafka, and a series of shorter book reviews intended to make the results of specialised research available to a wider audience. The subjects of the books reviewed range from the life of an eighteenth-century soldier and polymath in the Habsburgs' service to the continuing discussion on Austrian identity, and they include several further novelists in addition to those discussed in articles: notably the outstanding turn-of-the-century figure Richard Beer-Hofmann and the provocative present-day feminist Elfriede Jelinek.

Part One

An Austrian Jacksonian

Charles Sealsfield's Political Evolution, 1829–1833

Jeffrey L. Sammons

Charles Sealsfield (Karl Postl) is surely one of the most puzzling writers in the history of German letters. Despite a great deal of arduous if sometimes misdirected research and a body of thoughtful, nuanced critical writing in recent times, basic problems endure.[1] His biography remains inexplicable, his place in literary history, even to which national literature he belongs, contentious. Similarly elusive, though less often addressed, is what might be called the communication problem: what he supposed he was doing with his idiosyncratic novels, what intended effect on their audience American novels written in German and published in Switzerland and Germany were meant to have and to what extent they were suited to such purpose. This question has regularly been taken to be simpler than I believe it is. There is an extensive if imperfect consensus that Sealsfield meant to hold up to his German and Austrian audience a model of democracy, that he was thus a didactic political writer and to that extent related to the Young German movement and the politicised literature of the Vormärz. Sealsfield himself, in his sporadic comments on his purposes, tended to speak of his works as popular social novels striving for a true picture of America. In the dedication to the second edition of *Lebensbilder aus der westlichen Hemisphäre* he came closest to defining a didactic political purpose: 'Der zum Bewußtseyn ihrer Kraft und Würde erwachenden deutschen Nation sind diese Bilder des häuslichen und öffentlichen Lebens freier Bürger eines stammverwandten, weltgeschichtlich groß werdenden Staates als Spiegel zur Selbstbeschauung hochachtungsvoll gewidmet' (XI, [5])[2] ('These pictures of the domestic and public life of free citizens of a racially kindred state achieving world-historical greatness are respectfully dedicated to the German nation, as it awakens to its strength and dignity, for the purpose of self-contemplation'). Contemporary reviewers, hungry for any kind of democratic discourse, praised Sealsfield as an inspiration, although some doubted his relevance to German conditions.[3] The first German history of the novel in 1850 concluded with praise of Sealsfield for having introduced the democratic principle into the genre.[4] Some modern commentators have been more emphatic, arguing that his whole effort was directed toward confronting inhabitants of the timid and oppressed petty German states with a representa-

3

tion of the strong, free and confident American people; that his fiction formed an explicit contrast to Europe; that his didactic purpose was to teach liberty to Europe; that the often articulated hostility to Mexico was in fact directed against the Holy Alliance and Austria; that the origins and aims of his work were rooted in 'Austro-German culture'; that his narrated America is always a representation of Europe and particularly of Austrian conditions.[5] But when we look carefully at the texts, we may ask ourselves how they can be expected to have had these effects and whether they in fact did. The Austrian Americanist Walter Grünzweig, one of today's outstanding Sealsfield scholars, has had occasion to observe that Sealsfield's conception of his audience remains largely unclear to us and that *Der Legitime und die Republikaner* (*LR*) continues to be one of the least accessible of his works for the European reader.[6]

As far as I know, Sealsfield is the only European author of German-language fiction about the United States to have located himself explicitly in an American political context. To be sure, some German authors exhibited solidarity with the movement to abolish slavery (as Sealsfield emphatically did not), but abolition was not strictly a party issue; it tended, rather, to divide parties. Other German or, more likely, German-American authors have been committed to socialism, which, however, has rarely been a significant element of American party politics. But, as is well known, Sealsfield allied himself from an early date with the Jacksonian movement, which understood itself as refounding democracy on more egalitarian and populist principles against what were perceived as the aristocratic and centralising policies of the Federalist founders. In the 1820s the most vulnerable object of Jacksonian hostility to the cautious and conservative East Coast establishment was John Quincy Adams, prominent as the son of one of the chief architects of the constitutional order, the second president, John Adams. Sealsfield arrived in the United States in the year before the controversial election of 1824, which, because the outcome had to be negotiated in the House of Representatives, was widely regarded by Andrew Jackson and his supporters as having been 'stolen' by John Quincy Adams; the 'corrupt bargain' of February 1825 remained the most crucial political experience in Jackson's mind for the remainder of his career, as a subversion of egalitarian and majoritarian principles.[7] The English version of Sealsfield's first book on America, *The United States of North America as They Are* (1828), has very much the appearance of a political tract, if not so much in Jackson's favour, then certainly against President Adams, who 'if he had been sent by Metternich himself ..., could not pursue more closely the principles of the Holy Alliance' (II, 21). The critical political allegiance did not go unnoticed in Europe. Sealsfield's English publisher, in order to distance himself from the odour of Jacksonianism, had an attack on the book printed in his own *Quarterly Review*, and a letter of evaluation on the German version elicited by the publisher Cotta castigated Sealsfield's blatant partisanship.[8] But Sealsfield's fiction is so intensely assimilated to the details, not just of the Jacksonian movement in general, a large, evolving, incoherent and often opportunistic political phenomenon, but of its Southern and Southwestern agrarian faction, that one wonders whether European readers, not notable in those times for their interest in the details of the American scene, would have found them fully intelligible, while subsequent scholars have sometimes not looked closely enough at the context and have contented themselves with generalities about freedom and democracy, concepts that have quite specific delineations in the Jacksonian context and consequently in Sealsfield's fiction.

Sealsfield's first novel was written and anonymously published in English, as *Tokeah: or the White Rose* in Philadelphia in 1829, and later that year, in a slightly revised version, in London as *The Indian Chief: or, Tokeah and the White Rose* (IC). The book was probably written largely during the presidential campaign of 1828, in which Jackson achieved the victory he believed had been denied him four years earlier. It opens when a band of Indians in Georgia, led by the Oconee chief Tokeah, bring a baby girl for safekeeping to a backwoods trader named Copeland. After seven years Tokeah, filled with bitterness against the whites, takes her back, moves the remnant of his tribe across the Sabine River into what he later realises is the Mexican province of Texas and raises the 'White Rose' as a companion to his daughter Canondah, subsequently betrothed to the young, heroic Comanche chief El Sol. Again seven years later, a young English aristocrat, Arthur Graham, who had been taken captive by the pirate Jean Lafitte, turns up as a fugitive near the encampment, where he is badly wounded by an alligator and secretly tended by Canondah and Rosa. Restored to health, Arthur is helped to escape, but is recaptured by Tokeah, who is enraged at what he believes to be the treacherous harbouring of a probable spy. But, because Arthur does not kill the Indian who attacks him, Tokeah realises that he is not an enemy of the red men and allows him to seek to return to his people, extracting from him, however, his word of honour that he will not reveal the tribe's location. Tokeah, who has made an unwise alliance with Lafitte and promised Rosa to him as a wife, comes to fathom his true character, whereupon the pirate and his men attack the encampment. Owing largely to El Sol's battle skills, the pirates are defeated and captured, but Canondah is killed. Arthur, meanwhile, has found his way to Opelousas, where he is detained as a British spy and collaborator with the Indians, for the British are about to invade New Orleans in a critical battle of the War of 1812. However, Copeland, now mellowed into a country squire and justice of the peace full of rough-hewn wisdom, recognises the lad's good qualities and puts him in the care of a prosperous Creole planter and state senator named Gentillon, who lectures the still benighted aristocrat on American principles of freedom and democracy, after which Copeland is obliged to bring him to Jackson's camp for examination. There Tokeah, who has been commanded in a dream to recover his father's bones in Georgia, appears with El Sol, Rosa and the captured pirates; after several complications Tokeah releases Arthur from his word so that he can clear himself. Tokeah does recover the bones but is killed in an attack by an another Indian tribe on his way to an alliance with El Sol in Texas. Rosa is revealed to be the lost daughter of a Spanish aristocrat and in the last chapter she is shown living contentedly as Lady Graham with Arthur on his plantation in Jamaica.

It seems likely that, if it were not for Sealsfield's remarkable subsequent career, this book would be remembered, if it all, as no more than a bibliographical curiosity. The style, as has been pointed out with pedantic thoroughness, is riddled with Germanisms and other off-centre turns of phrase, though anyone who has written a book in a foreign language might show some sympathy for what Sealsfield managed to achieve. But in structure, characterisation and sensibility it is notably inferior to the antebellum American fiction from which he drew; for example, to the novels of Timothy Flint and James Kirke Paulding, and particularly to Catharine Maria Sedgwick's fine Indian captivity novel, *Hope Leslie* (1827).[9] The close resemblance of Sealsfield's novel to James Fenimore Cooper's *Leather-Stocking Tales*, three of which had appeared, and especially to *The Last of the Mohicans* (1826), was remarked at once and has been much discussed since, though not always in complete recognition of Sealsfield's deviation from Cooper's model in his evaluation of the Indian fate and of westward expansion. American reviews were few, superficial and very mixed (reprinted XXIV, 1–13).

Although the story begins at the end of the eighteenth century and the main action occurs prior to the Battle of New Orleans in January 1815, at the narrative level the novel is clearly set in the Jacksonian context and, as has been rightly argued, is not to be understood without Jackson.[10] He himself is, for the most part, indirectly present – as in the novels of Sir Walter Scott, another of Sealsfield's important models, the heroic historical figure is seen primarily in the middle distance and from below – though he makes one important appearance in a confrontation with the Indian chiefs Tokeah and El Sol. That the attitude towards the Indians is generally Jacksonian in spirit can be obscured for readers by a pervasive rhetoric of sympathy with the Indians' tragic fate, 'these unfortunate Parias of the west' (V, 3, 131), and by the castigation of the pillaging by the whites. Nevertheless, the novel accepts that their cause is lost and that their removal from settled territory is a necessity. At the very outset Copeland is resentful of the Indians' agricultural settlements and hostile to the philanthropists who encourage them (IV, 1, 21–3). There is an odd but, for its time, characteristic incoherence between the ascription of Indian suffering and decadence to the greed and violence of the whites on the one hand and the clear implication on the other that Indian character and level of civilisation improve by assimilation to white culture. The older the Indians, especially the women, the more savage and hideous they are, while the younger ones have benefited from contact with civilisation. White influence, for example, has caused the Cherokees to treat their women better and has made Canondah and the other Oconee girls 'well formed and graceful' (IV, 1, 93–4, 96). If Tokeah had not been a savage, he would have been a hero or benefactor of men, but, as it is, he is morbidly suspicious (IV, 1, 205–6); yet we are also told that he has been made more savage by persecution (IV, 2, 65–6). El Sol, for his part, has become less savage owing to his 'warlike intercourse with the Spaniards' (IV, 2, 97). Jackson is fairly severe toward Tokeah, whom he accuses of savage conduct in the past, but friendlier to El Sol, to whom he gives a medal, doubtless because he and his Comanches are at home where they are supposed to be, in the far West outside the boundaries of the United States (V, 3, 158–65). Jackson tells the chiefs that the red men 'should remember that we are as lawful possessors of the land as they are, and certainly the strongest. We could have made them slaves' (IV, 3, 161). There can be no doubt that *IC* is in consonance with the Jacksonian policy of Indian removal, counting but also accepting its cost in suffering and injustice.[11]

IC contains much of Sealsfield's customary rhetoric in praise of American freedom, of the sovereign people, their energies, initiative and public-spiritedness unshackled from European despotism and bureaucracy, in this case explicated largely by the Creole Gentillon to cure Arthur of his aristocratic prejudices. The doctrine as propagated here is marked by an insistence upon property and its preservation, a Jacksonian obsession as it was for Sealsfield. It is always understood as landed property along with its exploitation through agriculture and trade. Wealth of any other kind and its pursuit are always represented pejoratively in Sealsfield's fiction. It is the acquisition and maintenance of property that is causing the backwoodsmen to become more civilised (V, 2, 179; V, 3, 6–8). Jackson in his farewell address in 1837 stressed that the Constitution had 'secured the rights of property'.[12] In fact, the Constitution says nothing about the preservation of private property, except, by implication, intellectual property by means of copyright and patents.

Der Legitime und die Republikaner was published in 1833, in the first year of Jackson's second term. As a translation or adaptation it follows about half of *IC*, after which it deviates almost completely, employing only a couple of scenes of the earlier work.[13] The revision is a clear improvement, in the first instance stylistically, since the author was now writing in his native German, although, as in all of his subsequent works, the text is peppered with Americanisms of which it is often difficult to say how intentionally and consciously they are employed. Structurally the novel is better integrated. In *IC*, Tokeah rather implausibly takes Lafitte and the pirates as prisoners to Jackson's headquarters. In *LR* they are released because the Indians believe that such nasty characters will do evil to white people. To Tokeah's shock and horror, they turn up as volunteers in Jackson's forces at the Battle of New Orleans, as was the case historically. Arthur Graham has been displaced by James Hodges, no longer a disdainful aristocrat but the son of a wealthy merchant. A British midshipman who had been captured by Lafitte while clamming, he is a rather impetuous and disrespectful lad, thus better suited for conversion to Americanism. At the same time his moral character is heightened. Unlike Arthur, James realises that his flight from the Indian village has put Canondah in danger of her father's rage and he endeavours to return, swimming back across the Sabine before he is recaptured by the Indians (VI, 1, 291). The sentimental, trivial love story is dispensed with. The ultimate discovery of Rosa's Spanish parentage is pushed into the background and Rosa herself disappears from the end of the novel; James marries one of Squire Copeland's daughters. Sealsfield no longer has any use for Spanish and

British aristocrats in his concluding idyll. However, it is no longer class consciousness that needs to be overcome, but national traits, the conditioned arrogance and false sense of superiority of an Englishman. In this as in many other details Sealsfield has elaborated the political and, one must say, nationalistic fabric of the work. *LR* deviates from *IC* at the point where, in the latter, Copeland conducts Arthur to the Creole planter Gentillon for his instruction in American doctrine. Gentillon does not recur in *LR*; his role is taken over by a wealthy American colonel and his wife, who, although suspected of 'Tory' sentiments, nevertheless are true Americans who help James understand the rules of the democratic environment. (Actually they appear to hold Whig sentiments, but it was a rhetorical device of Jacksonian democracy to denote all opponents as 'Tories' if not monarchists.) Evidently Sealsfield no longer wished to employ a Creole in such an ideologically foregrounded role; in *LR* the Creoles' courage and loyalty in the face of the British invasion are called into question (VII, 2, 134–6), while Copeland tells James that Jackson treats Creoles like negroes (VII, 2, 170). In the rest of Sealsfield's fiction set in the Louisiana territory, Creoles are depicted as a harmless, frivolous and rather feckless lot, to be tolerated as long as they subordinate their Frenchy habits to the American way of life.

The specifically Jacksonian aspect is intensified through a number of details. The War of 1812 is now defined in the American understanding as an imposed and necessary war of independence from Britain (VI, 1, 156) and Jackson's role in it is more explicitly heroised. He is introduced descriptively much earlier in the novel (VII, 2, 136); his debate with Tokeah and El Sol is expanded and is placed for greater emphasis closer to the end (VII, 3, 271–93). While John Adams was fleetingly mentioned in *IC* among the 'great men' who founded the nation and came 'from the people' (V, 3, 11, 13), he and his son now clearly represent the enemy faction. Copeland in the first episode of the novel wishes the elder Adams to the devil (VI, 1, 30); the wealthy colonel is suspected of attachment to Adams's false doctrines (VI, 3, 112). Sealsfield's pejorative vocabulary of Tories, monarchists and the like is sometimes seen as evidence of an imposition of European political concepts on the American context, but in many places he appears quite consonant with American usage. When the opposition of the colonel's wife to free immigration exposes her as a crypto-'Tory' (VII, 3, 132), that, too, exactly reflects a Jacksonian position of the time.[14] However, when large-scale immigration, especially of the Irish, was perceived as an economic threat, the movement became more nativist, and Sealsfield would loyally follow it in that direction. Sealsfield's depiction of John Quincy Adams, especially in *The United States*, as a monarchist seeking to establish a hereditary presidency in his family reads like over-wrought campaign propaganda, but his biographer has observed:

> he had been accustomed since youth to look upon that office as a family inheritance. In his tall pride he desired it to come to him as it had come to Washington: unsolicited, unconnived for, without commitments or bargains with any man, a prize for which he, the son of President John

Adams and Abigail, would not lift a finger or make a nod. 'If my country wants my services, she must ask for them.'[15]

There is one more motif that is quite minor here but appears significant in retrospect: the association of the Southern yeomanry in its energy of expansion, land-taking and conquest with the Normans. Barely adumbrated in *IC* (IV, 1, 180), it appears more explicitly in *LR* (VII, 3, 249), where Copeland describes the inhabitants of Louisiana as a million masters on conquered land. The motif was to be a major element of the Alkalde's definitive ideological harangue in Colonel Morse's narration in *Das Kajütenbuch*. It, too, is a well-attested discourse of the antebellum South.[16]

Another change is Sealsfield's evidently increased willingness to grapple with the issue of slavery. His views on and representations of slavery have been a quite contentious topic in modern scholarship. The dispute cannot be reviewed here, except to say that it sometimes appears to me that European observers are less sensitive to the issue than Americans are obliged to be. My own opinion is that it is, again, best understood in the Jacksonian context. In *IC* slavery is barely visible. The few black characters receive, by Sealsfield's standards, neutral, even friendly treatment. The cultivated Creole complains that Copeland's men brutally beat a slave, to which Copeland, who 'thought it his duty to take the part of his countryman against a negro', replies: 'But them negroes are such beastly creturs' (V, 2, 228). But in *LR* Sealsfield begins to mount the defence of slavery common in the discourse of his environment. The narrator, not one of the characters, explains that, although the sight of slavery 'dem menschenfreundlichen Auge wehe that' ('pained the philanthropic eye'), 'die kleinen Wollköpfe' ('the little wool-heads') are in a cheerful and contented condition that many in the Old World might envy; the horrors claimed by abolitionists are rare, while the slaves' treatment in general redounds to the credit of the American character. Southerners do the best they can with their duties as slaveholders, which have been imposed on them; the thought of emancipation must cause one to shudder (VII, 3, 7–9). In any case, slaves were property, in which according to Jacksonian doctrine government must not interfere: 'For the government to legislate abolition would strike at the very foundation of American principles and institutions'; abolitionism was regarded as a partisan conspiracy of John C. Calhoun and John Quincy Adams.[17] Furthermore, as the great scholar of the American South, C. Vann Woodward, has shown, slavery, rather than appearing to be a contradiction within the ideology of democracy and equality, could actually be made to support it: 'When all who were white were invited to join the brotherhood of the free and equal and look down upon all who were black, unfree, and unequal, then American slavery did take on an ironic reconciliation with American equality as its underpinning, the underpinning of a strictly white egalitarianism.'[18] It would be useful if Sealsfield scholars, especially European ones, would become more familiar with this contextual discourse, as it would help them comprehend his violations of our current horizon of expectations of where a 'democratic' writer is supposed to stand. A recognition of his underlying and, indeed, intensifying racism would also contribute to clarity. In *LR*, for example, it is asserted not only that the white race is superior to the Indians, but also that even the proudest Indians must acknowledge this superiority (VII, 3, 30, 38–9).

In addition to these adjustments and changes, *LR* exhibits two ingenious innovations. The first of these has not been much noticed by criticism, perhaps because it is a subplot that takes place largely offstage. Jackson, while preparing his defences on his way to becoming the Hero of New Orleans, is at the same time being prosecuted for violating the rights of the State of Louisiana by arbitrarily imposing martial law and imprisoning a judge who defied him (VII, 2, 226–38).[19] Copeland's militiamen spend a good deal of valuable time in democratic session debating this issue and deciding whether to obey the order to join the defence forces, going on record as censuring the commander while continuing to serve loyally under him. A regular army officer, who, significantly, spent his youth in aristocratic, hierarchical England, is shocked and offended by this insubordination, but he, in turn, is told that he is offending the democratic spirit of his countrymen, thereby putting his standing in the community and his career in jeopardy. It is difficult to imagine any other moment in the historical record better suited to Sealsfield's purposes. The people, constantly alert to the threat of despotism and encroachment upon their liberties, govern their rulers, even their military commanders in a time of crisis. The local colonel is confident that Jackson himself will decide the matter justly (VII, 2, 289–90) and it turns out that he is more democratic in spirit than the officers who defend his authority; he yields to the censure and the fine, if not enthusiastically, then with reasonably good grace (VII, 3, 63, 251–2, 291). Needless to say, his authority is not damaged but enhanced by the episode. Here, if anywhere, is a message from America to Europe; such an event is, as Sealsfield supposes, unimaginable in any European country, unless one were to dredge up the memory of Frederick the Great's public-relations stunt in the matter of the miller of Sanssouci. The narrator sends the message quite explicitly:

> Es ist schwierig dieses republikanische Leben, das schwierigste das es gibt; denn zart ist die Grenzlinie des Rechtes, und leicht ist sie überschritten, wenn nicht die Millionen mißtrauisch wachen. Darum ist es nur bei einem Volke möglich, wo die Verstandeskräfte die höchste Stufe erreicht, wo selbst positiver Widerstand gegen den Machthaber noch die Grenzlinie seiner Pflicht erkennt, und so, ohne in Verwirrung und Anarchie auszuarten, seine Rechte behauptet oder die verlorenen wieder erobert (VII, 2, 237–8).

> [Republican life is difficult, the most difficult there is, for the boundary of justice is delicate and easily transgressed if the millions are not mistrustfully alert. Therefore it is possible only among a people whose rational capacity reaches the highest stage, where even positive resistance to the ruling powers recognises the boundary line of duty, and who thus, without degenerating into confusion and anarchy, maintain their rights or reconquer those that have been lost.]

Sealsfield's other innovative device, by contrast, cannot be missed by any reader, as it becomes a kind of leitmotif: the appellation of the Indian chief as 'der Legitime', thus paralleling him to the despots of Europe who claimed to rule legitimately by divine right. This metonymy is a concentrate of the intensification in two directions of the Indian theme in *LR*: on the one hand the heightened pathos of oppression, suffering and defeat; on the other a tightened insistence upon the inevitability and ultimate rightness of removal. Sealsfield establishes the first of these tones by setting to each of the three volumes a motto in which Thomas Jefferson is made to say that he trembles for his people when he considers the injustices that have been perpetrated against the original inhabitants. As we know, this remark of Jefferson's concerned not the Indians, but slavery, a sentiment for which Sealsfield had no use.[20] The bitterness of lost lands, of having been continually lied to and exploited, subverted by firewater, despoiled by relentless white greed, is passionately articulated by the Indians. Rosa, from her experience as Tokeah's forcibly adopted daughter, repeatedly defends him against the charge of savagery (e.g., VII, 3, 166). But Rosa is no longer a definitive voice in the novel, in which the images of savagery have been amplified. In the Indian camp James likens a dance to the sort of portrayal of Hell with which the Church has tried to terrify believers; the Indian girls burn a Yankee in effigy, a scene not in *IC* (VI, 1, 172, 177). Tokeah is made considerably more savage and is also diminished in stature. It appears more explicitly than in *IC* that his poor judgment in allying himself with the thieving pirate Lafitte and his humiliating incompetence in battle are causes of the loss of his daughter (VI, 2, 110, 118). At one point Tokeah charges the Great Spirit with injustice and wishes a curse on his own people (VII, 3, 39–40). In a lengthy scene entirely new to *LR*, Tokeah, after having recovered his father's bones in Georgia, makes a detour through Alabama, encountering the rest of his tribe, which has repudiated him because of his persistence in making futile war against the whites. Increasingly he is presented as blinded by paranoia. Instead of generously renouncing Rosa, as in *IC*, Tokeah refuses to accept her return to white society, seizes her and threatens her with a knife; she must be rescued by the wiser and cooler El Sol, to whom Tokeah has absurdly promised her, but who does know how to renounce (and to remove himself). Tokeah answers Rosa's plea for forgiveness with silence (VII, 3, 297–308). Jackson's lecture to the chiefs is now augmented with material drawn from his 'Second Annual Message' of December 1830 and his 'Message on Indian Affairs' of February 1831:[21] the progress of civilisation cannot tolerate a nomadic people wandering about the land; the Indians are welcome to settle as civilised farmers but otherwise must be removed. The Indians are silenced by the truth of what he says (VII, 3, 278–82). Historians believe that Jackson's apparent acceptance of Indian agricultural settlement was a hypocritical sop to liberal opinion;[22] he had been hostile to Indians all his life, he had made his first national reputation fighting the Seminoles in Florida and he probably was consistently determined to remove all Indians from the southern states. But Sealsfield may have taken his statements at face value. Copeland, identifiable as a stand-in for Jackson in the novel, asserts that the Indians are disappearing by their own fault (VII, 3, 296). In a probably fictive letter of dedication to 'A. J. Smith, Esq.' prefacing the novel, Sealsfield states that even though the sight of Indian removal is painful, they must for their own welfare be separated from the squatters and merchants (VI, 1, 2–3).

No model for Sealsfield's identification of Indian chiefdom with legitimacy has been found, which does not mean that there was none. The notorious eighteenth-century purveyor of misinformation about America, Cornelius de Pauw, associated the degenerate and effeminate beardlessness of Indians with the clean-shaven fashion of European aristocrats.[23] But Sealsfield's ingenious device is to literalise the cliché of the noble savage. Eloquence, the stoic style and the solemnity of hierarchical authority are noble *and* savage, archaic and obsolete like the European aristocracy. The chief's 'medicine' is revered by the Indians as a symbol of power just as sceptres, tiaras and crowns used to be by the European peoples (VI, 1, 98). It is, on the other hand, the *legitimate* principle of Spanish and French satraps to look upon populations as herds of sheep (VII, 2, 133–4). Jackson tells the chiefs they are bloodsuckers like the tyrants of the Old World (VII, 3, 279–80). One of the colonel's daughters, while giving Rosa a geography lesson, explains that kings are like Tokeah, only greater; childish peoples require such rulers to govern them, make wars, sell their territories (as Tokeah has done) and fool the people into thinking they have been appointed by God (VII, 3, 124–5). Later Rosa is taught that she will find living with American whites better than with Indians or with kings (VII, 3, 295).

Might this concept of legitimacy not be a link to the European relevance commentators seek in Sealsfield? The novel takes place shortly before the convening of the Congress of Vienna, where legitimacy was one of the basic principles; the legitimacy of Louis-Philippe's accession in 1830 was a disputatious matter at the time it was written. Public discussion of such matters was tabu under the Metternichian censorship; might not Sealsfield have smuggled it in from an exotic perspective?[24] If that had been the case, however, one would think that the censors would have been the first to notice. In fact, there is no reason to think that Sealsfield ever had any measurable political effect, and it has been argued that his republicanism was hardly registered in the Vormärz.[25] Generally speaking, there is little republicanism to be found among the writers of the Vormärz at all, at least after the death of Ludwig Börne in 1837. It is by no means clear that Sealsfield ever intended to have a political effect; rather his posture is one of holding up the American example for contemplation and understanding, to Europe's more or less eternal shame. He does not propose the exportation of American liberty to Europe; even in Latin America he sees no potential for republican government because of its Spanish character, as he asserts in *The United States* (II, 44–55); and in *Der Virey* he endeavours to show that there is no hope of American democracy in Mexico (IX, 2, 242–3; IX, 3, 306–7). On the whole, he seems to turn his back on Europe as irrelevant to the progress of mankind, at least until his late novel *Die deutsch-amerikanischen Wahlverwandtschaften*, but there he was unable to complete his intercultural chiasmus.[26] Furthermore, in that novel his hope for an elective affinity is placed in a Prussian, not an Austrian. He seems to have directed his attention toward Germany in general rather than Austria in particular and to have lost interest in Austria after his polemical essay of 1828, *Austria as It Is*, the Sealsfield work most anticipatory of the Young German spirit. A chubby scoffer with thick Austrian lips appears briefly in *Das Kajütenbuch* (XVII, 148; whether the editor's note, XVII, 398*, is correct that the thick lips are an allusion to the Habsburg physiognomy is difficult to decide). In *Die deutsch-amerikanischen Wahlverwandtschaften* the fashionables, who find Jackson and patriotism obsolete, regard the Louis-Philippes, the Metternichs and the Wellingtons as among their friends (XXII, 3, 65–67, 71); such sentiments are infallibly a sign of assimilation to aristocratic degeneracy. Sealsfield does not direct much attention at all to Central Europe. From within his American perspective, the first European object of concern and contrast is, of course, Britain; then France; then Spain. In Rosa's geography lesson, the rest of Europe is an undifferentiated collection of petty kingdoms (VII, 3, 123–4). It is well to bear in mind also that in Sealsfield's account American liberty, as his insistence on the development of landed property and 'Norman' conquests shows, is logically dependent upon the taking and cultivation of vast tracts of land empty except for disposable aboriginal inhabitants. Such circumstances cannot, of course, be replicated in Central Europe.

The inward turn of *LR* appears also in many American allusions that must have been difficult for Central European readers. For example, Copeland grumbles: 'Das alte Weib in der Bundesstadt schreibt und schwatzt Staatsrecht trotz Einem ...; wenn es aber darauf und daran kommt, so ist er Hamiltonianer über den alten John, und verliert den Kopf, wie er ihn hinter Baltimore verloren hat' (VII, 2, 231) ('the old woman in the Federal city writes and gabbles political theory with the best of them ...; but when it comes down to it, he is more of a Hamiltonian than old John, and loses his head as he did at Baltimore'). One wonders whether many readers will have recognised the allusion to President James Madison, whose brilliance as a constitutional theoretician was not equally matched by competence as an administrator and commander-in-chief, or have understood that he is being charged with susceptibility to the Federalist doctrines of the Adams faction and with confusion at an engagement at Baltimore after the burning of Washington (which the Americans won, incidentally, and which was the occasion for the writing of 'The Star-Spangled Banner'). There are two allusions to the Hartford Convention, an episode right at the time of the Battle of New Orleans, when a number of New England Federalists opposed to the war and the hegemony of the South discussed secession (VII, 2, 232; VII, 3, 144–5). The matter is undoubtedly relevant to the states-rights issues raised by Jackson's high-handedness in New Orleans but of no detectable relevance to European politics. James, faced with the prospect of hanging, thinks of Major André, the British officer who was hanged as the contact with the traitor Benedict Arnold (VII, 3, 190). American readers would probably

13

have recognised the name, and perhaps many British ones also, even though the event was a good half-century in the past, but what about Germans, Austrians and Swiss? Since the editors of the modern edition did not find it convenient to annotate *LR* with any thoroughness (even though many of the materials were prepared for the Riederer edition of 1937), interested non-American readers of today may still find the text intermittently inaccessible. It is hard to see how any political inspiration could have emanated from it in its time. The political dimension of Sealsfield's writings came to be ignored, so that they were classified as 'ethnographic' novels, as though his purpose had been to transmit Indian lore and the mores of backwoodsmen. This may not be entirely owing to the depoliticisation of the German bourgeoisie after 1848, as Steinecke argues,[27] but also to an original incongruity with any conceivable readership in their time. Thus Ritter seems right to me to conclude that Sealsfield's image of America is 'weniger das Amerikabild eines europäischen Schriftstellers denn eines amerikanisierten Autors der Neuen Welt'[28] ('less the American image of a European writer than of an Americanised author of the New World').

Many, if not almost all, of the German (as opposed to German-American) writers about America have been regarded as never having quite left home and have often been criticised for a parochial inability to penetrate the variety and nuances of American life; this is true even, perhaps especially, of the exiles of the 1930s. Sealsfield's case is the opposite; he became so deeply involved in an important but circumscribed area of American society and politics that, while he was able to represent it with unusual mimetic fidelity, he could not find, and perhaps did not even seek, efficacious political and ideological resonance in his readership. In the last analysis, an Austrian Jacksonian is an eccentric, and eccentrics maintain themselves in literary history only with difficulty, no matter how original and powerful their writing may be.

Notes

1. For an overview of some of the problems, see my article, 'Charles Sealsfield: A Case of Non-Canonicity', in Gerhard P. Knapp (ed.), *Autoren damals und heute. Literaturgeschichtliche Beispiele veränderter Wirkungshorizonte* (Amsterdam and Atlanta, 1991), pp. 155–72, and, forthcoming, 'Charles Sealsfield und das Freimaurertum: Mehr Fragen als Antworten.'
2. All references to Sealsfield's works are cited from Charles Sealsfield, *Sämtliche Werke*, ed. Karl J. R. Arndt et al. (24 vols, Hildesheim and New York, 1972–91) with volume number, original volume number where necessary and page number, a procedure required by the circumstance that organisation by volume of the edition does not always correspond to that of the reprinted originals.
3. Reviews are collected in Reinhard F. Spiess, *Charles Sealsfields Werke im Spiegel der literarischen Kritik: Eine Sammlung zeitgenössischer Rezensionen mit einer Einleitung* (Stuttgart, 1977). See Hartmut Steinecke, *Romanpoetik von Goethe bis Thomas Mann: Entwicklungen und Probleme der 'demokratischen Kunstform' in Deutschland* (Munich, 1987), pp. 124–9, and Jerry Schuchalter, 'Charles Sealsfield's "Fable of the Republic"', *Yearbook of German-American Studies*, 24 (1989), 20–1.
4. Steinecke, *Romanpoetik*, p. 33.

5. Franz Riederer, afterword to his edition, Charles Sealsfield, *Gesamtausgabe der Amerikanischen Romane* (Meersburg am Bodensee and Leipzig, 1937), V, 449; Hildegard Emmel, 'Recht oder Unrecht in der Neuen Welt. Zu Charles Sealsfields Roman "Der Legitime und die Republikaner"', in Sigrid Bauschinger, Horst Denkler and Wilfried Malsch (eds), *Amerika in der deutschen Literatur: Neue Welt-Nordamerika-USA* (Stuttgart, 1975), p. 76; Friedrich Sengle, *Biedermeierzeit: Deutsche Literatur im Spannungsfeld Restauration und Revolution 1815–1848*, Vol. III: *Die Dichter* (Stuttgart, 1980), p. 759; Walter Grünzweig, *Das demokratische Kanaan: Charles Sealsfields Amerika im Kontext amerikanischer Literatur und Ideologie* (Munich, 1987), p. 225; Peter Michelsen, 'Americanism and Anti-Americanism in German Novels of the XIXth Century', *Arcadia*, 11 (1976), 277; Günter Schnitzler, *Erfahrung und Bild: Die dichterische Wirklichkeit des Charles Sealsfield (Karl Postl)* (Freiburg, 1988), p. 12.
6. Grünzweig, *Das demokratische Kanaan*, pp. 219, 223.
7. Robert V. Remini, *The Life of Andrew Jackson* (New York, 1988), p. 304.
8. Eduard Castle, *Der große Unbekannte. Das Leben von Charles Sealsfield (Karl Postl)* (Vienna, 1952), pp. 218, 209.
9. On Sealsfield's relationship to and dependence upon his American literary context, see Grünzweig, *Das demokratische Kanaan*, and, with a somewhat different perspective, my article, 'Charles Sealsfield: Innovation or Intertextuality?' in Nancy Kaiser and David E. Wellbery (eds) *Traditions of Experiment from the Enlightenment to the Present: Essays in Honor of Peter Demetz* (Ann Arbor, 1992), pp. 127–46.
10. See especially Walter Grünzweig, '"Where Millions of Happy People Might Live Peacefully": Jacksons Westen in Charles Sealsfields *Tokeah: or the White Rose*', *Amerikastudien / American Studies*, 28 (1983), 219–36.
11. Cf. Emmel, 'Recht oder Unrecht', pp. 75, 78; Walter Grünzweig, *Charles Sealsfield* (Boise, 1985), pp. 14–15.
12. Edwin C. Rozwenc (ed.), *The Meaning of Jacksonian Democracy* (Boston, 1963), p. 2.
13. For a comparison of the two versions, see Bernd Fischer, 'Baumwolle und Indianer: Zu Charles Sealsfields *Der Legitime und die Republikaner*', *Journal of German-American Studies*, 19 (1984)) 85–96, esp. p. 88.
14. Arthur M. Schlesinger, Jr., *The Age of Jackson* (Boston, 1946), pp. 320–1.
15. Samuel Flagg Bemis, *John Quincy Adams and the Union* (New York, 1956), p. 18.
16. See Rollin G. Osterweis, *Romanticism and Nationalism in the Old South* (Gloucester, MA., 1964), pp. 6, 45–8, and Reginald Horsman, *Race and Manifest Destiny: The Origins of American Racial Anglo-Saxonism* (Cambridge, MA., 1981), pp. 164–6.
17. Remini, *The Life of Andrew Jackson*, p. 307; Remini, *The Legacy of Andrew Jackson: Essays on Democracy, Indian Removal and Slavery* (Baton Rouge and London, 1988), p. 89.
18. C. Vann Woodward, *The Old World's New World* (New York and Oxford, 1991), p. 121.
19. For this episode, see Remini, *The Life of Andrew Jackson*, pp. 109–10. The critical events occurred after the battle, not before and during it, as Sealsfield places them to heighten the effect. Jackson was fined $1,000, not, as Sealsfield has it, $2,000.
20. Thomas Jefferson, *Notes on the State of Virginia*, ed. William Peden (Chapel Hill, 1955), p. 163; see Grünzweig, *Das demokratische Kanaan*, p. 157.
21. Grünzweig, *Das demokratische Kanaan*, pp. 160–2; Emmel, 'Recht oder Unrecht', p. 80.
22. Edward Pessen, *Jacksonian America: Society, Personality, and Politics*, rev. edn (Urbana and Chicago, 1985), pp. 296–8.
23. Susanne Zantop, 'Dialectics and Colonialism: The Underside of the Enlighten-

ment', in W. Daniel Wilson and Robert C. Holub (eds), *Impure Reason: Dialectic of Enlightenment in Germany* (Detroit, 1993), pp. 314-15.

24. See Steinecke, *Romanpoetik*, p. 124.
25. Alexander Ritter, 'Charles Sealsfield: Politischer Emigrant, freier Schriftsteller und die Doppelkrise von Amerika – Utopie und Gesellschaft im 19. Jahrhundert', *Freiburger Universitätsblätter*, No. 75 (April 1982), 47; Bernd Steinbrink, *Abenteuer-literatur des 19. Jahrhunderts in Deutschland: Studien zu einer vernachlässigten Gattung* (Tübingen, 1983), p. 6.
26. For some speculations on Sealsfield's inability to complete the novel, see my essay, 'Charles Sealsfields "Deutsch-amerikanische Wahlverwandtschaften." Ein Versuch', in Anselm Maler (ed.), *Exotische Welt in populären Lektüren* (Tübingen, 1990), pp. 49–62.
27. Steinecke, *Romanpoetik*, pp. 127–8.
28. Ritter, 'Charles Sealsfield: Politischer Emigrant', p. 51.

German Idealists and American Rowdies

Ferdinand Kürnberger's Novel
Der Amerika-Müde

Ritchie Robertson

Ferdinand Kürnberger (1821–79) is perhaps Austria's most noteworthy literary exile of the nineteenth century. While Karl Postl, alias Charles Sealsfield, deliberately fled from Austria's reactionary government and clerical tyranny, Kürnberger was obliged to leave after his involvement in the 1848 revolution, and his eight impoverished and insecure years in Germany made him more attached to his homeland. And in contrast to Sealsfield's American books, based on direct and detailed knowledge, Kürnberger's best-known work, the novel *Der Amerika-Müde* ('The Man Weary of America', 1855), is a violently polemical but second-hand account of the United States. As such it anticipates the imaginary Americas depicted by Kafka in *Der Verschollene* (known in English as 'America') and Brecht in *Die heilige Johanna der Schlachthöfe* ('Saint Joan of the Stockyards'). In all three works, the American setting is less a subject for realist representation than it is a vehicle for satire. Kafka's satire brings out the oppressive character of industrial society and the unavoidable incrimination of the innocent; Brecht brings out the logic of capitalism and the supposed inadequacy of philanthropy; Kürnberger satirises a society which has discarded European culture in favour of narrow materialism. In previous studies of *Der Amerika-Müde* this satirical perspective has received too little attention. If one judges the novel as attempting a serious portrayal of American society, then one can only agree with Jeffrey L. Sammons in finding it ridiculous.[1] The most substantial study to date, the relentlessly Marxist account by Rüdiger Steinlein, ignores not only Kürnberger's satire but the fact that his critique is not primarily social or political, but cultural.[2]

The relation between politics and culture in Kürnberger's thought can be shown by a brief account of his activities and writings in 1848 and in exile. Unable to study at university because of inadequate school results, Kürnberger attended lectures and educated himself, while trying to establish a literary career with aphorisms and 'Novellen'. He belonged to the intellectual proletariat which played such a large part in the Vienna Revolution.[3] The bulk of this group were students living in poverty, who read liberal and radical publications, imported from Germany, surreptitiously in lectures. His own

17

marginality made Kürnberger all the readier to join the students who in March 1848 demonstrated against oppression and formed an Academic Legion. After Metternich had resigned and the government had promised freedom of the press, a parliament, and a constitution, Kürnberger wrote ecstatically: 'Die akademische Jugend sprach: es werde Licht und es ward Licht. In sechs Tagen ward die Welt erschaffen, in zwei Tagen Österreich. Der große Völkerpferch der Monarchie hat sich in einen civilisirten Staat verwandelt, die Hunde-Wache der geh. Polizei und Censur hat aufgehört, die Heerden sind Nationen geworden' ('The students said "Let there be light", and there was light. The world was created in six days, Austria in two. The monarchy's great corral of peoples has turned into a civilised state, the secret police and the censorship have stopped being watchdogs, the herds have become nations').[4] As a member of the Academic Legion, however, Kürnberger tried to keep under control the real proletariat, the propertyless urban mass, which was widely feared as an anarchic force. The danger of internal conflict among the revolutionary forces seemed confirmed when in August 1848 workers' demonstrations were suppressed by the citizen militia, who killed more people than had fallen in the March uprising. Kürnberger now withdrew from active politics, and his disillusionment was strengthened when in October the Minister of War, Latour, was beaten to death by an uncontrollable crowd.[5]

Throughout 1848 Kürnberger's writings on politics are interwoven with reflections on culture. His essay 'Gedanken über die Lyrik der Zukunft' ('Thoughts on the Lyric Poetry of the Future'), published on 17 April 1848, begins with the bold statement: 'Die Kunst ist die unbewußte Geschichts-schreibung der Menschheit' ('Art is the unconscious historiography of human-kind').[6] Art, according to Kürnberger, reveals that history is tripartite: ancient literature (that of Athens and republican Rome) dealt with public affairs; modern poetry, from the troubadours to Goethe, deals with the human heart. Now, however, the private ecstasies of the Romantic poet are less interesting than the prospect of political emancipation: Romanticism is over, and a new poetry, represented by Heine, Béranger, Byron, and Lenau, has begun to express our hopes of changing the world. However, we still lack a great hymnic poet who will apply classical rhetoric to humankind's struggle for freedom. Of such poetry, Kürnberger says in conclusion: 'Sie wird der Schiller der Realität sein' ('It will be the Schiller of reality', ii. 383). Even earlier, in February 1848, Kürnberger showed his belief that art could change consciousness and promote emancipation by urging that the Burgtheater should stage political plays instead of domestic dramas and thus educate its public as citizens: 'Der Geist der Freiheit, der politischen Selbständigkeit, der Bürgerwürde, der eigenen Macht und Größe muß tief und tiefer ins Volk dringen ... wenn wir das heilige Palladium der Konstitution wie Männer schätzen und schützen sollen' ('The spirit of freedom, of political independ-ence, of civic dignity, of one's own power and greatness, must penetrate deeper and deeper into the people, if we are to value and defend the sacred palladium of the constitution like men').[7] Just as the philosophy of the

Encyclopaedists had heralded the French Revolution, so the humble realism of German village fiction was a symptom of revolution in Germany, threatening the supremacy of kings and parliaments (ii. 395).

After Vienna had been reconquered by Imperial troops, Kürnberger escaped on 10 November 1848 with a forged passport. Having reached Dresden, Kürnberger was arrested in May 1849 on suspicion of involvement in the uprising there, simply because his 'revolutionary' appearance, with a broad-brimmed hat and long hair, excited the suspicion of an army officer who detained him in the street. He was imprisoned without trial in a fortress until February 1850, when he was released just as he and some fellow-prisoners had concerted a plan for escape. He then lived in Hamburg, initially under a false name. Meanwhile, the authorities in Vienna listed Kürnberger as 'highly suspicious' in the Police Register of Politically Suspect Persons, and tried repeatedly to have him extradited.[8] His letters from exile are full of understandable complaints about his poverty, his difficulty in getting his plays, essays and stories published, and his tussle with the authorities in order to obtain a passport.[9] He returned to Vienna in 1856, but his continuing struggles with Austrian bureaucracy required him periodically to seek refuge in Germany or Hungary.

In exile, Kürnberger remained proud of the achievements of the Revolution. His views became more radical. On 8 December 1850 he set out his political ideas in a long letter to his brother. Socialism is the attempt to rectify the present imbalance between the freedom and luxury of the few and the poverty of the many. 'Der Sozialismus ist nichts anderes als die Forderung: die ganze Grundlage der heutigen Gesellschaft möge revidiert (geprüft) und Einheit, Gerechtigkeit, Ordnung, Maß und Ziel hineingebracht werden' ('Socialism is nothing but the demand that the entire basis of modern society should be re-examined and that unity, justice, order, moderation, and purpose should be introduced').[10] Only in a republic can Socialism and freedom flourish: monarchy should be swept away like rubble. A republic without Socialism permits only limited freedom: 'Aber wer ist denn frei in einer Republik ohne Sozialismus? Bloß der Bürger, nicht der Mensch; bloß der Besitz, nicht die Arbeit; bloß eine Partei, nicht die Gesellschaft' (p. 111). He thinks the constitutional separation of power is a farce, and has equal scorn for its liberal and radical proponents. At this period he shows sympathy with *individual* conspirators such as Catilina and Aaron Burr.[11] In 1851 he wrote a play on Catilina, which he refers to as 'mein (sozialistischer) Catilina'.[12] He thought that if performed it would be ranked close to Grillparzer's *Ottokar,* but his prolonged efforts to get it staged were unsuccessful. Kürnberger's Catilina represents Rome as oppressing its provinces; the conspiratorial gathering at his house includes representatives of various subject nations (obviously alluding to the Habsburg Empire). He declaims: 'Die Republik der Welt sei unser Ziel, / Freiheit für alle, das ist die Verschwörung!' ('Our goal shall be the republic of the world, / Freedom for all is our conspiracy!')[13] In keeping with Kürnberger's Socialism at this period, Catilina's arch-enemies are the reactionary Cicero and the plutocrat Crassus. Kürnberger also considered a play about William of Orange, a revolutionary leader who, like himself, fled into exile.[14]

Exile disillusioned Kürnberger not only with politics but also about the power of culture in modern society. The commercial city of Hamburg struck him (as it had Heine) as cold and selfish: he complains in June 1850 that its inhabitants have 'den echten Egoismus einer Krämerkommune' ('the real egoism of a community of hucksters') and cause him 'Berserkerwut über den Geist der hiesigen karthaginiensischen Geld- und Handelsrepublik' ('fury at the spirit of this Carthaginian republic of finance and commerce').[15] Worse still, Hamburg seemed to typify the modern world, in which poetry had no place. Kürnberger became convinced, as he told Heinrich Laube, 'daß das Opfer der Poesie gefordert wird vom Zeitalter der rationellen Zivilisation' ('that the age of rational civilisation requires the sacrifice of poetry').[16] These views find expression in *Der Amerika-Müde*.

Kürnberger wrote this novel from spring 1854 till autumn 1855, with great reluctance, simply because he hoped to make money from it; like many other nineteenth-century German authors, he was obsessed by the prestige of classical drama, and would much rather have worked on his play *Firdusi*. Despite pressure from his publisher, Kürnberger did not fulfil his contract, which required him to deliver a portion of manuscript every month; he got behind, and early chapters were being printed while he was still writing the later ones. When published at the end of 1855, the novel was immensely successful: the first printing, of 10,000 copies, was sold out in a few years.

Der Amerika-Müde has a simple plot. The hero, a German aristocrat and poet called Moorfeld, arrives in New York full of enthusiasm for American liberty, but is disillusioned by his acquaintance with the country. He stays with a puritanical businessman and glimpses the coldness and vulgarity of American domestic life; visits the German settlers in the area of New York called 'Kleindeutschland' or Little Germany; and discusses current affairs in the elegant house of a wealthy New Yorker, Mr Bennet. He finds that German immigrants are generally despised. He then makes an uncomfortable journey to Ohio via Pennsylvania, where he observes how the German settlers have lost contact with their original culture but not gained a new one. After encountering bad inns and interfering clergymen, he arrives at New Lisbon, a dismal settlement in a swamp, which boasts a 'City Hall' and a Gothic cathedral built of planks. Here he buys some land on impulse, in order to help an unfortunate German settler called Anhorst, but is soon cheated out of it by unscrupulous locals; the law protects them instead of the rightful owner. Everything goes wrong, with an inevitability that becomes almost farcical. Anhorst is drowned in Lake Erie after a collision between two steamers: one had no warning bell and was sunk, while the captain of the other did not stop to look for survivors. A little German girl Moorfeld is fond of is frightened into insanity by a Methodist preacher. Back in New York, Moorfeld finds that his German acquaintances have either become unscrupulous materialists or fallen victim to the terrorism of American 'Rowdies'. He also meets Mozart's librettist Lorenzo da Ponte just as the latter is collapsing from hunger in a

Manhattan street; da Ponte tells how, having found Americans too prudish for Mozart, he became a businessman, but became bankrupt and was reduced to penury. (In fact, as Jeffrey Sammons has pointed out, da Ponte [1749–1838], who founded an Italian opera-house in New York and taught Italian at Columbia College, made an adequate if precarious living and praised New York in his memoirs.[17]) On the day Moorfeld leaves New York, thousands of xenophobic rioters burn down the German quarter. As his ship passes through the Narrows, an immigrant ship arrives full of Germans who point to the smoke rising from Little Germany and shout: 'Vivat das freie Amerika!' ('Long live free America!', iv. 567).

The very title of Kürnberger's novel announces its opposition to the current enthusiasm for America. He wrote to the Viennese man of letters Ludwig August Frankl in May 1854: 'Mein Roman wird der Amerika-Müde heißen, ein Titel von ostentativer Gegensätzlichkeit wie Sie sehen zu dem Europa-Müden und in einem Focus zusammenfaßen [sic], was von materiellen wie ästhetischen Enttäuschungen die überkommene Kenntniß des Westens uns bis jetzt zugeführt hat' ('My novel will be called The Man Weary of America, a title conspicuously opposed, as you can see, to The Man Weary of Europe, and it will comprehend in a single focus the material and aesthetic disappointments brought us hitherto by the knowledge of the West that has reached us').[18] The word 'europamüde' was apparently first used by Heine in his *Englische Fragmente* (1828): he describes how he enjoyed talking to Lascar sailors in the London docks because he felt 'des dumpfen abendländischen Wesens so ziemlich überdrüssig, so recht Europa-müde' ('thoroughly fed up with the dreary character of the West, really tired of Europe').[19] The word was given added currency when Ernst Willkomm used it as the title of his novel *Die Europa-Müden* (1838), which praises America extravagantly. At this period many thousands of Germans hoped to find relief in America from political frustration and material misery. In the 1830s some 150,000 emigrated to America; the crop failure and famine of the 1840s increased the number to 434,000; and in the 1850s almost a million emigrated. Many writers celebrated America as the land of freedom. In *Schutt* ('Rubble', 1835) the Austrian liberal aristocratic poet Graf Auersperg, alias Anastasius Grün, represented America as the land of the future: his 'Cincinnatus' sequence takes the ruins of Pompeii to represent an oppressive but crumbling Europe and contrasts it with the pastoral idyll of a tea-drinking American planter in the Appalachians, the solemnity of the primeval forest on the Ohio River, and the patriotic solidarity surrounding the figure of Washington.[20] And in later nineteenth-century German fiction it is the most spirited characters, like Judith in Keller's *Der grüne Heinrich* ('Green Henry') and Gideon Franke in Fontane's *Irrungen, Wirrungen* ('Error and Confusion'), who emigrate to America and achieve success there.

However, there were also dissentient voices that drew attention to the absence of tradition, the existence of slavery, the pressure of public opinion, the ruthlessness of capitalism, and the treatment of the American Indians. Dickens's *Martin Chuzzlewit*, with its hilariously scathing American episodes, was known in Germany and even adapted by Nestroy as *Die Anverwandten* (1848). The two opposing views on America, as on much else, are represented by Ludwig Börne and Heinrich Heine. On 15 January 1833, in number 97 of his *Briefe aus Paris* ('Letters from Paris'), Börne celebrates America as the land of freedom whose very existence angers the European aristocracy.[21] Heine, in his book on Börne, pointed out that this freedom did not extend to the black population of the South, and reported how, even in the North, the daughter of a New York clergyman had been tarred and feathered for marrying a black man.[22] His poem 'Jetzt wohin?' ('Whither now?') anticipates Kürnberger in imagining America as an egalitarian land of uncivilised boors – 'dem großen Freiheitsstall / Der bewohnt von Gleichheitsflegeln' ('Freedom's great stable, where the boors live equally').[23]

Two writers in particular may be discussed, as they had both travelled in America and experienced the transition from euphoria to disillusionment, and as Kürnberger alludes to both in his book: Nikolaus Lenau and Gottfried Duden.

Lenau, well known as a poet of 'Weltschmerz' or cosmic suffering, conceived the idea of visiting America at a time of deep depression and financial uncertainty.[24] Having lost half his inheritance in an ill-judged financial speculation, he hoped to become rich rapidly in America, and also had grandiose ideas about exploring unspoiled nature. After a sea journey of over two months, during which he fell ill with scurvy, he landed at Baltimore on 8 October 1832, intending originally to stay for no more than six weeks. He visited the interior and bought land at New Lisbon, Ohio (Kürnberger takes over this name). After visiting his property at Christmas 1832, he rented it for eight years to Ludwig Häberle, a Swabian who had made the crossing with him. Lenau made further journeys, visiting Niagara in March 1833, then travelling down the Hudson to New York; early in May he embarked for Europe again, disappointed with the New World. He paid little attention to his farm; Häberle abandoned it after a year and a half, and Lenau, by not paying taxes, lost his legal claim to it. It seems clear that, as Manfred Durzak points out, Lenau had no serious intention of settling in America but regarded his farm simply as an investment which an employee would run; Durzak may even be justified in alleging that Lenau projected his own cupidity on to the Americans.[25] Certainly Lenau seems to have made no serious attempt to sympathise with American life. On 16 October, within a few days of landing, we find him denouncing the Americans for soulless commercialism:

> Bruder, diese Amerikaner sind himmelanstinkende Krämerseelen. Todt für alles geistige Leben, maustodt. Die Nachtigall hat Recht daß sie bei diesen Wichten nicht einkehrt. Das scheint mir von ernster, tiefer Bedeutung zu seyn, daß Amerika gar keine Nachtigall hat. Es kommt mir vor, wie ein poetischer Fluch. Eine Niagarastimme gehört dazu, um diesen Schuften zu predigen, daß es noch höhere Götter gebe, als die im Münzhause geschlagen werden. Man darf die Kerle nur im Wirthshause sehen, um sie auf immer zu hassen.[26]

[Brother, these Americans are money-grubbing souls that stink to high heaven. Dead to all spiritual life, dead as doornails. The nightingale is right not to visit these scoundrels. I see a deep and serious significance in the fact that America has no nightingale. It seems like a poetic curse. It would take the voice of Niagara to preach to these villains that there are higher gods than those coined in the mint. One need only see the fellows in the inn to hate them for ever.]

This cultural critique of America continues in subsequent letters. America lacks any traditional, organic culture. Its typical inhabitant is 'der praktische Mensch in seiner furchtbarsten Nüchternheit' ('practical man in his most terrible sobriety').[27] The human spirit cannot cross the Atlantic. Americans are unbearably crude; even German immigrants soon lose their character and sink to the general level. Nature shares in this degeneracy: there are no nightingales, indeed no song-birds (in fact, since it was autumn, the song-birds had migrated southwards); Lenau quotes approvingly Buffon's opinion that all animate beings degenerate on American soil, and adds: 'Ich habe hier noch keinen muthigen Hund gesehen, kein feuriges Pferd, keinen leidenschaftlichen Menschen' ('I have not seen a single courageous dog here, nor a spirited horse, nor a passionate person').[28] These absurd views would not be worth quoting except to show that Lenau brought to America a conviction that as a new, inorganic society it must be in a state of cultural decline, and that, as a late-Romantic poet, he then abused the poetic fallacy to impute such degeneracy to the entire natural world found in America.

Kürnberger models his hero on Lenau and adopts Lenau's view of America. He makes matters worse by representing Moorfeld as having been cheated by American barrack-room lawyers, whereas Lenau was in fact let down by the German Häberle. However, as Kürnberger explained in a letter to Frankl of 25 June 1854: 'Die Intention dieser Dichtung geht nämlich in *erster* Linie darauf aus, die Verunglückung meines Auswanderers der *amerikanischen* Lebenspraxis zur Last zu schreiben' ('You see, the *principal* aim of this work is to blame my emigrant's misfortune on the *American* way of life', iv. 578); the fact that Lenau was ruined by a fellow-German and by his own negligence had therefore to be suppressed.

Gottfried Duden (1785–1856) was a German lawyer who lived from 1824 to 1827 at Montgomery, Missouri, and wrote a much-read book describing his experiences and urging other Germans to follow his example and emigrate to America.[29] Duden had a maize plantation, with many vegetables and a cow; he did not clear the ground himself, but waited while it was being done; he employed a cook and a hired farm-hand; he himself spent the time hunting, reading, and visiting other planters, but did no manual labour. However, he enthusiastically recommends emigration as the solution to over-population in Germany. He claims that German settlers are prosperous and well-liked. He especially recommends the Missouri region for settlement, dismissing fears about floods, yellow fever, and wild beasts, and repudiating a book by one Friedrich Schmidt which warns German readers that the area is subject to flooding (pp. 55–6). Discussing the American Indians, he deplores their cruelty and childishness, defends the current policy of compelling them to abandon nomadism and form settlements, and says they are well treated, despite the mistaken beliefs of 'philantropische Schwärmer' ('philanthropic enthusiasts', p. 107). The Missouri alone, not to mention its neighbouring rivers, has room for millions of plantations. More generally, he praises rapturously the happiness of Americans in general:

> Die große Fruchtbarkeit des Bodens, dessen ungeheuere Ausdehnung, das milde Klima, die herrlichen Stromverbindungen, der durchaus freie Verkehr in einem Raume von mehreren tausend Meilen, die vollkommene Sicherheit der Personen und des Eigenthumes, bei sehr geringen Staatslasten, das ist es, was man als die eigentlichen Pfeiler der glücklichen Lage der Amerikaner zu betrachten hat (p. 231).

> [The great fertility of the soil, its enormous extent, the mild climate, the splendid network of rivers, the entirely free traffic in a space of several thousand miles, the complete security of persons and property, with very slight taxes – these are to be regarded as the real pillars of the Americans' happy situation.]

Duden's book, however, contains some warnings. The first two years are bound to be hard. Settlers need plenty of money. They should emigrate in a group, under strong leadership and with a doctor attached, and should make sure there are other German settlers in the neighbourhood. Nor should they expect anything like European culture in America, except in the seaports: '*Dem Beurtheilenden ist nämlich scharf einzuprägen, daß an eben der Cultur der Amerikaner das practische Leben den vorzüglichsten Antheil hat.* Sie ist ein Erzeugniß der unternehmenden Thätigkeit und *im Ganzen dieser dienend*; wogegen in *Europa umgekehrt* die Bildung fast allein aus dem Unterricht in Schulen, oder doch aus Büchern, hervorgeht' ('*Anyone trying to make up his mind must be firmly assured that American culture is dominated by practical life.* It is a product of active enterprise and *serves this purpose as a whole;* whereas in Europe, by contrast, education proceeds almost exclusively from school instruction, or at least from books', p. 293). The relentlessly practical character of American life is one of the main charges Kürnberger makes in *Der Amerika-Müde.*

Duden's *Bericht* was immensely successful.[30] By combining travel narrative and practical information, it founded a genre of handbooks for emigrants. It undoubtedly helped to encourage the enormous wave of emigration from Germany to America in the 1830s. Emigrants infected by Duden's enthusiasm were often disappointed by their experiences: thus the nationalistic Germans who founded the town of Hermann on the Missouri in 1836 soon had to sell off their land. In response to such people's complaints, Duden published an ironic recantation.[31] Here he affects to repent of believing that his readers could understand German properly. He repeats his practical advice to would-be emigrants and also savages those who can find nothing good in America.

Kürnberger mentions Duden's book twice, unflatteringly, in *Der Amerika-Müde*. It is among the books on America that are dismissed as amateurish (iv. 77). Later Moorfeld meets some settlers who were cheated by a land agent and now live on a barren, barely habitable prairie; they are cultured people whose books include 'deutsche und englische Klassiker, Chateaubriands Natchez, Dudens Missouri und ähnliche Phantasiewerke über Amerika' ('German and English classics, Chateaubriand's *Les Natchez*, Duden's *Missouri*, and similar works of fantasy about America', iv. 333). Nevertheless, Kürnberger seems to have used Duden's book both as a structural model and as a source of information. Duden's book consists of a series of informative letters, supposedly written on his travels. His journey from Baltimore via Cincinnati and Louisville to St Louis seems to have served Kürnberger as the model for Moorfeld's journey from New York via Philadelphia, Harrisburg and Pittsburgh to Ohio. Some of the details he mentions are also taken over by Kürnberger. For example, in the sixth letter Duden describes the construction of fences, explaining that the zig-zag arrangement of rails uses more wood in order to dispense with the labour of carpenters (p. 21). Kürnberger uses this information, but in a negative tone. After complaining of the desolate appearance of American farmland, he adds: 'Die Zickzack-Zäune, die sog. Virginia-Fenzen vollenden den widerwärtigen Anblick' ('The zig-zag fences, known as Virginia fences, complete the repulsive sight', iv. 321). Similarly, the grand names given to American towns (Lisbon, Paris, etc.), and the grid pattern on which they are designed, are interpreted positively by Duden, whereas Kürnberger sees such features as pretentious, artificial, and unimaginative.

Besides showing particular disapproval of Duden's book, Kürnberger's narrator criticises the German literature on America available in the early 1830s, the period in which the novel is set. He says that books of travel were uninformative, amateurish, and fanciful. Yet they were still more misleading through their political tendency:

> Der Liberalismus der Restaurationsepoche fand in Wort und Schrift über Amerika eines seiner wenigen erlaubten Ausdrucksmittel. Er benutzte es eifrig. Er feierte die Sternbanner-Republik als die praktische Verwirklichung seines geächteten Ideals. Er hätte es für politische Unklugheit, ja für Verrat gehalten, die Flecken seiner Sonne zu gestehen (iv. 77).

> [The liberalism of the (post–1815) Restoration period found one of the few means of expression permitted to it in talking and writing about America. It celebrated the Republic of the Star-Spangled Banner as the practical fulfilment of its prohibited ideal. It would have thought it politically unwise, if not treacherous, to acknowledge the spots on its sun.]

This passage forewarns us that *Der Amerika-Müde is* the work of a disillusioned liberal. Kürnberger thinks that the liberalism of the Vormärz overestimated the importance of politics at the expense of culture. He therefore shows us America through the eyes of a poet, in order to demonstrate that cultural decline necessarily brings political degeneracy. The poet, as Moorfeld explains, can best judge how far the ideal has been realised in any political system. Alluding implicitly to Schiller's poem 'Das Ideal und das Leben', which stresses how remote the ideal is from life, he tells his New York hosts that as life and the ideal have now drawn closer together, modern poets have the task of exploring the ideal on earth by examining various societies:

> Der Poet wird künftig Tourist sein. Er sucht das Ideal auf Erden, oder vielmehr er lernt die Realität gründlicher kennen, eh' er sie verdammt und zum Recht der Verzweiflung greift. – Byron ging nach Griechenland, ich nach Amerika. Er besuchte ein absterbendes Volk, ich ein aufblühendes (iv. 171).

> ['The poet in future will be a tourist. He will seek the ideal on earth, or rather he will become more thoroughly acquainted with reality, before he condemns it and resorts to the right of despair. Byron went to Greece, I to America. He visited a dying nation, I a nation that is growing.']

If Moorfeld had been satisfied by his experiences, he might have become the 'Schiller of reality' that Kürnberger hoped for in 1848. But his idealistic naiveté is clearly heading for disappointment.

Not only Kürnberger's ideals, but also his powers of representation, are determined by his allegiance to German classicism. His classical aesthetics preclude him from giving an adequately realistic depiction of American life. Thus Kürnberger was delighted when Laube described his play *Quintin Messis* as 'goethisch', and told him that Goethe had been his early ideal, 'der Mentor meiner dichtenden Lehrjahre' ('the mentor of my poetic apprenticeship').[32] He demands symmetry, totality, and the identity of the outer form with the inner content. In an essay on the 'Dorfgeschichte' or village tale, written in October 1847 and published in January 1848, he accepted detailed realism only if it fitted into a harmonious and idealised totality: 'Die Aufgabe der Kunst ist die volle und erschöpfende Repräsentation der Weltidee in einer gewissen Summe sinnlicher Erscheinungen, die in idealen, bedeutenden Linien den Charakter des Ganzen ausprägen' ('The task of art is the full and exhaustive representative of the cosmic idea in a certain sum of sensory phenomena which determine the character of the whole in significant, ideal lines', ii. 352). He has no interest in the contingent details of everyday life or in the homely truthfulness that his contemporary, George Eliot, praised in the painting of Dutch realism. He would not have appreciated her famous appeal in chapter 17 of *Adam Bede:* 'All honour and reverence to the divine beauty of form! Let us cultivate it to the utmost in men, women, and children – in our gardens and in our houses. But let us love that other beauty, too, which lies in no secret of proportion, but in the secret of deep human sympathy.'

In *Der Amerika-Müde*, Moorfeld's appearance is described in terms of

German classical aesthetics: 'Sein Wuchs, mit Winckelmann zu reden, sein Stamm ist fein, wir möchten sagen *artistisch* gebaut' ('His stature, or to use Winckelmann's term, his trunk, is finely, we might say *artistically* built', iv. 5). Even his clothing is suited to his personality, as form to content: 'Sie stellt eine Persönlichkeit dar, welche über die Identität von Gestalt und Gehalt durch ein natürliches Gefühl, durch eine angeborene Poesie belehrt ist' ('It represents a personality that is informed of the identity of form and content by a natural feeling, an innate poetry', iv. 5–6). Mr Bennet's house in New York, where Moorfeld attends a reception, reveals its classical simplicity in its façade: 'Seine Verhältnisse waren einfach, seine Ornamente schicklich, jede Linie mit dem Takt des Genies getroffen. Das Auge lief auf und ab daran und empfand nichts Störendes, nur Harmonie und höchste Idealität der Formen' ('Its proportions were simple, its ornaments seemly, every line was drawn with the tact of genius. The eye surveyed it and felt nothing discordant, only harmony and supreme ideality of forms', iv. 208). It turns out to be modelled on a Florentine palace designed by Raphael. The interior matches the exterior: the hall has only one ornament, a classical statuette of Apollo.

Judged by such aesthetic standards, everyday America must of course seem ugly and grotesque. Kürnberger's didactic purpose excludes Eliot's human sympathy. Dutch realism might have been a suitable model for the scene in the Green Tree, an inn frequented by German immigrants; after all, Lenau adopts this mode for the earlier part of 'Das Blockhaus', one of the best of his American poems, and Grün uses it in describing the Independence Day celebrations in no. 7 of his 'Cincinnatus' sequence. Instead, Kürnberger favours Dickensian caricature, so that the landlord is described as ludicrously fat, and the clerk Henning is exaggeratedly tall and skinny. On the train to Philadelphia, Moorfeld is surprised that the conductor has not even a badge to mark his status, and mentions this to another traveller, who is described grotesquely:

> Mein Nachbar war ein langer, hagerer Mann, aber meine Frage blähte ihn auf wie eine frische Brise ein schlappes Segel. Er streckte Arme und Beine aus wie ein Bachkrebs, der an einer schwierigen Stelle am Ufer klettert, spuckte weit von sich, zog seinen Vatermörder in die Höhe und sagte 'mit Sonnenschein in der Brust': 'Ich rate, Mister, ein Kondukteur ist kein Hund, das ist ein Faktum; wozu ein Abzeichen?' (iv. 297).

> ['My neighbour was a tall, lean man, but my question puffed him up, as a fresh breeze swells a slack sail. He stretched out his arms and legs like a fresh-water crab climbing up a difficult part of the bank, spat a long way, pulled up his stiff collar, and said sunnily: "I guess, Mister, a conductor ain't a dog, that's a fact; why a badge?"']

Even nature in America lacks classical sublimity, as Moorfeld finds when he explores the forests: 'Dabei mangelte dem Walde aber doch auch der Ausdruck der ruhigen Größe und Erhabenheit. Die Baumasten standen charakterlos in unendlicher Buntheit durcheinander' (iv. 361–2: 'The forest also lacked the expression of quiet greatness and sublimity. The tree-trunks were jumbled up in endless variety without character').

The literary conventions by which Kürnberger represents America already dictate the outlines of his social and ideological criticism. If classical beauty and traditional culture are not to be found, Kürnberger cannot represent what America does offer in a sympathetic or respectful way. He can only depict it with grotesque exaggeration. In keeping with his polemical purpose, therefore, he selects those aspects of social life that lend themselves to such depiction.

Kürnberger's Americans have even worse manners than those in *Martin Chuzzlewit*. He intimates that when travelling by train in America it is normal to stretch out your legs and put your feet on the shoulders of the person opposite you. On the steamer there is only one towel for all the passengers. Travelling, Americans are coarse and unkempt; they spit and tell endless dirty jokes. At home they are painfully respectable. Mr Bennet illustrates American prudery by recounting how he tried to introduce the waltz: one lady fainted, another screamed, and even Colonel Burr, a social outcast, refused to visit his house in future. Yet the average middle-class household is devoid of taste or politeness. The house of Moorfeld's New York landlord, the businessman Staunton, is crudely decorated, and it emerges that the choice of decor is left to the tradesman. The ill-furnished parlour contains no books except an ostentatiously displayed Bible. Before dinner, Mrs Staunton is found at the table reading the *New York Tribune,* and does not lower the paper when the gentlemen enter the room. Table manners are repulsive: the host puts a soft-boiled egg in his mouth and spits out pieces of shell. The food is almost uneatable: the meat is fat; the host drinks champagne mixed with brandy. This strikes Moorfeld as an allegory of American culture: 'Trinkt der Amerikaner seine Champagner mit Brandy, wer garantiert hier das Genie gegen die Prosa? fragte sich der Fremdling' ('"If the American drinks his champagne with brandy, who will safeguard genius here against prose?" wondered the stranger', iv. 39).

American cultural life is represented as entirely vulgarised and commercialised. The freedom of the press is constantly abused for the sake of sensational journalism. On landing in New York, Moorfeld listens to the newsboys and gathers that half the nations of Europe are in revolt, a number of kings have been deposed, many ministers executed, several cities swallowed up by the earth; the list is rounded off by 'ein teuflisch-raffinierter Doppel-Gattenmord' ('the double murder of a married couple, carried out with devilish cunning', iv. 10). At the theatre, Moorfeld sees a crude, exaggerated, violent melodrama whose success is determined by a vociferous claque. Religion is joyless and sanctimonious: Moorfeld is rebuked for playing his violin on a Sunday, and even for taking a Sunday stroll. The only amusement permitted on Sunday is watching the fire-brigade put out fires. His New York host's wife, who belongs to innumerable benevolent organisations, gets her pleasure from shopping on Saturday and attending church on Sunday to hear, and be sexually stimulated by, an elegant preacher: 'aus Sabbat und Shopping zogen die Damen Newyorks die Kraft, eine Woche lang zu Hause so langweilig zu sein, als es ihnen die Landessitte vorschrieb' ('Sabbath and shopping gave the ladies of New York the strength to be as dull at home for a week as the national custom prescribed', iv. 81). In the interior of America we find a camp-meeting, which is an orgy of howling and weeping, adroitly stage-managed by a revivalist preacher.[33] To show that all these aspects of culture are driven by cynical, hard-sell commercialism, Kürnberger makes his hero encounter the same character, Hoby, first as the noisiest of the news-boys, then as the leader of a theatre claque, and finally as the preacher at the camp-meeting.

The obvious targets, such as the treatment of slaves and Indians, also receive due criticism. Kürnberger condemns slavery and makes Moorfeld predict a slave rebellion. On his journey to Lake Erie, Moorfeld meets an Indian who tells him how the whites cheat the Indians, get them drunk, and induce them to fight and kill each other. Like Dickens, Moorfeld visits the Philadelphia penitentiary, which subjected its inmates to solitary confinement; here he finds captives reduced almost to imbecility, and obsessed by sadistic fantasies which in normal life would easily be dispelled. This 'progressive' mode of punishment was notorious: some years earlier Kürnberger wrote to a friend who had been condemned to death, 'Da Sie nicht dem pennsylvanischen System verfallen, das Granit und Basalt zerreibt, so wird mir nicht bange um Sie' ('As you have not fallen in to the hands of the Pennsylvanian system that wears down granite and basalt, I am not worried about you').[34]

More penetrating comment on America is placed in the mouth of Benthal, a German immigrant who had to flee after taking part in the public demonstration of liberalism known as the Hambach Festival. Moorfeld first finds him working as an assistant teacher in a school kept by one Mr Mockingbird. In his spare time Benthal helps German immigrants to find jobs and tries to persuade them to be more adaptable, learn English, and get used to the greasy food. However, he also urges them to retain their German qualities:

> Ihren deutschen Tiefsinn stemmen Sie entgegen der routinierten Flachheit, Ihr deutsches Gemüt der höflichen Herzenskälte, Ihre deutsche Religion dem trocknen Sektenkram, Ihr deutsches Persönlichkeitsgefühl dem herdemäßigen Parteitreiben, Ihr deutsches Gewissen dem Humbug und Yankee-Trick, Ihre deutsche Sprache dem Mißlaut und der Gedankenarmut, Ihr deutsches Weinglas der Mäßigkeitsheuchelei, Ihre deutsche Sonntagslust dem Sonntagsmuckertum Amerikas (iv. 147).

> ['Oppose your German profundity to routine shallowness, your German warmth to polite coldness, your German religion to the dry rubbish of sects, your German sense of personality to herd-like party politics, your German conscience to humbug and Yankee trickery, your German language to ugly sounds and intellectual poverty, your German wine-glass to hypocritical abstinence, your German enjoyment of Sunday to America's sabbatarian bigotry.']

If the Germans remain true to their national identity, Benthal foresees a providential union between American materialism and German 'Geist', which will enable Germany to dominate not only America but also the world. In the context of the novel as a whole, these prophecies seem to be extravagant, doomed to frustration by the power of American materialism, to which Benthal himself falls victim. By the end he has gone into business with Mr Staunton, adopted American dress, manners, and commercial outlook, and dropped his German fiancée in favour of Mr Staunton's daughter Sarah; he has fantasies of becoming 'ein Cäsar in der Wall Street' (iv. 540), but it is clear that the dubious Staunton will get the better of him.

Earlier in the novel, however, Benthal is presented in a thoroughly positive light. He reads aloud an essay on American society, in which he tries to explain its stability. His main argument is that Americans overpraise their constitution and do not realise that their security from revolutionary upheavals comes from the wide distribution of property. Despite this safeguard, America's stability may not last: the size and diversity of the Union, with 26 states, makes Benthal (rightly) predict fragmentation and civil war, which he thinks may be followed by military dictatorship and monarchy. It is tempting to suppose, as Hildegard Meyer does, that this analysis is indebted to Tocqueville's *Democracy in America*.[35] However, Tocqueville dismisses the danger of military dictatorship and, less judiciously, the likelihood that any part of the Union might secede; he thinks that the tendency is towards ever-increasing democracy, and that the state, by diminishing its citizens' initiative, may come to exercise a quiet tyranny which is compatible with formal democracy.[36]

By 1854, when he wrote *Der Amerika-Müde*, Kürnberger's political views had evidently swung a long way from his Socialism of 1851. He now espouses a form of liberalism with strongly conservative features. In rejecting the democratic liberalism of the Vormärz in favour of a more practical, conservative, nationalistic liberalism, Kürnberger's novel resembles Gustav Freytag's *Soll und Haben* ('Debit and Credit'), which likewise appeared in 1855.[37] Freytag undertook to show the German people at work, and placed his upright hero Anton Wohlfart in the firm of T. O. Schröter, which was supposed to exemplify humane capitalism; though the modern reader will be struck by the stunted lives of Schröter's employees, the one-dimensionality of the hero, the imperialist attitude towards the Poles, and of course the projection of the negative side of capitalism onto the villainous Jew Veitel Itzig. Kürnberger provides a negative counterpart by depicting the horrors of unrestrained democracy. Few readers will find his novel convincing, least of all Americans, who have always responded to it with patriotic indignation. It seems to me that Kürnberger's critique of materialism, however persuasive in the abstract, has not received convincing fictional form. Kürnberger is hampered by numerous deficiencies. Most obviously, his attempt at a serious critique of America is mixed up with trivial objections to American table manners, zig-zag fencing, and so forth, and with national stereotypes which are still widely current one hundred and fifty years later. More significantly, his allegiance to German classicism leads him to over-estimate the importance of culture and to confuse it with politics and with morality. And, most importantly for the literary critic, his negative judgement on American life is already implicit in his mode of representation: unable to escape from classical aesthetics, he can represent American life only by means of grotesque satire, which is insufficient to sustain a full-length novel and makes what should be tragic events mechanically and laughably predictable.

However, Kürnberger's imaginary America is ultimately an allegory for the progress of liberalism in Austria. It is generally agreed that Austrian liberalism went through two phases.[38] Before and after 1848 it was an emancipatory movement which fought against absolutism and urged the introduction of constitutional government and the establishment of human rights. When liberalism itself attained power in the 1870s, its emphasis shifted to safeguarding the dominance of the wealthy bourgeoisie and its economic freedom against the demands for political participation and social security that came from below – from the lower middle classes and working classes who were to find their political voice in the Christian Social and Socialist movements. Even earlier, however, in the decade 1849–59, economic liberalism, with laissez-faire policies freed from political controls, operated without any advance towards political emancipation. This disjunction of economic from political liberalism seems to be a characteristic feature of late nineteenth-century Austrian and, still more, of German history, distinguishing both from the development of liberalism in Britain and France.[39]

In the reflective passages of Der *Amerika-Müde*, Kürnberger is attacking the tendencies already present in the liberalism of the early 1850s: the development of economic laissez-faire unimpeded by culture and morality. Thus he introduces into the novel the Boston clergyman Dr Channing, who delivers a speech on America's defects. Its education is too limited: 'Der Geist unsrer Pädagogik ist nicht der, Menschen zu bilden, sondern Rechen-maschinen zu machen' ('The spirit of our teaching is not to form human beings, but to make calculating machines', iv. 245). At the end of the novel we see democracy degenerating into mob rule. As the mob burns down Little Germany with no attempt at interference by the police, thousands of 'Rowdies', including youthful members of the fire-brigades, surround City Hall and squirt water at the Mayor when he tries to calm them. These satirically exaggerated events fulfil Dr Channing's prophecy, hundreds of pages earlier, that an emphasis on profit, with no attention to moral restraints and too little provision for the security of property and the individual, must threaten civil society:

Wir sind mit dem *Gewinne* als mit unserem höchsten Gute eine Ehe eingegangen und niemanden darf es wundern, daß aus dieser Ehe die gemeinsten Leidenschaften entsprossen sind, welche alle bessern moralischen Stützen unsers Gemeinwesens entfestigen, während selbstische Berechnung, Neigung nach äußerm Schein, Verschwendung, unruhige, neidische und niedere Begierden, wilder Schwindelgeist und tolle Spekulationswut die Stelle dafür einnehmen. In Wahrheit, es geht ein Geist der Zügellosigkeit und der Verwilderung durch unser Land, der, wenn er nicht unterdrückt wird, der gegenwärtigen Gestaltung der bürgerlichen Gesellschaft die Auflösung droht (iv. 244).

['We have entered into a marriage with *profit* as our supreme good, and nobody should be surprised that this marriage has given birth to the vilest passions, which are slackening all the better moral supports of our community, while their place is taken by selfish calculation, concern with external appearance, extravagance, restless, envious and base desires, unchecked dishonesty and the rage for speculation. Indeed, a spirit of intractable savagery pervades our country, and, if not suppressed, it threatens the present form of civil society with dissolution.']

Such arguments must find a sympathetic response from anyone who has observed how the idolatry of the free market in the 1980s has in many countries served to unravel the social fabric for the sake of individual profit. Kürnberger developed these views in an essay which he wrote in 1861 but did not publish, entitled 'Was ist Freiheit?'. Here he makes a familiar distinction between active freedom, which permits the individual active participation in politics, and passive freedom, which allows the individual to avoid interference. Constitutional government (in which Vormärz liberals placed their hopes) does not bring freedom by itself; it merely puts power into the hands of a bureaucracy and removes it from the people. The model that Austria should follow is that of Great Britain, which permits active freedom through parliamentary democracy and ensures the liberty of the person:

England, welches trotz aller menschlichen Unvollkommenheiten der unbestrittene Musterstaat ist, ist es einzig deshalb, weil es seine historischen Bestände am treuesten bewahrt hat. So besitzt England seine Freiheit in der doppelten Fülle ihrer zwei großen, geschichtlich charakteristischen Kulturformen: es hat in seinem Parlamente die grandios-kostümierte, modern-theatralische Freiheit des Redehaltens und Gesetzemachens; es hat in seiner Habeas-Korpus-Akte die simple, altväterische, aber nicht minder nützliche Freiheit des Ungeschoren-bleibens (i. 470).

['England, which despite all human imperfections is the undisputed model state, is so solely because it has maintained its historic resources most faithfully. Thus England possesses its freedom in the twofold plenitude of its two great and historically distinctive cultural forms: in its parliament it has the freedom of oratory and legislation, grandly costumed, modern and theatrical; in its Habeas Corpus Act it has the simple, traditional, but no less beneficial freedom of remaining unmolested.']

The emphasis here on tradition recalls the depiction of America as a country fatally estranged from cultural traditions. This criticism reappears, with reference to religion, in Kürnberger's other (and far inferior) novel, *Das Schloß der Frevel* ('The Castle of Crimes'), completed in 1875 but published only posthumously. It is about the 'Kulturkampf' and the place of the Catholic Church in a Europe of nation-states. Kürnberger, though highly anticlerical, introduces a cultured and intelligent Jesuit who puts the case for religious tradition and cites America as a horrible warning: 'Amerika, das republikanische, angelsächsisch-protestantische Amerika, das Paraderößlein aller demokratischen Musterreiter, erzeugte sich gar die Wunder des Tischrückens und Geisterklopfens und macht nicht übel Miene, den Spiritismus wie eine Religion zu instituieren' ('America, republican, Anglo-Saxon, Protestant America, the parade horse of all democratic horsemen, even brought forth the wonders of tableturning and spirit-rapping and is in a fair way to institute spiritualism as a religion', v. 138).

Other continuities have recently been pointed out by Karlheinz Rossbacher in his study of late nineteenth-century Austrian liberalism. Rossbacher analyses the Feuilleton 'Ich suche im Nebel meinen Weg' ('I seek my way in the mist', 1875) in which Kürnberger conducts an imaginary conversation with 'Master Vorwärts', a personification of progress whose English title associates this ideology especially with the Anglo-American world. Kürnberger complains that capitalism cannot include beauty in its calculations, and Rossbacher shows that this critique is continuous with the attack on philistine capitalism carried out in *Der Amerika-Müde*.[40] It was his critique of liberalism from the inside that made Karl Kraus call Kürnberger the 'größten politischen Schriftsteller, den Österreich je gehabt' ('the greatest political writer Austria has ever had').[41]

However, the presentation of an ideology in literary form can expose limitations which remain concealed by discursive prose, and the enormous importance that *Der Amerika-Müde* assigns to culture may give one pause. Although it might be hoped that literature and art would extend one's imaginative sympathies, in Kürnberger's case they have a limiting effect. He refuses to take Americans seriously insofar as they lack European culture. His classical aesthetics contradict the implicit democratic thrust of his politics and enable him to represent ordinary people only as harmless grotesques or as a threatening mob. To imagine and represent the turbulent democracy of America would require not classical harmony but Walt Whitman's 'barbaric yawp'.

Notes

1. Jeffrey L. Sammons, 'Land of Limited Possibilities: America in the Nineteenth-Century German Novel', *Yale Review*, 68 (1978), 35–52; reprinted in id., *Imagination and History: Selected Papers on Nineteenth-Century German Literature* (New York, 1988), pp. 217–36 (esp. pp. 231–2).
2. Rüdiger Steinlein, 'Ferdinand Kürnbergers *Der Amerikamüde*. Ein "amerikanisches Kulturbild" als Entwurf einer negativen Utopie', in Sigrid Bauschinger, Horst Denkler and Wilfried Malsch (eds), *Amerika in der deutschen Literatur* (Stuttgart, 1975), pp. 154–77.

3. See R. J. Rath, *The Viennese Revolution of 1848* (Austin, TX, 1957).
4. Ferd. Kürnberger, 'Die Wiener Revolution, fragmentarischer Bericht', *Wiener Sonntagsblätter*, ed. Ludwig August Frankl, 7, no. 12 (no. 1 of new series), 19 March 1848, pp. 13–16 (p. 13).
5. For Kürnberger's reaction, see Hubert Lengauer, *Ästhetik und liberale Opposition. Zur Rollenproblematik des Schriftstellers in der österreichischen Literatur um 1848* (Vienna, 1989), p. 219. The chapter on Kürnberger here (pp. 203–42) is identical with Lengauer's 'Nachwort' to the reissue of *Der Amerikamüde* [sic] in the 'Österreichische Bibliothek' (Vienna, 1985), pp. 565–615.
6. Ferdinand Kürnberger, *Gesammelte Werke*, 4 vols (numbered 1, 2, 4, 5), ed. O. E. Deutsch (Leipzig and Munich, 1910–14), ii. 376. Wherever possible, Kürnberger's works are quoted from this edition, and references by volume and page number are given in the text.
7. 'Das Burgtheater und seine Mission', quoted from Lengauer, *Ästhetik*, p. 220.
8. Lengauer, *Ästhetik*, pp. 228–9.
9. See Ferdinand Kürnberger, *Briefe eines politischen Flüchtlings*, aus dem Nachlaß herausgegeben von Otto Erich Deutsch (Leipzig and Vienna, 1920); 'Die Geschichte meines Passes. Eingabe an Se. Exzellenz den Staatsminister Grafen Belcredi. Persönlich überreicht im Sommer 1866', *Die Fackel*, 214–15, 22 December 1906, 7–38. Karl Kraus printed this document after an editorial dealing with recent injustice and headed 'Aus dem dunkelsten Österreich'.
10. *Briefe eines politischen Flüchtlings*, p. 105.
11. Catilina (108–62 B.C.) tried to overthrow Cicero's government in Rome; Aaron Burr (1756–1836) plotted to found a Western American empire, including Mexico, with New Orleans as its capital.
12. Letter to Heinrich Laube, 24 Sept. 1852, in Otto Erich Deutsch, 'Briefe Ferdinand Kürnbergers an Heinrich Laube', *Deutsche Rundschau*, 181 (Oct.–Dec. 1919), 144–52, 286–304 (p. 286).
13. *Catilina. Drama in fünf Aufzügen* (Hamburg, 1855), p. 35.
14. For William of Orange, see the letter to L. A. Frankl quoted in Deutsch, 'Briefe Kürnbergers an Laube', p. 286n. For Kürnberger's interest in Aaron Burr, whom he compared to Catilina, see *Gesammelte Werke*, vol. 4, p. 216, and Lengauer, *Ästhetik*, p. 235.
15. *Briefe eines politischen Flüchtlings*, p. 92.
16. Letter of 24 September 1852, in Deutsch, 'Briefe Kürnbergers an Laube', p. 288.
17. See 'The Lorenzo Da Ponte Episode in Ferdinand Kürnberger's *Der Amerika-Müde*' in Sammons, *Imagination and History*, pp. 237–46.
18. Quoted in Hansgeorg Schmidt-Bergmann, 'Über die Gegenwärtigkeit von Literatur in literarischen Werken. Leben und Werk Lenaus als Modell für Ferdinand Kürnberger, Peter Härtling und Gernot Wolfgruber', *Lenau-Forum*, 16 (1990), 77–84 (p. 77).
19. Heinrich Heine, *Sämtliche Schriften*, ed. Klaus Briegleb, 6 vols (Munich, 1968–74), vol. 2, p. 594; also used at vol. 5, p. 206, and vol. 6, p. 59.
20. See Anastasius Grün, *Gesammelte Werke*, ed. Ludwig August Frankl, 5 vols (Berlin, 1877), vol. 3, esp. pp. 269, 275, 302.
21. Ludwig Börne, *Sämtliche Schriften*, ed. Peter and Inge Rippmann, 5 vols (Dreieich, 1977), vol. 3, pp. 714–15.
22. Heine, *Sämtliche Schriften*, vol. 4, p. 39.
23. Ibid., vol. 6, p. 101.
24. See the informative article by Eduard Castle, 'Amerikamüde. Lenau und Kürnberger', *Jahrbuch der Grillparzer-Gesellschaft*, 12 (1902), 15–42. More generally, on Kürnberger's sources, see Hildegard Meyer, *Nord-Amerika im Urteil des deutschen Schrifttums bis zur Mitte des 19. Jahrhunderts. Eine Untersuchung über*

Kürnbergers Amerika-Müden (Hamburg, 1929). This important book contains an astonishing bibliography of the contemporary German literature dealing with America.

25. Manfred Durzak, 'Nach Amerika. Gerstäckers Widerlegung der Lenau-Legende', in Bauschinger, Denkler and Malsch (eds), *Amerika in der deutschen Literatur*, pp. 135–53 (esp. p. 136).

26. Nikolaus Lenau, *Werke und Briefe*, ed. Hartmut Steinecke and András Vizkelety, vol. 5 (Vienna, 1989), pp. 230–1.

27. Ibid., p. 244.

28. Ibid., p. 235. For Buffon's view, see Michèle Duchet, *Anthropologie et histoire au siècle des lumières* (Paris, 1971), pp. 264–6.

29. Gottfried Duden, *Bericht über eine Reise nach den westlichen Staaten Nordamerika's [sic] und einen mehrjährigen Aufenthalt am Missouri (in den Jahren 1824, 25, 26 und 1827), in Bezug auf Auswanderung und Übervölkerung* (Elberfeld, 1829).

30. See Peter Mesenhöller, '"Auf, ihr Brüder, laßt uns reisen fröhlich nach Amerika". Reisebericht und Reiseschilderung im Kontext der deutschen Amerika-auswanderung des frühen 19. Jahrhunderts', in Peter J. Brenner (ed.), *Der Reisebericht* (Frankfurt, 1989), pp. 363–89 (esp. pp. 368–74 on Duden).

31. See *Die nordamerikanische Demokratie und das v. Tocqueville'sche Werk darüber, als Zeichen des Zustandes der theoretischen Politik* [etc.; to which is appended] *Duden's Selbst-Anklage wegen seines amerikanischen Reiseberichtes, zur Warnung vor fernerem leichtsinnigen Auswandern* (Bonn, 1837).

32. Letter, 9 August 1850, in Deutsch, 'Briefe Kürnbergers an Laube', p. 149.

33. These meetings were a favourite subject for satire in nineteenth-century America: see e.g. Mark Twain, *Huckleberry Finn*, ch. 20.

34. *Briefe eines politischen Flüchtlings*, p. 94.

35. Meyer, *Nord-Amerika im Urteil des deutschen Schrifttums*, p. 86.

36. See Alexis de Tocqueville, *Democracy in America*, tr. George Lawrence, ed. J. P. Mayer (London, 1994), esp. pp. 370, 690.

37. The two are compared by Castle, 'Amerikamüde', p. 36, and Steinlein, 'Kürnbergers *Der Amerikamüde*', pp. 169–70.

38. See Karlheinz Rossbacher, *Literatur und Liberalismus. Zur Kultur der Ring-straßenzeit in Wien* (Vienna, 1992), p. 47.

39. See David Blackbourn and Geoff Eley, *The Peculiarities of German History* (London, 1984).

40. Rossbacher, *Literatur und Liberalismus*, pp. 229–34. A complete edition of Kürnberger's journalism is being prepared by Hubert Lengauer.

41. *Die Fackel*, 214–15, 22 December 1906, p. 5.

Unconscious Poesy?

Marie von Ebner-Eschenbach's
Die Poesie des Unbewußten

R. C. Ockenden

Marie Ebner's slender work of 1881 *Die Poesie des Unbewußten, Novellchen in Korrespondenzkarten* (*The Poesy of the Unconscious, A Short Novella in Post-cards*) seems to have begun life as an exercise in concentrated form. Certainly her own early references to the work call it 'the postcard novella', rather than naming its title.[1] However, it is a work of interest for its thematic as well as its formal aspects, although it has attracted little critical attention, possibly because of its slight appearance and unpretentiousness. It was one of the earliest successful works by the then 51-year-old author: Julius Rodenberg was happy to publish it at once in his *Deutsche Rundschau* – and we know that he did not accept all her work of this period;[2] the author records with delight a favourable review in a periodical she regarded as hostile to her – *Bohemia* praised it for the 'Feinheit ihrer psychologischen Beobachtungsweise' (the subtlety of its psychological observation);[3] and after securing Rodenberg's permission, Paetel published the novella in the collection *Dorf- und Schloßgeschichten* of 1883.[4] However, important friends of Marie Ebner's, whose judgement generally meant more to her than that of critics, were not won over by the story. Louise von François found it the first work of her friend which disappointed her, and Betty Paoli could not get on with it at all.[5] Ferdinand von Saar, the slightly younger friend whom Ebner treated as a mentor, contrasted the 'delightful basic idea of the story' with the 'naivety of its execution'.[6] My contention is that both the composition of the story and the character of the heroine are much more artful than Ebner's first readers realised.

In terms of theme, this novella echoes many of Ebner's other works. A large proportion of her stories is concerned, directly or indirectly, with marriage and its successes or (more usually) failures. Even though in this instance we witness less than two months of a marriage, one particular feature of it represents a recurring circumstance in Ebner's writing: it has been arranged with little more than the nominal consent of the bride. The young woman begins her correspondence with her mother by remarking that the latter has 'sent her off into the world with an unknown gentleman', whereas the mother claims to know him very well.[7] In several stories the husband 'selected' for a young woman is contrasted with a man (generally younger than the husband) who would or might have been her own choice. This is a situation Fontane would hint at in *Effi Briest,* some thirteen years later: jolly cousin Dagobert represents an ideal youthful companion, and hence possible marriage-partner, for Effi, just as Innstetten could have been for her mother twenty years before. But it is built into the social structures of the time that young men, however attractive, lack the necessary wealth, substance or social position to be considered as husbands; hence a pattern of older husbands and younger wives is set up, which tends to repeat itself.

Ebner offers various illustrations of this motif. Even when a young woman feels positively about marrying an older, established man, as in *Nach dem Tode,* there is a disappointed man of her own age in the wings (Eberstein's nephew, Alfred). Coerced marriages can happen, of course, at any social level, as Ebner's work illustrates: in *Die Resel,* for example, an attempt is made to persuade the peasant heroine to marry someone other than the man she loves, a situation the aristocratic Countess evidently identifies with.[8] Perhaps the most telling examples are the central figures of the two juxtaposed stories *Comtesse Muschi* and *Comtesse Paula.*[9] The latter, bolstered by her sister who has suffered deeply from an arranged marriage, defies parental pressure and makes her own choice of husband; Muschi, a less courageous figure, supposes she is interested in the Swabian suitor selected by her father but is clearly more happy in the company of cousin Fred.[10] At first sight, *Die Poesie des Unbewußten* does not accord with this pattern. The heroine's husband, Albrecht, is clearly older than she; but her evidently young cousin Hans, who is referred to only in one letter, attracts her censure for his immoral behaviour rather than any sign of affection. [10] Hans has become embroiled with an (older?) married woman – as, of course, had Albrecht: a system which makes men wait before they are entitled to marry is one that presumes that they will become involved in illicit affairs. However, as we shall see, the heroine's disparaging remarks about Hans should not necessarily be taken at face value. Be that as it may, there is no sign of a 'struggle against parental authority'[11] on the part of this heroine; she is not, like Paula, a rebel.

Characterisation in this novella is unusual in several respects. Parental authority here is represented by the mother, rather than the more common authoritarian father;[12] but she shares with male authority figures in other of Ebner's works a dislike of any show of emotion [1 and 10] – a trait which indicates that they choose to repress their own emotions.[13] The mother in *Die Poesie des Unbewußten* is a strong, manipulative woman who appears to have her son-in-law as well as her daughter completely under her thumb, and who is committed to old-fashioned, patriarchal views of marriage and its roles. The husband, Albrecht, is more conventional: his stupidity is a quality he shares with many powerful male figures in Ebner's work, and a warning sign of his potential violence is given when he mistreats his horse. [9][14] On the other hand, although we see him being groomed for patriarchal authority by his stepmother, he is as yet insecure enough to need her assistance. The 'other woman', Albrecht's former mistress Blanka, is a more unusual figure.[15] She seems a veritable Orsina, a 'rasendes Weib' [raging woman] who has come back, bent on revenge, to plague her faithless lover; yet her final gesture (turning over to the young wife the love letters Albrecht wrote to Blanka) is ambivalent: does she wish to destroy the marriage, and, possibly, Albrecht? or is she genuinely seeking to empower her fortunate rival? Her last words, accompanying the letters, are: 'All life is a struggle, and marriage especially. Here are some weapons' [25].[16]

But the most unusual figure is the unnamed heroine of this story, the writer of 19 of the 26 pieces of correspondence – all but the last being postcards[17] – which make it up. Her cards create an impression of colossal naivety and total subservience – still to her mother, and now to her husband as well. The only other attribute emphasised by the text is her bookish intelligence: she offers, as light evening conversation for her husband, the question of whether he prefers *Götz* or *Wallenstein;* when Albrecht, who has clearly read neither, declares a liking for Schiller's treatise on the Seven Years' War, she points out that no such work exists, and then supposes that Albrecht must have been making a joke. Albrecht, writing to his sister to complain that his new young wife is too good for him, mentions her 'Verstand' and 'Gelehrsamkeit' (intelligence and erudition) among her chief qualities. [7] She is, in fact, a bluestocking, and it might seem that the text mocks her for having too much book-learning and insufficient understanding of the world. Ebner is not above mocking bluestockings, as she was conscious of having done in her satirical sketch *Die Visite.*[18] But in general, and notably in the two *Comtessen* pieces, we see Ebner sympathetic to women whose education exceeds that of the men in their environment. Her two most famous aphorisms seem further to reinforce that stance: 'Als eine Frau lesen lernte, trat die Frauenfrage in die Welt' (The issue of women's rights came into the world the day a woman learned to read) and 'Eine gescheite Frau hat Millionen geborener Feinde:– alle dummen Männer' (A clever woman has millions of born enemies – each and every stupid man).[19]

And yet the common view of this text, going back at least to Richard M. Meyer, has been one which takes at face value the naivety of the heroine, and hence, in my view, endorses Saar's judgement on the naivety of the work's execution.[20] In her 1913 study, Riemann appreciates that 'man liest so vieles zwischen den Zeilen dieser Karten' (we read so much between the lines of these cards); comparing the novella with Ebner's *Der Nebenbuhler,* she comments on the two stories: 'Die Schreiber lassen unabsichtlich so mancherlei durch-blicken, daß der Leser trotz der anscheinend so sprunghaften Form die Situation deutlich übersieht. Scheinbar deutlicher und klarer als der Schreiber.' (The writers unintentionally signal so much to us that the reader, despite the form being apparently so disjointed, has a clear grasp of the situation. Seemingly much clearer and more distinct than the writer has.)[21] In her book on Ebner, Alkemade claims that the 'education of the central character' is the basis of this novella's development (as it is of other works by the author), and she cites the heroine as one of those young girls who are married off without love but gradually achieve sympathy or even love in their marriages.[22] Alkemade thus sees the heroine as learning from her experiences, and in her reading the novella would fit with those 'Erziehungsgeschichten' (stories of education) which early critics regarded as Ebner's favourite mode.[23] Later scholars rather stress the education the young wife has received *before* her marriage: in his afterword to the Winkler edition Klein thinks that the heroine's good upbringing is responsible for her not reading the letters which Blanka smuggles to her and thus avoiding a catastrophe.[24] Edgar Gross, in his afterword to the Nymphenburg edition, sees the heroine vanquishing Albrecht: 'Indem die junge Frau die Briefe ihrem Gatten ungeöffnet zurückgibt, trägt sie mit dem ihr angeborenen und durch gute Erziehung gestärkten fraulichen Gefühl den Sieg über die nur vitale Überlegenheit des Mannes davon.' (By giving her husband his letters back unopened, she scores a victory, through that womanly feeling natural to her and strengthened by her good upbringing, over the sheer vitality and superiority of the husband.)[25] In lauding the heroine's upbringing, Gross and Klein are endorsing the mother's support of patriarchal values.

According to such readings of the novella, the machinations of the mother and the new husband are defeated by the sheer innocence of the young wife. It does not occur to her that the recently-widowed Blanka, whose return to the vicinity so disturbs her husband, could be a former mistress; she expresses disgust at the thought of anyone who (like her cousin) pays court to a married woman. The arrival of Emilie, Albrecht's sister, whom he summons, she attributes to chance; she does not piece together Blanka's language of betrayal and revenge, and the lengths Albrecht and Emilie go to to keep her apart from Blanka. She presumes the letters Blanka keeps referring to are some written by Albrecht to Blanka's late husband, and that Albrecht is reluctant to let her see them because they are full of misspellings and inaccuracies of history, geography and culture generally. Hence when Blanka smuggles them to her under a pile of cut roses it does not occur to her to investigate them, since Albrecht has already shown he is embarrassed about them and she would never do anything to contradict his wishes. The heroine's innocence, then, seems total, and the last words of the novella indicate what has happened during the seven weeks encompassed by the tale. As her husband kneels at her feet, his eyes filled with tears (at his escape and at the extraordinary naivety of his wife), he exclaims and whispers '"O mein Weib! mein Kind!"' ("O my wife! My child!") The two terms extend what the heroine has just written about Albrecht: 'mein bester Mann, mein teurer Herr' (my dearest husband, my dear master). [26] The union of man and wife seems to have been rescued, but what in fact has been established is a relationship between a beloved master and a child. Albrecht has stepped into the mother's shoes.

But what makes this novella more than a slight piece, for all its brevity, is the fact that a quite different reading emerges once we presume the heroine to be *aware* of the sensational events unfolding around her, but reluctant to join in the melodrama. If we suppose that the young bride, having made a good marriage to a weak but biddable husband, sees no advantage in forfeiting that position by creating a scandal, then we can see why she writes as she does even when she has seen through the charade and understood Albrecht's relationship with Blanka. Marriage may be, as Blanka claims, a battle-ground, but the young wife has no intention of fighting on that ground. She has few options: brusquely to expose Albrecht and bring his past life out into the open would yield her little profit within the social system she belongs to; instead, she can use the advantage she possesses, without falling to the level of those around her. By the end of the novella she holds a permanent threat over the head of Albrecht; he cannot be sure how much she knows, but he is aware that she is his intellectual superior, and he must always harbour the suspicion that she has seen through him. That we, the readers, are also left in some uncertainty derives from the fact that we are only privy to the letters the heroine writes to her mother, that domineering personality from whom, she must know, no support will be forthcoming for anything but observance of the conventions, and who, moreover, is in league with Albrecht. It is that uncertainty which makes much of the fascination of this novella.

The form of the novella has, as we have seen, suggested parallels with other shorter pieces by Ebner, like *Comtesse Muschi*[26] and *Der Nebenbuhler*. In the former case, all the letters are written by Muschi herself, which at once makes her an easier target for satire through her false understandings and ignorance of what is going on, but also helps to make her someone we can sympathise with.[27] In *Der Nebenbuhler*, the boundless and stupid egotism of the central character is well brought out in his letters, and the only divergences from his authorship are provided by a note from his academic patron (which serves both to heighten the ridiculousness of the main character and to make the patron sound foolish) and two brief letters, just before the end of the tale, which fulfil a technical plot function. The looser structure of *Die Poesie des Unbewußten*, in which we have letters not only from the young wife but from the mother and the husband as well, enables the latter to become more interesting characters. As for the heroine herself, she seems neither to be a pathetic self-deluding figure like Muschi, nor arrogant and wilfully ignorant like the hero of *Der Nebenbuhler*. Riemann, who like other critics draws attention to Ebner's brilliant ability to catch the distinctive voice of a first-person narrator,[28] diagnoses the voice of the young bride as one of 'reiner Kindlichkeit in Denk- und Ausdrucksweise' (childlike innocence of thought and expression). However, unlike Muschi, who is writing to a chum and tells her (nearly) everything, the young wife writing to her mother is, as I have stressed, in a very different situation.

But the form is also a part of the story which unfolds. The heroine's mother has imposed on her newly-married daughter the condition that if she writes to her, it should be only on postcards which (a splendid touch of tyrannical kindness) her mother has provided her with.[2] The mother evidently wishes her daughter to devote herself entirely to her husband and to the process of getting to know him. But we can see that she is also discouraging her daughter from any intellectual appraisal of her situation, and, by keeping her at arm's length in this way, ruling out any possibility of the daughter appealing to her mother for help when difficulties arise.

40

However, the last entry in the novella is not a postcard but a letter: 'Heute muß es ein Brief sein, und heute mußt du es mir verzeihen.' (Today it has to be a letter, and today you must forgive me the liberty.) [26] How has the subservient daughter arrived at such a point of rebellion?

The turning-point in this short novella comes with the first mention of Blanka, and Albrecht's bad temper when he realises that she has returned to haunt him. [8 and 9] Here for the first time the heroine disobeys her mother, by allowing her communication to spill over on to a second postcard: in the light of the strong words of the mother earlier: 'Murre nicht gegen meine Anordnungen' (Don't grouse about my directives) [3], this disobedience seems bold. We also see the heroine for the first time here protesting to Albrecht about something – in this case the violent treatment of his horse; and immediately afterwards she wishes Blanka were elsewhere [9][29] – does she really have no inkling of the part Blanka has played in her husband's life? And is it mere chance that in her very next postcard she raises the question of her cousin Hans's adulterous behaviour, and tells her mother how she pressed Albrecht for his views on such behaviour?[10] The double postcard also contains landscape description, the only such passage apart from the apparently perfunctory scene-setting of the first postcard. In this later card, the heroine's description of the setting of Blanka's country house is charged with an uncharacteristic and suggestive sensuality which seems to relate to what we later learn about the relations between Albrecht and Blanka: '[Das Tal] zieht sich lange schmal hin, breitet sich dann plötzlich aus und umfängt sammetne Wiesen und einen kleinen See, den unser Waldbach tränkt, am Ufer des Sees liegt ein Garten, und in diesem ein allerliebstes Schlößchen' (The valley is narrow for quite a long way, then suddenly it opens out to embrace velvet meadows and a small lake, which is fed by our forest brook; on the shore of the lake is a garden, in which there is an exquisite little country house) [8].

From this point onwards, belief in the heroine's complete innocence and incomprehension is increasingly undermined by the detail of the text. We are struck by the fact that as the intrigue begins to reach its climax with the revelation that Blanka still has Albrecht's love-letters, and Albrecht, in panic, begins sending desperate letters to his mother-in-law, the heroine ceases to write to Mama for a while. After ten days, evidently in reply to an enquiry from her mother, she writes: 'Alles gut, mehr als gut' (Everything's fine, better than fine) [23], and next day writes twice on the same day in clear contravention of her mother's ordinance. In the second card she copies out Blanka's last message to her, acknowledges that Blanka's declaration about marriage being a battle-ground is 'quite clever', and adds: 'I would have preferred a simple, warm word of farewell' [25]. These words can be read either as a naive, good-hearted comment, or as a more profound wish for reassurance that Blanka has indeed gone out of her life. The last communication to her mother, as well as being a letter rather than a card, begins with a rather stiff mode of address – 'Meine geliebte Mutter' (My beloved mother) as though to suggest the distance of independence [26].

A structural device frequently employed by Ebner is that of mirroring, comparison and contrast, which is used, especially in the shorter fiction, in striking ways. Contrasting scenes are set up, as in *Er laßt die Hand küssen:* the true idyll of young Mischka with his sweetheart, and the false one of the grandmother's rococo literary effusion.[30] Unexpected links are suggested between people of different classes, like the Countess and the young heroine in *Die Resel*, or the first and second owners of the dog in *Krambambuli*, and between different generations, as in *Ob spät, ob früh.* Above all Ebner enjoys bringing together contrasting characters who illuminate each other, and provide an opportunity for lively dialogue. Her work often exemplifies the close relationship between novella and drama, most famously formulated by Storm in the words 'The novella is the sister of the drama'.[31] The claim that Ebner turned to writing fiction because she was unable to make her way as a dramatist is commonly made, but often has a belittling or pitying flavour to it. Ebner herself was positively aware of these links, as is shown by her choice of the term 'dialogisierte Novelle' for some of her one-act dramas.[32] *Die Poesie des Unbewußten* offers no such contrast in characters, apart from the superficial one between the former mistress and the young wife; but it does juxtapose two figures, in the young wife and the husband, who create expectations through the cliché of the helpless, innocent girl and the strong, experienced man. It is this cliché which the novella subverts, as its title hints.

Critics have not been kind to the title: Gross finds it 'rather ill-conceived' and Klein regards it as simply misleading.[33] What neither observes is that the title clearly refers to Eduard von Hartmann's *Philosophie des Unbewußten.* This was a work very famous in its time, though its continued celebrity came to rest on the patronising comments made about it by Nietzsche, particularly in the ninth section of *Vom Nutzen und Nachteil der Historie für das Leben* of 1873–4. In his work, Hartmann dilates with Schopenhaurean pessimism on the disadvantages of love, of marriage and of child-bearing. His fundamental proposition about love, sex and marriage is that there is a powerful (above all male) procreative instinct at work, which totally defeats reason and common sense. Hence humans (in particular males) are drawn, against their better judgement, into relationships which they decorate with the language of love. Hartmann observes that all such talk of love is an illusion; and he notes that since the only marriages that last are those that replace passion with friendship, it is impossible after a few years of wedlock to distinguish between those couples who chose each other voluntarily and those who made what he terms 'conventional', i.e. arranged marriages.[34]

Ebner's diaries reveal that she knew *Philosophie des Unbewußten*, though her own view of it is not divulged there.[35] What does draw comment from her is one of Hartmann's ventures into creative writing, his drama *Tristan and Isolde* of 1871, on which she delivered the verdict 'elendes Machwerk' (miserable concoction). She adds the comment: 'Praxis u. Theorie, lieber Hartmann, unbewusster! bleiben sie [sic] bei der Theorie'. (Theory and practice, my dear Hartmann, you unconscious man! Stick to theory!)[36] These sharp words about Hartmann's (truly dreadful) play are presumably those of a craft practitioner whose guild has been invaded by a bungler; but they also betray some reservations about Hartmann's philosophy. We notice that Hartmann's key concept of the Unconscious is turned against him in her comments by being personalised: he is someone unconscious of what he is doing. Ebner was fascinated by Schopenhauer, but objected to the idea that human beings have no free will;[37] Hartmann's theory of the priority of blind forces must have been equally unacceptable to her. The heroine of our novella may have no choice but to accept things as they are; what she is rebelling against is the role of victim which everyone seems to have assigned to her. The link to Wagner provided by Hartmann's play (which owes a great deal to the opera) also reminds us that Wagner's *Tristan und Isolde* finishes by rhyming and equating the Unconscious with the height of ecstasy ('Unbewußt – Höchste Lust' are Isolde's last words). Such celebration of the unconscious is precisely not, in my view, the aim of this novella.

In carrying the ideas of Hartmann's title to Ebner's novella, I want to suggest that it is the apparently 'aware' characters, notably the husband, Albrecht, and not the heroine, who are in reality the 'unconscious' persons. And whereas the young wife maintains a largely matter-of-fact approach, it is Albrecht and Blanka who indulge in romanticism and 'poesy'. In her first card the heroine describes the white brook as 'whipped soapsuds'; meanwhile her husband claims that the sounds in the treetops are a greeting from the trees. [1] When he takes up his pen, Albrecht positively peppers his cards with exclamation marks and italics,[38] including desperate cries such as 'damit werde ich allein nicht fertig' (I can't cope with this situation alone) and 'Die Reue ist etwas Schreckliches' (Remorse is something terrible). [11 and 21] Blanka seems trapped in the rhetoric of cheaper romantic fiction, as exemplified by her ploy with letters smuggled in under roses and her melodramatic 'Ich bin gekommen, um Gericht zu halten'. (I have come to sit in judgement.) [25 and 17] For her part, the heroine dismisses the intense dialogue between Blanka and Emilie, Albrecht's sister, as 'kindische Reden' (childish talk). [17]

It is Albrecht, the husband, who is shown to be the 'unconscious' figure, as the form 'des Unbewußten' in the title suggests. He, not the young wife, is really the child in this novella. With hindsight, what appeared to be a conventional description in the first postcard conceals the wife's suspicion of this beneath a topographical reference: Albrecht's country house stands on 'ein Kind von einem Berge' (a child of a mountain). [1] It is he who undergoes an education. He starts off, as we see from his two letters to his sister, terrified of being 'found out' and trying to uphold a false image of himself towards his new wife, and this very attempt ultimately gives her power. [7 and 11] As Ebner's aphorism puts it: 'Wo wäre die Macht der Frauen, wenn die Eitelkeit der Männer nicht wäre?' (Where would women's power be, if it weren't for men's vanity?)[39] The stern exhortations to deceit, tyranny and male chauvinism he receives from his mother-in-law [20 and 22] are not the real lessons of the story, but rather his coming face to face with his own failings, his remorse, and his very real admiration, possibly love, for his new wife. Her lesson for him at the end of the text is 'daß *ich* deine einzige Freundin und Vertraute bin und sein muß ' (that *I* am and must be your only friend and confidante) [26]. There is no place here for a mistress – but none for an interfering parent either. If the manipulators in this story, including the mother, are defeated by someone who observes their rules better than they do – or at least appears to – it is not, as critics have supposed, because the young wife is naive, but because she is using her intelligence in a subtle way. As an aphorism of Ebner's claims: 'Es gibt mehr naive Männer als naive Frauen' (There are more naive men than naive women).[40]

Unconscious poesy is not Ebner's business; she is committed to alert and aware prose. At the end of the day, her heroine is not a radical, attempting to overthrow social structures; instead, she has asserted herself and established benign power within an existing structure. She has achieved what Necker, writing in the year of Ebner's death, saw as the modern woman's ideal: 'sich nicht abhängig vom Manne zu machen' (not to make oneself dependent on man).[41] As a more recent critic has pointed out, the 'major concerns of "old [pre-1920] feminism" were the oppression of wives, the economic dependence of women and the suppression of female "selfhood" or self-esteem.'[42] This may seem a limited achievement; but in the context of the late 19th century world in which Ebner was writing, it is something worthwhile. The heroine may finish up being as powerful a mistress in her own house as her mother has been, but the signs are that she will be a more humane one. The source of her authority will be a sympathetic understanding of individuals, their complexities and weaknesses, not the bolstering force of illiberal social conventions.

Notes

1. See the first references to it in: Marie von Ebner-Eschenbach, *Tagebücher III, 1879–1889*, ed. Karl Konrad Polheim and Norbert Gabriel, with Markus Jagsch and Claus Pias, Tübingen 1993, pp. 143, 144, 146. The title *[Die] Poesie d[es] U[nbewußten]* is first used on 5 September 1881, see *Tagebücher III*, p. 148.
2. See the diary entry for 28 September 1881, *Tagebücher III*, p. 153. In the sub-title of the *Deutsche Rundschau* version, the work was called a 'Novelletchen'. Helmut Brandt, 'Marie von Ebner-Eschenbach und die "Deutsche Rundschau"', in *Die Österreichische Literatur: Ihr Profil von der Jahrhundertwende bis zur Gegenwart (1880–1980)*, ed. Herbert Zeman, Graz 1989, pp. 1001–1015, discusses the rejection of *Bozena*, of *Die Freiherrn von Gemperlein* and of *Margarethe*, and Rodenberg's presumed reasons, on pp. 1011–12.
3. *Tagebücher III*, p. 91.
4. *Tagebücher III*, pp. 204 and 342: on 19 October 1883, on receipt of her free copies of the collection, Ebner declares in her diary her doubts about 'the whole writing business'. *Contra* Ferrel V. Rose in *The Guises of Modesty: Marie von Ebner-Eschenbach's Female Artists*, Columbia, SC, 1994, p. 194, it was *Die Resel*, not this novella, which was added to the second (1890) edition of the collection.
5. *Tagebücher III*, pp. 152 and 161.
6. *Briefwechsel zwischen Ferdinand von Saar und Maria* [sic] *von Ebner-Eschenbach*, ed. Heinz Kindermann, Vienna 1957, pp. 66–67.
7. See postcards numbered 1 and 3. Individual items of the correspondence will henceforward by referred to by numbers (following the numbering in the text) in square brackets.

8. See *Das Gemeindekind – Novellen – Aphorismen*, Winkler Verlag, Munich 1978, [henceforward cited as *Gemeindekind*] pp. 220f., 224.

9. The two stories were published together under the title *Zwei Comtessen* (in some editions modernised to *Komtessen*) in 1885.

10. As Ferrel Rose notes in *Guises of Modesty*, p. 121.

11. The phrase is used by Edith Toegel, 'Daughters and Fathers in Marie von Ebner-Eschenbach's Works', in *Oxford German Studies*, 20/21, (1991–921), p. 125.

12. The text strongly implies that she is a one-parent child; this may link her to Ebner's own situation, but it also aligns her with many chief characters in literature, notably 19th-century novels. On relations between fathers and daughters in Ebner's work, see the article listed in note 11.

13. This motif appears in many Ebner stories, especially later ones. In *Nach dem Tode*, *In letzter Stunde* and *Erste Trennung* the theme of (male) repression of feelings is central; it is at its most poignant in the tiny sketch *Das Lied*.

14. Violence to animals, a regular motif in Ebner's work, is often used to indict male heartlessness; a telling example occurs in *Die Freiherren von Gemperlein*, see *Gemeindekind*, pp. 315–16, which contradicts the common critical view of Ludwig as one of a pair of amiable eccentrics. For a re-evaluation of that story, see Agatha C. Bramkamp, *Marie von Ebner-Eschenbach: The Author, Her Time and Her Critics*, Bonn 1990, pp. 102–108.

15. It should be noted that she is not 'eine gefahrliche Kokotte' ('a dangerous higher-class prostitute'), as Johannes Klein suggests: Marie von Ebner-Eschenbach, *Erzählungen – Autobiographische Schriften* (Munich, 1978) [henceforward cited as *Erzählungen*], p. 925. She is an unhappily-married woman who starts an affair with the unmarried Albrecht in some hope of a better future with him. It is his mother-in-law who advises Albrecht, should the truth come out, to refer dismissively to Blanka as a flirt ('Kokette').

16. Klein, *Erzählungen*, p. 925, is mistaken to think that these are letters written *to* Albrecht.

17 In response to trivial enquiries about whether the postcards were open or sent in envelopes (see *Tagebücher III*, p. 362), Ebner concocted a humorously elaborate reply in her foreword to the collection *Dorf- und Schloßgeschichten*.

18. See *Tagebücher III*, p. 796. The piece may be found in *Sämtliche Werke*, (Paetel), Berlin n.d. [1920], V, pp. 306–16. Although it was not published in book form until 1901, it was finished at least by May 1888, see *Tagebücher III*, p. 795.

19. *Gemeindekind*, pp. 888 and 875.

20 Richard M. Meyer, *Die deutsche Literatur des neunzehnten Jahrhunderts*, 3rd, revised edition, Berlin 1906, p. 607, sees 'das naive Kinderherz' (the naive childlike heart) at the core of this novella.

21. Else Riemann, *Zur Psychologie und Ethik der Marie von Ebner-Eschenbach*, Hamburg 1913, p. 71.

22. Zr. Mechtildis Alkemade, *Die Lebens- und Weltanschauung der Freifrau Marie von Ebner-Eschenbach*, Graz 1935, pp. 86, 50–51.

23. Meyer (see note 20) p. 606 sees all her works in this light; his view is echoed by Moritz Necker, *Marie v. Ebner-Eschenbach*, Munich 1916, p. 209.

24. *Erzählungen*, p. 925.

25. Edgar Gross in his afterword in: Ebner-Eschenbach, *Gesammelte Werke Band 3 = Erzählungen III*, Nymphenburger Verlagshandlung, Munich 1960/1961, p. 315.

26. Rose, *Guises of Modesty*, p. 120. Rose makes a reference to *Comtesse Paula* on that page which I think should be to *Comtesse Muschi*.

27. Rose, *Guises of Modesty*, pp. 119–135 deals at length with the two *Comtessen* stories; she goes well beyond the standard view of Muschi, that 'her heart's in the right place' (see e.g. Anton Bettelheim, *Marie von Ebner-Eschenbach*, Berlin 1900,

p. 149) in presenting her very positively. Rose's view of Muschi's relationship with Nesh seems to me overdone, and Ebner's own verse comment on Muschi is unfortunately not given in full: see pp. 119 and 133; p. 135.

28. Necker (see note 23), pp. 204–5 mentions some of the best examples of this skill.
29. The heroine uses a double euphemism by wishing Blanka were 'where the best-known spice grows' – the German imprecation despatching someone to 'where the pepper grows' itself involves a euphemism for hell.
30. *Gemeindekind*, pp. 235 and 244–5.
31. The phrase appears in *Eine zurückgezogene Vorrede aus dem Jahre 1881* and in Storm's letter to Keller of 14 August 1881; the correspondence with Keller was first published in *Deutsche Rundschau* of 1903/4.
32. For example *Ohne Liebe* and *Bettelbriefe* (which is a genuine 'dialogue'), *Erzählungen*, pp. 487–510 and 635–650.
33. Gross, *loc.cit.* (see note 25); Klein in *Erzählungen*, p. 925 .
34. See Eduard von Hartmann, *Philosophie des Unbewußten*, (2nd, enlarged edition), Berlin 1870, pp. 181–198, especially pp. 181–190 and 195–6 and pp. 586–607, especially pp. 593f., 603 and 606f.
35. Marie von Ebner-Eschenbach, *Tagebücher I, 1862–1869*, ed. Karl Konrad Polheim with Rainer Baasner, Tübingen 1989, p. 287.
36. Marie von Ebner-Eschenbach, *Tagebücher II, 1871–1878*, ed. Karl Konrad Polheim with Markus Jagsch, Claus Pias, Georg Richard, Tübingen 1991, p. 29.
37. Rose, *Guises of Modesty*, p. 138.
38. The Winkler edition removes all the emphases indicated by the 'Sperrdruck' (spaced printing) in Ebner's text; the Nymphenburg edition is correct here.
39. *Gemeindekind*, p. 872.
40. *Gemeindekind*, p. 880.
41. Necker (see note 23), p. 218.
42. Helga H. Harriman, 'Marie von Ebner-Eschenbach in Feminist Perspective', *Modern Austrian Literature*, 18/1,1985, p. 33, with footnote 34 on p. 37.

Ferdinand von Saar's
Doktor Trojan
Politics, Medicine and Myth
Ian Foster

Somehow Ferdinand von Saar (1833–1906) has never really arrived. Nor has he ever entirely gone away. During the author's own life-time the reception given to his work was mixed. The prodigious efforts he expended on monumental historical tragedies like the two-part *Kaiser Heinrich IV*, *Die beiden De Witt* or *Thassilo* were never rewarded. Few of his stage works were even performed. More successful were the thirty-two Novellen he published between 1873 and 1906. However, the sale of these slender works to newspapers and in collected volumes was in no way enough to sustain Saar after his retirement from the army in 1860, when, as an impoverished junior lieutenant weighed down with debts and lacking the aristocratic 'Protektion' necessary in those days to advance a military career, he first hoped to earn a living by his pen.[1] Such independence was never granted. The limited freedom he did enjoy came about through patronage. His wealthy benefactors were liberal aristocratic women, many from a Jewish background: Caroline von Gomperz-Bettelheim, Baroness Todesco or the Princess Hohenlohe. He was a regular at the prestigious literary salon of Josephine von Wertheimstein, also frequented by the young Hofmannsthal.[2] Among the most significant of Saar's patrons was the Princess Salm (née Liechtenstein), at whose country estates in Moravia – Raitz and Blansko – Saar was given his own rooms, an arrangement that continued after her death in 1894, by which time Saar was very much part of the family retinue. Saar's most enthusiastic champions during the 1880s and 1890s were to be found among these landed and titled folk. It was through their intervention that he received numerous state grants and eventually was made a peer of the realm in 1902, becoming only the second writer after Grillparzer to sit in the 'Herrenhaus'.

The reception given to Saar's fiction during his lifetime has in a sense been perpetuated since his death. The significant readership he enjoyed among his patrons and the relatively restricted readership of liberal newspapers and journals has been succeeded by an academic readership. It may surprise readers to learn that there have been some 27 doctoral dissertations written on Saar since 1918, 18 of them dealing exclusively with the Novellen. Nor has our author's work ever been completely out of print.[3] In 1908, the Vienna branch of the Schiller Society, in accordance with the author's last will and testament, published an edition of the writer's complete works that has become a familiar standard version. This version, edited by Jakob Minor, with a short biography by Anton Bettelheim, presents the reader with a packaged 'life and works'.[4] The very neatness of the package, its apparent completeness and definitive status, provided commentators with a ready catalogue of starting points for interpretation for the first fifty years after the author's death. Bettelheim's biography was supplemented by the limited published correspondence.[5] A number of the dissertations of the 1930s and 1940s would win prizes in our own ecologically-conscious age for their adept recycling of material. A decisive break with the established and largely antiquarian view of Saar was James Lee Hodge's 1961 dissertation 'The Novellen of Ferdinand von Saar: Anticipations of Twentieth Century Themes and Techniques', whose title alone indicates a change of perspective. One should also single out Franz Karl von Stockert's doctoral study *Zur Anatomie des Realismus*, which draws extensively on unpublished manuscripts to investigate Saar's working methods and the structure of a number of key stories.[6] It is only relatively recently, however, that the status of the Minor edition has been thoroughly undermined. Under the supervision and editorship of Professor Polheim of Bonn, historical-critical editions of the Novellen 'Mariannen', 'Innocens', 'Seligmann Hirsch', 'Die Geigerin' and 'Der Brauer von Habrovan' have shown not only that there are significant manuscript and textual variants to many of Saar's Novellen, but also that existing readings of the stories can be justified and, in some cases, improved upon through a detailed study of such variants and related material.[7] In most cases, these readings have concentrated on interpreting Saar's fiction at the level of the author's symbolism and the mythological backdrop which may be discerned in some stories. Polheim's own interpretation of the story 'Der Brauer von Habrovan' is a model example. As a result, it might be said that the contemporary references in Saar's work, perhaps less apparent to a modern reader, have been played down in favour of a reading that draws on Western culture from the Greeks onwards.

As a contrast to this development, I would like to draw attention to one of Saar's stories that has received little critical examination: the Novelle *Doktor Trojan*. The story was first published in the *Neue Freie Presse* as a Feuilleton on 24, 25, 26 and 29 September 1896. In two letters written a few weeks later Saar refers to this story as one he considers to be among his best work. To the journalist and critic Moritz Necker on 5 October 1896 he wrote: 'Ich halte den Trojan für meine wirklich beste Arbeit, und daß sie [sic] Ihnen nicht mißfällt, bestärkt mich in diesem Glauben' ('I consider *Trojan* to be my best work [underlining in original], and the fact that it does not displease you strengthens me in my conviction'.[8] To probably his closest friend and confidant, the writer and fellow former officer Stephan Milow (von Millenkovic) he wrote on the same day: 'Daß Euch der "Trojan" gefallen hat, freut mich sehr. Ich halte ihn selbst für eine gelungene runde Arbeit' ('I am very pleased that you like *Trojan*. I consider it a well-rounded and successful piece of work').[9] What can have motivated an author as scrupulous as Saar to describe a story that now only occasionally features among those anthologised by modern critics in such glowing terms? The answer may, I believe, lie in its thematic range, something I have indicated in my title.

The Minor edition describes the text as having been written in three weeks in August and early September of 1896, and commentators on the story have accepted this account. For Saar, whose working methods were meticulous in the extreme, this would have been unusual. And in fact it comes as no surprise to discover that the writer had been carrying the idea for the story around with him for some months previously. In his letter to Milow on 5 October he wrote: 'Ich war schon, wie ich Dir angedeutet, im Frühjahr damit beschäftigt; die Geschichte ging aber nicht recht weiter; erst in der zweiten Hälfte des August, wo ich wieder in Raitz war, machte ich mich neuerdings daran, und da gelang es mir, das Ganze in 3 Wochen fertig zu schreiben. Schickte es, frischweg, an die Neue Presse, die es (zu meinem Erstaunen, da ich mich auf ein Refus gefaßt) auch sofort gebracht hat' ('As I had already indicated to you, I was working on the story in the early part of the year. I couldn't complete the story properly. Only in the second half of August, when I was in Raitz again, did I try again, and then I succeeded in finishing the whole thing in three weeks. Sent it straight to the *Neue Presse*, who (to my astonishment, since I was expecting a rejection) published it immediately').[10] The text was subsequently revised by the author and included in the collection *Nachklänge* in 1899.[11]

Like many of Saar's Novellen, *Doktor Trojan* is the story of an individual's fate confronted with historical change. Saar's typical hero or heroine is destroyed like Trojan by an irresolvable entanglement of personal weaknesses and forces beyond his or her control. Trojan's tale is related by a writer who arrives in the castle of R..., where an apartment has been prepared for him. Irritated to discover that the writing materials provided are not suitable, he sets off into the nearby village to buy replacements.[12] The biographical parallels with Saar's own stays at Blansko and Raitz are obvious. As in numerous other stories this framework narrative is deployed with great skill and subtlety. The story is in fact pieced together by the narrator from four separate witnesses: the local shopkeeper Nezbada, the retired doctor Wanka, his successor Dr Hulesch, and Trojan himself.

In the village shop the narrator encounters Trojan for the first time. From the proprietor Nezbada he learns that Trojan is doctor to the village and surrounding countryside, though he holds no formal medical qualification. The following day the narrator learns more about Trojan from Dr Wanka, former family doctor to the narrator's hosts and authority on the archaeology of the region's caves. Wanka relates how Trojan's father had tended to the medical needs of the population. In contrast to his son, however, Trojan senior did have a medical degree of sorts. The young Trojan spent a dissolute youth and found his vocation too late in life to acquire proper training. On a ramble to the Horic – a nearby plateau – the narrator again meets Trojan. This time Trojan tells his own story and reveals that the real reason for his giving up medical studies was a horror of cutting into human flesh. Years later, while reading medical texts aloud to his ageing father, he had rediscovered his vocation and begun to practise medicine, at first under his father's supervision, then independently. After this meeting there is a break in the narration.

Eight years pass before the narrator returns to R.... What awaits him is a transformation of the formerly impoverished, sleepy village into a smart, thriving settlement. On returning to the castle, the narrator enquires of Dr Hulesch what has become of Trojan. Hulesch relates that, as his colleague Dr Wanka had feared, Trojan's unlicensed practice brought him into conflict with the authorities, particularly since the arrival in R... of an ambitious young doctor named Srp. Prosecuted and imprisoned at Srp's instigation for failing to diagnose a case of diphtheria, Trojan became increasingly marginalised and took up with a woman deserted by her drunken and violent husband. One night Trojan appeared at Hulesch's door, requesting his assistance in an emergency. The patient was Trojan's lover. The young woman died shortly after Hulesch's arrival of a severe case of undiagnosed anthrax. While Hulesch returned to R... to report the case to Srp as district medical officer, Trojan killed himself out of grief and guilt.

The story can be interpreted in a number of ways. As my title suggests, I am concerned with two levels of significance within the Novelle: the political and the medical. There is also scope for a mythological interpretation. Trojan is repeatedly associated with the figure of Mercury – the narrator first encounters him under the sign of Mercury: Nezbada's shop carries a sign with 'Mercury's emblems' (p. 170).[13] Mercury's main emblem is of course the caduceus, or wand with two serpents entwined around it. As the emblem of the Greek god associated with healing, the caduceus is a long-established symbol of the medical profession. Trojan even carries a gnarled stick or 'Knotenstock' (p. 175) reminiscent of this. There are repeated references to his crossing the countryside with long strides in high boots (pp. 184–5). This symbolism would tend to support a positive view of Trojan as the true spirit of medicine. Other references are more ambivalent. Trojan's 'laboratory', where he prepares his medicines, is compared to a 'Hexenküche' or witches' den. Like the hero of another Saar Novelle, *Leutnant Burda*, Trojan is compared to Don Quixote (p. 170). His appearance and mannerisms are grotesque. He has a nose like a duck's bill (p. 170), hands like bird claws (p. 176) and a high, reedy voice.

The description of his suicide maintains this double view. Trojan is described as having cut his throat with a rusty sickle, almost separating head from body, like some sacrificial god of the harvest with outstretched arms, spilling blood on the ground (p. 199). The text, however, does not end with this scene, one which shocks even the vengeful Dr Srp into silence, but with the final remarks of Dr Hulesch and the main narrator. Hulesch's words 'Er hatte ja längst den Kopf verloren' ('He had lost his head a long time ago'), with their crass pun on Trojan's dismal fate, puncture the momentary pathos of the hero's demise.

In many of Saar's stories there is a temptation to read the text solely with a view to unpicking the mythological backdrop and constructing alternative meanings. Mythological references are adumbrated to produce an authoritative interpretation. While this may prove persuasive, by concentrating on such elements we may miss others. I would suggest that *Doktor Trojan* can be read as a Novelle in which Saar addresses social and political issues. The mode of address is perhaps characteristically indirect, but such issues are at the heart of the story.

At the political level, the story is slightly unusual among Saar's Novellen in that no exact date can be given for the action. Saar seldom gives a year, but he does often provide information that contemporaries would have found easy to interpret as signalling a particular period in Austria-Hungary's recent history.[14] All his stories are set within his own lifetime. In a historical context the most obvious marker in *Doktor Trojan* is the change that takes place in the eight-year gap between the narrator's visits to the village of R...:

> Fast acht Jahre hatten verstreichen müssen, eh' ich zum zweiten Male nach R... kam. Aber wie überrascht war ich, als ich, den Bahnhof verlassend, dem Orte zufuhr. Er war kaum mehr zu erkennen, so sehr hatte er sich inzwischen erweitert und verschönert (p. 186).

> [It was to be almost eight years before I was to return to R... and how surprised I was when I left the station to travel into the village. The place was barely recognisable, as it had been extended and improved so much.]

The improvements and additions include a public park, pavements, new modern houses and new businesses. Among the new buildings the narrator notes a pharmacy, a doctor's surgery and a new town hall. All have signs in both Czech and German. The old R... has disappeared. Nezbada's humble shop has been replaced by an attractive general store in the ground floor of a new town hall. Even the duck-pond has been transformed into a decorative lake with dainty wrought-iron surround and ornamental fountain! The narrator's comment is 'Fortschritt! Überall Fortschritt!' (p. 187). One should not interpret this as a negative judgement, though there is more than a hint of irony in the description of the fountain and the rather showy new town hall.

Too frequently, Saar has been portrayed as simply an antiquarian writer, somehow unable to deal with the present, to make the radical break with narrative tradition that a younger generation, in particular Schnitzler of course, were able to achieve. The famous opening of his story *Die Geigerin* (1875) almost invites such a view:

> Ich bin ein Freund der Vergangenheit. Nicht daß ich etwa romantische Neigungen hätte und für das Ritter- und Minnewesen schwärmte – oder für die sogenannte gute alte Zeit, die es niemals gegeben hat, nur jene Vergangenheit will ich gemeint wissen, die mit ihren Ausläufern in die Gegenwart hineinreicht und welcher ich, da der Mensch nun einmal

seine Jugendeindrücke nicht loswerden kann, noch dem Herzen nach
angehöre (p. 157).[15]

[I am a friend of the past. Not that I have romantic tendencies or go
into raptures at the thought of knights or courtly love – nor am I
enthusiastic about the good old days that never were. No, what I mean
is the past whose tributaries reach into our present and to which I still
belong in my heart, since one cannot deny the impressions of one's
youth.]

The typical Saar narrator rejects on the one hand a romanticised distant past
and on the other hand a nostalgic recent past. He is aware of the dangers of
bathing in a warm nostalgic glow, in which disparate elements of the recent
past coexist in an artificially comfortable sequence of images. Saar's subject is
precisely the tension between impersonal ineluctable historical forces and the
notion of individual human destiny. In these terms, and as a writer who found
much of his own world view in the philosophy of Schopenhauer, Saar does
not believe in progress. But unlike Schopenhauer, who wrote that the
'chapters of human history differ essentially only in the names and years
attached to them' and that the 'essential content [of human history] is
everywhere the same',[16] Saar does believe that change is important and that at
times change may be change for the better. At the same time, narratorial
sympathies are by and large with those who come to grief through the
processes of historical change. A further sentence from the opening of *Die
Geigerin* makes this clear. The narrator tells us that he is interested in failures
and people who have led tragic lives because 'alles das, was sie
zurückwünschen oder mühsam aufrecht erhalten wollen, hat doch einmal
bestanden und war eine Macht des Lebens, wie so manches, das heutzutage
besteht, wirkt und trägt' ('everything that they wish would return or labour to
maintain once existed in its own right and held the power of life, like so many
things that now exist, have their effect and maintain things', p. 157). The
implicit warning against arrogance that these words contain should not be
overstated: Saar's narrators are not continually wagging a reproving finger at a
decadent present.

In Saar's fiction the choice of settings counteracts false nostalgia, an effect
summed up in the striking phrase 'the good old days that never were'. The
significance of the precise temporal and physical settings has been elaborated
by a number of critics, the most recent and persuasive account being Alfred
Riemen's interpretation of the story *Schloß Kostenitz* (1892).[17] Riemen points
out the importance of the reader recognising the symbolic elements: '... the
apparent mere description in fact contains an interpretative attribution of the
places which may function as a foreshadowing device'.[18] Another relevant
aspect highlighted by Riemen is the narrator's standpoint. In *Schloß Kostenitz*,
and indeed in *Doktor Trojan*, the teller of the tale places himself in the
proximity of the local landowner. He is part of the aristocrat's retinue – not
exactly a hanger-on, for he is not dependent on any one benefactor, but he is
a guest of the family who is allotted quarters in an adjacent building or a wing

of the castle. In the Marxist analysis of Gerhard Rothbauer, the standpoint of the narrator is explained as a coded expression of Saar's own dependence on his patrons. He too was forced to live 'adjacent to the castle'. However, this position offered a vantage-point that made a disinterested narratorial style possible. When it comes to registering the tremors and seismic shocks of change, Saar's Novellen are impartial. Compassion for the victims does not blind the narrator to their complicity and fallibility.

Looking at the detail of the setting, the arrival of signs in Czech in the village of R... suggests that the narrator's first visit occurs around or before 1880 and his return at some time in the middle of the 1880s. The division of the Empire in 1867 into two parts, ruled respectively from Vienna and from Budapest, gave minority groups within the 'Austrian' part of the Empire an opportunity to advance their cause by political means. While Czech-speakers represented only around 12% of the Empire's total population in the period 1880 to 1910, in the 'Austrian' part of the Empire they made up 23% of the population. Indeed, within the Czech lands of Bohemia and Moravia they formed approximately two-thirds of the population.[19] As such, they were an important constituency that had to be appeased. At first, following the rejection in 1871 of a new nationality law and plans to create a general diet for the Czech crownlands of Bohemia, Moravia and Silesia (where the Czechs numbered only 22% of the total), Czech representatives stayed away from the Vienna parliament in protest. The collapse of the German Liberal government in 1878 led to their return to the Reichsrat during the period of the Taaffe ministry, known as the 'Iron Ring', which held office from 1879 to 1893. Taaffe's 'ring' was intended to fence in the German Liberals with a coalition of German, Polish and Czech feudal aristocrats. It also found allies among the moderate Czechs. Czech politicians were promised concessions on the issue of language – for example, the teaching of Czech in schools – and the creation of a Czech university in Prague.

The electoral reform of 4 November 1882 extended the franchise to sections of the petit bourgeoisie previously unrepresented in the Reichsrat by lowering the property qualification from 10 Gulden to 5. This had the effect of further undermining the position of the bourgeois German Liberals, who now found themselves outflanked by the newly-organised Christian Socials and German Nationals. For the Czechs the reform ultimately meant that the more moderate 'Old Czech' party was superseded by the 'Young Czechs' in the elections of 1890. What the Christian Socials, German Nationals and Young Czechs had in common was that they represented less well-educated sections of their respective societies who were more open to chauvinistic doctrines and ideas of a national struggle for existence.[20] The baleful consequences of those doctrines and the attendant anti-Semitic potential in the case of the Christian Socials are well-known.

The language question was at the centre of political struggle. It is no accident that the great Czech leader Thomas Masaryk is known to have characterised the inability to use one's native tongue as a 'mark of political slavery'.[21] In *Doktor Trojan*, the development of the township of R... is associated with an emergent Czech bourgeoisie and the shift in the demographic balance of the urban population in favour of Czech-speakers. The ambitious newcomer Dr Srp finds political support from the Young Czech faction. When Trojan continues to practise medicine despite the warnings of Dr Wanka and fails to diagnose a case of diphtheria, he becomes the subject of political debate:

> Es kam zu lebhaftem Meinungsaustausch – und schließlich senkte sich die Wagschale zu Gunsten Srps, der ja ein *wirklicher* Doktor war und überdies zur extremen tschechischen Partei hielt, welche im Gemeinwesen allmählich die Oberhand gewonnen hatte. Aus ihr ging jetzt auch ein neuer Bürgermeister hervor, ein sehr wohlhabender Mann, der es um so mehr unter seiner Würde hielt, für den Kurpfuscher einzustehen, als dieser eigentlich ein Deutscher war, wenn er auch seit jeher eine vollständig neutrale Haltung bewahrt hatte (p. 192).

> [There was an animated exchange of views – and in the end the balance tipped in favour of Srp, who was after all a *real* doctor and furthermore a supporter of the extreme Czech party, which had gradually gained the upper hand in communal affairs. It had then produced a new mayor, a very wealthy man, who considered it beneath his dignity to stand up for a quack, particularly since that quack was a German, even if he had always maintained a completely neutral attitude.]

Two points are worthy of note in this account. Firstly, the narrator notes the credibility attached to Srp's qualifications. Only a few pages before, he had noted that Srp '– unter uns gesagt – in der Tat nicht viel mehr Kenntnisse besaß, als man eben bei oberflächlich und notdürftig zurückgelegtem Studiengange erwirbt' (p. 190) '– between you and me – he in fact possessed scarcely more knowledge than one might expect someone to obtain from meagre and superficial studies'). Secondly, while the 'extreme Czech party' supporters are partisan in taking their decision against Trojan, Trojan himself is said to have remained neutral. The classic predicament of the German-speaking minority in the late Habsburg period – of not having a nation to support, other than the supranational state and its organs – also applies to him. Like his father, he has served the local population out of a sense of duty rather than in expectation of any reward. While Saar's narrator underlines Trojan's medical failings, he also makes clear that something has been lost with the rise of new partisan forces in Moravian society, however much these might contribute to economic and social development. The rise of a more aggressive Czech nationalism is integrated into the story in a subtle and ambivalent manner.

Srp's arrival in R... is part of the town's economic development and is inevitably followed by a tightening of the regulations for medical practitioners. But it is Trojan's horror of surgery that precipitates the crisis and not the mere fact of a qualified competitor. This dread of the knife is more than a simple plot device. In a letter to Stephan Milow, Saar wrote:

Die Anregung gab mir ein Vorfall, der sich vor einigen Jahren in Blansko ereignete; das 'gelehrte' Material aber lieferte mir die Broschüre 'Unter der Herrschaft des Messers' von dem bekannten Masseur Dr Reibmayr. Dieses Schriftchen hatte bei seinem Erscheinen viel Staub in medicinischen Kreisen aufgewirbelt, und eine Entgegnung des Professors Albert hervorgerufen.[22]

[An incident that happened in Blansko some years ago gave me the impulse to write the story. The brochure 'Under the Reign of the Knife' by the noted masseur Dr Reibmayr provided me with the 'learned' material. This booklet had stirred up things in medical circles when it appeared and prompted a reply from Professor Albert.]

Albert Reibmayr's tract, subtitled 'Ein Mahnwort von einem Freunde der leidenden Menschheit' ('A Word of Warning from a Friend of Suffering Humanity') was first published in Vienna in 1892.[23] Its essential argument was that despite the much vaunted advances in medicine in the previous twenty years there had been only a marginal improvement in the mortality rates among patients admitted to hospital and, more importantly, a decrease of around 10% in the number of patients regarded as fully cured. Provocatively, Reibmayr took the official statistics of the Allgemeines Krankenhaus, Vienna's historic general hospital, from the year 1859 – a year in which the Habsburg Empire had fought a major war – and compared them with the statistics from 1888. Reibmayr's case, that a patient still had roughly the same chance of dying in hospital but a worse chance of actually getting better, was bound to stir up trouble among the doctors of the day. Yet he went even further in seeking a culprit for this unsatisfactory state of affairs. The guilty party as far as he was concerned was surgery.

The discovery of antisepsis, mainly associated with Joseph Lister around 1880, and the use of carbolic acid to sterilise operating theatres and surgical instruments had ushered in a surgical boom. Vienna was one of the great surgical centres during this period. The eminent German surgeon Theodor Billroth (1829–1894) arrived in Vienna from Zürich in 1867. He was chosen by his colleagues as the candidate most likely to advance medical research in Vienna.[24] Many of the techniques that were to become standard surgical practice for the early twentieth century were pioneered in the capital of the Dual Monarchy. Where previously doctors had only operated in the direst cases, they were now able to operate with some degree of confidence that their patients' wounds might heal safely. Reibmayr's figures illustrate this dramatic shift. In 1856, there were 184 operations at the Allgemeines Krankenhaus, by 1867 the figure was 443 (an initial rise that may be associated with the introduction of anaesthesia), but by 1888 there were 2,122 operations in one year. The overall number of patients admitted annually remained more or less constant throughout.[25]

Reibmayr concluded his case – stated in 40 pages – with seven summary points. In respect of *Doktor Trojan* the sixth of these points seems apposite: 'We believe that we have discovered the probable cause of the failures noted in the infinitely greater readiness of modern surgeons to operate.'[26] Throughout his argument, Reibmayr makes it clear that he does not object to surgery *per se*. Indeed, he takes care to praise the improved standards of hygiene and care in modern hospitals and their positive effects on mortality rates. He does, however, question the wholesale application of surgery as a panacea. It is not far-fetched to imagine Saar seeing in Reibmayr's case against surgery affinities with his own views on the benefits and drawbacks of modern civilisation. Reibmayr's seventh and concluding summary point might have come from the lips of one of Saar's narrators:

> The final result of our statistical research is that at this point we cannot but express our admiration for what the professors of the Allgemeines Krankenhaus were able to achieve in former times in relatively unfavourable hygienic conditions, where operative techniques were little developed and so forth. We would consider it a great benefit to young doctors if these figures were brought to their attention in order that they should learn the necessary modesty and not look down with contempt on an earlier period with the arrogance of modernity, but see in those figures a spur to achieving better results for the good of suffering humanity with the assistance of the advances that have been made.[27]

In fact, the narrator of *Doktor Trojan* explicitly places the discussion of Trojan's aversion to cutting into flesh in the context of medical advances in the Dual Monarchy. When the narrator comments on Trojan's failing to the effect that he considers some degree of surgical knowledge to be a vital part of a doctor's training, Trojan is scathing in reply:

> Anatomische Kenntnisse sind allerdings notwendig, aber die kann man sich aufs gründlichste aus jedem guten Atlas verschaffen. ... Man braucht nicht erst Kadaver zu zerstücken. Das ist etwas für die eigentlichen Anatomen, wie Hyrtl und Rokitansky – oder für die Physiologen, wie Brücke. Oppolzer und Skoda haben niemals eine Lanzette berührt, das überließen sie den Chirurgen, den Schuhs und Pithas. Sie waren eben *Internisten* (p. 181).

> [A knowledge of anatomy is necessary in any case, but one can gain that knowledge quite thoroughly from any good medical atlas. ... One does not need to go as far as cutting up cadavers. That is something for the real anatomists, like Hyrtl and Rokitansky – or for the physiologists, like Brücke. Oppolzer and Skoda never touched a lancet. They left that to the surgeons, to men like Schuh and Pitha. They were *specialists in internal diseases*.]

The names would of course have been familiar to contemporary readers. With the exception of Franz Freiherr von Pitha, who was Professor of Surgery in Prague from 1841, these were the great and the good of the Viennese medical world in the middle of the nineteenth century.[28] To them Vienna owed its reputation as a great medical centre. Trojan points out that these names were associated with different fields, and some of them had nothing to do with surgery. When Trojan comes to his own relations with Dr Hulesch he again makes reference to this medical context. He explains that Hulesch is a 'fanatical admirer' of Billroth and goes on to characterise Billroth's influence as follows:

> Bei aller Hochschätzung dieses genialen Mannes und seiner erstaunlichen Leistungen muß ich doch sagen, daß er die Medizin ganz unter die Herrschaft des Messers zu bringen droht. Er selbst hat ja ganz gewiß den Blick dafür, ob und wann eine Operation notwendig ist ... Aber für seine Schüler gibt es keine sonstige Therapie mehr; den alten kostbaren Pflanzen-Arzneischatz verachten sie ganz und gar. Es sind ungeduldige Leute, sie wollen der Natur vorgreifen und tun ihr Gewalt an. Aber *natura non facit saltus* – und auch der Arzt darf keine Sprünge machen (p. 182).

> [Despite my admiration for his genius and his astonishing achievements, I have to say that he is threatening to bring medicine totally under the reign of the knife. He certainly has the skill to recognise whether and when an operation is needed ... But for his students there is now no other therapy than surgery. They have nothing but contempt for valuable old herbal medicines. They are impatient people who want to interfere with the course of nature and do violence to her. But *natura non facit saltus* – and neither should the physician take shortcuts.]

Not only does this passage allude directly to the title of Reibmayr's critique of modern surgical practice, it borrows directly from Reibmayr's text. The first section of *Unter der Herrschaft des Messers* has the title 'On the Lack of a Genuine Philosophical Spirit in Modern Medicine' ('Mangel an echt philosophischem Geist in der heutigen Medicin'). In a footnote on the second page, Reibmayr remarks that his argument refers principally to the present Vienna Medical School and the Allgemeines Krankenhaus, that is, mainly the successors to the names given by Trojan in his diatribe against surgery as a prerequisite for doctors. Though Billroth is not referred to by name by Reibmayr, there can be little doubt that he and his methods are the main target. Reibmayr then complains that the inductive methods of modern medicine have led to 'den ganzen pflanzlichen Heilschatz' ('the whole store of herbal medicines' – I quote the German to show the similarity in the phrasing) being thrown on the scrap-heap.[29]

Of course, not all of Trojan's character and ideas are drawn from Reibmayr's text. For example, Trojan emphasises that a country doctor may need to become a Samaritan to his patients and contrasts this with the easy lot of the city physician. Some of the bitter criticism of urban medics may be more than conventional dislike of doctors. Saar himself suffered from a number of chronic illnesses, and his most intimate letters are full of remarks about his condition and the prescriptions of doctors who want him to go to Carlsbad.

Given the charged nature of the subject and the appearance of the story as a 'Feuilleton' in the *Neue Freie Presse*, there was bound to be a reaction to Saar's taking up of Reibmayr's ideas. Indeed, he says as much in his letter to Milow:

> So wurde dann auch schon aus Wien geschrieben, daß der 'Trojan' böse Reden von Seiten der Ärzte auf sich gezogen habe. So geht's! Ich habe die Geschichte mit rein künstlerischer Harmlosigkeit verfaßt – und nun sieht es aus, als hätte ich die Ärzte angreifen wollen![30]

> [I heard from Vienna that *Trojan* had attracted some bad remarks from the doctors. That is the way it goes! I wrote the story in a harmless artistic spirit – and now it looks as if I set out to attack doctors!]

Rereading *Doktor Trojan* in the light of this remark, one might well share Saar's surprise. Trojan's failure to diagnose and treat a serious condition does not speak well for the opponents of surgery. The narrator remains neutral. He has sympathy for Trojan, considering the punishment far greater than the crime, and, while disliking Srp's personal ambition and aware of his lack of competence, he can see the inevitable conflict between the new and the 'past whose tributaries reach into our present'.

The example of *Doktor Trojan* suggests that in Saar we have a major writer whose achievement has been denied due recognition, partly, at least, because so much of it found expression in the small-scale form of the Novelle. Yet within the confines of this form, Saar fused mythical archetypes with contemporary history. *Doktor Trojan* demonstrates his awareness not only of controversies concerning the medical profession but of the national conflict, particularly the transfer of power from Germans to Czechs in Bohemia and Moravia, which were embittering Austrian politics at the turn of the century and modifying the meaning of the word 'Austrian'.

Notes

1. See Ian Foster, *The Image of the Habsburg Army in Austrian Fiction, 1888 to 1914* (Berne, 1991), pp. 157–9, for a brief survey of Saar's military career and its significance.
2. See Hugo von Hofmannsthal, *Sämtliche Werke I. Gedichte I*, ed. Eugene Weber (Frankfurt, 1984), pp. 226–9. Hofmannsthal was a regular guest at the Wertheimstein home in Döbling from 1892 to the death of Josephine von Wertheimstein in 1894, an event which inspired the celebrated poem 'Über Vergänglichkeit'.
3. The *Verzeichnis Lieferbarer Bücher* as of 15 June 1993 lists eight separate collections (excluding the scholarly versions under Polheim's editorship):
Ferdinand von Saar, *Dissonanzen. Die Familie Worel* (Reclams Universalbibliothek 7681)
Ferdinand von Saar, *Die Steinklopfer. Tambi* (Reclams Universalbibliothek 8663)
Hansres Jacobi (ed.) *Ferdinand von Saar. Meisternovellen* (Manesse, 1982)
Karlheinz Rossbacher (ed.) *Ginevra und andere Novellen* (Ullstein, 1983)
Karl Konrad Polheim (ed.) *Sündenfall und andere Erzählungen* (Bouvier, 1983)

Hans-Heinrich Reuter (ed.) *Reqiem der Liebe und andere Novellen* (3rd ed., Leipzig, 1988)

Burkhard Bittrich (ed.) *Ferdinand von Saar. Mährische Novellen.* (Dt. Bibl. d. Ostens, 1989)

Ferdinand von Saar, *Novellen aus Österreich* (Insel, 1990)

4. Jakob Minor (ed.), *Ferdinand von Saar. Sämtliche Werke in zwölf Bänden* (Leipzig, 1908).

5. Saar's correspondence with Princess Marie zu Hohenlohe has been available for many years: Anton Bettelheim (ed.), *Fürstin Marie zu Hohenlohe und Ferdinand von Saar. Ein Briefwechsel* (Vienna, 1910). Also of relevance is Moritz Necker's 'Briefe von Ferdinand von Saar' in *Österreichische Rundschau*, 16 (1908), 194–207. The letters between Saar and Marie von Ebner-Eschenbach appeared as Heinz Kindermann (ed.), *Briefwechsel zwischen Ferdinand von Saar und Marie von Ebner-Eschenbach* (Vienna, 1957). More recent publications are *Briefe an, von und um Josephine von Wertheimstein. Ausgewählt und erläulert von Heinrich Gomperz 1933. Für die Drucklegung neu bearbeitet und herausgegeben von Robert A. Kann* (Vienna, 1980/81) and the correspondence between Saar and a young Jewish law student in Czernowitz: Jean Charue (ed.), *Ferdinand von Saar. Briefwechsel mit Abraham Altmann* (Bonn, 1984). The latter is especially valuable as Saar's deference towards his patrons at times leads him to censor himself. For this reason, some of the unpublished correspondence in the Vienna City and State Library Manuscript Collection is rather more revealing of the writer and his interests than the better-known material.

6. Franz Karl von Stockert, *Zur Anatomie des Realismus: Ferdinand von Saars Entwicklung als Novellendichter* (Göppingen, 1970).

7. For the most recent detailed bibliography on Saar, see Karl Konrad Polheim (ed.), *Ferdinand von Saar. Ein Wegbereiter der literarischen Moderne* (Bonn, 1985), pp. 326–8. Polheim's edited text of 'Der Brauer von Habrovan' also appears in the same volume (pp. 291–319). Further texts in the series 'Ferdinand von Saar. Kritische Texte und Deutungen' are Detlef Haberland (ed.), *Ferdinand von Saar: Seligmann Hirsch* (Tübingen, 1987) and Lydia Beate Kaiser (ed.), *Ferdinand von Saar: Herr Fridolin und sein Glück* (Tübingen, 1993).

8. Letter to Moritz Necker in collection of Vienna City and State Library, Inventory Number 143.664.

9. Unpublished letter to Stephan Milow dated 5 October 1896 in collection of Vienna City and State Library, Inventory Number 68.153.

10. Ibid. The elliptical phrasing is typical and reflects Saar's army years.

11. These details, given by Minor, *Sämtliche Werke*, vol. X, p. 167, have been checked by the present author.

12. The references to 'purple ink' in the text may in fact be a private joke between Saar and his patrons – there are a number of letters in the collection of the Vienna City and State Library which are indeed written in purple ink. Saar usually wrote exclusively in black.

13. The text of *Doktor Trojan* may be found in the edition by Jakob Minor, *Sämtliche Werke* (Leipzig, 1908), pp. 165–200. All quotations are from this edition.

14. See Alfred Riemen, 'Schloß Kostenitz und sein Erzähler', *Euphorion*, 82 (1988), 25–50, p. 31 for a discussion of this aspect.

15. The text of *Die Geigerin* may be found in the Minor edition, vol. VII, pp. 153–7.

16. Arthur Schopenhauer, *Die Welt als Wille und Vorstellung*, ed. Paul Deussen (Munich, 1911), vol. II, pp. 503–4. The original reads: 'Die Kapitel der Völkergeschichte sind im Grunde nur durch die Namen und Jahreszahlen verschieden: der eigentliche wesentliche Inhalt ist überall der selbe.'

17. Alfred Riemen, 'Schloß Kostenitz und sein Erzähler'.

18. Ibid., p. 32. My translation.
19. See R. A. Kann, *A History of the Habsburg Empire, 1526–1918* (Berkeley, 1974), pp. 606–7.
20. See Friedrich Prinz, 'Die Ära Taaffe und die böhmischen Ausgleichsversuche' in Karl Bosl (ed.), *Handbuch der Geschichle der böhmischen Länder*, vol. III, pp. 154–74 (Stuttgart, 1968), p. 156: 'German Nationals and Schönerer supporters on the one side and Young Czechs on the other reflected a similar social structure. Their petit-bourgeois nationalism that rose to a pitch of intransigent chauvinism and their doctrinaire ideological stance resulted from the entry of new, politically immature sections of the populace into parliamentary life' (my translation).
21. See Stanley B. Winters, 'The Young Czech Party (1874–1914): An Appraisal', *Slavic Review*, 28 (1969), 426–444, p. 440.
22. Unpublished letter to Stephan Milow dated 5 October 1896 in collection of Vienna City and State Library, Inventory Number 68.153. Bettelheim's biographical introduction also identifies *Unter der Herrschaft des Messers* and mentions the incident in Blansko as sources of inspiration for the story, but does not identify the author of the treatise. See Anton Bettelheim, 'Ferdinand von Saars Leben und Schaffen', in Jakob Minor (ed.), *Ferdinand von Saar. Sämtliche Werke in zwölf Banden* (Leipzig, 1908) vol. I, pp. 162–3.
23. Albert Reibmayr, *Unter der Herrschaft des Messers. Ein Mahnwort von einem Freunde der leidenden Menschheit* (Vienna, 1892).
24. See Wolfgang Genschorek, *Wegbereiter der Chirurgie. Johann Friedrich Dieffenbach. Theodor Billroth* (Leipzig, 1982), pp. 165–6.
25. See Reibmayr, *Unter der Herrschaft des Messers*, p. 32.
26. Reibmayr, *Unter der Herrschaft des Messers*, p. 39. Translations from this text are my own.
27. Reibmayr, *Unter der Herrschaft des Messers*, p. 4.
28. See Hans-Heinrich Reuter (ed.), *Ferdinand von Saar. Requiem der Liebe und andere Novellen* (Leipzig, 1958), pp. 677–8.
29. Reibmayr, *Unter der Herrsschaft des Messers*, p. 3.
30. Letter to Stephan Milow, 5 October 1896.

Knowing the Other

Leopold von Andrian's *Der Garten der Erkenntnis* and the Homoerotic Discourse of the Fin de Siècle

Jens Rieckmann

In 1918, when Leopold von Andrian was being considered for the appointment of general director of the Burgtheater and the Vienna opera, Count Colloredo-Mansfeld, then the president of the Austrian cabinet, indicated to Hofmannsthal that he knew 'was man aus dem "Garten der Erkenntnis" herauslesen könne, wenn man wolle' ('what one could gather from *The Garden of Knowledge*, if one wanted').[1] The count was alluding to rumours circulating in the Austro-Hungarian foreign service, which Andrian had joined in 1899, that Andrian's 1895 novel was a veiled representation of its author's sexual orientation. Andrian was concerned that these rumours would preclude his appointment. When serving in the diplomatic corps, he had lived in constant fear that he would be exposed as a homosexual or would be blackmailed because of his sexual orientation. Looking back on his career he wrote that he was constantly asking himself: 'Pourquoi est ce qu'il me bat froid? Aurait-il découvert qq [quelque] chose? – Solang V.[erfasser, i.e. Andrian] in der Carrière war ... bei jedem Bf [Brief] mit unbekannter Handschrift, den er bekam ... Bei jeder Unfreundlichkeit des Ministeriums ...' (Why does he cut me dead? Has he discovered anything? As long as the author was pursuing his career ... every time he received a letter in an unknown handwriting ... every time the ministry treated him coldly').[2] In the War Ministry Andrian was known as the 'sweet Semite', i.e. he was subjected to twofold stigmatisation as a homosexual and as a Jew.[3] As Sander Gilman has shown, this linkage of sexual and racial 'otherness' was typical in the anti-Semitic discourse of the time.[4]

Andrian both internalised and rejected the generally accepted view of homosexuality as unnatural, as a sign of the Jew's sexual perversity. The conflict thus created in his psyche is reflected in *Der Garten der Erkenntnis* and led to his breakdown after the completion of the novel. It ultimately caused him to abandon the attempt to resurrect his literary career in the 1930s. In his notes for the unfinished autobiographical novel *Der Lauf zum Ideal. Des Gartens der Erkenntnis zweiter Teil* ('The Approach to the Ideal: Part Two of The Garden of Knowledge'), which he began working on in 1933, he repeatedly addresses the problem of how to represent his sexual

61

desires and experiences, which inspired his poetic imagination, in his fictional alter ego's sexuality. How, he asks himself, 'könnte man G[abriel]'s Figur hinstellen, ohne das zu berücksichtigen, was ihm, wenn er zurückdenkt, die Hauptsache scheint' ('how could the figure of Gabriel be portrayed without taking account of what seems to him, looking back, the heart of the matter?'). He answers his own question by saying: 'Man muss, unzweifelhaft, die ganze Figur erschauen ... u. wie sollte man das ohne α [Andrian's code denoting homosexuality] thun' (TUA 183, p. 175: 'One must undoubtedly behold the figure as a whole, and how is that to be done without alpha?'). Although he was aware that this aspect could not be ignored, 'Furcht u. Scham u. Ehrgefühl' (TUA 183, p. 174: 'fear, shame and honour') prevented him from dealing with it openly, as the following note reveals:

> So kommt er zur Arbeit ... die Arbeit soll es mir klar machen α u. Gnade ... hier habe ich das *notwendige* Sujet ... man schreibt wie es gewesen ... ein Dichter befreit sich indem er dichtet. ... Das auch ganz schön, wenn nicht α in seinen Tiefen rumoren würde, u. wenn nicht der Bruch zwischen unterbewusst u. oberbewusst bestünde. Weil er besteht, kann er das α nicht in Worte bringen, u. weil er inzwischen wieder sündigt ... kann er nicht die relig.[iösen] Dinge (Gott) rein u. stark genug fühlen. So muss die Arbeit misslingen (TUA 174, p. 68).

> ['Thus he gets down to work ... the work must clarify alpha and grace for me ... here I have the *necessary* subject-matter ... one writes as it really was ... a writer frees himself by writing. ... That would be fine if it were not for alpha murmuring deep down inside him, and if there were not a split between unconscious and conscious. As there is a split, he cannot put alpha into words, and as he sins again in the meantime, he cannot have a strong and pure enough awareness of religious matters (God). Hence the work must fail.']

For the same reason Andrian toward the end of his life abandoned the idea of writing altogether. In 1948 he noted: 'Alles mehr oder weniger, ist Gegenstand für die Litteratur, c'est entendu. Die ganze, gradezu monstrose Natur V. [des Verfassers] könnte auch dargestellt werden. Aber nie als Autobiographie, dazu ist es zu horrendum u. pudendum' (TUA 189, p. 5: 'Practically anything is a subject for literature, that goes without saying. The author's entire, positively monstrous nature could be depicted too. But never autobiographically, it is too appalling and shameful for that'). In this note Andrian significantly establishes the same link between his sexuality and his Jewish heritage that his detractors in the War Ministry had established. Having rejected the idea of writing his autobiography, he considers creating a 'freierfundene Figur' ('imaginary figure'), but dismisses this possibility as well:

> aber wie gesagt, auch eine solche wäre zu monstros, zu hässlich als dass V, sogar wenn er könnte, sie darstellen möchte, u. außerdem: ein Ausnahmsfall, ein singularer Fall, ein monstroses Mischproduct, zweier

alter ausgelebter u. untereinander heterogener Rassen, interessant für den Betroffenen, aber kaum für die Anderen (TuA 189, p. 50–1).

['but as I said, even such a figure would be so monstrous, so hideous, that the author would not wish to depict it, even if he could, and besides: an exceptional case, a unique case, a monstrous cross-breed of two old, effete and incompatible races, interesting for the person concerned, but hardly for anyone else.']

Similar doubts had already assailed the young Andrian. A note written in the spring of 1894, when he was working on his short novel *Der Garten der Erkenntnis*, reads: 'Sie waren Sclaven der Natur das erkannten sie jetzt. Und die Natur hatte sie gestraft, weil sie eine Schönheit gesucht hatten, die nicht zugleich den Frondienst [?] ihrer Nützlichkeit in sich trug' (TuA 52, p. 175: 'They were nature's slaves, as they now realised. And Nature had punished them for seeking a kind of beauty that did not subject them to the servitude of utility'). The note is related to the explicitly homoerotic relationship between Erwin, the protagonist of Andrian's novel, and Clemens, a fellow student: 'einen Augenblick standen sie sich gegenüber in ihrer unfruchtbaren Schönheit, von der sie einander nichts geben konnten' ('for a moment they stood facing each other in their sterile beauty, which neither could transmit to the other').[5] At the same time, however, Andrian also gave expression to the Platonically inspired thought that the renunciation of procreation represented an advance over the 'Nützlichkeit' of heterosexual love: 'Das Sich-nicht-Fortpflanzen müssen – ein Erkenntnisfortschritt des Menschen' (TuA 47, p. 23: 'Not having to beget one's kind – a gain in human knowledge').[6]

In the 1890s Andrian's defiance of conventional sexual norms, combined with his sense of mission and martyrdom, generally prevailed over the sense of guilt that his upbringing had instilled in him. At this time Andrian saw a significant connection between his mission as an artist and his sexual orientation. In his 1894 diary he recorded the impression a statue of Antinous had made upon him; the figure of Antinous was frequently evoked in turn-of-the-century art to signal homoeroticism: 'Gefühl des Märtyrertriumphes ... soviel habe ich schon gelitten soviel werde ich noch leiden für diese Sache: aber jetzt ist mir klar geworden, daß darin die Zukunft der Welt ... liegt und daß ich ein Apostel dieser Religion und daher ein großer Künstler bin' (TuA 55, p. 35: 'a feeling of triumphant martyrdom ... I have suffered so much and will suffer so much more for this cause: but now I realise that that is where the future of the world lies and that I am an apostle of this religion and hence a great artist'). The link Andrian establishes between homoeroticism and creativity was commonly made by apologists and advocates of homoeroticism in the late nineteenth century. Both Walter Pater and John Addington Symonds based their justification of this linkage on Platonic thought.[7] In the *Symposium*, Diotima in her remarks on 'creative souls', on poets and artists, 'men who are more creative [are more pregnant] in their souls than in their bodies', argues 'with all the authority of a sophist' that such a man 'wanders about seeking beauty that he may beget offspring ... and when he finds a fair and noble and well-nurtured soul ... he gladly embraces him ... and at the touch and presence of the beautiful he brings forth the beautiful'.[8]

The new religion, as Andrian conceived it – and in this respect his thoughts were very similar to those of Pater, whom he read in 1894[9] – was characterised by a new sensibility with the potential of bringing about a cultural regeneration. In March 1894, Andrian expressed his hope that the 'ganze Umwälzung im Fühlen, in der Kunst eine [neue] Cultur schaffen würde' (TUA 52, p. 52: 'that the complete revolution in feeling, in art, would create a new culture'). The 'Cultus der Frau', which had 'die Freundschaft [between men] aus der Welt geschafft' (TUA 52, p. 51: 'the cult of woman, which had abolished male friendship'), would be replaced in this neo-Hellenistic culture by homosocial relations. Andrian based this belief in an 'Umwälzung im Fühlen' primarily on his reading during this spring. Concluding his notes on the hoped-for cultural renaissance he writes: 'Es geschehen ... noch Wunder: Verlaine, Oscar Wilde, Pierre Loti – und viele andere' (TUA 52, p. 52: 'Miracles still happen: Verlaine [etc.] and many others'). Reading Verlaine, he felt a 'große Sehnsucht nach der Antike' ('great yearning for antiquity') and desired to write 'Stücke ... die als ganze Stücke das tragen, was Verlaine in lyrischen Gedichten, den Duft der ganzen Zeit d.h. des Zaubers dieser Zeit. Da wären zwei Möglichkeiten, klassisch und hellenistisch' (TUA 52, p. 30: 'plays that as whole works convey what Verlaine has done in lyric poems, the atmosphere of that whole age, i.e. of its magic'). Loti's novel *Mon frère Yves*, the story of a homoerotically charged friendship between two sailors, made a deep impression on him, in part because it was the first text he had read in which he found 'so etwas wirklich künstlerisch geschildert' (TUA 52, p. 175: 'such a thing described with true artistry'). At the same time he was reading Oscar Wilde, probably *The Picture of Dorian Gray*. In April 1894, he wrote to Hofmannsthal: 'Hast Du etwas vom Dichter Oscar Wilde gelesen? Der ist auch merkwürdig' ('Have you read anything by the poet Oscar Wilde? He's remarkable, too').[10] Two years later, when he had read an account of the Wilde trials, he spoke to Hofmannsthal of the 'so wunderbare Verteidigung Wilde's' ('Wilde's wonderful defence').[11] Most likely he was referring to Wilde's defence of 'the love that dare not speak its name' as the love which 'Plato made the very basis of his philosophy ... that deep, spiritual affection that is as pure as it is perfect.'[12]

Andrian's sense of being part of a regenerative, homoerotically grounded European cultural movement based on the Platonic ideal of 'spiritual procreancy' was reinforced through an encounter in Nice in March 1894 with a young Englishman. This person identified himself as a 'Hellenist' writer belonging to a 'Schule von jungen Leuten in London', 'die alle keinen Schnurrbart tragen' (TUA 52, p. 44: 'a school of young people in London, none of whom has a moustache'), the Uranian writers associated with Oscar Wilde who exalted the 'heavenly' love between males.[13] Andrian's detailed account of his conversation with the Englishman, who is not identified in the diary, leaves no doubt that he was familiar with the coded homoerotic discourse of the 1890s. The Englishman's remark, 'Die Hellenisten nennen wir uns' ('We call ourselves the Hellenists'), has a revelatory significance for him: 'in dem Moment fällt mir ein was B – [Bahr?] über Wilde erzählt hat – und in der einen Minute ist mir ganz klar, was das heißt, – warum der Name – und warum der rasierte Schnurbart [sic]' (TUA 52, pp. 44–5: 'At that moment I remember what B. told me about Wilde – and in a single moment I realise quite clearly what it means – why the name – and why shave off one's moustache'). The coded reference to the 'Hellenisten' opens up the conversation, begun as a '[T]asten, wie Künstler immer zu Anfang' (TUA 52, p. 44: 'tentative, as always when artists begin'). It turns into an exchange of two artists whose identical sexual orientation is signalled by glances and coded language designed both to reveal and to veil a common interest and to establish a sense of solidarity: 'natürlich gibt's auch eine Menge Leute die uns hassen', the Englishman continues with a 'bezeichnender Blick' ('significant look'), 'Wir müssen alle zusammen stehen, international muß die Bewegung sein. ... ich glaube Sie gehören zu den *unsern*, Sie schaun so aus. Ich erkenne alle die zu uns gehören auf den ersten Blick – es ist eben die eine große Idee, die uns bindet' (TUA 52, pp. 45–6: 'naturally there are lots of people who hate us; we must all stand shoulder by shoulder, the movement must be international. I think you are one of us, you have that look. I recognise all those who belong to us at the first glance – for we are linked by one great idea').

The impact of this exchange on Andrian is indicative of his ambivalent and complex attitude toward his sexuality. He is drawn toward the subculture that the Englishman reveals to him, ashamed of the attraction he feels, and bent on rationalising his desire to explore this secret world as a longing peculiar to the artist's nature:

> und ich habe das gewisse große Gefühl der Neugier, der Erwartung, des Gefühls, [sic] eine neue Welt zu sehn – ein physisches Gefühl, so wie die Angst vor eine[r] Prüfung. Ich habe das Gefühl in eine Welt neben der Welt einzutreten, ein ganz anderes Gefühlsleben vor mir zu sehen, eine Welt, von der unsre Welt keine Ahnung hat, und die sie verachten würde, und der große Männer angehören – und mein unruhiger Traum ist von solchen Bildern verfolgt, ich fühle, daß dies für mein Schicksal entscheidend sein kann, für mein ganzes Leben – schäme mich vor mir selbst, daß ich so ganz diesem dumpfen Gefühl hingegeben bin. – Und sage zu meiner Entschuldigung, daß ja da sich ein Leben von Geheimnis[,] Räthseln, Gefahren, verborgenen Schönheiten sich mir öffnet, und kann es einem Dichter etwas Interessanteres geben – so als wäre ich im vorgen [sic] Jahrhundert in den Freimaurerorden aufgenommen worden (TUA 52, pp. 46–7).

[and I have that great feeling of curiosity, of expectation, the feeling of seeing a new world – a physical feeling, like the fear before an examination. I have the feeling of entering a world alongside the world, seeing a quite different emotional life in front of me, a world of which our world has no inkling, and which it would despise, and which includes great men – and my restless dream is pursued by such images,

I feel that this may be decisive for my destiny, for my entire life – am ashamed of myself for being so caught up in this obscure feeling. – And I excuse myself by saying that a life of mystery, enigmas, dangers, concealed beauties is opening up before me, and can there be anything more interesting for a poet – as though in the last century I had been received into the Order of Freemasons.]

But Andrian's desire to use his writings as a vehicle for the advancement of the new Hellenism collided with traditional, internalised strictures. Initially Andrian subjected himself to a kind of self-censorship. In the poems he submitted in 1893 for publication in Stefan George's *Blätter für die Kunst* ('Pages for Art'), he systematically changed the male third person pronouns of the original into female ones. In the poem 'Klage der verfolgten Liebenden' ('Lament of the Persecuted Lovers'), for example, the original lines 'Mein Herz, was hast du denn gethan? / Du sahst *ihn* viel zu lange an' ('My heart, what have you done? You looked at *him* for far too long') were made to read 'Mein Herz, was hast du denn gethan / Du sahst *sie* viel zu lange an' in the printed version of 1894 ('... You looked at *her* for far too long').[14] The original third person male pronoun was restored only in 1919, after Andrian had left the foreign service. In other works he was writing or planning to write in 1893, he also transposed same-sex relationships into heterosexual ones.[15] In the fragmentary cycle of poems *Erwin und Elmire*, written in 1893–94, his 'sündig süss[e]' love for Erwin Slamecka, a cadet at a military academy in Vienna, is recast as the 'Nervenliebe' of a fin-de-siècle poet for Elmire, a naive, Ingeborg Holm type of woman.[16] A planned novel with the title *Und die Philister banden ihn* ('And the Philistines bound him') was to depict 'die Geschichte E[rwin Slameckas] transformirt [sic] ins Weibliche' (TUA 42, pp. 44–5: 'the story of E. transposed into the feminine'), though Andrian conceived it as a representation of the suffering of the homosexual artist.

Despite these concessions to the repressive practices and bourgeois sexual niceties of the nineteenth century, the homoerotic implications of Andrian's love poetry were not entirely erased. The replacement of the speaker's male love object with a female one in 'Klage der verfolgten Liebenden' not only deprives the poem of its poignancy, but the speaker's lament 'Drum wirst mit Steinen du beworfen' loses its meaning if the love that is expressed is not of a kind which bourgeois morality castigates.[17] The poem 'Sonett', which George published in 1901, suggests that physical heterosexual union, dictated by mere instinctual desire for reproductivity, is a tainting of a higher form of love, the homoerotic spiritual bond between males:

> Ich denke derer, die wir einstmals kannten,
> Mit lichten Augen und mit lichten Haaren,
> Da mit der Sehnsucht wir von sechzehn Jahren
> Der Seele gleiches Zittern Liebe nannten. –
>
> Die sich von uns zu einem Weibe wandten,
> Bis sie des Daseins Niedrigkeit erfahren,

Und wir sie wiedersahen und das Mal gewahren,
Das in ihr Leben jene Lippen brannten.[18]

[I think of those whom we once knew, with light-blue eyes and golden hair, when, with the yearning of sixteen, we called the soul's like trembling by the name of love – those who turned away from us for a woman, until they learned the baseness of existence, and we saw them again and perceive[d] the brand that those lips burnt into their lives.]

In one fragmentary poem in the *Erwin und Elmire* cycle Andrian breaks the bonds of these self-imposed strictures. The poem gives an indication of what the cycle might have been without the concessions Andrian felt he had to make to the temper of the times. It is an undisguised advocacy of the naturalness of homoerotic love; the doubts that the beloved has voiced about its justification are rejected as the prejudice of the ignorant Nietzschean 'herd':

O lass mich, lass mich
Mit dem Abnormalen, was
ist normal in dieser kranken Zeit

Du häufst Sophismen weich gen unsre Liebe
Die auch in Deinem Innern dennoch lebt

Was hat die Wandlung wohl
In Dich vollzogen

Banalen Maasstab der banalen Menge[19]

[O leave me, leave me with the abnormal; what counts as normal in this diseased age? You gently pile up sophisms against our love, which nevertheless dwells also within you. I wonder what brought about the change in you? The banal standards of the banal crowd.]

With *Der Garten der Erkenntnis* Andrian overcame unsophisticated transcriptions in his early love poetry, of homoerotic desire into acceptable heterosexual forms. In this key text of fin-de-siècle sensibilities the quest for 'Erkenntnis', with its biblical connotations of carnal knowledge, is inextricably related to knowing the Other, the emissary from an unknown, seductive, hidden world. This hidden world is first revealed to Erwin by his fellow student Heinrich Philipp, a holy sinner, who speaks 'sonderbar und geheimnisvoll' in 'verbotenen Worten' of a 'Seite im Wiener Leben [die] mit diesen verbotenen Worten irgendwie zusammenhing' (*Garten* 14–15: 'strangely and mysteriously, in forbidden words, of a side of Viennese life that was somehow connected with these forbidden words'). It is Erwin's first intimation of a world which he perceives as 'schlecht und verboten' ('bad and forbidden'), according to the value system of bourgeois morality, and at the same time as 'reizvoll' ('alluring', *Garten* 14), because it promises satisfaction of his sexual longings, his 'Drang nach dem "Anderen"' ('urge for the "Other"'): 'Er sagte das "Andere" und hatte dabei das Gefühl, nach irgendeiner Richtung erstrecke sich eine Welt, in der alles verboten und geheim sei, gleich groß mit der, die er kannte' (*Garten* 19–20: 'He said "the Other", feeling as though in some direction there extended a world in which everything was forbidden and secret, a world just as big as the one he knew'). He associates this world of the 'Other' with the 'Opernbälle, die Sofiensäle, der Ronacher und das Orpheum und der Circus und die Fiaker' (*Garten* 14, 15, 20). Significantly, the chain of associations moves from bourgeois respectability (Opera balls and 'Sofiensäle') to the less reputable vaudeville and music halls of late nineteenth-century Vienna (Ronacher and Orpheum).

The most striking link in this chain is the 'Fiaker' on whom Erwin's fantasy about the 'Other' fixates: 'Besonders die Fiaker schaute er mit einer eigentümlichen ängstlichen Aufregung an. Manche sahen den jungen Herren sonderbar ähnlich, daß in dieser Ähnlichkeit der Gegensatz lag, müßte mit der Beschaffenheit des "Anderen" zusammenhängen' (*Garten* 20: 'He looked at coachmen, in particular, with a curious fearful excitement. Many bore a strange resemblance to their young masters; the fact that the contrast lay in this very resemblance must be linked to the nature of the "Other"'). 'Das Andere', signifying the forbidden and seductive realm of sexuality, is concretised in 'der Andere', signifying the object of Erwin's longing:

Einer [der Fiaker] besonders gefiel ihm, wenn er im Frühling in den Prater fuhr; … er … saß da, etwas nach vorne gebeugt, die Zügel hoch und weit auseinandergehalten, mit einer gesuchten Gebärde der Arme, starr und doch seltsam lebend, wie eine graciöse und etwas manirierte Zeichnung in der manirierten Eleganz seines Zügels (*Garten* 20).

[He particularly liked one [of the coachmen] when he drove to the Prater in the spring; he sat there, bending forward slightly, holding the reins high up and far apart, with a deliberate gesture of his arms, rigid and yet strangely living, like a graceful and somewhat mannered drawing in the mannered elegance of his reins.]

As Scheible has pointed out, Erwin's imagination here 'fixiert … den Fiaker [zur Imago] in der Gebärde der Umarmung' ('fixates the coachman as an imago in the gesture of embrace').[20] The image is, however, not only one of embrace but also of domination, indicated by the 'hoch und weit auseinandergehalten[en] Zügel'. Implicit in this image then is not only the expectation of finding 'Das Andere' in a male, but also the desire to be subjugated by the socially inferior 'Fiaker'.[21] The amalgamation of the sexual 'Other' and the social 'Other' is explicitly stated in Andrian's 1893 notes 'Ideen zu künftigen Arbeiten' ('Ideas for future pieces of work'): 'Manchmal abends … überkam ihn eine unwiderstehliche Versuchung, an die Andern zu denken; die Andern, das waren die Niedrigen' (TUA 46, pp. 38–9: 'On some evenings he was overcome by an irresistible temptation to think of the others; the others – they were the low-born').[22]

The conjunction of the sexual 'Other' and the social 'Other' was grounded in part in the homoerotic discourse of the turn of the century,[23] in part in the consciousness of the fin-de-siècle dilettante, and in part in Andrian's biography. A passage in Andrian's 1894 diary, for example, expresses the longing for the imaginary unconscious naiveté of the lower classes in terms that are familiar from literary renditions of the dilletante syndrome such as Hofmannsthal's *Der Tor und der Tod* ('The Fool and Death'), Thomas Mann's *Tonio Kröger*, and Hermann Bahr's *Die Mutter* ('The Mother'), to name just a few:

> Und auf der ganzen Stadt liegt der Sonntag, und in den Straßen gehn Matrosen und Soldaten und Stritzis und Mädeln in Gruppen und paarweise, und auch da werd ich traurig und ich schaue den Matrosen nach mit einer Art Sehnsucht – es ist eben ein so ganz, ganz anderes, wahrscheinlich befriedigteres Leben, dessen Parfum mich einen Augenblick anweht, eines Lebens, das seinen Weg von Anfang zu Ende geht, ohne zurück- und vorzuschaun, in den Freuden und Leiden des Augenblicks. (TUA 52, p. 26)

> [And Sunday lies upon the whole city, and in the streets sailors and soldiers and spivs and girls are walking in groups and couples, and again I feel sad and I gaze after the soldiers with a kind of yearning – for it is such a very, very different and probably a more satisfied life whose perfume reaches me for a moment, a life that goes on its way from beginning to end, without looking back or forward, in the joys and sorrows of the moment.]

It is hardly coincidental that Andrian's longing attaches itself particularly to the sailors; they had become part of the homosexual iconography by the end of the nineteenth century.[24] The 'Other' is attractive because it is socially dissimilar and at the same time perceived as complementary. Reflecting on his encounter with guides on a mountain hike, Andrian writes: 'Und dasselbe Gefühl, wie bei den L[akaien], der wehmütige Reiz eines Lebens, dessen Schönheit man empfindet und mit dem man nichts gemein hat, und wie eine Art [Liebe] zu denen, wie zu den dementsprechenden, die die Ergänzung dazu bilden sollten.' (TUA 52, p. 71: 'And the same feeling as I had with the servants, the melancholy charm of a life whose beauty you feel and with which you have nothing in common, and something like a kind of love for them, as for the equivalent people who should complement them'). Also, the lower classes were of course sexually available for money, as is evident from the Wilde trials.

The ultimate cause of this attraction, however, lies in Andrian's masochistically tinged sexuality which he explored in a long self-analytic passage in his 1897 diary under the heading 'Der Gang von α bei mir' (TUA 62, p. 156). In this passage he traces the origin of his sexual identity to the 'Idee der Erniedrigung bei der das Ganze angefangen hat ... die Idee des Umgangs mit "der Hefe" ... de coucher avec les valets' (TUA 62, pp. 156–7: 'idea of degradation with which it all began ... the idea of intercourse with the dregs, of sleeping with the servants'). Originally the idea of humiliation is equated with sexuality as such, 'ohne Wissen von α und ohne irgendein directer Gedanke [sic] daran' (TUA 62, p. 157: 'without knowledge of alpha or any direct thought of it'). The equation of sexuality with humiliation can be traced to Andrian's distinction between a '1. und ... 2. Seele' ('first and second soul'); the former is 'geistig' ('spiritual'), the latter 'triebhaft' ('sensual': TUA 54, pp. 70–1).[25] This distinction is probably based on Plato's concept of the tripartite soul represented in the image of the charioteer guiding the white horse and the black horse. It is also reflected in Hofmannsthal's 1891 review of Bourget's *Physiologie de l'amour moderne*: 'Claude Larcher schreibt mit der ... geistfunkelnden ... "oberen" Seele; und stirbt an der "unteren", der Tier-seele' ('Claude Larcher writes with his witty, sparkling "upper" soul/ and dies of his "lower"/ animal soul').[26] In Andrian's conception of the divided soul, however, there is no 'charioteer'; the 'first and second souls' are engaged in a constant battle, and their aspirations are irreconcilable, as the following entry in Andrian's 1894 diary indicates:

> Und was merkwürdig war, wenn ich so einen ganzen Tag Ludwig XIV oder dgl. vorgestellt hatte, so waren die Vorstellungen, die ich abends im Bett beim V [Andrian's code for masturbation] producirte, ganz entgegengesetzter Natur. Schmutz vereinigt mit Demüthigungen aller Art. Also die erste Wollust, die ich kennen lernte, war ... jener Punkt, wo Schmutz und Lust sich treffen (TUA 52, p. 19).[27]

> [And the curious thing was that when I had spent a whole day imagining Louis XIV or someone similar, the ideas I produced in bed while masturbating were of a completely opposite nature. Dirt associated with humiliations of all kinds. Thus the first voluptuous enjoyment that I became acquainted with was the point where dirt and pleasure meet.]

The idea of the humiliation of the 'first soul' and the longing for that degradation eventually became associated in Andrian's imagination with homosexual practices: 'mir combinierten sich die beiden [Erniedrigung und α] so, daß ich mir sagte il n'ya pas de possibilité plus grande que celle' (TUA 62, p. 157: 'the two [degradation and alpha] became combined in such a way that I would say to myself: there can be no greater possibility than that'). This association was reinforced through conversations and sexual experimentation with his fellow students at the Schottengymnasium: 'Und das Reden über alle nicht gekannten Sachen; – weißt Du was v-[ögeln] heißt? –; bei alledem *immer mehr die Rede vom Verbotenen Geheimen Niedrigen Unanständigen als von der Frau*; und zum Schlusse eben das' (TUA 62, p. 159; my emphasis: 'And talking about all the things we didn't know; "do you know what screwing is?"; at the same time, much more talk about forbidden, secret, base, indecent things than about women; and finally, just that').

For Andrian, then, the desire for humiliation, the 'Vorstellung sich = [gleich] machen dem Niedrigen' (TUA 62, p. 158: 'idea of putting oneself on a

level with the base') became unalterably intertwined with his sexual orientation as the following diary entries indicate: 'Dieses Gefühl der Erniedrigung
war verkleidet und abgeschwächt und vermischt mit anderem, in dem was ich
später die "verschiedenen Stände und Lebensberufe kennenlernen" nannte; es
waren hauptsächlich die unteren Schichten' (TUA 62, p. 161: 'his feeling of
degradation was disguised and diluted and mingled with something else, in
what I later called "becoming acquainted with the various classes and
professions in society"; mainly the lower classes'). The 'Hintergedanke' in
these encounters was always 'wie schön das wäre, wenn sie [homosexuell]
wären' (TUA 62, p. 161: 'how nice it would be if they were homosexual').

Andrian obviously shared the nineteenth-century belief that, as Havelock
Ellis put it in his *Sexual Inversion: Studies in the Psychology of Sex*, 'the
uncultured man of civilisation is linked to the savage', particularly in his
sexual attitudes.[28] In 1893 Andrian wrote in his diary: 'Dem Bauern ist es
natürlich, wenn ein Mädchen, das noch nicht – hat, sich Befriedigung ihres
Triebes sucht – so wie etwa ein Hungriger ißt, weil er hungrig ist' (TUA 42, p.
50: 'The peasant considers it natural for a girl who hasn't yet – to seek to
satisfy her urge – just as a hungry man eats because he is hungry').
Furthermore it was generally believed, as Alan Sinfield has pointed out in a
recent study, that '[t]he lower classes [had] little anxiety about same-sex
practices'.[29] Both these views are reflected in *Der Garten der Erkenntnis* when
Erwin, overcome by the 'Wahnsinn des Erlebnisses, den die heißen Nächte
bringen' ('the madness of experience that comes with hot nights'), leaves his
bed in the attic of a mountain cabin hoping that one of the 'Senner und
Führer' would follow him: 'dort schliefen Senner und Führer ... nur
manchmal wälzte sich einer von ihnen um oder seufzte oder stöhnte ein Wort;
unten aber brüllte das Vieh stoßweise und schmerzlich ... Lange blieb er
stehen und wartete, doch es kam niemand' (*Garten* 40–1: 'herdsmen and
guides were sleeping there ... sometimes one of them would roll over or sigh
or groan out a word; but down below the cattle were uttering short, painful
bellowings ... He stood there waiting for a long time, but no-one came'). The
juxtaposition of the 'Senner und Führer' with the bellowing cattle suggests
the animalistic and indiscriminate sexuality to which Erwin succumbs: 'und
zitternd vor Begierde lehnte er an die Wand, und seine Seele genoß die
Erinnerung an die Lust seines Leibes und gestand, daß es der wahrhaftigste
Drang des Menschen sei, seinen Leib an den Leib eines andern Menschen zu
pressen' (*Garten* 42: 'and trembling with desire he leaned against the wall, and
his soul savoured the memory of his body's pleasure and confessed that it was
man's truest urge to press his body against another person's body'). Later
Erwin is to remember this night in which he was tempted to give in to the
promptings of the 'second soul', had the opportunity presented itself, as a
transgression of the moral order of a heterosexual society: 'er war gefallen'
(*Garten* 43: 'he had fallen'), thus putting himself in the position of the 'fallen
woman', the emblem of sexual transgression in nineteenth-century society and
literature.

The most enigmatic figuration of the sexual and social 'Other' is the

Stranger whom Erwin encounters three times. Initially following him 'sehnsüchtig nach Erkenntnis' (*Garten* 43: 'yearning for knowledge'), Erwin later believes him to be his '*Feind*' ('enemy': *Garten* 55). Shortly before he dies, 'ohne erkannt zu haben' (*Garten* 58: 'without having attained knowledge'), the memory of the first encounter with the Stranger is evoked, suggesting that the Stranger could have been the key to the knowledge that Erwin was searching for: 'Jeden Tag nahm die Dürre seiner Seele zu, und mit ihr wurde die Sehnsucht nach Erkenntnis trockener und quälender; jeden Tag sehnte er sich mehr nach dem Regen wie er an *jenem* Abend gewesen war' (*Garten* 57, my emphasis: 'Each day the desiccation of his soul increased, as the yearning for knowledge grew ever more dry and tormenting; each day he yearned more for the rain as it had been on that evening').

The initial encounter with the Stranger takes place in a disreputable 'Heurigenlokal' in a Vienna suburb ('Vorstadt'). The location functions, as has been pointed out in the more recent literature on Andrian's text, as a topographical sign of the association Erwin makes between the 'Other' and the lower classes.[30] The Stranger, whose 'Kleider waren dürftig' (*Garten* 36: 'his clothes were shabby') is socially linked with Clemens, the earlier object of Erwin's narcissistic love, who is 'arm und sehr einfach ... verdorben wie ein Gassenbub' (*Garten* 22: 'poor and very simple, as corrupt as a street-arab'), and is also linked with the 'nicht sehr elegant[e]' lieutenant, whom Erwin meets on his journey to Bozen, the first male figure to whom Edwin is attracted (*Garten* 10). In addition, the social milieu of the 'Vorstadt' is correlated with sexuality and the promise of sexual experience, just as the 'Führer and Senner' in the mountains were earlier in the text. Affected by the songs sung by a young man who is marked by make-up and artificially curled hair as a homosexual,[31] and by a woman with bare shoulders, the men and women in the 'Heurigenlokal' fall into a kind of sexual trance: 'sie neigten ihr Haupt auf die Seite, ihre Lippen öffneten sich, ... wie verzaubert starrten ihre Augen ... so wurden sie willig sich hinzugeben' (*Garten* 34: 'they inclined their heads to one side, their lips parted ..., their eyes stared as though entranced ... thus they grew willing to surrender themselves'). Erwin's crossing into this realm of lower-class life and sexuality is prompted by a vague erotic longing ('er fühlte Sehnsucht nach der Fülle der Erlebnisse, deren Möglichkeit in ihm war' [*Garten* 33]: 'he felt a yearning for the wealth of experience that was potentially in him'), and on his journey into this realm he encounters sexual signs. He sees prostitutes, and the perfumes arising from the flowering plants 'hatten sich noch nicht gemengt, streiften einander und wollten sich vereinigen' (*Garten* 33: 'had not yet mingled, brushed against one another and wanted to unite'). Such textual elements combine to signal to the reader the veiled sexuality that marks Erwin's encounter with the Stranger.

The narration of this central episode is modelled on Andrian's chance encounter with a young man in Venice. His notebook account of this ('Meine Italienische Reise' [7 October 1894–3 November 1894]) serves as the blueprint for its later encoded fictional transposition.

Und wie er mich anschaut: ohne zu lächeln, aber en face, als wollte er sein Gesicht darbieten, sagen, das bin ich, ... Dieses Gesicht: ja alles ist darin alle die Nuancen, die gegeneinander gehalten ein so unglaublich reizvolles Bild für die Hellenen gab, ihren Dionysos ... in dem sie den ganzen Zauber des großen weiten ... Asiens hineinlegten ... und die Augen mit der ruhig blühenden Sinnlichkeit der Morgenträume ... Und er fängt nicht an zu reden. Er schaut mich nur wieder mit dem Blick an, der nicht provocirt, der mir sagt: so bin ich, willst Du mich so nehmen; wenn er spricht hat er etwas vom Kind, vom gutmüthigen, das fast junges Thier ist. Den Thurm geht er hinauf mit so schlaffen Tritten daß ich denke, es ist eine Frau. Nachdem die paar Worte erledigt sind, stehn wir uns einen Moment gegenüber. Er lächelt ein vages, feiges, dionysisches Lächeln, mit Augen, die weit weg sind ... das ganze Phantastische der Situation, so lebendig, durch unsere beiden Wesen dahinter ... ein Moment. Und dann zögernd mit Gesprächen dazwischen: ob er gedient hat? Erst nächstes Jahr ... ob er auch zu Frauen geht? Ja manchmal. Was ihm mehr Spaß macht? *Es ist das gleiche.* / Dionysos. (TUA 55, 69–70)

[And how he looks at me: without smiling, but directly, as though he wanted to present his face and say 'that's me' ... This face: it contains everything, all the nuances that, in combination, gave the Hellenes such an incredibly alluring image, their Dionysus ... in which they placed all the magic of vast Asia ... and his eyes with the calmly blooming sensuality of early-morning dreams ... And he does not begin to talk. He only looks at me again with that gaze that, without provoking, says to me: 'This is how I am, if you will accept me'; when he speaks he is rather like a child, a good-natured one that is almost a young animal. He climbs the tower with such languid steps that I think he's a woman. After dealing with our few words, we stand for a moment facing each other. He smiles a vague, cowardly, Dionysiac smile, with eyes that are far away ... the fantastic quality of the situation, so alive, through our two natures that lie behind ... a moment. And then, hesitantly, with intermittent conversation: has he served in the army yet? Not until next year. Does he also go to women? Yes, sometimes. Which does he enjoy more? *It's all the same.* / Dionysus.]

The notebook entry makes the sexual nature of the encounter in Venice explicit, whereas in the account of Erwin's encounter with the Stranger it can only be inferred from the signs that permeate its narration:

Ganz ernst blieb auch Einer, der neben dem Erwin saß. Nur von Zeit zu Zeit sah er den Erwin an, und als man ihn seinen Wein brachte, reichte er das Glas dem Erwin, damit er zuerst daraus trinke. Als ihm dann der Erwin eine Cigarette gab, schien sein Körper in seltsam schmeichelnder und demütiger Dankbarkeit kleiner zu werden, indeß sein Auge flehend aber ruhig zum Erwin sah. ... In seinen Gliedern war die Weichlichkeit eines, der des Morgens erwacht ... Als der Erwin hinausging, kam ihm der Fremde nach und bat ihn um Feuer; sie gingen durch die Vorstadt gegen die Bahnen zu ... Endlich waren sie draußen, wo das Land anfängt, dessen farbloses zertretenes Gras von Planken umschlossen wird. Der Fremde fragte ihn, wohin sie gingen; das wußte der Erwin nicht und er bekam Angst und wandte sich gegen die Stadt zu. Der Fremde bettelte ihn um ein Almosen an (*Garten* 34–6)

[There was someone sitting beside Erwin who also remained perfectly serious. Only from time to time did he glance at Erwin, and when his wine was brought he handed Erwin the glass, so that the latter should drink from it first. When Erwin then gave him a cigarette, his body seemed to shrink in strangely obsequious and humble gratitude, while his eyes looked at Erwin beseechingly yet calmly. ... His limbs had the relaxed quality of someone waking up in the morning ... When Erwin went out, the stranger followed him and asked for a light; they went through the suburb towards the tram-lines ... At last they were outside the city, where the country begins, its colourless, trampled grass enclosed by planks. The stranger asked him where they were going; Erwin didn't know, and he grew frightened and turned towards the city. The stranger begged him for alms.]

The passage contains a number of homosexual signs. The eye contact between Erwin and the Stranger, the ritualistic sharing of the wine and cigarettes, the request for a light, the Stranger's sexual overtures – in the context his request for an 'Almosen' takes on obvious sexual connotations – all are encoded signs which signal the homoerotic nature of the encounter, which is heightened by the spatial symbolism. In the repressed sexuality of the late nineteenth century the encounter can find its potential realisation only in a place far removed from the 'civilised' space of the city.

The notebook entry describing the encounter in Venice shows how Andrian's poetic and mythologising imagination was already engaged in transforming the anonymous young man into a representation of Dionysos. As I have shown elsewhere, the narrator of the fictional text is engaged in this transfiguration as well.[32] The association of the Stranger in both texts with Dionysos and of homoeroticism with the unlocking of nature's secrets can be adduced from Nietzsche's *Geburt der Tragödie*. Nietzsche argues that the 'Urgrund' of Greek tragedy represents an 'Objektivation eines dionysischen Zustandes ... das Zerbrechen des Individuums und sein Einswerden mit dem Ursein' ('an objectivation of a Dionysiac state ... in which the individual is shattered and becomes one with primordial being').[33] Such a lifting of the veil of Maya can only be achieved by committing an 'ungeheure Naturwidrigkeit' ('a monstrously unnatural act').[34] Nietzsche bases his argument on an analysis of the Oedipus myth which, in his interpretation, illustrates the causal connection between incest and the acquisition of knowledge. Andrian, in a note in his diary, took this argument one step further when he wrote: 'Der stärkste Grad der Hybris nach den Alten war die Selbsterkenntnis Narcissus

... [d]er dritte Grad war den Hellenen schon kein Frevel mehr: die Liebe zum gleichen Geschlecht' (TUA 48, p. 31: 'According to the ancients, the most extreme degree of hubris was the self-knowledge of Narcissus ... the third degree was not a crime for the Hellenes – love for one's own sex').

Erwin's rejection of the Stranger's overtures is an indication of the conflict between the desire to give in to his homosexual longings and his internalised Platonic idealisation of homoerotic feelings. Seen in this context, the meaning of one of the mottoes for *Der Garten der Erkenntnis*, 'Ego Narcissus', needs to be reevaluated. Critics of Andrian's novel have interpreted this motto negatively from the vantage point of the meanings that the Narcissus myth has taken on in our post-Freudian age. Scheible, for example, argues that Erwin's 'völlige Distanzierung von der Außenwelt die Möglichkeit schafft, alle Energien auf das eigene Ich zu konzentrieren', the I, 'das sich selbst das einzige Libido-Objekt ist' ('his complete detachment from the outside world makes it possible to focus all his energies on his own ego').[35] Looked at from a pre-Freudian perspective, however, the narcissistic impulse takes on a quite different meaning, particularly in the homoerotic discourse of the late nineteenth century. I have already quoted the homoerotically and narcissistically charged lines from Andrian's poem 'Sonett': 'Da mit der Sehnsucht wir von sechzehn Jahren/Der Seele gleiches Zittern Liebe nannten.' These lines are echoed in Andrian's diary where he characterises his love for Erwin Slamecka in similar terms: 'Sein Gesicht ist für mich die Verkörperung meiner Seele' (TUA 45, p. 114: 'To me his face is the embodiment of my soul').[36] This is not so much an anticipation of the Freudian analysis of the Narcissus syndrome as a reflection of Platonic thought. In his explication of the tripartite soul Plato has Socrates say in *Phaedrus*: 'the lover is his [the beloved's] mirror in whom he is beholding himself'.[37] This *Platonic* narcissism forms the basis for two possible realisations of homoerotic love: one spiritual, the other carnal:

> when they [the lovers] are side by side, he [the beloved] is not in a state in which he can refuse the lover anything, if he ask him, while his fellow steed and the charioteer oppose him with shame and reason. ... if the better elements of the mind which lead to order and philosophy prevail, then they pass their life in this world in happiness and harmony, masters of themselves and orderly – enslaving the vicious and emancipating the virtuous elements; ... If, on the other hand, they leave philosophy and lead the lower life of ambition, then ... the two wanton animals take the two souls when off their guard and bring them together ...[38]

I would argue that the Stranger is a projection of Erwin's 'second soul', of his sexuality, which he perceives as the 'enemy' of the 'first soul', because he cannot reconcile its promptings with the aspirations of the 'first soul'. The failure of Andrian's protagonist to gain knowledge then represents the inability to solve the conflict which is indicated early in the novel: 'sein Körper und seine Seele lebten ein fast zweifaches Leben geheimnisvoll in einander' (*Garten* 4: 'his body and his soul led an almost double life mysteriously in each other'). How much Andrian would have wanted to resolve this conflict is indicated in a diary entry that was written shortly after the completion of *Der Garten der Erkenntnis*:

> Was meine Person betrifft, so wünsche ich die Vielheiten in ihr in eine Einheit zu verwandeln; es soll in meiner Seele keinen Gegensatz geben zwischen Empfindungen die ich liebe und Empfindungen deren ich mich schäme, zwischen äußerem u. innerem Leben ... es soll endlich keinen Gegensatz zwischen meinem Körper und meiner Seele geben, ich will physisch ebenso bewußt wie psychisch leben; ich will in meinem ganzen Dasein die absolute Einheit besitzen, wie ich glaube, daß sie die Griechen besessen haben (TUA 184, p. 3).

> [As far as my personality is concerned, I wish to transform its diverse qualities into a unity; my soul ought not to contain any opposition between feelings that I love and feelings of which I am ashamed, between outer and inner life ... there should, finally, be no opposition between my body and my soul, I want to lead my physical life as consciously as my psychic life; I want to possess absolute unity in my entire existence, as I believe the Greeks possessed it.]

As early as 1895 he was aware that as a homosexual he could achieve this harmony of body and soul only in a 'neuen Cultur' (TUA 184, p. 2), 'in der die Frau nicht mehr auf dem Pedestal steht – eine quasi antike Cultur' (TUA 52, p. 52: 'a new culture in which woman no longer stands on a pedestal – the culture of antiquity, as it were'). These sentiments link Andrian's reflections with the Platonically inspired homoerotic discourse extolling male friendship which found an eloquent expression in a letter that Winckelmann wrote in 1762 to Reinhold Friedrich von Berg:

> eine solche Freundschaft, die bis an die äussersten Linien der Menschlichkeit gehet ... ist die höchste Tugend, die itzo unter den Menschenkindern unbekannt ist, und also auch das höchste Gut, welches in dem Besitze derselben besteht. Die christliche Moral lehret dieselbe nicht; aber die Heiden beteten dieselbe an, und die größte [sic] Thaten des Altertums sind durch dieselbe vollbracht.[39]

> [Such a friendship that goes to the utmost limits of humanity is the supreme virtue that is now unknown to the human race, and hence also the supreme good consisting in the possession of this virtue. Christian morality does not teach this; but the pagans worshipped it, and the greatest deeds of antiquity were accomplished by it.]

Notes

1. Hugo von Hofmannsthal – Leopold von Andrian, *Briefwechsel*, ed. Walter H. Perl (Frankfurt, 1968), p. 273.
2. Quoted from Andrian's unpublished *Tagebücher und Arbeitshefte*, vol. 189, p. 49. These are cited in the text as TUA followed by the volume and page number.

Doubtful readings are indicated by [?]. I would like to thank the Deutsches Literaturarchiv for permission to quote from these unpublished materials.

3. See Steven Beller, *Vienna and the Jews 1867–1938: A Cultural History* (Cambridge, 1989), p. 205.
4. See Sander L. Gilman, *Freud, Race, and Gender* (Princeton, 1993), pp. 162–5 and passim.
5. Leopold von Andrian, *Der Garten der Erkenntnis* (Frankfurt, 1970), p. 25. This edition is cited in the text as *Garten* followed by the page number.
6. Quoted in Ursula Renner, *Leopold Andrians 'Garten der Erkenntnis'. Literarisches Paradigma einer Identitätskrise in Wien um 1900* (Frankfurt, 1981), p. 146.
7. See Linda Dowling, *Hellenism and Homosexuality in Victorian Oxford* (Ithaca, NY, 1994), p. 80.
8. Eugene O'Connor, ed. *On Homosexuality: Lysis, Phaedrus and Symposium* (Buffalo, NY: Prometheus Books, 1991), pp. 141–42. All passages from Plato's works are quoted from this edition.
9. See Hofmannsthal – Andrian, *Briefwechsel*, pp. 104 and 304.
10. Hofmannsthal – Andrian, *Briefwechsel*, p. 29.
11. Ibid., p. 61.
12. H. Montgomery Hyde, ed., *The Three Trials of Oscar Wilde* (New York, 1956), p. 236.
13. For a discussion of the Uranian writers see Dowling, *Hellenism*, pp. 114–16, 134–7.
14. Walter H. Perl (ed.), *Leopold von Andrian und die Blätter für die Kunst* (Hamburg, 1960), p. 67.
15. The same process of transformation occurs in Thomas Mann's notes for his planned novel *Die Geliebten*. See Peter de Mendelssohn, *Der Zauberer. Das Leben des deutschen Schriftstellers Thomas Mann* (Frankfurt, 1975), pp. 481–90.
16. This cycle has recently been published by Joelle Stoupy. Leopold Andrian, *Fragmente aus Erwin und Elmire* (Amsterdam, 1993). Quotations from pp. 84, 91.
17. *Leopold von Andrian und die Blätter für die Kunst*, p. 67.
18. Ibid., p. 79.
19. *Erwin und Elmire*, p. 91.
20. Hartmut Scheible, *Literarischer Jugendstil* (Munich, 1984), p. 42. For a discussion of the 'Fiaker' as the personification of 'das Andere' see also Renner, *Andrians 'Garten der Erkenntnis'*, pp. 110–15, and Gabriella Napoli Rovagnati, *Leopold von Andrian. Poeta dimenticato del fine secolo viennese* (Milan, 1985), p. 69.
21. Gert Mattenklott, referring to another passage in *Der Garten der Erkenntnis*, speaks of Erwin's 'Sehnsucht [nach] Überwältigung durch die rohe Lust der einfachen Leute'. See Mattenklott, *Bilderdienst. Ästhetische Opposition bei Beardsley und George* (Munich, 1970), p. 277.
22. Quoted in Renner, *Andrians 'Garten der Erkenntnis'*, p. 111.
23. See Alan Sinfield, *The Wilde Century: Effeminacy, Oscar Wilde and the Queer Moment* (New York, 1994), pp. 138–56.
24. Karl Heinrich Ulrichs, the first analyst of homosexuality, for example, published a collection of homoerotic stories entitled *Matrosengeschichten* in 1885.
25. Quoted in Renner, *Andrians 'Garten der Erkenntnis'*, p. 113.
26. Hugo von Hofmannsthal, *Gesammelte Werke. Reden und Aufsätze I*, ed. Bernd Schoeller (Frankfurt, 1979), p. 94.
27. Quoted in Renner, *Andrians 'Garten der Erkenntnis'*, p. 104.
28. Quoted in Sinfield, *The Wilde Century*, p. 137.
29. Ibid., p. 137.
30. See Renner, *Andrians 'Garten der Erkenntnis'*, pp. 154–7; Scheible, *Literarischer Jugendstil*, p. 45; Mattenklott, *Bilderdienst*, p. 276; Iris Paetzke, *Erzählen in der Wiener Moderne* (Tübingen, 1992), p. 45.

31. See Andrian's 1897 diary entry where he discusses his homosexual feelings: 'Damit hängt auch zusammen die Art Schönheit qui me mouvait [?] le plus, das [sic] glänzende glatte Haut, blondes gebranntes Haar' (TUA 62, pp. 158–9).

32. Jens Rieckmann, 'Narziß und Dionysos: Leopold von Andrians *Der Garten der Erkenntnis*', *MAL* 16 (1983), 65–81.

33. Friedrich Nietzsche, *Gesammelte Werke in drei Bänden*, ed. Karl Schlechta (Munich, 1969), vol. I, p. 53.

34. Ibid., p. 57.

35. Scheible, *Literarischer Jugendstil*, p. 35. Cf. Fischer's argument that Erwin and Andrian can be understood as 'klinisch korrekte Ausprägungen dessen … was Freud unter dem Begriff Narzißmus faßt' (Jens Malte Fischer, *Fin de Siècle: Kommentar zu einer Epoche* [Tübingen, 1978], p. 150). Similarly Paetzke writes: 'Wirklich weist der "Garten der Erkenntnis" in der Gestaltung seiner Hauptfigur auf den "narzißtischen Typus" [Freuds] voraus, nach dem man "liebt: a) was man selbst ist (sich selbst), b) was man selbst war, c) was man selbst sein möchte"' (Paetzke, *Erzählen in der Wiener Moderne*, p. 40). See also Renner, *Andrians 'Garten der Erkenntnis'*, pp. 120–4.

36. Quoted in Renner, *Andrians 'Garten der Erkenntnis'*, p. 119.

37. Plato, *Phaedrus*, p. 74.

38. Ibid., pp. 74–5.

39. Letter of 9 June 1762, quoted in Paul Derks, *Die Schande der heiligen Päderastie. Homosexualität und Öffentlichkeit in der deutschen Literatur 1750–1850* (Berlin, 1990), p. 181.

Note

Leopold von Andrian's *Nachlaß* is at the Deutsches Literaturarchiv, Marbach, Germany. It comprises numerous volumes of diaries and notebooks. Among these are six notebooks with poems and drafts for poems (1893/94), notes and drafts for *Der Garten der Erkenntnis* and its unfinished continuation *Gabriels Lauf zum Ideal*, several volumes of manuscript containing Andrian's late unpublished work *De Anima*, as well as approximately 2,000 letters. Roughly half of these are by Andrian, the others were addressed to Andrian by writers, artists, publishers, politicians, scientists, and journalists.

Kafka, Homosexuality and the Aesthetics of 'Male Culture'

Mark M. Anderson

For Richard Plant

The new, unexpurgated edition of Kafka's diaries, which includes a number of explicitly homoerotic entries, raises a question that few critics have been willing to address publicly – namely, the question of a closeted homosexuality and its impact on his writing.[1] While not nearly as extensive or as unambiguous as the Thomas Mann diaries, the material is too explicit to be denied, especially since it seems to throw light on murkier but no less suggestive homoerotic spaces in the literary texts such as the Stoker's cabin in the American novel *Der Verschollene*, the lumber-room ('Rumpelkammer') and Titorelli's studio in *The Trial*, or Bürgel's bedroom in *The Castle*. Max Brod, who originally excised the diary passages, maintained an understandable silence about his friend's sexuality that subsequent commentators, generally uninterested in the relation between biography and text, have effectively if unwittingly enforced. But in light of the historical turn in recent literary criticism, the restored biographical material clearly merits investigation, especially since it relates Kafka and his texts in unexpected ways to specific debates about homosexual identity in Austria and Germany at the beginning of the century.[2]

Until recently, the two major attempts to interpret Kafka's work in light of a 'secret' homosexuality were Ruth Tiefenbrun's *Moment of Torment* and Günter Mecke's *Kafkas offenbares Geheimnis*, both of which share the reductive premise that all of Kafka's writings, with their bizarre and enigmatic imagery, can be unlocked with the key of a presumed homosexual practice.[3] That these two studies have found hardly any echo is only too comprehensible, given their unrepentant biographical reductionism, and I will refrain from any systematic criticism. Two points should be noted, however. First, both studies explicitly assume that Kafka's sexuality *isolated* him from prevailing social practices, thus occasioning feelings of guilt and shame as a moral deviant. What I propose to show is that Kafka's sexual drives, including a physical attraction to men, emerged from and were sustained by a structure of social relations peculiar to *fin-de-siècle* German culture. To be sure, Kafka was isolated in many respects, and homosexuality was far from being an accepted practice either in Habsburg Bohemia or Wilhelminian Germany. But the

79

German tradition of male friendship, the segregation of the sexes in school and university, and specifically German forms of male camaraderie such as the 'Männerbund' (male group) and the 'Wandervogel' movement, encouraged a homosociality that in scope and intensity was quite different from that of other European countries.[4] A second, related misconception is the assumption that Kafka was theoretically naive about homosexuality. This is clearly not true: in addition to the well-known political scandals that brought this question into public view in the first decade of the century,[5] Kafka's culture produced an astonishingly rich body of theoretical studies, from Freud and Krafft-Ebing to Otto Weininger, Magnus Hirschfeld, Hans Blüher and Otto Gross, which laid the groundwork for a non-normative view of same-sex relations between men. Like other members of the Expressionist avant-garde, Kafka came into contact with many of these theories and in several instances freely speculated about his own homoerotic impulses. Consider for instance the following passage from a letter to Max Brod of mid-November 1917 in reference to Hans Blüher's book *Die Rolle der Erotik in der männlichen Gesellschaft*: 'Wenn ich jetzt noch hinzufüge, daß ich vor einiger Zeit Werfel im Traum einen Kuß gegeben habe, falle ich mitten in das Blühersche Buch hinein' ('If I add that some time ago I kissed Werfel in a dream, I shall fall right into Blüher's book').[6] This is hardly the voice of a closet homosexual, anxiously suppressing any trace of his 'shameful' longings, even though Kafka admits that Blüher's book 'excited' him ('es hat mich aufgeregt') and he had to lay it aside for two days. Whatever homoerotic drives may have informed Kafka's sexuality, he was most probably not a practising homosexual who simply 'translated' biographical experience into coded literary form. In a new study that is both theoretically and historically more astute than these earlier works, Sander Gilman looks at the question of sexual identity from the perspective of 'Kafka, the Jewish patient'. Reacting against the binary oppositions of male/female, straight/gay in these studies, he takes Magnus Hirschfeld's notion of the homosexual as a 'drittes Geschlecht' harbouring a 'woman's soul in a male body' and adapts it to contemporary stereotypes of Jews. 'For the Jewish male was another version of the "third sex"', Gilman writes. 'His circumcised body was neither "straight" in a normative sense nor was it "gay", except by extension and metaphor.'[7] Gilman points to a wide range of contemporary medical authorities who posited a link between sexual orientation and racial origin. Moses Julius Gutmann observed for instance that 'all of the comments about the supposed stronger sexual drive among Jews have no basis in fact; most frequently they are sexual neurasthenics. Above all the number of Jewish homosexuals is extraordinarily high.'[8] According to a professor of anthropology at the University of Vienna, among Jews 'the physical signs of the sexual characteristics are noticeably vague. Among them, the women are often found to have a relatively narrow pelvis and relatively broad shoulders and the men to have broad hips and narrow shoulders.'[9] In Kafka's case, Gilman thus posits a culturally constructed identity based on three mutually reinforcing characteristics – medical illness (tuberculosis), homosexuality and Jewish origins – with the last element outweighing and in some sense determining the first two. As a Jew, Gilman argues, Kafka was perceived as an 'effeminate', 'castrated' male: as the 'drittes Geschlecht' that, far from not daring to speak its name, was being trumpeted in political scandals, newspaper articles and learned scientific journals.

Gilman's argument that racial and sexual identity should be thought of as related aspects of the same problem rings true for the academic and popular discourse of Kafka's period, and is reflected in contemporary use of the term *Art* (type, kind, species) to refer to sexual orientation as well as 'racial' origin. Somewhat surprisingly, Gilman does not discuss another, competing account of homosexual identity, although it too relies on the same kind of racial and sexual stereotypes that his work so effectively foregrounds: that of the virile 'Aryan' or 'Greek-German' male who formed physical as well as emotional bonds with men of his 'kind'. In 1899 Adolf Brand founded what has been called the 'world's first gay journal', *Der Eigene. Ein Blatt für männliche Kultur*, which emphatically rejected Hirschfeld's notion of the 'third sex' or feminised male.[10] Although politically allied with Hirschfeld in the fight against Paragraph 175 of the Prussian Penal Code outlawing sexual relations between men, Brand and his circle took issue with Hirschfeld's medical and legal definition of homosexuality, with its focus on physical acts and arcane terminology, developing instead poetic terms like 'Jünglingsminne' and 'Männerliebe' to emphasise the spiritual quality of male love. Whereas Hirschfeld took pains to point out the separateness of a homosexual identity, contributors to *Der Eigene* considered same-sex relations between men to be one part of a broad spectrum encompassing ancient Greek forms of male love, the eighteenth- and nineteenth-century German tradition of male friendship, the aesthetic appreciation and cultivation ('Pflege') of the naked male body (hence their interest in gymnastics, nudism or 'freie körperliche Kultur', clothing reform, etc.). In their view the friendships between Socrates and Plato, Goethe and Schiller, Nietzsche and Wagner embodied the culturally fertile union of virile male sensibilities that they sought to promote in their own culture.

Generally disdainful of the women's liberation movement and what they called the 'Gynökokratie' of the West, Brand and his circle celebrated 'männliche Kultur' as a specifically German, or 'Greek-German' phenomenon that would help revitalise German youth, German educational institutions, and ultimately the German state. Often invoking the Greek notion of 'pedagogical eros' or the anthropological construct of the 'Männerbund', popularised by Heinrich Schurtz's study of 1902, they saw signs of an awakening male culture in contemporary German culture that was strongly hierarchical, disciplined and culturally fertile. In the 'Wandervogel' clubs that sprang up in the decade before the First World War, in poetic groups like the Stefan George circle, or in alternative educational institutes like Gustav Wyneken's school in Wickersdorf, a small group of enlightened leaders ('Führer') would channel 'natural' homoeroticism among youths into meaningful personal relationships and cultural achievements.[11]

'Male culture' was hence seen as German or Greek, female culture as

Western or Jewish – a normative polarisation that in some cases anticipated Nazi racial ideology. As the historian of *Der Eigene*, Harry Oosterhuis, has recently observed, the conservative philosophers Benedict Friedländer and Eduard von Mayer were 'obsessed by the notion that female influence in culture and in politics was devastating for the vigor of civilisation'. Their interest in the 'Männerbund' was meant as a bulwark against a democratic, 'feminine' and 'Jewish' modernism. 'According to Mayer's philosophy of culture,' Oosterhuis writes,

> the rise of culture had only become possible when *Männerbünde* broke through the torpor of matriarchal rule. By waging war, the all-male brotherhood-in-arms had subjugated women and 'inferior races,' thus laying the foundation for aristocratic states. Male bonding was the proper means, Mayer said, to settle accounts with modern egalitarianism and 'slave morality.' For Mayer, a healthy culture was inherently masculine, aristocratic, and racist. ... Friedländer ... elaborated theoretical types of male and female cultures, imputing to the latter all signs of degeneracy, such as democratic levelling, desire for luxury, sexual hypocrisy, and also monogamy for men. ... It was clear to Friedländer that the German nation had to stop further feminisation of Western civilisation by making the *Männerbund* the core of the state, safeguarding the exalted goals of male friendship such as moral strength, self-sacrifice, and spirit.[12]

Though extreme, these views were by no means atypical of *Der Eigene*, many of whose contributors (and how many of its readers?) became Nazis in the 1920s and '30s. Even the liberal physician Edwin Bab, who supported women's rights and an Enlightenment view of cultural progress, maintained that 'die Frauenbewegung führt uns zu altjüdischen, die Bewegung für männliche Kultur zu altgriechischen Idealen zurück' ('the women's movement leads us back to ancient Jewish ideals, the movement for male culture back to those of ancient Greece').[13]

There is no evidence that Kafka had any direct knowledge of Brand and his journal, although anti-modern and anti-feminine impulses in his writing after 1914 (especially evident, as we shall see, in *In der Strafkolonie*, 'In the Penal Settlement') evoke aspects of Friedländer's and Mayer's attack on the 'feminised' West. But the conception of male culture promoted by *Der Eigene* is closely related to the rise of the 'Wandervogel' movement and to the views of its first historian Hans Blüher, whose writings Kafka did know. In his 1912 study of the 'Wandervogel' as an 'erotic phenomenon', Blüher claimed for instance that the centres ('die Centren und Wirbelpunkte') of the movement were men who loved boys in the ancient Greek manner and for whom 'der Wert des Weibes in der äußersten Ecke des Bewußtseins lag' ('the value of woman was in the remotest corner of their consciousness').[14] In his book on male society, he combined Schurtz's notion of the 'Männerbund' with Freud's theory of sexual drives, arguing that women had only a sexual or 'family' drive, whereas men had both a sexual and a social drive; the one served to propagate the species, the other led to the formation of all social groups, from the primitive 'Männerhaus' (men's house) to the modern state.[15] In his view 'Platonic' love between ⌐ was morally and culturally superior to heterosexual, conjugal relations. Ra her than as a symptom of effeminacy or degeneracy, as some had claimed, Blüher interpreted male bonding in the 'Wandervogel' movement as the sign of a healthy 'racial' impulse in the German 'Volk':

> Der Wandervogel war eine völkische Begebenheit ... Die hier auftretenden Erastenverhältnisse mit ihrer heroischen Note widersprechen allen voreiligen Ansichten von Femininität und Weichlichkeit, sie widersprechen auch der gelegentlich auftauchenden Meinung, daß die 'Homosexualität' mit dem Niedergange und der schlechten Rassemischung eines Volkes parallel laufe. Ich konstatiere, daß unter den ausgeprägtesten Erastennaturen des Wandervogels die Mehrzahl einen stark betonten germanischen Rassetyp vertrat, der hie und da geradezu bewundert wurde.[16]

> [The rambling movement was an event rooted in popular instincts. ... The erastic relationships [Blüher's Greek term for male-male relations] that appeared here with their heroic overtones contradict any hasty assumptions about femininity and softness; they also contradict the view occasionally expressed that 'homosexuality' runs parallel with a people's decline and miscegenation. I can state that the majority of the most markedly erastic characters among the ramblers represented a strikingly Germanic racial type which sometimes met with positive admiration.]

Blüher's racial gloss on the 'Wandervogel' movement was not lost on Max Brod, who announced his discovery of Blüher's book on male society, and also the same author's *Volk und Führer in der Jugendbewegung*, in an enthusiastic letter to Kafka of 4 October 1917.[17] The books, he reported, are

> eine Hymne auf die Päderastie, von der aller Kulturfortschritt erwartet wird. Ich las die Bücher, ohne aufhören zu können. Heute aber bin ich doch schon etwas ernüchtert und sehe in ihnen mehr die Deskription des deutschen Mannes als des Mannes überhaupt. Blüher findet, daß nur der Eros zwischen Männern wahre soziale Arbeit schaffen kann, daß dagegen der Mann, der von Natur aus zur Frauenliebe neigt, nicht an der Gesellschaft, sondern nur im Kreise der Familie schaffen kann, also ein niedriger Typ ist. Wenn du nach Prag kommst, gebe ich dir die Bücher. Du mußt sie unbedingt lesen.[18]

> [a hymn to pederasty, from which all progress in civilisation is expected. I read the books without being able to stop. Today, however, I have sobered up somewhat, and see in them rather the description of the German man than man as such. Blüher thinks that only Eros between men can create real social labour, but that the man who is naturally

inclined to the love of woman cannot work creatively in society, only in his family circle, and therefore he is a low type. I'll give you the books when you come to Prague. You absolutely must read them.]

Kafka responds a few days later that he is eager ('begierig') to read Blüher; traces of this reading then appear in the above-quoted letter of November in which he admits his homoerotic attraction to Franz Werfel: '[das Blühersche Buch] hat mich aufgeregt, zwei Tage lang mußte ich deshalb das Lesen unterbrechen' (p. 196: 'Blüher's book got me so excited that I had to stop reading it for two days'). But although he promises to write Brod more about his reaction, the extant letters contain no further mention of Blüher until 1922, and then only with regard to the latter's anti-Semitic pamphlet *Secessio judaica*.

Though sparse, these passages clearly indicate Kafka's awareness of Blüher's theories about 'male society' and the role of homoeroticism in the formation of the state – theories that would seem to have played a significant role in the depiction of the castle officials and the 'Herrenhof' in *Das Schloß* (1922). Here, however, I would like to stress the matrix of early social and cultural experiences that had already situated Kafka within the 'German-Greek' tradition of male culture and thus predisposed him to a sympathetic hearing of Blüher's theses. In a same-sex German gymnasium in Prague, he cultivated literary, aestheticised friendships with his classmates; his early letters to Oskar Pollak clearly show the erotically charged nature of this friendship, which he would later develop with Franz Werfel and Jitzhak Löwy (though not in any significant way with Max Brod). As I have attempted to detail more extensively elsewhere, Kafka also participated in those aspects of turn-of-the-century German culture celebrated by *Der Eigene*, from gymnastics and the reform clothing movement to nudist health colonies cultivating a 'Hellenic' appreciation for the male body.[19] From roughly 1909 until 1917, twice daily, he followed a gymnastic regimen developed by the Danish athlete J. P. Müller that was based on Greek ideals; the cover of the exercise manual showed a sculpture of a naked Greek athlete. Finally, Brod himself relates an episode from Kafka's youth that, in its celebration of eroticised male friendship, nature and literature, seems to jump straight out of the pages of *Der Eigene*:

> Kafka and I were keen hikers. Every Sunday, often Saturdays as well, we were in the forests surrounding Prague whose beauty encouraged a cult of innocence and enthusiasm … We swam in the forest streams, for Kafka and I lived then in the strange belief that we hadn't possessed a countryside until a nearly physical bond had been forged by swimming in its living, streaming waters … Soon Werfel was introduced into our secret clan of nature worshippers. One beautiful summer Sunday we took the train to the pure silver waters of the Sazawa, undressed in the middle of a forest, in nature (which we greatly preferred to the public swimming pools), listened to the resounding new verse of [Werfel's] *Weltfreund* as naked river and mountain gods, and swam for hours in the

rushing waters. This sublime, Hellenic summer day lingers forever in my memory.[20]

Though undoubtedly tinged by his nostalgia for pre-war Prague, Brod's account nonetheless suggests that the boundaries between 'German-Greek' and 'Jewish' identity were far more fluid than is sometimes assumed. In the Nietzschean context of 1900, even (or perhaps especially) young German Jews aspired to a 'Hellenic' enjoyment of art, nature and the naked male body.[21]

This is, I would submit, the dominant cultural and social grid through which Kafka came to apprehend his own sexual identity and through which we need to read the restored homoerotic passages in the diaries. While Kafka undoubtedly perceived as 'Jewish' or 'urban' certain aspects of his identity – his 'nerves', his body's 'fragmented' state and weakness – an eroticised homosociality was part of the German youth culture that informed his early friendships and first attempts to define his identity as a (German) writer. To put it in somewhat exaggerated terms, normative heterosexuality was represented to him by the world of his parents, by their 'Jewish' household, by the injunction to marry and have children within the community. An escape from this world was represented by the space of male companionship, literature, vacations and travel outside Prague – the space of German culture where Kafka could experiment with his identity, develop his 'peculiar' or 'eigentümliche' self without being observed by his parents, and, at least temporarily, put their normative, bourgeois expectations on hold.[22] As we shall see, 'travel' or 'traffic' ('Verkehr'), and especially the travel diary, played a fundamental role in this process of experimentation and self-definition.[23]

Most of the censored homoerotic passages stem from the travel diaries. For instance, during his trip to Friedland in 1911 Kafka describes the five male travellers in his train compartment, including the physiognomy of a skinny man eating ham and sausages. The censored passage is the final sentence referring to the latter: 'Das scheinbar umfangreiche Glied macht in den Hosen einen starken Wulst' (pp. 931–2: 'His apparently sizeable penis makes a large bulge in his trousers'). By itself this detail is merely descriptive, and Kafka characteristically refrains from connecting a physical observation with an emotional or psychological content. But in context it becomes quite intriguing. Kafka calls the man a 'Windbeutel', a term that suggests loose personal morals, and notes admiringly his disrespect for train regulations in disposing of his garbage. He also welcomes the man's aggressive physical proximity (in contrast to the 'Reichenberger Jude' whom he guiltily mocks):

> Während des Essens hat er in dieser unnötigen mir so sympatischen, aber erfolglos nachgeahmten Hitze und Eile zwei Abendblätter mir zugewendet ausgelesen. Abstehende Ohren. Nur verhältnismäßig breite Nase. Wischt mit den fetten Händen Haare und Gesicht, ohne sich schmutzig zu machen, was ich auch nicht darf. Das scheinbar umfangreiche Glied macht in den Hosen einen starken Wulst.

[While he was eating, he sat facing me and finished reading two evening papers with a haste and energy that appeal to me, though I can't imitate them. Protruding ears. Only a relatively broad nose. Wipes his hair and face with his greasy hands, without dirtying himself, which I can't do either. His apparently sizeable penis makes a large bulge in his trousers.]

Here the desired other is decidedly not the Jew from Reichenberg, who is concerned primarily with the cost and speed of the express trains, but the non-kosher German eating his ham and two sausages – 'zwei Würste, deren Haut er mit einem Messer durchsichtig kratzt' ('two sausages whose skin he scrapes with a knife until it is transparent') – who can wipe his hair and face with greasy hands 'without dirtying himself' – an ability that Kafka, presumably as a Jew, is not 'able' or 'allowed' to do without contaminating himself ('was ich auch nicht darf'). At the same time, the final homoerotic 'Pointe' to this description makes us question the nature of his reference to the 'unreines' (impure matter) mentioned in the entry immediately preceding this one:

Ich müßte die Nacht durchschreiben, so viel kommt über mich, aber es ist nur unreines. Was für eine Macht dieses über micht bekommen hat, während ich ihm früher soviel ich mich erinnere mit einer kleinen Wendung … auszuweichen imstande war.

[I ought to write all night, there's so much I want to say, but it is only impure matter. What power this has gained over me, while formerly, so far as I remember, I was able to avoid it by a slight turn.]

Is this 'impure matter' merely a poor quality of literary inspiration, or is it sexually explicit (homosexual) fantasies that interfere with his writing, and that he can no longer elude with 'a slight turn'? Brod excised a similar passage from the travel diary for Jungborn, a Christian health resort in the Harz mountains that Kafka visited in the summer of 1912. Guests slept in open-air huts, did group calisthenics outdoors, sang hymns, and engaged in various 'Naturheilkunde' activities. Separated from the women except for meals and social activities, the men spent most of the day in the nude: 'einige Nackte liegen still vor meiner Tür. Alles bis auf mich ohne Schwimmhosen. Schöne Freiheit' ('some naked people are lying motionless outside my door. Nobody is wearing trunks, except me. Lovely freedom'), Kafka notes approvingly on the first day of his visit (p. 1040, 8 July 1912). The excised passage is located in the entry for 9 July after the description of the nude calisthenics, washing, and singing of 'einiger Choräle' ('a few chorals'): '2 schöne schwedische Jungen mit langen Beinen, die so geformt und gespannt sind, daß man nur mit der Zunge richtig an ihnen hinfahren könnte' (p. 1041: 'two beautiful Swedish boys with long legs whose shape and posture is such that one could only really stroke them with one's tongue'). More expansive than the first in its exhibition of a sexual fantasy, the passage reveals the homoerotic tension in subsequent, apparently innocuous entries from the same diary, such as the brief mention of the Swedish boys' bending movements ('Verbeugungen') or Kafka's awkwardness in talking with a 'good-looking' or 'beautiful' aristocrat named Herr Guido von Gillhausen, an army captain ('Hauptmann') and author of the poem 'An mein Schwert' ('To my Sword'):

> Schöner Mann. Wage aus Respekt vor seinem Adel nicht zu ihm aufzuschauen, habe Schweissausbruch (wir sind nackt) und rede zu leise. Sein Siegelring. – Die Verbeugungen der schwedischen Jungen (p. 1048, 16 July).

> [Good-looking man. Out of respect for his nobility I don't dare look him in the face, break out in a sweat (we are naked) and speak in too low a voice. His seal-ring. – The bending movements of the Swedish boys.

Here we should recall that most of the guests at Jungborn were Christian, as was its founder, Adolf Just, who formulated its back-to-nature ideology in explicitly revivalist Christian terms. Fear of being recognised as a Jew may have been part of Kafka's reluctance to shed his swimming trunks and of his general anxiety about the nudity at Jungborn. In any case, the Swedish boys – presumably blond and blue-eyed – as well as Captain Guido von Gillhausen, are clearly not Jews. His objects of desire appear as the distant, 'hygienic' Other whose naked legs exert a special fascination (without provoking any trace of disgust); or as the imposingly military, virile German, the aristocratic 'Hauptmann' with his sword and seal-ring before whom Kafka, the 'humble Jew', lowers his gaze and speaks 'in too low a voice'.

Kafka's simultaneous enjoyment and fear of his homoerotic impulses surface in the remarkable dream scenario he includes at the end of the diary entry for 15 July. After noting his reading of Plato's *Republic* as well as his posing nude for a guest and amateur painter named Dr Schiller, he records the following erotic association: 'Modell gestanden für Dr. Schiller. Ohne Schwimmhosen. Exhibitionistisches Erlebnis. – Die Seite in Flaubert über die Prostitution. – Die grosse Beteiligung des nackten Körpers am Gesamteindruck des Einzelnen' ('Was a model for Dr Schiller. Without trunks. Exhibitionistic experience. The page in Flaubert about prostitution. – The large part played by the naked body in the overall impression made by the individual'). The dream is as follows:

> Ein Traum: Die Luftbadgesellschaft vernichtet sich mittelst einer Rauferei. Nachdem die in zwei Gruppen geteilte Gesellschaft mit einander gespaßt hat, tritt aus der einen Gruppe einer vor und ruft der andern zu: 'Lustron und Kastron!' Die andern: 'Wie? Lustron und Kastron?' Der eine: 'Allerdings.' Beginn der Rauferei (p. 1047, 15 July 1912).

> [A dream: the air-bathing party destroys itself by means of a brawl. After the party, divided into two groups, has been larking about, someone steps forward from one of the groups and calls to the other: 'Lustron and Kastron!' The others: 'What? Lustron and Kastron?' The first: 'Certainly.' The brawl begins.]

The manifest dream imagery would seem to issue from the neo-Hellenic, gymnasium-like character of male companionship at Jungborn: playful yet competitive, eros dissolved into sport and games. Less determinable is the pair of Greek-sounding names that sets off the fight. Though meaningless to the reader, they seem instantly intelligible to all participants in the dream as a gross insult, and once the names are repeated the group of men 'destroys itself' in a brawl. The names are also marked by repetition: both within the narrative itself where one group echoes the other, but also as a name pair composed of two-syllable, rhyming units – Lust-ron / Kast-ron. With their Greek appearance, the paired names may recall Castor and Pollux, the inseparable twin brothers who embodied an ideal male love (and thus could seem offensive on another level). But if so, the dream formation has evidently grafted this mythological content and linguistic form onto the German words for pleasure and castration, 'Lust' and 'Kastration'. The dream narrative would thus seem to turn on the conflict between pleasure and castration, which in this case is not motivated by a Medusa's head but by an all-too-literal proliferation of male genitalia. The ensuing 'Rauferei' (with the connotation of terms like 'Rauflust', love of scrapping) could be a male orgy as well as a brawl; both involve the violent loss of separation between the two groups, between two brothers, perhaps between (Jewish) Self and (Greek-German) Other, between 'Lust' and 'Kastration'.

The violence in this dream scenario suggests that Kafka's homoerotic tendencies were not without ambivalence; indeed, in the concluding section I will analyse several literary texts in which homoerotic fantasies are charged with extreme violence and cruelty. Nonetheless, the above passages from his travel diaries are striking precisely because they lack the feelings of filth and disgust that heterosexual relations invariably provoked in Kafka, traces of which abound in both the literary and biographical writings.[24] Take for example the extensive, newly restored diary passage concerning the artist Alfred Kubin and his heterosexual conquests:

> Über Weiber: Die Erzählungen über seine Potenz machen einem Gedanken darüber, wie er wohl sein großes Glied langsam in die Frauen stopft. Sein Kunststück in früheren Zeiten war, Frauen so zu ermüden, daß sie nicht mehr konnten. Dann waren sie ohne Seele, Tiere. Ja diese Ergebenheit kann ich mir vorstellen.

> [On women: his stories about his potency make you think about how he stuffs his great penis slowly into women. His trick in the past was to exhaust women until they couldn't do any more. Then they were without a soul, animals. Yes, I can imagine this submission.]

Kafka then describes in graphic and rather revolting detail nude photos of Kubin's mistresses and concludes with an admiring reference to his orgy-like exploits with 'ausgehungerten Kaufmannsfrauen' ('the starved wives of businessmen') and the unaccompanied women who go to Munich during the carnival season 'offenbar nur um sich koitieren zu lassen. Es sind

Verheirathete, Mädchen, Witwen aus ganz Bayern' ('obviously just to get laid. They are married women, girls, widows from all over Bavaria', pp. 275–6, 28–9 Nov. 1911). In contrast to the 'lovely freedom' and bucolic tranquillity of the Jungborn experience, to the inviting legs of Swedish boys, Kafka here focuses on details that highlight the crude, depersonalised nature of heterosexual couplings. Women appear as animals or as pornographic images that men exchange between themselves: as 'vehicles' in the 'traffic' of power relations between men.[25] Significantly, the focus of Kafka's imagining gaze is not so much Kubin's mistresses as the artist's sexual member and its subjugating power.

This same discrepancy between 'disgusting', 'animal-like' heterosexual intercourse on the one hand, and seductive, eroticised fantasies about powerful men on the other, informs much of Kafka's literary work. For instance, in *The Castle*, K.'s actual sexual relations with Frieda are dirty and crude; their first encounter takes place on a bar-room floor in puddles of beer. By contrast, Klamm and the castle officials – all 'Frauenjäger' (skirt-chasers) who behave literally like pigs in their sexual appropriation of women – exert a powerful erotic attraction on K. that, in one key instance, is associated metaphorically with Greek art and has a flirtatious, almost child-like innocence. Late in the novel K. has an interview with the secretary Bürgel, who lies naked in bed and is about to tell him something important when K. falls asleep:

> K. schlief, es war zwar kein eigentlicher Schlaf, ... aber das lästige Bewußtsein war geschwunden, er fühlte sich frei, nicht Bürgel hielt ihn mehr, nur er tastete noch manchmal nach Bürgel hin, er war noch nicht in der Tiefe des Schlafs, aber eingetaucht in ihn war er, niemand sollte ihm das mehr rauben. ... Ein Sekretär, nackt, sehr ähnlich der Statue eines griechischen Gottes, wurde von K. im Kampf bedrängt. Es war sehr komisch und K. lächelte darüber sanft im Schlaf, wie der Sekretär aus einer stolzen Haltung durch K.'s Vorstöße immer aufgeschreckt wurde und etwa den hochgestreckten Arm und die geballte Faust schnell dazu verwenden mußte um seine Blößen zu decken und doch damit noch immer zu langsam war. Der Kampf dauerte nicht lange, Schritt für Schritt und es waren sehr große Schritte rückte K. vor. War es überhaupt ein Kampf? Es gab kein ernstliches Hindernis, nur hie und da ein Piepsen des Sekretärs. Dieser griechische Gott piepste wie ein Mädchen, das gekitzelt wird.[26]

> [K. was asleep, though it was not real sleep, ... but his burdensome consciousness had vanished; he felt free, Bürgel no longer held him, but occasionally he groped for Bürgel; he was not yet in the depths of sleep, but he had dived into it, and nobody should deprive him of it. ... A secretary, naked, very similar to the statue of a Greek god, was being hard-pressed by K. in a fight. It was very funny, and K. smiled gently at it in his sleep, how the secretary kept being frightened out of a proud pose by K.'s attacks and had quickly to use his raised arm and clenched fist to cover up his exposed parts and yet was always too slow. The fight

did not last long; K. was advancing step by step, and they were very big steps. Was it a fight at all? There was no serious obstacle, only the occasional squeal from the secretary. This Greek god was squealing like a girl being tickled.]

Jungborn revisited? A 'fight' with a naked Greek god who 'squeals' like a girl when tickled? If nothing else, this passage should tell us something about the homoerotic nature of K.'s struggle with the Castle officials and their 'Herrenhof'.

In the following remarks I will discuss three literary texts by Kafka that are not usually grouped together and that, at first sight, might not seem to relate to the question of homosexuality or even 'male culture' in the direct way that the above quotation from *The Castle* does. I do so for several reasons: to show just how specific and pervasive a certain kind of homoerotic fantasy is in Kafka's writing; and secondly, to point to a specific aesthetic quality related to this fantasy. In one of the earliest and still most perceptive studies of Kafka, Günther Anders refers to the frozen, petrified beauty that results from the terror of 'a flash of lightning which still persists' and that he links to the Gorgonic beauty of the Medusa head, the vision of which literally petrifies the viewer in a state of continuous terror. 'Time stands still for the man who is frightened', Anders writes and points out that the resulting 'eternal moment' is experienced not as a desired, 'classical' timelessness, but as a curse.[27] This insight will help us negotiate the passage from historical context to imaginative and literary fantasy, where the boundaries between the 'Jewish' home and the 'German' outside world become blurred or disappear entirely, giving way to Freud's realm of the 'Unheimliche' (the uncanny) and to what Kafka termed 'das Eigentümliche'. At the same time these texts ascribe to this 'flash of lightning' the fantasmatic scenario of a homosexual rape that violates and inscribes a helpless protagonist with punishing male force.

My first example is from *Die Verwandlung* ('The Metamorphosis'), the paradigmatic text in Kafka's work where an escape from the family and bourgeois normalcy is figured as the eruption of the monstrous – 'das ungeheure Ungeziefer' ('the monstrous insect') – within the domestic confines. At the end of the second section Gregor has left the privacy of his room and exposed himself, his 'eigentümliche' self, to the view of his horrified family. In order to drive him away, his father begins pelting him with apples which, strangely enough, seem to have been given an electric charge: 'Diese kleinen Äpfel rollten wie elektrisiert auf dem Boden herum und stießen aneinander' ('These little apples rolled about on the floor and bumped into one another as though they had been electrified'). One of the apples 'thoroughly penetrates' Gregor's back ('drang … förmlich in Gregors Rücken ein') and 'nails' him in a Christ-like position of vulnerability to the floor where he 'stretches himself out' in a daze: 'Gregor wollte sich weiterschleppen, als könne der überraschende unglaubliche Schmerz mit dem Ortswechsel vergehen; doch fühlte er sich wie festgenagelt und streckte sich in vollständiger Verwirrung aller Sinne' ('Gregor wanted to drag himself further, as though the astonishing and unbelievable pain would vanish when he got to a different place; but he felt as though he had been nailed down, and stretched himself out with all his senses in a complete daze').[28] This confusion is then followed by a vision of his parents copulating: Gregor's mother drops her petticoats ('Röcke') one after the other, and merges in 'gänzlicher Vereinigung' ('complete union') with the father.

One of the defining characteristics of this bizarre scene is the gradual reduction of Gregor's visual acuity. To begin with, his visual field is cropped by his insect body, which positions him flat on the floor with his head down. Further, the struggle with his father has so exhausted him that he can barely keep his eyes open. The scene ends in classic Freudian fashion in which vision of the primal scene results in the child's blindness and symbolic castration: 'nur mit dem letzten Blick sah er noch, wie ... die Mutter hervoreilte ... und wie sie stolpernd über die Röcke auf den Vater eindrang ... in gänzlicher Vereinigung mit ihm – nun versagte aber Gregors Sehkraft schon ...' (only with a final glance did he see his mother hurrying forward ... stumbling over her petticoats, merging with on his father ... in complete union with him – but now Gregor's vision gave out'). This progressive loss of sight, which actually intensifies the visual, plastic quality of the scene, is also what gives the physical punishment its special terror: that of being surprised from behind by an unexpected, invisible, 'electric' charge, which Gregor 'stretches out' to receive. And what seems like the gratuitous ending of this passage – there is no realist narrative need for the mother to copulate with the father in full view of the children – underscores the sexual nature of the punishment and the child's masochistic pleasure: the same verb ('eindringen') is used to refer to the apple 'penetrating' Gregor's back and to the mother 'merging' with the father. Like many of his texts, this most famous Kafka story depends on a fantasy of homosexual violence and masochistic pleasure which, perhaps because it is not explicitly figured as sexual, can be acted out in even more extreme form.

My next example is the less well-known text 'Die Brücke' ('The Bridge'), an originally untitled, diary-like passage which Max Brod published in 1931.[29] The protagonist is a bridge that is stretched over an abyss, its feet bored into the earth on this side, its hands 'jenseits' ('beyond'). The setting is mountainous, remote from the normal 'Touristenverkehr' ('tourist traffic'), and not yet inscribed on a map, although with a decidedly German (even German Romantic) 'Forellenbach' ('trout-stream') below the bridge. Despite their obvious differences, the position and mental state of the bridge is not unlike that of Gregor during the apple bombardment: it lies face-down, its vision is cropped, its extremities are 'stretched out', its senses are in a 'Wirrwarr' ('confusion') that disrupts the normal sense of time. Suddenly the sound of 'manly' steps produces in the bridge a longing for contact, a longing to 'stretch out' and receive the traveller: 'Gegen Abend im Sommer, dunkler rauschte der Bach, da hörte ich einen Mannesschritt! Zu mir, zu mir. – Strecke dich, Brücke ...' ('Towards evening in summer, the stream was darkening as it rushed along, I heard a manly step! To me, to me. – Stretch out, bridge'). Complicating the nature of this encounter is not just the human/non-human identity of the bridge but also a confusion of gender: the confusion of the feminine noun 'die Brücke' with the ostensibly masculine voice of the unnamed narrator; but also the confusion of the bridge's 'Rock' (is this 'skirt' or 'coat'?) and its 'buschiges Haar' ('bushy hair'). The encounter with this 'traveller' is an odd sort of 'Fremdenverkehr' (or 'Wandervogel' excursion?) that is unmistakably sexual:

> Er kam, mit der Eisenspitze seines Stockes beklopfte er mich, dann hob er mit ihr meine Rockschösse und ordnete sie auf mir. In mein buschiges Haar fuhr er mit der Spitze und liess sie, wahrscheinlich weit umherblickend, lange drin liegen.

> [He came, he tapped me with the iron tip of his stick, then he lifted my skirts and arranged them upon me. He thrust the tip into my bushy hair and left it lying there for a long time, probably gazing all round.]

In the middle of this German Romantic reverie – 'gerade träumte ich ihm nach über Berg und Tal' ('I was just dreaming in his wake over hill and dale') – this pleasurable, almost caressing touch of the male traveller turns violent as he attacks the 'unknowing' bridge with brutal force from behind:

> Dann aber ... sprang er mit beiden Füssen mir mitten auf den Leib. Ich erschauerte in wildem Schmerz, gänzlich unwissend. Wer war es? Ein Kind? Ein Turner? Ein Waghalsiger? Ein Selbstmörder?

> [But then ... he leapt onto the middle of my body with both his feet. I shuddered in furious pain, completely unknowing. Who was it? A child? A gymnast? A daredevil? A suicide?]

The bridge then tries to turn around to see its aggressor and plunges into the abyss where it is impaled ('aufgespiesst') on the pointed stones in the stream.

On one level the bridge's motion recalls the mythological gesture of Orpheus turning around to glimpse his beloved – the epistemological impulse to 'see' the other that results in separation and loss. Within the intertextual realm of Kafka's own literary production, 'Die Brücke' also gestures toward the conclusion of 'Das Urteil' ('The Judgement'), where Georg Bendemann executes a perfect (and suicidal) gymnastic 'turn' over a bridge, which at that moment is crossed by a powerful surge of city 'traffic' or 'Verkehr'. For almost half a century this intertextual link was obscured by Brod's misreading of the word 'Turner' in the manuscript of 'Die Brücke' (he mistakenly read, and published, 'Traum' ['dream']). The new edition restores this link to the child gymnast and suicide victim in 'Das Urteil' and to Kafka's 'Turner' figures in general. (Indeed, on one level the story can be read as the literalisation of the gymnastic term 'Brücke', which refers to the arched position of the body, stomach up, hands and feet on the floor.) As a structure facilitating passage from one realm to the other, the bridge can also be associated with metaphor and with the figurative language of literary texts. But 'Die Brücke' literally turns 'Das Urteil' around, 'inverting' the urban 'traffic' of Georg Bendemann's marriage to the 'Wandervogel' encounter between male traveller and bridge. The narrative motion of the bridge ('Brücke dreht sich um!' – 'Bridge turns round!') literalises the sexual inversion that leads to a lethal inscription/impalement. The innocent, child-like bridge, which at the beginning of the text is not yet 'inscribed' in maps ('in den Karten noch nicht eingezeichnet'), is physically penetrated by the 'Eisenspitze' of the man's walking stick and then impaled on the pointed, 'zugespitzte' rocks in the stream below. Traffic no longer flows, the German Romantic reverie is over.

In der Strafkolonie recounts a similar tale of sadistic inscription, impalement and death far from this 'Wandervogel' setting, on a sandy island in the tropics. To be sure, the narrative's textual syncretism, in which the archaic merges with the technologically modern, the 'primitive' natives with the colonising power, the German text with ostensibly French dialogue, resists any facile historical contextualisation. Nonetheless, the officer's speech is clearly organised around the dichotomy between a glorious past and a sordid present; between the 'old Commandant' who created the penal apparatus and the 'new Commandant' who is destroying it; between the harsh military and 'Oriental' justice of the former and the 'Enlightenment', 'European' views of the latter. This dichotomy is also gendered: the officer celebrates the male order which has produced the machine and its highly aestheticised spectacles of corporeal inscription and punishment, while denigrating the female order of the New Commandant that threatens the Old Commandant's 'life work': "'Soll wegen dieses Kommandanten und seiner Frauen, die ihn beeinflussen,'" the officer asks the traveller, "'ein solches Lebenswerk" – er zeigte auf die Maschine – "zugrunde gehen?"' (p. 196: "'Is such a life's work" – he pointed to the machine – "to be ruined by this commandant and the influence of his women?"')

The officer presents us, in other words, with the antimodernism and antifeminism of turn-of-the-century theorists of male culture like Mayer, Friedländer and Blüher. On the one hand he celebrates a 'Männerbund' with its charismatic leader, military discipline, spiritual strength and cultural achievement; on the other, he evokes the threat posed to this order by the 'liberal', 'feminine' views of the new Commandant. The fulcrum for these two struggling forces is the European scholar and 'traveller' ('Forschungs-reisender'), whom the officer attempts to seduce into his cult of the machine with almost coquettish means. He takes him by the arm, embraces him, lays his head on his shoulder, but most of all describes with incredible emotional investment the magnificent spectacle of the machine as it inscribes its victims with the 'schöne Schrift' ('beautiful script') and 'Verzierungen' ('embellishments') of military judgment: 'Ein Anblick,' as the officer claims, thus anticipating his own self-destructing fate, 'der einen verführen könnte, sich mit unter die Egge zu legen' (p. 193).

The cruel centre of the story is the 'peculiar' ('eigentümlich') machine, which is introduced as the strange object of the officer's desire and admiration, at once his 'property' and something foreign, incomprehensible, uncanny: '"Es ist ein eigentümlicher Apparat", sagte der Offizier zu dem Forschungsreisenden und überblickte mit einem gewissermaßen bewundernden Blick den ihm doch wohlbekannten Apparat' ('"It's a peculiar apparatus", said the officer to the traveller, surveying with a somewhat admiring gaze the apparatus with which he was surely familiar'). The gender of the machine, like that of the bridge, is ambiguous: it contains the 'male' needles and spikes ('Spitzen') that penetrate the prisoner's skin, but also the 'female' bed that cradles him and the immense 'Truhe' with its multiple gears. This gender confusion increases during the story, as 'der Apparat' is increasingly referred to as 'die Maschine', and culminates in the final scene of execution with the female apparatus running amok, stabbing the officer while holding him in its embrace. At the same time the machine's 'feminine' attributes are clearly differentiated from the organic, material sexuality of the women who give candy to the prisoner and silk scarves to the officer: it represents a kind of mechanical, technological feminine, always 'frisch geputzt' with its gleaming steel, glass and brass parts, and powered by an invisible electric battery.

This last detail provides the link to the punishment scenarios of *Die Verwandlung* and 'Die Brücke'. For the terrible fantasy of this tropical 'Männerbund' is again a kind of homosexual rape, complete with electric charge, iron spike and unwitting victim: a rape that inscribes into the immobilised and helpless body a knowledge of sin and guilt. The prisoner is stripped and placed face-down on a 'bed', strapped with leather thongs so that he cannot move, and then penetrated from behind by the electric machine's needles and spike: 'Also hier ist das Bett', explains the officer to the traveller. 'Auf [das Bett] wird der Verurteilte bäuchlings gelegt, natürlich nackt' (p. 184: 'So here is the bed. On [the bed] the condemned man is laid face down, naked of course'). Later the condemned man has his clothing cut off by the soldier from behind – 'der Soldat [durchschnitt] mit einem Messer hinten Hemd und Hose' – before being placed in the machine's grip. When the 'Spitzen' of the needles first touch his naked back, he shudders and 'stretches out' his hand to the traveler. Like Gregor and the bridge, the soldier is ignorant of the reason for his punishment. The court's sentence is not told to him beforehand and the officer's entire explanation of the machine is said to take place in French, a language he doesn't understand.

When the officer takes the prisoner's place, however, the 'normal' inscription and 'Erlösung' ('redemption') fail to take place, giving way to a grotesque murder whose enactment foregrounds the naked male body as a sexual object. With the traveler watching, the officer undresses, takes his 'Degen' ('sword') out of the sheath, breaks it and throws clothing and sword into a pit. 'Nun stand er nackt da. Der Reisende biß sich auf die Lippen und sagte nichts' (p. 208: 'Now he was standing there naked. The traveller bit his lips and said nothing'). I will omit a detailed description of the execution process itself, which, rather than follow the slow, progressive model of inscription and sexual climax described by the officer, impales his body on the tip ('Spitze') of a giant spike and leaves it hanging, motionless, over the pit. The final description of the corpse is worth quoting however, as it constitutes an extreme example of the 'frozen', horrible beauty of Kafka's texts evoked by Günther Anders:

> Es war, wie es im Leben gewesen war; kein Zeichen der versprochenen Erlösung war zu entdecken; ... die Lippen waren fest zusammengedrückt, die Augen waren offen, hatten den Ausdruck des Lebens, der Blick war ruhig und überzeugt, durch die Stirn ging die Spitze des großen eisernen Stachels (p. 211).

> [It was as it had been while he was still alive; there was not a sign of the promised redemption to be discerned ... his lips were pressed tightly together, his eyes were open with a living expression, his gaze was calm and convinced, through his forehead went the point of the great iron spur.]

This is perhaps the most terrifying 'rape' in Kafka's writing: one in which the self eternally contemplates its own phallic impalement.

The above readings are not meant to reduce Kafka's literary texts to the level of biographical experience and a presumed 'homosexual' identity. To use Kafka's own term, I have tried to establish a kind of 'Verkehr' between personal and literary documents, between biography and aesthetics, that will link Kafka's texts to what Brand, Blüher and others understood by 'männliche Kultur' and an expanded notion of homoerotic desire. For Kafka, Blüher, and the contributors to *Der Eigene*, what mattered was not so much a fixed sexual identity or the exclusivity of male-male relations, but a radical *expansion* of individual freedom to include emotional and physical relations of all kinds. In epistemological terms, this expansion coincided with the contemporary redefinition of sexuality advocated by psychoanalysis in which virtually all psychic and physical activity were seen as being motivated in some way by the sexual drives. In political terms it coincided with contemporary calls for personal freedom, including the freedom to engage in non-normative sexual behaviour. In both senses Adolf Brand's notion of 'der Eigene' and Kafka's notion of 'das Eigentümliche' occupy a common ground in the claim for the individual's unrestricted development and autonomy: a radical freedom of the self that harks back to the founding text of political anarchism, Max Stirner's *Der Einzige und sein Eigentum* ('The Individual and his Property', 1844).[30] 'Male culture' in this sense means simply the individual male's freedom to do with his 'property', his body, whatever he likes – whether 'proper' or not.

More disturbing than this rather idealistic vision of individual freedom is the undercurrent of nationalist, anti-Semitic and anti-feminine sentiment that often accompanied it. Although not all contributors to *Der Eigene* became ardent Nazis, the journal played a role in the increasingly militarist and racist forms of male bonding that developed in Germany in the 1920s and early 1930s.[31] In 1924 and 1925 Brand published anti-Semitic attacks on Hirschfeld and his associate Kurt Hiller, including an article by Karl Heimsoth, a psychoanalyst who invented the conception of 'homophile', who asserted that the 'homosexual feminism' of Hirschfeld's 'Jewish Committee' was dangerous to 'German eros'.[32] The subsequent Nazi attack on Ernst Röhm – in 1931 a Munich newspaper denounced the head of the SA as a homosexual and a danger to the party – marks a moment of crisis in the history of *Der Eigene* from which it never recovered, although Brand appealed to party officials not to deny the importance of 'male culture' and the 'Männerbund' in the Nazi movement.[33] Blüher too became increasingly racist and anti-Semitic, as Kafka was to learn to his dismay in 1922 when he read *Secessio judaica*. That Blüher's readership extended from Jewish-German figures of the avant-garde to leading Nazis and even Hitler himself, who read his work intensively while in prison, points not to an irony of history but to a complexity and imbrication of historical phenomena that retrospective categorisation often obscures.

This brings us back to the public acceptability of Kafka's homoerotic fantasies. Brod's censorship of the diaries is one of the many ways in which he tried to shape his friend's literary legacy. Not just the protective gesture of a friend, his decision to leave out certain 'compromising' homoerotic entries was also, perhaps primarily, a critical and editorial effort to present Kafka as a religious writer for the modern, post-Nietzschean age. Kafka's disgust with (hetero-)sexual relations fits conveniently into this image: a saint who eschews all earthly temptation for the sake of his writing. But disgust is precisely what is lacking in Kafka's characterisation of desire between men. Though it may provoke a variety of emotional responses ranging from simple affirmation and childlike fascination to near-sublime moments of terror and pain, homosexual desire does not trigger the same order of emotional denial that the mere thought of marriage and heterosexual relations induced. '[J]edes Hochzeits-reisepaar,' Kafka admitted to Brod in reference to his engagement to Felice Bauer, 'ob ich mich zu ihm in Beziehung setze oder nicht, ist mir ein widerlicher Anblick und wenn ich mir Ekel erregen will, brauche ich mir nur vorzustellen, daß ich einer Frau den Arm um die Hüften lege' ('I find every newly-wed couple going on their honeymoon a revolting sight, whether I relate myself to them or not, and if I want to arouse disgust in myself, I need only imagine putting my arm round a woman's waist').[34] Ironically, what Brod left untouched were precisely these 'disgusting' heterosexual relations that Kafka repeatedly characterised as a violation of his identity, as a journey away from the strange or 'eigentümliche' self that marked him as a writer. One is tempted to recall K.'s thoughts in *The Castle* as he lies in an embrace with Frieda on the filthy bar-room floor:

> Dort vergiengen Stunden, Stunden gemeinsamen Atems, gemeinsamen Herzschlags, Stunden, in denen K. immerfort das Gefühl hatte, er verirre sich oder er sei soweit in der Fremde, wie vor ihm noch kein Mensch, eine Fremde, in der selbst die Luft keinen Bestandteil der Heimatluft habe, in der man vor Fremdheit ersticken müsse und in

deren unsinnigen Verlockungen man doch nichts tun könne als weiter gehn, weiter sich verirren (pp. 68–9).

[There hours went past, hours in which they breathed as one, in which their hearts beat as one, in which K. kept feeling that he was losing himself or wandering into a strange country, further than anyone before him, a strange country where even the air had nothing in common with the air of his home, where one must be suffocated by strangeness and yet a senseless allure meant that one could do nothing but go on and lose oneself still further.]

Whatever he may have thought of 'male culture', Kafka was never able to conceive of heterosexual 'Verkehr' as anything but a betrayal of his 'eigentümliche' self, as a journey into 'die Fremde'.

Notes

1. *Tagebücher in der Fassung der Handschrift*, ed. H.-G. Koch, M. Müller and M. Pasley (Frankfurt, 1990); all subsequent references will be to this edition.
2. An informative discussion of Kafka's sexuality is provided by Frank Möbus' recent study, *Sünden-Fälle. Die Geschlechtlichkeit in Erzählungen Franz Kafkas* (Göttingen, 1994). Like earlier critics, however, Möbus downplays the issue of homosexuality even in passages where it is clearly important.
3. R. Tiefenbrun, *Moment of Torment: An Interpretation of Franz Kafka's Short Stories* (Carbondale, IL, 1973); G. Mecke, *Franz Kafkas offenbares Geheimnis. Eine Psychopathographie* (Munich, 1982). Tiefenbrun announces for instance that, although Kafka never openly admits it, once one reads the totality of his writings it becomes clear that the predicament of all his heroes 'is based on the fact that they are all homosexuals' (p. 21). Mecke also insists that a simple translation of Kafka's coded language results in 'Klartext', the 'secret-yet-open' confession of Kafka's 'shame' as a homosexual in a repressively heterosexual culture (p. 15).
4. For the notion of homosociality and its literary manifestations in Victorian England, see Eve Kosofsky Sedgwick, *Between Men: English Literature and Male Homosocial Desire* (New York, 1985).
5. In addition to the Oscar Wilde trial, which received close media attention in Austria and Germany, the highest profile German scandal was the Eulenburg affair, which exposed important political figures close to the Kaiser as homosexuals. See J. Steakley, *The Homosexual Emancipation Movement in Germany* (Salem, 1993; first pub. in 1975), and I. Hull, *The Entourage of Kaiser Wilhelm II 1888–1918* (Cambridge, 1982).
6. *Briefe 1902–1924*, ed. M. Brod (Frankfurt, 1958), p. 196. The more recent edition of Kafka's correspondence with Brod includes Brod's letters as well: see *Max Brod und Franz Kafka, Eine Freundschaft*, vol. 2, ed. M. Pasley (Frankfurt, 1989).
7. Gilman, *Franz Kafka: The Jewish Patient* (London, 1995), p. 79.
8. Quoted ibid., p. 80.
9. Quoted ibid.
10. First published in 1897 under the name *Der Eigene. Monatsschrift für Kunst und Leben*, the journal took on the subtitle of 'männliche Kultur' in 1899 and appeared regularly until 1931. Selections from the journal have been reprinted and edited by Joachim S. Hohmann in *Der Eigene. Ein Blatt für männliche Kultur. Das Beste aus der ersten Homosexuellenzeitschrift der Welt* (Frankfurt, 1981). A similar volume in

English was edited by Harry Oosterhuis in a special issue of the *Journal of Homosexuality*, vol. 22 (1991), nos. 1/2, entitled 'Homosexuality and Male Bonding in Pre-Nazi Germany. The Youth Movement, the Gay Movement and Male Bonding before Hitler's Rise. Original Transcripts from *Der Eigene*'. Unless otherwise noted, all references are to the German reprint and will be noted in parentheses.

11. Schurtz's study, *Altersklassen und Männerbünde. Eine Darstellung der Grundformen der Gesellschaft* (Berlin, 1902), posited contrary 'Triebe' in man and woman: a 'Familientrieb' and a 'mannmännlichen Geselligkeitstrieb'. 'Darum ist das Weib der Hort aller Gesellschaftsformen, die aus der Vereinigung zweier Personen verschiedenen Geschlechts hervorgehen, der Mann dagegen der Vertreter aller Arten des rein geselligen Zusammenschlusses und damit der höheren sozialen Verbände' (p. iv). For a discussion of Schurtz's study and its impact, see Jürgen Reulecke, 'Das Jahr 1902 und die Ursprünge der Männerbund-Ideologie in Deutschland' in G. Völger and K. von Welck (eds), *Männerbund, Männerbünde: Zur Rolle des Mannes im Kulturvergleich* (Cologne, 1990), vol. 2, pp. 3–10.

12. H. Oosterhuis in *Journal of Homosexuality*, 22 (1991), p. 187.

13. 'Frauenbewegung und männliche Kultur', 1903, 407; reprinted in *Journal for Homosexuality*, 22 (1991), 134–44.

14. Blüher, *Die deutsche Wandervogelbewegung als erotisches Phänomen* (Jena, 1912) , p. 30.

15. Blüher, *Die Rolle der Erotik in der männlichen Gesellschaft. Eine Theorie der menschlichen Staatsbildung nach Wesen und Wert*: vol. I, Der Typus Inversus, vol. II, Familie und Männerbund (Jena, 1919 and 1920: first published 1917). Blüher's theory of 'male society' and the 'Männerbund' are in the second part of vol. II, which also offers a reprise of his book on the 'Wandervogel' (pp. 91–131).

16. *Die deutsche Wandervogelbewegung*, pp. 114–15.

17. I have not been able to consult this latter volume, which was also published at Jena by Diederichs during the war. Its proto-fascist tendency can, however, be inferred from an advertisement listing the book's subtitle as 'Eine Auseinandersetzung mit der Demokratie' and the following chapter headings: 'Der geborene und der gewählte Führer / Der demokratische Wahlirrtum ... Gustav Wynekens Führertum.'

18. *Max Brod/Franz Kafka. Eine Freundschaft*, vol. 2, p. 176.

19. Mark Anderson, *Kafka's Clothes: Ornament and Aestheticism in the Habsburg Fin de Siècle* (Oxford, 1992).

20. *Streitbares Leben* (Frankfurt, 1979), pp. 22–3, my translation.

21. See Steven Aschheim, *The Nietzsche Legacy in Germany 1890–1990* (Berkeley, 1992), and J. Le Rider and D. Bourel (eds), *De Sils Maria à Jerusalem: Nietzsche et le judaisme, les intellectuels juifs et Nietzsche* (Paris, 1991).

22. The passage begins 'Jeder Mensch ist eigentümlich und kraft seiner Eigentümlichkeit berufen zu wirken ...' and describes the negative effects that family and school have on this 'peculiarity'. See *Nachgelassene Schriften und Fragmente*, vol. II, ed. J. Schillemeit (Frankfurt, 1992), pp. 7ff.

23. See my discussion of 'traffic' in Kafka's writings, *Kafka's Clothes*, pp. 22–3. Freud attributes sexual meaning to railway traffic and motion in particular in a usage consistent with Kafka's literary exploitation of the trope; see his 'Drei Abhandlungen zur Sexualtheorie', *Studienausgabe*, vol. 5 (Frankfurt, 1989), pp. 106–7.

24. 'Fast immer, wenn Kafka sich mimetisch mit der Sexualität beschäftigt, sieht sich der Leser mit einer Wortwahl konfrontiert, die Ekel, Schmutz, animalische Gewalt suggeriert' (Möbus, *Sünden-Fälle*, p. 8). One should note, however, that these associations are provoked by heterosexual intercourse, and are strikingly

absent from Kafka's depiction of homoerotic encounters.

25. See Sedgwick, *Between Men*.
26. *Das Schloß*, ed. M. Pasley (Frankfurt, 1989), pp. 415–16. Kafka heightens the sexual implications of this encounter by specifying that Bürgel is the 'Verbindungssekretär' between Castle and village, a job which requires constant 'travel' (a 'Reisetasche' lies next to the bed as a metonymic signal of the meaning of 'Verkehr'). K. later falls into bed with Bürgel and clasps the latter's foot, which Bürgel 'allows' him to hold. Significantly, the dream ends with K. stepping on the shards of a champagne glass, a gesture that Möbus links to the Jewish marriage ceremony (*Sünden-Fälle*, p. 122), thereby downplaying the scene's 'evident' homoeroticism. But the marriage symbolism (or the castration symbolism of broken class) could just as easily be understood as heightening the scene's sexual import.
27. Günther Anders, *Franz Kafka*, tr. A. Steer and A. K. Thorlby (London, 1960), pp. 58–9. First published as *Kafka – Pro und Contra* (Munich, 1951).
28. *Gesammelte Schriften. Erzählungen und kleine Prosa* (New York, 1946), p. 109. Except where otherwise noted, all references to Kafka's stories will be to this edition.
29. All quotations are from *Nachgelassene Schriften und Fragmente*, vol. I, ed. M. Pasley (Frankfurt, 1993), pp. 304–5. According to Pasley, 'Die Brücke' was written sometime in mid to late January 1917.
30. See particularly the chapter entitled 'Mein Verkehr' in which Stirner advocates that the individual cut off 'intercourse' with family and bourgeois society.
31. On this subject see the last two chapters of the *Journal of Homosexuality*, 22 (1991), 'Political Issues and the Rise of Nazism' and 'Male Bonding and Homosexuality in German Nationalism', pp. 183–264. In his pathbreaking study, Richard Plant deals with the subsequent Nazi persecution of homosexuals during the Third Reich; see *The Pink Triangle: The Nazi War against Homosexuality* (New York, 1986).
32. 'Freundesliebe und Homosexualität', *Der Eigene*, 1925, no. 9, 415–25, as quoted by Oosterhuis, ibid., p. 188. Heimsoth was a member of the Nazi party and a friend of Ernst Röhm, a known homosexual whom Brand defended in *Der Eigene* in 1931. Other contributors to the journal who became Nazis were Hans Heinz Ewers (the official biographer of Horst Wessel), Heinrich Pudor (the pioneer of nudism or 'Nacktkultur') and the well-known *Jugendstil* illustrator Hugo Höppener ('Fidus').
33. Brand, 'Political Criminals: A Word about the Röhm Case (1931)', in *Journal of Homosexuality*, 22 (1991), 235–240.
34. Letter of 18 October 1913, *Max Brod/Franz Kafka. Eine Freundschaft*, vol. 2, p. 131.

The First World War Fiction of
Andreas Latzko

Andrew Barker

Narrative fiction about the First World War remains a relatively unexplored area of modern Austrian literature, even though two of its greatest works (albeit on very different scales) were inspired by the war: Kraus's *Die letzten Tage der Menschheit*, written 'für ein Marstheater' ['a theatre on Mars'],[1] and Trakl's battle-poem 'Grodek' (1914). Trakl apart, however, Austrian war poetry has none of the cachet of its English equivalent,[2] while for most readers First World War fiction in German begins and ends with two works which only appeared years after the cease-fire: Arnold Zweig's *Der Streit um den Sergeanten Grischa* (1927) and E. M. Remarque's *Im Westen nichts Neues* (1929). In this essay, however, I shall suggest that above all in the collection of stories entitled *Menschen im Krieg* (1917) and to a lesser extent in the episodic novel *Friedensgericht* (1918), Andreas Latzko produced works worthy of comparison with Zweig and Remarque which are the more remarkable for being written while the war still raged.[3]

While several canonical Austrian novelists experienced life at the front – Musil, Roth and Doderer spring to mind – warfare subsequently found relatively little resonance in their imaginative writings. When it did, as in the depiction of the youngest Trotta's death in *Radetzkymarsch* (1932), Roth was writing from a post-war perspective and to an agenda which was not primarily a literary response to war. However, as the examples not only of Andreas Latzko but also of Ernst Weiss reveal, there were some notable Austrian writers who both saw action and wrote about it at the time. Weiss, the problematic friend of Kafka, now attracts some critical attention,[4] but the once-celebrated Latzko, a soul-mate of Stefan Zweig and Romain Rolland, has disappeared virtually without trace.

Born in Budapest in 1876, baptised a Roman Catholic, but of Jewish descent with a Hungarian father and a Viennese mother, Latzko first wrote in Hungarian, only turning to German in 1901. After studying philosophy and chemistry in Berlin, he worked first as a journalist in Egypt, India, Ceylon and Java, but by 1914 *Kürschners Deutscher Literatur-Kalender* reveals a Munich address, and there can be little doubt this is the unnamed South German city portrayed in the first chapter of *Friedensgericht*. Called up in

100

1914, Latzko served as an officer on the Italian front, but having contracted malaria, and with his nerves in shreds, was released from military service in 1916 and allowed to go to Davos in Switzerland. There he composed the six stories comprising *Menschen im Krieg*. In his war diaries Romain Rolland records Latzko telling him that he had not been wounded, but had seen:

> wie zwei Ochsen und drei Männer von einer Granate in Stücke gerissen wurden. Im ersten Augenblick spürte er nichts. Aber zwei Tage später, als man eine Platte mit noch blutigen Steaks auf seinen Tisch stellte, begann er zu heulen, spie, wurde von Krämpfen geschüttelt. Sechs Monate lang zitterte er am ganzen Leibe und verweigerte jede Nahrung.[5]

> [how two oxen and three men were ripped to shreds by a grenade. At first he felt nothing. But two days later, when they put before him on the table a platter with still bloody steaks, he began to howl, vomited, was racked by convulsions. For six months his whole body shook and he refused all food.]

The memoirs of the Swiss publisher Max Rascher recall Latzko's relief at settling in Zürich, which, as he admitted in a letter to Carl Seelig, he had no intention of quitting after his recall to the Boroevics Corps in Northern Hungary at the end of 1917. After Latzko's application to the Austrian authorities for a general discharge (he had already been demoted after the publication of *Menschen im Krieg*), his books and furniture arrived at his flat in the Kurhausstrasse early in 1918. Nevertheless, even in the safety of Switzerland police enquiries continued throughout the year, and Latzko felt constantly threatened until the cessation of hostilities.

The letters between Zweig and Rolland reveal Latzko as a sympathetic but neurotic character. A surviving photograph indicates a man of mournful and haunted disposition,[6] but he was also someone whose convictions overrode personal tragedy. Writing to Rolland on 21 November 1918, Zweig noted: 'Latzko will nach Deutschland gehen, ich verstehe ihn nicht mehr. Er will seine sterbende Frau verlassen, nur ... um dorthin zu gehen, aus dem Bedürfnis zu handeln.'[7] (Latzko wants to go to Germany, I no longer understand him. He intends leaving his dying wife ... to go there, just because of a need to do something.)

Writing from St Moritz in January 1918 Zweig, for whom Latzko was 'ein wunderbarer Mann'[8] ('a wonderful man'), describes meeting him at a reading in Davos: 'Er ist sehr leidend, Morphinist im höchsten Grade, sehr nervös und überreizt. Aber ein menschlicher Mann. Wir haben uns gut verstanden.'[9] (He suffers greatly, a complete morphine addict, very nervous and over-wrought. But a humane man. We got on well.) Almost a decade later, in September 1927, Zweig observed that Latzko lacked the gift of happiness. He was attracted by unhappiness, and it was precisely this attraction which made him creative: 'Er liebt alles, was gegen etwas ist, und wäre unzufrieden, wenn Harmonie sich verwirklichte.'[10] (He loves everything which is contrary, and would be dissatisfied, were harmony to be achieved.)

To make matters worse, Latzko was still an addict, now confined to a sanatorium in Hungary. Things were so serious that Zweig believed he had only a short time to live.[11] Four years later, however, Latzko published his last novel *Sieben Tage* (1931). This appeared in English as *Seven Days* in the same year; thereafter came a biography of Lafayette (English translation 1936). Latzko went into exile in Amsterdam as early as 1931, remaining there until his death in 1943. In 1948 a memorial was erected to his memory in that city, and in 1951 his autobiography *Levensreis* ('Life's Journey'), co-authored with his Georgian second wife Stella Otarowa-Latzko, was published in the Netherlands.[12]

The reasons for Latzko's present neglect are complex, but János Szabó has suggested that whereas erstwhile Marxists found him too little concerned with issues of class, his views are unpalatable in a climate of triumphal capitalism. For Hungarian literary historians Latzko is of scant interest because he wrote chiefly in German and lived abroad, while Austrianists cannot squeeze him into the straitjacket of the 'Habsburg Myth'. Although he published his war works in Switzerland, he does not belong to Swiss literature, and he is certainly not a 'German-German' author. To complete the picture of neglect, his cause has been taken up neither by 'Exilforschung', nor by scholars researching the relationship of Jews to Austro-German culture.[13] Szabó concludes that the underlying reason for this neglect is, however, twofold. Not only was he an outsider wherever he went, he was also the type of socially critical author often denounced as a 'Nestbeschmutzer', and such artists have habitually been ignored in Austro-German critical circles.[14]

Although neglected today, Latzko remains a writer of considerable power, as the French pacifist Henri Barbusse acknowledged in a letter to Carl Seelig after reading *Menschen im Krieg*:

> J'ai lu et relu l'oeuvre de Latzko. C'est admirable et cet homme a un talent de tout premier ordre ... Il doit être maudit dans toutes les sphères militaristes allemands et autrichiens, pour avoir bâti un tel livre de vérité poignante et vivante.[15]

> [I have read and re-read Latzko's work. It's admirable, and the man has a talent of the first order ... They must curse him in all the militaristic spheres in Germany and Austria for having constructed a book of such poignant truth and vivacity.]

Comparing *Menschen im Krieg* with Stefan Zweig's *Jeremias*, a more recent critic judges that as a 'social protest against the War and those who live by it it is more urgent and more compelling than Zweig's stylised Old Testament epic'.[16]

Alongside Leonhard Frank's *Der Mensch ist gut* (1917), *Menschen im Krieg* is the earliest example of anti-war fiction published by non-Swiss authors in the safe haven of Zürich at precisely the same time as Dada was born there. Latzko appeared in the pacifist Max Rascher Verlag, founded in Zürich with the specific aim of disseminating pacifist literature. Although tolerant enough to permit pacifist artists to emigrate to Switzerland, the authorities in Germany and Austria took increasing exception to anti-war works, but apart from banning their import could do little about books which only appeared in Switzerland. *Menschen im Krieg*, dedicated to friend and foe alike ('Freund und Feind zu eigen'), was the first work to appear under Rascher's new imprint, and its success was phenomenal. Within a few weeks 8,000 copies had been sold in Switzerland; by 1919 it had reached 33,000.[17] English and French translations were quickly prepared. The individual stories in *Menschen im Krieg*, whose strikingly authentic ambience is that of the Austro-Hungarian Empire at war, had originally appeared anonymously in such organs as René Schickele's *Die weißen Blätter*, and only with the third edition did the book carry the author's name. In *Die Fackel* on 9 October 1917 Karl Kraus greeted the book with great enthusiasm, exclaiming that it was 'ein Schrei, vor dem kunstrichterliche Einwendungen gern verstummen' ('a scream which silences aesthetic reservations').[13] The satirist reckoned it to be the duty of all those seeking confirmation of a European dimension in German war literature to inveigle their bookseller into obtaining a copy of *Menschen im Krieg*. The day would not be long in coming, so he erroneously believed, when 'das offizielle Österreich darauf stolz sein wird, daß es auch durch diese Tat am Weltkrieg beteiligt war' ('Austria will officially be proud that through this act too it partook of the World War') (p. 175).

Although the style of Latzko's war fiction is for the most part realistic, the impact of literary Expressionism can also be discerned, for example in the extended depictions of the minutiae of physical violence and mental turmoil. The direct nature of Latzko's emotional appeal to the reader, the often disjointed, staccato sentences, the exuberant punctuation with its frequent use of multiple dashes are further indications of the author's stylistic proximity to Expressionism. As Szabó has pointed out, however, he is never tempted to present a splintered reality in the manner of the Dadaists, remaining content with linear plots. The overall impact of Latzko's war fiction, Szabó concludes in obvious allusion to Munch's most celebrated Expressionist canvas, is akin to a single, long-drawn scream.[19]

'Der Abmarsch' ('The march-off'), the opening story of *Menschen im Krieg*, is set in the autumn of 1915 in a small provincial town. The title seems initially misleading, for the soldiers here have long since been marched off to death or glory. Only later will its significance be revealed. In Expressionist-tinged language which personifies both the town and the war itself, Latzko is at pains to underline the incongruity of a civilisation confronted by the 'große Wut' ('great rage') of the 'anspruchsvollen, lärmenden Gesellen' ('demanding noisy fellow') which is war:[20]

Aber die schönen, schmiedeeisernen Brunnen auf den Plätzen rauschten doch gleichmütig weiter, plauderten mit beruhigender Ausdauer von den Tagen ihrer Jugend, da die Menschen noch Zeit und Sorgfalt für edel geschwungene Linien gehabt, Krieg eine Angelegenheit für Fürsten und Abenteurer gewesen. (p. 11)

[But the beautiful cast-iron fountains in the piazzas splashed serenely on, talked at soothing length about the the days of their youth, when people still had time to care about nobly curved lines, when war was an affair of princes and adventurers.]

This 'sleepily peaceable' town, nestling in the hills, is the incongruous setting for a military hospital housing the casualties of the battle raging on the Doberdo plateau some fifty kilometres distant.

The central character of the novella is an unnamed officer conscript, a famous opera composer in civilian life, who has lost his sanity at the front. Betraying further the impact of Expressionism on Latzko's narration, none of the major characters is specifically named, but merely designated by function or rank. The cause of the composer-lieutenant's madness, the 'unerhörte Begebenheit' of the novella's structure, is a gruesome one, related by Latzko with unsparing detail. While showing the composer the latest photograph of his wife, a fellow officer had been killed when a dismembered, booted leg came hurtling through the air, lodging its spur in his skull. All this is related by the suddenly eloquent composer himself, who until then had communicated neither with his fellow officers nor with his pretty young wife who has come to be with him, but whose concern is met with blank hostility. The 'spur' to relating the incident (Latzko is obviously aware of the mordant pun on 'Sporn' which works in German as it does in English) is the wife of a major, doing her bit as a military nurse, who pruriently asks the assembled officers what had been 'their most horrible experience at the front': 'Was aber war das Gräßlichste, das Sie draußen erlebt haben?' At this point the composer suddenly finds his voice:

– Gräßlich? Gräßlich ist nur der Abmarsch – rief er – Man geht, – – – und daß man gelassen wird, das ist gräßlich! – (p. 23).[21]

['Horrible? Only marching off is horrible', he cried. 'You go – – – it's being left that is horrible! –']

What unbalanced him initially was the grotesque death of a comrade, but in his madness he unleashes a criticism not against the war as such, but against those who let it happen. And here Latzko springs a surprise. For the blameworthy are not the politicians, the industrialists, or the battle-thirsty High Command, but the women who wave their menfolk off into battle, throwing roses into the compartments as the trains steam away. In convoluted counterpoint to Aristophanes' *Lysistrata*, Latzko has his mad composer blame woman for the carnage. War is not the most terrible thing – for what else would one expect war to be? – rather, it is the realisation that women are cruel:

Die Frauen haben uns geschickt! Kein General hätt' was machen können, wenn die Frauen uns nicht hätten in die Züge pfropfen lassen, wenn sie geschrieen hätten, daß sie uns nicht mehr anschaun, wenn wir zu Mördern werden. Nicht einer wär hinaus, wenn sie geschworen hätten, daß keine von ihnen ins Bett steigt mit einem Mann, der Schädel gespalten, Menschen erschossen, Menschen erstochen hat. (p. 30f.)

[The women sent us! No general could have done a thing if the women hadn't had us stuffed into the trains, if they had screamed that they wouldn't look at us again if we became murderers. Nobody would have gone off if they had sworn that not one of them would get into bed with a man who had split skulls, shot people, bayonetted people.]

As the story unfolds, it becomes evident that the composer is fired by contempt for women who for the sake of obtaining the vote are prepared to throw themselves in front of trains, to attack politicians and commit arson, but who do nothing to protect their men:

Für das Stimmrecht, hörst du? Und für ihre Männer nicht? Nicht einen Laut, nicht einen Schrei! (p. 32)

[For the right to vote, do you hear? And not for their menfolk? Not a peep, not a shout!]

Not for the first time in Austrian letters of the early twentieth century, the voice of Otto Weininger can be heard in the composer's dismissal of women as vain, sexually-motivated creatures of fashion devoid of ethical fibre.

A woman also plays a decisive and problematic role in 'Heimkehr' ['Homecoming'], the final story of *Menschen im Krieg*, where the disfigured and embittered Johann Bogdán returns from Kielce on the Russian front to his home on the Hungarian puszta. Already contemptuous of 'das vornehme Weiberpack' ('the bevy of posh women') in the hospital who try to convince him that his lover will feel proud because he has been mutilated in the name of the Fatherland (p. 181), Bogdán discovers that in his absence Marcsa has betrayed him with the local feudal baron. Her treachery may be a further indication of the Weiningerian view of woman as ethically void and dominated by sexuality, but an equally striking feature of this story is Latzko's readiness to use Bogdán's outrage both at his injury and his cuckolding to engage in a quasi-Marxist prophecy about the future of a whole society. A servile man by both temperament and social conditioning, Bogdán had been proud to be his master's servant, feeling only contempt for the Socialist views of the hump-backed Mihály. The latter is the village outcast, who had once tried to organise workers' protests in the local brickworks which now turns out shellcases. In the 'erlebte Rede' typical of this story, Mihály ponders:

Dieser Bogdán war immer schon eine elende Lakaiennatur gewesen, stolz darauf, den hohen Herrn dienen zu dürfen. Fühlte sich solidarisch mit seinen Unterdrückern, weil er in verschnürten Joppen mit silbernen Knöpfen zu ihrem Glanze beitragen durfte. (p. 184)

[This Bogdán was always a miserable lackey, proud of being permitted to serve his lords and masters. Felt solidarity with his oppressors because he could add to their lustre in his laced jackets and silver buttons.]

Aware of Marcsa's treachery, however, Bogdán revises his views of the hunchback, who had suggested that people like Johann Bogdán were merely cannon-fodder for a ruling class which has used the war to enrich itself:

> Der eine geht hinaus und läßt sich den Schädel kaput schlagen, der andere bleibt schön daheim, fabriziert Granathülsen und tapeziert sein Schloß mit Tausendkronenscheinen! (p. 186)

> [The one goes off and has his head smashed in, the other stays safe at home, makes shell cases and wallpapers his castle with thousand-crown notes!]

Recognising that 'the hunchback was actually not so stupid after all' ('Er war eigentlich gar nicht so dumm, der Bucklige') (p. 198), Bogdan confronts the feudal overlord:

> So maßlos war seine Wut, daß er wie der bucklige Sozi sprach, ohne sich zu schämen. (p. 199)

> [His rage was so extreme that he spoke like the hunchbacked lefty and felt no shame.]

Having already proved himself an efficient and cold-blooded killer in battle, Bogdán, his consciousness newly raised, then stabs him to death. Here, then, is the old order challenged from below by one who has been exploited both socially and sexually by the ruling class. This climax, which seems to echo the role of the peasantry in the Bolshevik Revolution, is not, however, the end of the story. For although the old order is now dead, the peasant's revolt is not allowed to triumph. Forgetting his military training and deserted by the instinct for survival honed in battle, Bogdán fails to guard his rear. Deprived by war of her once-handsome lover and then robbed of her rich protector by the vengeful returnee, the twice-bereft Marcsa exacts her own revenge by splitting open Bogdán's skull with a fearful blow from behind. At the end of the book, master and servant, the old feudal order, lie dead, victims both of the femme fatale.

In 'Der Sieger' ('The Victor') moral deficit accrues neither to unthinking women fired by enthusiasm for a war which takes away their sons and lovers, nor to a thwarted woman seeking revenge, but to a military commander scheming in luxurious safety far behind the front line while men perish at his imperious behest. War is for him a time of personal blessing upon which painful reality must not be allowed to intrude. Enjoying to the hilt the veneer of elegance and sophistication which the arrival of the Army High Command has imparted to what was once a boring provincial backwater, the vainglorious Commander-in-Chief forbids the walking wounded to sully its now bustling streets with their presence:

Der ganze Krieg präsentierte sich, von hier aus gesehen, wie ein lebensspendender Strom, der Musikkapellen heranschwemmt, Geld und Frohsinn unter die Leute bringt und von promenierenden Offizieren betrieben, von gemächlich verdauenden Generalstäblern dirigiert wird. Von seiner blutigen Seite war nichts zu sehen! Kein Geschützdonner schlug an's Ohr, kein Verwundeter trug sein persönliches Elend als störende Note in die allgemeine Lebenslust hinein. (p. 45)

[Seen from here, the whole war presented itself as a life-giving stream, washing up military bands, bringing money and merriment to the people, promoted by promenading officers and and directed by leisurely digesting types from the General Staff. No artillery thunder assaulted the ear, no casualty disturbed the general joie de vivre with his personal misery.]

Latzko's satire is at its most mordant in his deft portrayal of this choleric, superannuated soldier who at the end of a long peacetime career suddenly finds social, professional and financial fulfilment in the war. With rotund satisfaction he informs the wife of the Chief of the General Staff:

Und haben Sie sich schon die jungen Leute angesehen, die von der Front hereinkommen? Sonnenverbrannt, gesund und vergnügt! ... Glauben Sie mir, die Welt ist noch nie so gesund gewesen, wie heute. Nehmen Sie aber eine Zeitung in die Hand, dann lesen Sie von einer Weltkatastrophe; vom Verbluten Europas, und was die Herren sonst noch zusammenschmieren. (p. 105)

[And have you already had a look at the young people who come in from the front? Tanned, healthy and contented! ... Believe me, the world has never been as healthy as it is today. But pick up a paper and you'll read about global catastrophe; about Europe bleeding to death, and anything else these gentlemen can scrape together. –]

This story might have held a special appeal for Kraus not only because it closely reflects his views on the moral turpitude of the High Command, for whom the 'segensreiche Wirkung des Krieges' ('beneficial effect of war') (p. 105) is like a 'herrliches Märchen' ('splendid fairy-tale') (p. 109), but also for its portrayal of a credulous, supine journalist who when interviewing the 'allmächtige Märchenkönig' ('almighty fairy-tale king') (p. 50) fails to challenge his transparently hypocritical lament that modern generals, condemned to lead from the rear, have no chance of going into battle at the head of their troops (p. 53). The general's contemptuous mental dismissal of the journalist's timid enquiry as to when hostilities might cease rounds off the story. Listening at a safe distance to the sound of the barrage, the general is transfigured:

Das Trommelfeuer! ...
Die Augen der Excellenz leuchteten auf. Über das eben noch verärgerte

Gesicht huschte ein Schein innerer Befriedigung.
Gott sei Dank! Noch gab es Krieg. (p. 57)

[The barrage! ...
His Excellency's eyes lit up. Across the face still betraying annoyance
flitted a gleam of inner contentment.
Thank God! The war was still on.]

There is nothing subtle about Latzko's contempt for 'His Excellency',
which contrasts strongly with 'Der General', Joseph Roth's fond pen-sketch
of a similar figure published in in 1919.[22] Readers of Roth and Latzko might
be further tempted to establish certain links between 'Der Sieger' and Roth's
attempt in *Radetzkymarsch* posthumously to rehabilitate the regime which
Latzko despises. Noteworthy are the parallel descriptions of afternoon con-
certs in small provincial towns, where military bands entertain the local
populace as well as the Habsburg Establishment. In Roth's novel it is the
sound of the 'Radetzkymarsch', in 'Der Sieger' it is that other musical
epitome of Old Austria, the younger Strauss's 'Blue Danube' waltz, which
fills the old square in front of the town hall 'mit Trommelwirbel und
Tschinellenschlag' ('with the roll of drums and the crash of cymbals') (p.
102). At times even Latzko seems on the point of succumbing to the
'Habsburg myth', producing passages which would not be out of place in
Roth's epic of yearning for a Golden Age that never was:

Unter den hundertjährigen Platanen, die mit ihren riesigen, ineinander
greifenden Kronen den ganzen Platz wie ein Kirchenschiff überwölbten,
saß es sich sehr angenehm. Die Herbstsonne lag mit mattem Glanz auf
den Mauern ringsum, streute, wie durch Butzenscheiben, goldene
Ringe durch das dichte Laub, auf die kleinen, runden Tische, die in
langen Reihen vor dem Kaffeehaus standen. (p. 100)

[It was most pleasant sitting under the hundred-year-old plane trees
whose giant interwining crowns arched over the square like the nave of
a church. The autumn sun shone weakly on the surrounding walls,
spreading as if through bull's-eye windows rings of golden light through
the dense foliage onto the little circular tables standing in long rows
before the cafés.]

It is also tempting to see in Roth's incorruptible 'Hero of Solferino' a counter-
figure to Latzko's anonymous 'Victor of ***' who personifies the mendacious
military hubris of the latter-day Empire from which Joseph Trotta so
conspicuously dissociates himself. Whereas Trotta ensures the withdrawal of
the offending schoolbooks mythologising his saving the Emperor's life,
Latzko's self-serving coffee-house commander basks in the knowledge that
every child in the land now recognises him thanks to the patriotic postcards
bearing his portrait.

Whereas in 'Der Sieger' Strauss's waltz fills the air of a town which war
has made as 'lebendig und sorglos fröhlich' ('lively and happily carefree') as

Vienna's Graben on a spring day in peacetime (p. 100), 'Heldentod' ('A Hero's Death') rings to the sound of the 'Rácóczy March', music as redolent of Magyar patriotism as the 'Blue Danube' is of Viennese 'Gemütlichkeit'. It is, however, a bitter and intense narration whose hyper-realism teeters on the edge of surrealism. It traces the last, hallucinatory hours of the kindly Hungarian Reserve Lieutenant Otto Kádár as he lies in a field hospital swathed in mounds of cotton wool. He had lost half of his head when a shell came crashing through the dugout where he and his fellow officers were listening to a wind-up gramophone blaring out the Rácóczy March. As his life ebbs away, a single image dominates what is left of his mind: with grotesque precision the intact record had flown throught the air and landed precisely on the empty space above Cadet Meltzar's shoulders where seconds before there had been a head:

> Man hatte ihm den Kopf vertauscht! Den hübschen, blonden, achtzehnjährigen Kopf abgeschraubt und mit einer zerkritzelten schwarzen Scheibe ersetzt, die nichts konnte als den Rakoczymarsch krächzen. (pp. 161–2)

> [They had swapped his head! The handsome, blond, eighteen-year-old head had been screwed off and replaced by a scratched black disc which could only croak out the Rácóczy March.]

Meltzar had been a stereotypical young officer, conditioned by war propaganda and the values of the military caste with which he identified himself totally. Since he spoke like a recording in life, there is a horrible symmetry in the replacement of his head by the record. Obsessed by this image, the hallucinatory cries of the dying Kádár drive the other casualties to distraction. Yet when death finally comes, it is grotesquely misunderstood. Obsessed by the sound of the record and its transposition onto Meltzar's headless torso, the dying Kádár's final demented utterance is a rendition of the Rácóczy March. For his comrades, however, whose responses are also as predictable as the tracks on a gramophone record, this is not evidence of a shattered mind, but additional proof of unswerving patriotism:

> – Der arme Teufel dort unten hat endlich ausgelitten. Als echter Ungar! Mit dem Rakoczymarsch auf den Lippen! – (p. 168)

> ['The poor devil down there has finally suffered his last. As a real Magyar! With the Rácóczy March on his lips!']

Although Szabó omits 'Feuertaufe' ('Baptism of Fire') and 'Der Kamerad' ('The Comrade') from his recent anthology on the grounds that although readable they are not particularly original, these are the stories which most consistently reflect Latzko's direct experience of fighting in battle and the mental breakdown he subsequently suffered. It is no coincidence that characters who have lost their reason occur repeatedly in both *Menschen im Krieg* and in *Friedensgericht*. In the figure of the deeply humane yet militarily insufficient Captain Heinrich Marschner in 'Feuertaufe', the longest story in the collection, Latzko gives a disturbing insight into a necessary truth of war: that scrupulous, honest, caring officers do not necessarily make the best leaders of men or the most efficient protectors of the troops under them. In prose which graphically recreates the physical and mental realities of life on the Isonzo front, Latzko relates the horror and the pity of war.[23] The reader cannot but pity Marschner, as he himself pities the middle-aged Viennese conscripts condemned to death as they march into battle under his hesitant and compassionate command. His deputy, the fearless and fanatical twenty-year-old Weixler, is doubtless the 'better' officer, albeit a far inferior human being. He treats Marschner with a disdain tantamount to subordination. Both perish after a direct hit on their trench. Marschner, however, dies with a certain satisfaction: he survives just long enough to see the disembowelled Weixler realise the meaning of the suffering he has hitherto contemptuously refused to acknowledge all around him:

> – Er leidet! – ... durchflammte es Marschner. – Er leidet! ... jauchzte es in ihm. Und ein Leuchten ergoß sich über seine Blässe ...
>
> Die ersten Soldaten, die durch den hochgetürmten Erdwall endlich bis zu ihm vordrangen, fanden ihn schon entseelt; um seinen Mund schwebte, trotz der gräßlichen Verwundung, ein zufriedenes, fast glückliches Lächeln. (pp. 95–6)

> ['He's suffering!' ... the thought burnt within Marschner. 'He's suffering!' ... he felt exultantly. And a glow spread over his pallor ...
>
> The first soldiers who finally penetrated through the piled-up bank of earth found him already dead; despite the horrific wound a contented, almost happy smile hovered around his mouth.]

It is no coincidence that 'Feuertaufe', the story of an inadequate field-officer, dragged back into uniform from his successful career as a civil engineer, is followed by the biting satire of 'Der Sieger' and its non-combatant general. Nor is it a coincidence that 'Der Sieger' is followed by the howl of anguish which is 'Der Kamerad', the portrait of a personality destroyed by the events which have revitalised the absentee 'Victor of ***'. 'Der Kamerad' is the quasi-demented confession of an officer whose sanity has collapsed under the weight of his experiences on the Isonzo. Set in the Görz/Gorizia region, where Latzko himself spent time in a field hospital after the collapse of his own reason in 1916, this first-person narrative, frequently cast as an interior monologue, takes the form of an imagined report to the unimaginative doctors who believe their patient can be cured of his memories: 'Soll ich von meinem Gedächtnis geheilt werden, wie von einem Leiden?' ('Am I to be cured of my memory as if of some complaint? – p. 133). It is evident that Latzko's admiration for the medical profession was not enhanced by his experiences at their hands: 'Die Ärzte glauben nur an Dinge, die *sind*' ('Doctors believe only in things which are *tangible*' – p. 129).

Though ostensibly mad, endlessly haunted by the 'comrade' whose death he witnessed some fourteen months previously, this narrator is truly sane: for not to be driven crazy by the ceaseless violence, disfigurement and dismemberment which was the reality of the 1914–18 war was a deeper form of insanity, encouraged by the mindless inculcation of propaganda both within the military and through reports in the press. In language which reaches an almost lyrical intensity, the nameless narrator castigates the truly sick:

> Krank sind die anderen. Krank sind jene, die mit strahlenden Augen Siegesnachrichten lesen und eroberte Quadratkilometer leuchtend über Leichenberge aufsteigen sehen … Krank sind alle, die das Stöhnen, Knirschen, Heulen, Krachen, Bersten, – das Jammern, Fluchen und Verrecken überhören können, weil rings um sie der Alltag murmelt, oder selige Nachtruhe liegt.
> Krank sind die Tauben und Blinden, nicht ich! (pp. 132–3)

> [The others are sick. Sick are those whose eyes gleam as they read reports of victories and see conquered square kilometers rise radiantly over mountains of corpses … Sick are all those who can fail to hear the groaning, gnashing, howling, crashing, bursting, – the wailing, cursing and dying, because around them everyday life murmurs on or nocturnal peace reigns.
> Sick are the deaf and the blind, not me.]

Hardened though we may be by a century which has witnessed so much violence, much of it preserved on celluloid as well as in print, the directness of the narration in 'Der Kamerad' still sears into the imagination. For the narrator of 'Der Kamerad', cursed by a photographic memory, the imagination is the same as a camera,

> weil jeder Mensch aus seinen Erinnerungen gebaut ist und nur lebt, solange er wie eine geladene Kamera durchs Leben geht … Ja, muß man denn, um als 'geistig normal' zu gelten, sein Gehirn wie Schwamm und Schiefertafel handhaben, Bilder, die gräßlichste Not in die Seele gebrannt, auf Kommando wegwerfen können, wie man Seiten aus einem Photographiealbum reißt? (p. 133f.)

> [because everyone is built up of his memories and only lives as long as he goes through life like a loaded camera … Must we then, in order to count as 'mentally normal', handle our brains like a slate and sponge and be able on command to throw away images which deepest affliction has burnt into our souls, like tearing pages out of a photograph album?]

For the narrator of 'Der Kamerad', in truth the voice of Latzko himself, the long-term fate of *Menschen im Krieg*, in a century which was before long to endure even greater horrors than the Isonzo, would merely have been further confirmation of the insanity of the world. The time has still to arrive which will bear out the prophecy of the book's second motto: 'Ich weiß gewiß, die Zeit wird einmal kommen, wo alles denkt wie ich' ('I know for certain that the time will come when everyone thinks as I do').

The novel *Friedensgericht*, coming in the wake of Latzko's enormous success with *Menschen im Krieg*, is an altogether more ambitious piece of work. Composed between autumn 1917 and June 1918, with an English translation entitled *Judgment of Peace* following in 1919, the novel is sometimes overburdened with dialogue lifted out of an anti-war tract. However, Latzko has for the most part enough skill as a story-teller to drive his narrative along despite the discursive interludes. *Friedensgericht* is not, as has been maintained, a further collection of novellas, rather it is a prose equivalent of the contemporary 'Stationendrama', following the life story a single main character, Georg Gadsky, who provides the links between the six discrete sections. The novel bears a dedication which speaks for itself as an indication of the work's humanist, pacifist, internationalist stance: 'Meinem großen Landsmann in Menschenliebe: ROMAIN ROLLAND zu eigen' ('Dedicated to ROMAIN ROLLAND, my great compatriot in the love of mankind').[24] In a letter to Rolland of 30 October 1918, Zweig reveals that *Friedensgericht* was being distributed for propaganda purposes amongst German prisoners of war, but in an edition whose dedication, which might have been counterproductive, was missing:

> Ich kann nicht glauben, daß Latzko es weiß. Aber wenn er es nicht weiß und es sich wirklich so verhält (was man nachprüfen müßte), spielt ihm sein Verleger einen schändlichen Streich.[25]

> [I can't believe that Latzko knows about it. But should he not know, and if this really is the case (which would have to be checked out), his publisher is playing a dirty trick on him.]

Like the war writings of Karl Kraus, *Friedensgericht* is a protest against the ideology of heroic sacrifice peddled in the press. Unlike Kraus it does not attack the press as such, except in 'Kriegsgefangen' where a French character complains about the French press, and Gadsky expresses his contempt for the world of the newspapers:

> Hassenswert waren nur die verdammten Federhelden, die fern vom Schuß ihre Phantasie schweifen ließen, ohne nach den armen Teufeln zu fragen, die mit gebrochenen Knochen für das so verdiente Zeilenhonorar bezahlen mußten! (p. 222)

> [Worthy of hatred were only the accursed heroes in the war of words, who, well out of gunshot range, let their imagination roam without asking about the poor devils who had to pay with their broken bones while they are paid by the line!]

In the opening section, 'Feldgrau' ('Field grey'), two volunteer recruits in the German army await their commissions and first posting to the front: the arrogant and conservative Gadsky, 33 years old, an internationally acclaimed pianist, and the delicate, dreamy, but high-minded liberal poet, Artur Weiler, who is about three years younger (p. 54).[26] Weiler is representative of the many left-inclined German writers and intellectuals who joined up out of a vague sense of defending a threatened culture:

> Er war ja nie so richtig kriegsbegeistert gewesen, hatte sich nur mühselig eine Erklärung zurechtgezimmert; so etwa, als stände er vor seinen Regalen, und verteidigte mit Fäusten und Zähnen die Bücher, die Eindringliche zerfetzen und besudeln wollten. (p. 52)

> [He had never been all that enamoured of the war, only with difficulty had he knocked together an explanation; as if he were standing in front of his shelves and defending with fists and teeth the books which intruders wanted to shred up and defile.]

Chance has brought Gadsky together with Weiler, whom he had long admired, and whose works he had defended 'gegen unverständige Urteile ... Sofort war eine Zauberinsel um sie geschlossen' ('against ignorant judgments ... At once a magic isle had closed around them') (pp. 10–11). Once in the army, Weiler is horrified by the nature of Prussian militarism. Made to go over the top in battle, he kills a Frenchman and goes incurably mad, a development reminiscent of similar episodes in *Menschen im Krieg*. From the outset the novel attacks not so much things 'German' as Prussian militarism (wonderfully caricatured in the appalling figure of Feldwebel Stuff) and its dehumanising effects:

> Die Dümmsten selbst empfanden dumpf den Widerspruch zwischen dem stürmischen Bedürfnis der Bevölkerung, die Vaterlandsverteidiger zu ehren, und der Behandlung, die ihnen in der Kaserne zuteil ward. (p. 3f.)

> [Even the most stupid were dimly aware of the contradiction between the enthusiastic needs of the population to honour the defenders of the fatherland and the treatment meted out to them in the barracks.]

A problematic feature of 'Feldgrau' (and indeed of *Friedensgericht* as a whole) is the manner in which anti-war writing rubs shoulders with a 'Künstlerroman' based initially on generational conflict: Gadsky's lover, the Prussian officer's daughter and opera singer Mathilde von Moellnitz, has alienated her family not just by becoming an artist, but by living with a man without the blessing of church or state; Gadsky's artistic ambitions meet with resolute opposition from his philistine family; Weiler's mother has never forgiven him for not following the 'ehrbaren Beruf' ('honourable profession') of his father (p. 26). The painterly ambitions of the young and sensitive Ensign Krülow, a third major character introduced in this chapter, were thwarted by his family's expectations that he would join the army. Krülow's father is a Prussian general; his mother, however, was an Austrian,

und hat sich nie ganz bei uns eingewöhnt ... Wenn sie mit mir
spazieren fuhr, machte sie sich oft über unsere Kiefernwälder lustig, die
so kerzengerade ausgerichtet dastehen, wie Soldaten zur Inspizierung.
'Kein Grashalm' – sagte sie bitter, – 'darf hier so wachsen, wie es ihm
und dem lieben Gott Spaß macht!' (p. 35)

[and never really felt at home with us ... When she took me out for a
drive she often made fun of our pine forests, lined up as straight as
candles like soldiers on parade. 'Not a blade of grass' – she said bitterly,
– 'can grow here to please either itself or the dear Lord.']

It comes as little surprise in the context of Latzko's war fiction that such a
gentle and fine human being as Krülow should lose his life in battle. Indeed,
to a reader coming to *Friedensgericht* after reading *Menschen im Krieg*, his
death seems inevitable.

Weiler functions as the mouthpiece for an extended critique of the German
bourgeois attitude to war, where the sentimental jargon of personal sacrifice,
as enunciated by the generation of the fathers, is contrasted with their
hardheaded regard for money. How, Weiler asks, are they able to come to
terms with the loss of their human 'investment' on the battlefield while at the
same time demanding a good return on the capital they invest in the state by
means of war loans? Is their money really more important than their own flesh
and blood? How can they place so many conditions upon the use of their
money, but none upon the abuse of their children? (p. 28) Germany might
have prided itself on being the 'Land der Dichter und Denker', but Weiler
has his doubts:

Die meisten wollen stolz und selbstzufrieden sagen können: 'Mein Sohn
hat heute das Doktorat gemacht', oder ist 'Bureauchef, Regierungsrat,
Direktor geworden; hat die Tochter des reichen Kaufmann So und So
gefreit!' (p. 26)

[Most people want to be able to say with pride and self-satisfaction: 'My
son got his doctorate today', or 'he's been appointed office manager, has
been made a First Secretary, a director, has married the daughter of the
rich merchant so and-so!']

The inference is clear: a country which has sold out to conformist social
attitudes will have few ethical qualms about war.

The novel depicts the foulness of war with the same technique of intense
realism already employed in *Menschen im Krieg*. Only towards the end does
Friedensgericht stretch the credulity of the reader in its striving to make capital
out of Latzko's Rollandesque belief in the reconciliation of France and
Germany. Moving away from the field of battle, the penultimate chapter
'Kriegsgefangen' ['Captured in battle'] is set in Switzerland, where wounded
soldiers of all the warring nations were gathered together under the auspices
of the Red Cross. There they were given medical treatment, and once
convalescence was complete prisoners were exchanged. In a chapter which

calls to mind Schiller's verdict on the conclusion of *Egmont* as a somersault into the world of opera, the recuperating Gadsky remembers with fond regret the days of his captivity in a French POW camp. The commandant, one of his most fervent admirers, could remember the smallest detail from a Gadsky concert of five years before, and treated him not as an enemy but a friend, even providing him with a grand piano. In this episode, where a Frenchman honours the achievements of a German musician, Latzko may have been alluding to the work of Romain Rolland, whose aim had been above all to explain Germany, and especially German music and art, to the French people.

After his transfer to Lucerne, Gadsky strikes up another deep (and officially forbidden) friendship with a French soldier, an extended conversation with whom provides the bulk of 'Kriegsgefangen'. It is their last tête-à-tête, for the next day Gadsky will be shipped back to Germany and the waiting Feldwebel Stuff. Their debate is full of mutual tolerance and understanding, despite intellectual positions which are poles apart: as in earlier disputes with Weiler, Gadsky remains the often misanthropic cynic with a deep distrust of Germany. Merlier, on the other hand, recapitulates Weiler's faith in mankind, and even in Germany, a country where he received some of his education. This spirit of tolerance and reconciliation is not, however, allowed to conclude a novel which was written as war still raged. Sailing towards the German shore, returning to what he now realises is a true 'Kriegsgefangenschaft' ('imprisonment *by* war'), Gadsky throws himself into Lake Constance, but even before hitting the water he regrets his actions. However, the cries of 'man overboard' remain unheard amidst a cacophony of voices bellowing

> In der Heimat, in der Heimat
> Da gibt's ein Wiedersehn!
>
> [Back home, back home,
> There we'll meet again!]

Aesthetically speaking it would have been more satisfactory had Latzko ended his novel with the death of Gadsky. Instead, however, he leaves us with the delirium of the insane poet Weiler in the chapter entitled 'Die Rache' ('Revenge'). This final section is not lacking in elements bordering on kitsch as Weiler's nurse, with her 'welkendes Altjungferngesicht' ('wilting old maid's face') (p. 268) loses her heart to the hopelessly deranged artist. Believing in his delusion that peace has finally arrived, Weiler demands that the officer who had constantly threatened him with court martial ('Kriegsgericht') now be summoned before the tribunal of peace, the 'Friedensgericht' of the novel's title (p. 271). For his pains, he is constrained in a bath of freezing water, comforted by Sister Mally. His gaze boring through the walls of the asylum, he murmers defiantly words which are both hopeful and menacing: 'Warten!' ... 'Nur warten!' ... ('Wait!' ... 'Just wait!' ... – p. 278).

Latzko's (anti-)war fiction is most concise and hard-edged in *Menschen im Krieg*. To a large extent *Friedensgericht* merely recapitulates, at greater length, the motifs and devices already encountered in the earlier collection. The strengths of the novel are the same as those of *Menschen im Krieg*, but it is helped neither by its discursive passages nor by its proximity to the 'Künstlerroman'. There is also a loss of immediacy in Latzko's decision to shift the setting away from the Austrian front, of which he had intimate experience, to the Franco-German conflict which he only knew at second hand. Indeed, Stefan Zweig, whose admiration for Latzko was great, considered it a thoroughly bad book.[27] In both works, however, the vigour of Latzko's moral commitment to peace is beyond question, as is also his Krausian conviction that the enemy is just as much an internal as an external one. His works may have had no tangible impact on the readiness of Europeans to commit acts of martial barbarism, but at least his hope for a reconciliation between Germany and France has become the plank upon which a new Europe is now being built. Like Siegfried Sassoon, whose *Memoirs of an Infantry Officer* were only published in 1930, Latzko was a free spirit who deserves to be remembered for 'his bleak realism, his contempt for war leaders and patriotic cant, and his compassion for his comrades'.[28]

Notes

1. The drama was written during the war, appearing first in *Die Fackel* (1918/1919) before publication in revised form in 1922.
2. See W. E. Yates, 'Franz Werfel and Austrian Poetry of the First World War', in *Franz Werfel. An Austrian Writer reassessed*, ed. Lothar Huber (Oxford/New York/Munich, 1989), pp. 15–37. See especially the fine bibliography.
3. The only modern edition is the anthology *Andreas Latzko, Der Doppelpatriot. Texte 1900–1932*, ed. János Szabó (Munich and Budapest, 1993). The collection reprints out of sequence four of the six stories in *Menschen im Krieg* ('Der Sieger'; 'Der Abmarsch'; 'Heimkehr'; 'Heldentod') and 'Der Verräter', the fourth chapter of *Friedensgericht*. Latzko's order of publication in *Menschen im Krieg* is: 'Der Abmarsch'; 'Feuertaufe'; 'Der Sieger'; 'Der Kamerad'; 'Heldentod'; 'Heimkehr'.
4. Particularly noteworthy in this context is Weiss's story 'Franta Zlin'. For works on Weiss in general see Franz Haas, *Der Dichter von der traurigen Gestalt: Leben und Werk von Ernst Weiß* (Frankfurt, 1986); *Ernst Weiß – Seelenanalytiker und Erzähler von europäischem Rang*, ed. Peter Engel and Hans-Harald Müller (Berne, 1992).
5. Romain Rolland, *Das Gewissen Europas. Tagebuch der Kriegsjahre 1914–1919*, vol. 3 (Berlin, 1983), p. 543.
6. See Gustav Huonker, *Literaturszene Zürich. Menschen, Geschichten und Bilder 1914 bis 1945* (Zürich, 1986), p. 41.
7. *Romain Rolland/Stefan Zweig: Briefwechsel 1910–1940*, vol. 1, ed. Waltraud Schwarze (Berlin, 1987), p. 396. Paula Latzko died on 30 April 1919.
8. Ibid., p. 324.
9. Ibid., p. 296.
10. Ibid., vol. 2, p. 251.
11. Ibid., vol. 2, p. 291.
12. See Ferdinand Borges, *Andreas Latzko; rebel tegen het onrecht* (Antwerp, 1954).
13. *Andreas Latzko*, ed. Szabó, p. 219. The short story 'Ein Duell' (1911) (Szabó, pp. 18–24) portrays traditional Jewish values triumphant over Gentile capitalism, but the story has a strangely mythical tone which seems to divorce it from contemporary concerns.

14. J. Szabó, 'Ein Österreicher aus Ungarn oder ein Ungar aus Österreich? Zum Lebenswerk von Andreas Latzko', in: *'Kakanien'. Aufsätze zur österreichischen und ungarischen Literatur, Kunst und Kultur um die Jahrhundertwende*, ed. E. Thurnher, W. Weiss, J. Szabó and A. Tamás (Budapest and Vienna, 1991), p. 365.

15. Quoted Huonker, *Literaturszene Zürich*, p. 41.

16. C. E. Williams, *The Broken Eagle: The Politics of Austrian Literature from Empire to Anschluss* (London, 1974), p. 123.

17. Huonker, *Literaturszene Zürich*, p. 41. Demand fell away rapidly after the war, and Rascher was left with 15,000 unsold copies.

18. Karl Kraus, *Die Fackel*, nos. 462–71 (9 October 1917), 175. This translation appears in Williams, *The Broken Eagle*, p. 123.

19. *Andreas Latzko*, ed. Szabó, p. 226. See also: M. Stern, *Expressionismus in der Schweiz*, 1 (Berne and Stuttgart, 1981), p. 244; W. Krull, *Politische Prosa des Expressionismus* (Berne, 1982), pp. 127–141.

20. A. Latzko, *Menschen im Krieg*, 6–10 Tausend (Zürich, 1918), p. 9. All further page references will be to this edition, and follow the quotation.

21. Latzko retains the Hungarian convention of using dashes instead of quotation marks to indicate direct speech.

22. Joseph Roth, *Werke*, 1, *Das journalistische Werk 1913–1923*, ed. K. Westermann and F. Hackert (Cologne, 1989), p. 38.

23. It would be interesting to compare *Menschen im Krieg* with *Am Isonzo* by Kraus's *bête noire* Alice Schalek, also published in 1917.

24. Rolland had published a favourable review of *Menschen im Krieg* in *Les Tablettes* in December 1917. See William T. Starr, *Romain Rolland and a World at War* (Evanston, IL, 1956), p. 154.

25. *Rolland/Zweig. Briefwechsel*, vol. 1, p. 386.

26. All page references are to A. Latzko, *Friedensgericht* (Zürich, 1918).

27. *Andreas Latzko*, ed. Szabó, p. 229.

28. *The Oxford Companion to English Literature*, ed. Margaret Drabble (Oxford, 1985), p. 867.

Misogyny and the Myth of Masculinity in Joseph Roth's *Radetzkymarsch*

Martha Wörsching

Over the years, many critics have analysed Roth's work in the context of its time, as the product of a period of dramatic historical, socio-political and economic transformation in Europe between the two World Wars; they have focused on his political or literary themes and tried to explain his conspicuous political conversion from socialist and pacifist to Austrian monarchist. He has perplexed his readers as the author of both the 'arch-Austrian *Radetzkymarsch* and the arch-Jewish *Hiob*'.[1] At the same time he has been seen as the prophet of the coming Holocaust which in fact he only escaped by drinking himself to death, dying in exile in Paris just before the outbreak of the war. He has been praised by one of his editors and friends, Hermann Kesten, as one of the century's best narrators in the German language, although Kesten adds: 'Im Leben und in der Kunst hat Roth die "große Komödie" gespielt; und er hat viele Masken getragen' (Roth played 'high comedy' in both life and art; and he wore many masks).[2]

Most critics agree that his literary work at its best is a prime example of the depiction of the universal *human* condition of alienation and rootlessness. Yet Roth's very mythologising and mask-making in his life and work can be seen as a reflection of his own inner conflicts as a *man* trying to adapt to the demands of hegemonic masculinity. It is of course not surprising that any interpretation of Roth's work will begin to make sense of it by actively identifying with the male protagonist; but as a result of feminist theory this seemingly unproblematic identification with the hero or anti-hero has been challenged, and we can begin to question the fundamentally sexist equation between 'man' (as the male of the human species) and 'human being', thus rejecting man's particular experience as universal or as a manifestation of the 'human condition'. Thus, assertions like: 'Das grundlegende Problem im Werk Joseph Roths ist folgendes: Der *Mensch* befindet sich in einem Zustand der Isoliertheit' (The basic problem in Roth's work is the following: *The human being* exists in a state of isolation) may be typical for male-stream literary criticism, but at the same time it challenges us to consider more closely the gendered nature of his work, and to explain it not as a description of the universal human condition, but as a particular type of masculinity as ideology.[3]

Thus, on closer consideration, Roth's 'backward-looking utopia', as Marcel Reich-Ranicki has called it,[4] turns out to be a place inhabited by men only, being 'cleansed' of women; in this patriarchal mythology, women are dismissed in the asides or dealt with as exasperations, as diversions from the straight path towards male individual autonomy.

Therefore, in addition to the perspectives of race, class and history, Roth's *Radetzkymarsch* deserves to be analysed from the perspective of gender, as an ideology of Jewish 'non-hegemonic masculinity'.[5] This seems all the more worthwhile as this novel, published in 1932, is generally considered his most accomplished work; it brought him the acclaim he was waiting for – and, ironically, would have brought him the money he so desperately needed, but for the fact that soon after its publication the Nazis came to power; his books were burned and his publisher went bankrupt. Roth left Germany in January 1933 to live in exile until his death. The novel marks a high point in his writing, but also his turn towards Habsburg. It seems as if with the anti-heroic protagonist, Roth had produced a mask for himself which he increasingly filled, life strangely imitating art. The role of the 'k.u.k. Offizier', which he had never been in real life, became a projection which was taken at face-value by Austrian monarchists themselves; thus, Otto von Habsburg, the pretender to the crown, sent a delegation of Austrian legitimists to Roth's funeral.[6]

I propose to discuss the novel as masculinist myth, highlighting the misogynist depiction of women in relation to the main narrative of male individuation, and placing it in the context of the novel as a mythology of masculinity, as the product of an author with a problematic male socialisation, born into a Jewish community in a remote corner of the Habsburg empire, during the last years of the nineteenth century. I will then attempt to explain the particular content of this masculinist myth in the context of Roth's life-long search for the absent father and the struggle to free himself from maternal dependence, which, according to the author, could be achieved through the creation of a *spiritual* patriarchy, as Roth put it himself, an 'Aristokratie des Geistes ... ihr kann man niemals die *geistige* Herrschaft streitig machen' (an aristocracy of the mind ... whose *spiritual* rule can never be disputed).

The Novel as Masculinist Myth

Roth's 'historical' novel about the decline of the Austrian Empire is, of course, not a portrayal of the actual historical development of Emperor Franz Joseph's reign, but can be seen as a utopian construct of 'life praxis' which, in the author's view, is the only avenue left for the artistic (male) genius; it can be understood in the context of Roth's experiences as an individual who became politically and socially aware just before the outbreak of the war, who lived through the war and its aftermath, the formation and destruction of the first republican states and the rise of fascism in Germany and Austria. Yet the gendered nature of this construct should be investigated more deeply in the context of Roth's highly problematic identity as a Jewish man. The 'poetic reality' of the narrative in *Radetzkymarsch* is a quest for male individuation which is paradoxically achieved in the end by embracing the legacy of archetypal patriarchs.

At the centre of Roth's novel is the development of the male individual, searching for his rightful place in a number of male lines of biological or spiritual grandfather-father-son relationships: there is the simple Slovenian gendarme of farming stock, father of the 'Hero of Solferino' who risked his life for the young Emperor Franz Joseph and was elevated to the nobility; the latter's son, as high-ranking civil servant, is the father of Carl Joseph von Trotta, the central figure who, as a young officer, lives in the shadow of his famous grandfather, and, as the anti-hero, achieves individuation in death. Other lines of male relationships – and related in friendship and mutual trust to the main Trotta line – consist of Carl Joseph's Jewish friend Dr Demant with his 'biblical' grandfather; Jacques, the loyal old servant; and Carl Joseph's faithful Slav peasant orderly. The construct is held together by the spirit of Emperor Franz Joseph as the ageing 'father' of his loyal subjects.

The concepts of male 'dynasty' ('Geschlecht'), 'friendship', 'brotherliness' and 'personal loyalty between men' are poetic variations of the same theme of male mutual obligation and trust. The drama is played out in a homosocial world of the cadet school, the army, civil service, and the Imperial court. There is no room here to argue more clearly how far these relations are hierarchical and undemocratic;[8] what I want to do instead is to focus on what is hidden in the margins of the novel, namely the particular way in which women are depicted here and the function allocated to women in relation to the narrative which creates an edifice of male 'spiritual' rule.

In the novel, the drama of male individuation enacted by its central character is developed on a stage where women are for the most part marginal (for instance, mothers are mentioned only in asides and die an early death, in contrast to fathers who reach a biblical age) or are drawn as lifeless stereotypes; nevertheless, they are used to mark important stages in the development towards the autonomy of the male individual. Yet if women appear on the scene at all, they are depicted as superfluous and irritating, as temptation to male self-determination and autonomy, and as steps on the way to male adulthood. As objects in relation to the male protagonists, women have no subject status themselves. Sexual love is depicted as a risk to 'life', as engulfment and annihilation of individuality: thus, for instance, when the central figure, Carl Joseph, is made to renounce his 'maternal' first lover who dies in childbirth, he is described as being at the 'Grenzposten zwischen der Liebe und dem Leben ... wieder der Welt zurückgegeben', and he 'meldete seinem Vater die Rückkehr, blaß, kurz und entschlossen, wie es sich für Männer geziemt' (... at the frontier post between love and life ... given back to the world. ... reporting his return to his father, pale, concise and decisive, as is seemly for men).[9]

This first main 'temptation' on the way to 'becoming a man' prefigures the structure of the novel, and although the points where the path of male progress is temporarily held up by encounters with the female are treated as minor deviations and given very little space in the narrative as a whole, I want to draw them out here at some length to exemplify my suggestion that in this novel, hegemonic masculinity is predicated on the submission of the female. This gendered mechanism between male power and female powerlessness is described by the psychoanalyst Karen Horney in her article 'The Dread of Women' – published incidentally in the same year as *Radetzkymarsch* – where she takes issue with Freud's notions of gender, and where she underlines 'two key points: the extent to which masculinity is a structure of overcompensation and the fundamental connection of the making of masculinity with the subordination of women'.[10]

Roth's portrayal of women in *Radetzkymarsch* must be seen in its relation to his attempt to construct an image of the autonomous male. Thus, it is worthwhile to concentrate more closely on a number of typical depictions of women in the novel, which, in the narrative context, fall in a number of categories all implying different degrees or types of subordination.

First, women as sexual beings are objectified as commodities, animals or as types of food which may be tempting, appetising or nauseating; this is exemplified in the novel through the figures of prostitutes and adulterous lovers. Analogies are established between women and gambling (pp. 144, 302); women are portrayed as market goods to be picked or 'left on the shelf' by the discerning male, for instance:

> Er besuchte die Mädchen selten, wählte sorgfältig unter ihnen und besaß noch sechs Gulden, als er in den Sommerferien wieder heimkam (p. 153).

> [He visited girls seldom, chose carefully between them and still had six Gulden left when he returned home again for the summer holidays.]

Similarly, women are depicted as tainted consumables, as in the scene of the visit to the local brothel, when the officers are shown to feel obliged to follow the call 'zu saurer Freude. Kindermann war der Ohnmacht nahe, wenn er nackte Frauen roch, das weibliche Geschlecht machte ihm Übelkeiten' (p. 206: 'to sour joy. Kindermann was close to fainting when he smelled naked women, the female sex made him feel nauseous').

Though Kindermann is clearly depicted as homosexual (and generally in an unsympathetic way), physical disgust is nevertheless the feeling the narrator wants to convey in relation to the women, but not in relation to their customers:

> Die seidenen Röcke der Frau Resi Horwath raschelten gleichzeitig in allen Winkeln des Hauses. Ihre großen, schwarzen Augenbälle rollten ohne Richtung und Ziel in ihrem breiten, mehligen Antlitz herum, weiß und groß wie Klaviertasten schimmerte in ihrem breiten Mund das falsche Gebiß. ... Die nackten Mädchen schwirrten ihnen entgegen, eine emsige Schar von weißen Hennen (pp. 207–8).

[Frau Resi Horwath's silk skirts rustled in every corner of the house simultaneously. Her great black eyeballs rolled round and round without aim or focus in her broad, pasty face; her false teeth shimmered white and large like piano keys in her wide mouth. ... The naked girls fluttered towards them, a busy flock of white hens.]

The analogy between women and food combined with the object status of militaristic submission is evident in the following excerpt from the description of a lavish feast:

> Und die runden, rosafarbenen Schinkenräder, von einer großen, silbernen, dreizackigen Gabel bewacht, reihten sich gehorsam aneinander auf länglicher Schüssel, begleitet von rotbäckigen Radieschen, die an kleine knusprige Dorfmädchen erinnerten (p. 287).

> [And the round and pink wheels of ham, guarded by a large three-pronged silver fork, fell in line obediently on a long dish, accompanied by red-cheeked radishes, reminiscent of small crisp village girls.]

In a similar vein, the nostalgia for bucolic life and feudal gender relations is expressed in the portrayal of women as nature, as the following sentence shows: 'Daheim wohnten sie in niedrigen Hütten, befruchteten nächtens die Frauen und tagsüber die Felder!' (p. 195: 'At home, they used to live in low huts, inseminating the women by night and the fields by day!')

If women as sexual species are experienced as threatening and therefore have to be depicted as strictly controlled, thus reduced to the non-human and inanimate, then individual women also appear as a de-individualised, de-humanised sexual threat to the rational, spiritual male:

> Sie stand in den blauen Höschen, die Quaste, wie eine Waffe in der Rechten, gegen ihren Mann gewendet und sagte mit zwitschernder Stimme: .... Jetzt saß sie, den Oberkörper in den Hüften verrenkt, ein lebloses Wesen, Modell aus Wachs und seidener Wäsche. Unter dem Vorhang ihrer langen schwarzen Wimpern erschienen die hellen Augen, falsche, nachgemachte Blitze aus Eis. Ihre schmalen Hände lagen auf den Höschen wie weiße Vögel, gestickt auf blauseidenem Grund (pp. 216–17).

> [She stood in her blue briefs, holding the powder-puff like a weapon in her right hand, turned towards her husband and said with a twittering voice: .... Now she sat, with her upper body twisted from the hips, a lifeless being, a wax model in silk underwear. Beneath the curtain of her long, black eyelashes the bright eyes appeared, false, imitation flashes of ice. Her slim hands lay on her briefs like white birds embroidered on a blue silken background.]

A favourite way of depicting women as posing an existential threat through their sexuality is in their role as predatory, false and/or ageing ('pretending to be youthful') lovers, as the following passages may show:

Die angenehmen Polster glitten ... tückisch und behutsam gegen den Leutnant. ... Wie der gefährliche Befehlshaber all der Kissen und Polster sah sie aus. ... Zu dem gefährlichen Geschlecht der schwachen Mörderinnen gehörte sie höchstwahrscheinlich. Man mußte trachten, unverzüglich ihrem Bereich zu entkommen. ... 'Witwen gehören verbrannt!', ... kam dem Leutnant gleichzeitig in den Sinn (pp. 249–51).

[The pleasant bolsters slid ... slyly and carefully towards the Lieutenant. She looked like the dangerous commander of all the pillows and bolsters. ... She probably belonged to the dangerous race of weak murderesses. One had to endeavour to escape her sphere without delay. ... 'Widows should be burned!', ... was the thought that simultaneously entered the Lieutenant's mind.]

Frau von Taussig war schön und nicht mehr jung. ... Sie brauchte Geld, und er [Herr von Taussig] war bequemer als ein Kind. ... (Sie liebte die Zeiten, in denen ihr Mann krank war.) (pp. 315–16)

[Frau von Taussig was beautiful and no longer young. ... She needed money, and he [Herr von Taussig] was less bother than a child. ... (She loved the times when her husband was ill.)]

Frau von Taussig stellte dem nahenden Alter junge Männer entgegen wie Dämme (p. 317).

[Against the approach of old age, Frau von Taussig put up young men, like dams.]

The 'dread of women' is evident in the depiction of women in their maternal and/or sexual relation to men, seen as imprisoning, infantilising and domesticating. This applies in *Radetzkymarsch* particularly to the portrayal of older women, as in the case of mothers and lovers. For instance, the reader is encouraged to identify with the father who is critical of the educational aspirations his wife projects onto their young son, as is suggested by a reference to 'das erste Lesebuch seines Sohnes, der gerade fünf Jahre alt geworden war und den ein Hauslehrer, dank dem Ehrgeiz der Mutter, die Nöte der Schule viel zu früh schmecken ließ' (p. 145: 'the first reading book of his son who had only just turned five and whom a private tutor, thanks to the ambition of the mother, provided with a foretaste of the miseries of school all too early'). The mother's 'crime' here is to attempt to 'discipline' the child's mind, and since education is defined as a male sphere, her efforts must be ridiculed as transgression.

But the maternal and sexual are described as threateningly diffuse and inextricably linked with each other. Thus, the fear of losing autonomy through any relations with women is expressed in the novel in numerous ways. It is particularly apparent in the relationship between Carl Joseph and Frau von Taussig, as the following quotations demonstrate:

Als die Nacht einbrach, bekam er Angst wie ein Kind vor der Dunkelheit (p. 318).

[When night fell, he was seized by fear of the dark like a child.]

Der Leutnant lag an ihrer Brust wie ein Kind. Sie hatte keine Angst mehr vor dem Alter. ... Sie sah ihn an, von mütterlichem Stolz erfüllt, ... wie eine Mutter (pp. 319–20).

[The lieutenant lay on her breast like a child. She was no longer afraid of old age. ... She looked at him, full of maternal pride, ... like a mother.]

... sie machte Carl Joseph jünger, ebenso wie sich selbst, dümmer und ratloser, ebenso wie sich selbst (p. 375).

[She made Carl Joseph younger, just as she made herself younger, more stupid and lost, just as she was herself.]

And as he walks along the Ringstrasse in Vienna, Carl Joseph sees 'Damen, die ihre Kavaliere spazieren führten, wie an Leinen' (p. 322: 'ladies who took their beaus for a walk, as if on leashes').

It seems that in *Radetzkymarsch*, the only way in which women can be seen as 'good' is by portraying them as personified charity in the role of the 'fallen angel' in reverse. Thus Carl Joseph's 'aging lover' Frau von Taussig mends her ways by renouncing sexuality and becomes a nurse, though her description also suggests a nun:

Es war das Angesicht einer gealterten Frau, die immer noch schön war. Ja, die Schwesternhaube verjüngte sie wie alle Frauen, weil es in ihrer Natur liegt, von Güte und Mitleid verjüngt zu werden und auch von den äußerlichen Abzeichen des Mitleids (p. 449).

[It was the face of a woman who had aged, who was still beautiful. Yes, the nurse's [or: nun's] wimple made her younger, like all women, for it is in their nature to be made younger by kindness and pity and also by the outward signs of pity.]

The novel's main narrative may thus be seen as the protagonist's progress towards male autarchy: the hero extracts himself from the ties of emotional and sexual dependence on women, which he achieves in the novel by exorcising women as subjects, so that male subjectivity can prevail in the context of patriarchal relations of domination.

On the other hand, in explicitly sex-less roles, women are depicted as conventional, pretentious, arrogant, stupid or disloyal to their Austrian roots. This is evident in the scarce but very dismissive references to Joseph Trotta's wife or his son's housekeeper:

Wohl dachte der Baron manchmal daran, seinen Vater zu besuchen. ... Mit der Frau sprach er nie von seiner Abkunft. Er fühlte, daß die

Tochter des älteren Staatsbeamtengeschlechts ein verlegener Hochmut von einem slowenischen Wachtmeister trennen würde. Also lud er den Vater nicht ein (p. 150).

[Sometimes the Baron did think of visiting his father. ... He never talked to his wife about his origins. He felt that the daughter of the older dynasty of civil servants would be set apart from the Slovene gendarme by an embarrassed arrogance. Therefore he did not invite his father.]

Fräulein Hirschwitz, die viele Jahre in Deutschland gelebt hatte, immer hochdeutsch sprach ..., nickte schwer und langsam. Es kostete sie offensichtlich Mühe, das bedeutende Gewicht des Haarknotens vom Nacken zu lösen und ihr Haupt zu einer zustimmenden Neigung zu veranlassen (p. 162).

[Fräulein Hirschwitz, who had lived in Germany for many years and always spoke High German ..., gave a slow and laboured nod. It obviously cost her a great effort to lift the considerable weight of her hair-bun from her neck and to cause her head to incline in agreement.]

Von Fräulein Hirschwitz nahm er wohlgemut kurzen Abschied, mit der unbestimmten und kühnen Hoffnung, sie nie mehr wiederzusehen (p. 282).

[He took his leave of Fräulein Hirschwitz in excellent spirits with the vague yet bold hope of never seeing her again.]

These numerous quotations are necessary to illustrate the extreme misogyny of the novel which literary criticism generally overlooks; for an author praised as one of the best in the German language, the style of many of these passages is surprisingly close to kitsch and pornography. Women are portrayed as objects of subordination, and this is often accompanied by a tone of ridicule otherwise absent in the novel as a whole. With the exception of the category of 'woman as asexual charity', the images are all highly negative. The array of male figures inhabiting this homosocial world of the novel spans a wide range of characteristics, from the evil Kapturak to the noble anti-hero. But what Roth here describes as 'real men' are men who have freed themselves from female domination and have found their safe place within a hierarchy of relationships built on loyalty to the patriarchal 'father' which even transcends death. This can be illustrated from Dr Demant's words to Carl Joseph:

'Es ist nicht wegen meiner Frau', sagt er. 'Das ist ja unwichtig geworden! Damit bin ich fertig. Es ist deinetwegen.' Er wartet auf eine Antwort und weiß, daß keine kommen wird. 'Es ist gut, ich danke dir!' sagt er ganz schnell (p. 221).

['It is not because of my wife', he says. 'That's not important any longer! That's all behind me now. It is because of you.' He waits for an answer, knowing that there will be none. 'It's all right, thank you!' he says very quickly.]

A lttle later, before Dr Demant's fatal duel, we are told:

> Ausgelöscht war die kindische Liebe zu seiner Frau. Die Eifersucht, vor wenigen Wochen noch ein schmerzlicher Brand in seinem Herzen, war ein kleines Häufchen Asche (p. 236).

> [His childish love for his wife was extinguished. The jealousy, only weeks ago a painful fire in his heart, was a small heap of ashes.]

These intense relationships between men are charged with repressed emotions 'seemly for men', as is shown not only in scenes between the 'spiritual' brothers Carl Joseph and Dr Demant, but also on many occasions between father and son:

> Er schickte noch einen zärtlichen Blick zu seinem Sohn. Gleich darauf aber hatte er Angst, man würde diesen Blick bemerken, und er senkte die Augen. ... Er küßte den Sohn auf die Wangen. Und obwohl er sagen wollte: Mach mir keinen Kummer! Ich liebe dich, mein Sohn!, sagte er lediglich: 'Halt dich gut!' – Denn die Trottas waren schüchterne Menschen (p. 299).

> [He gave his son a last tender glance. But then he feared immediately that this glance might be noticed, and he lowered his eyes. ... He kissed his son on both cheeks. And although he wanted to say: 'Don't cause me any sorrow! I love you, my son!', he said only: 'Keep well!' – For the Trottas were shy people.]

And similarly:

> Der Alte saß, beide Hände hingen schlaff ... . Er ist jung und töricht, dachte der Sohn. Er ist ein lieber, junger Tor mit weißen Haaren. Ich bin vielleicht sein Vater, der Held von Solferino. Ich bin alt geworden, er ist nur bejahrt. ... Carl Joseph schob seine Hand unter den Arm des Vaters. Er fühlte jetzt den mageren Arm des Alten wie vor Jahren beim abend-lichen Spaziergang in Wien. Er entfernte die Hand nicht mehr. Sie standen zusammen auf. Sie gingen Arm in Arm nach Hause (pp. 429–30).

> [The old man sat, his hands hanging limply .... 'He is young and foolish', thought the son. 'He is a dear, young fool with white hair. Perhaps I am his father, the hero of Solferino. I have aged, he is only old in years.' ... Carl Joseph slid his hand under his father's arm. He felt now the thin arm of the old man, just as he had years ago when they used to take their evening stroll in Vienna. He did not take his hand away any more. They got up together. They went home arm in arm.]

Even the very last pages of the novel continue this theme of yearning for

126

parental acclaim and male bonding, mixed with suppressed emotions, namely
when 'what is seemly' in this confined world of patriarchal men is recalled at
the death of the last Trotta by his chess-partner and friend:

> Doktor Skowronnek wartete, das Porträt des Helden von Solferino auf
> den Knien. Nach einigen Minuten erhob er sich, nahm die Hand Herrn
> von Trottas, beugte sich gegen die Brust des Bezirkshauptmanns,
> atmete tief und schloß die Augen des Toten. ... Und er spielte mit sich
> selbst eine Partie, schmunzelnd, von Zeit zu Zeit auf den leeren Sessel
> gegenüber blickend ... (pp. 454–5).

> [Dr Skowronnek waited, with the portrait of the hero of Solferino on
> his knees. After a few minutes he got up, took the hand of Herr von
> Trotta, bent towards the District Commissioner's chest, took a deep
> breath and closed the dead man's eyes. ... And he played a game of
> chess with himself, smiling to himself, glancing now and again at the
> empty chair opposite ....]

Thus the patriarch is to live on in his loyal friends and servants.

On the political level, *Radetzkymarsch* is Roth's expression of despair with
democracy and his identification with a non-nationalistic but dead monarchy.
On an artistic level, he hopes to have found an authoritative voice. The
narrative of spiritual aristocrats as an attitude of defiance seems the only
possible artistic praxis in the face of Nazi inhumanity. In 1933, the 'democratic experiment' of the Weimar Republic followed the homosocial world of
feudal military power into its grave, while the new and brutal but equally
homosocial patriarchy of the industrial 'final solution' came into its own, to
which the spiritual and cultural hegemony of 'fathers' could be no match. Yet
the illusion survived among Roth's followers, when Hermann Kesten, his
friend and later editor, in the introduction to the collected works published in
1956, still professed that he has towards Roth and other dead or living poets
'das Gefühl eines jüngeren Bruders' (feelings of a younger brother) whom he
loves 'mit der ... Liebe, mit der man seine Ahnen, seine Väter und Brüder
liebt' (with the ... love one feels for one's ancestors, one's fathers and
brothers), and he thus claims his own place in this male 'spiritual dynasty'.[11]

Joseph Roth's identification with the lost world of the Austrian monarchy
at a time when he saw any hope of a humane and democratic political present
disappearing, can be seen as the result of his 'experience of not belonging'[12]
and as a desperate expression of *wanting to belong*. An analysis of the 'poetic
reality' of the novel as masculinist ideology, placed in the context of his
background and life, can tell us more about the inner reality of the man Roth.

Roth's Background and Life – Myths and Facts

'Der Leutnant Trotta, das bin ich' (Lieutenant Trotta, that's me) is what
Roth claimed on more than one occasion during the last years of his life.[13] Yet

this is only one of the many legends he spread about his own background and career. In his work as a whole, the authorial voice is elusive: 'Bewußt oder halbbewußt hat er es eher darauf angelegt, daß unsere lesende Sympathie durch seine geschriebenen Menschen, Szenen, Meinungen hindurch immer wieder den Autor sucht' (Consciously or half-consciously, he rather intended us again and again to read sympathetically in search of the author right through his fictitious people, scenes and opinions).[14] If his voice is indeed elusive, then nevertheless his legends and silences about his past speak for themselves, and they indicate his embarrassment with his own origins, as Bronsen points out: 'Zu dem Intimbereich, ... gehörte unter anderem seine ostgalizische Herkunft' (Part of this intimate area ... was, among other things, his East Galician [Jewish] background),[15] while the absence of a father who, because of the outbreak of mental illness, disappeared in a mental home even before Roth was born, was experienced as one of the 'peinlichste Lücken seiner Kindheit' (most embarrassing gaps of his childhood).[16]

Bronsen's biography of Roth, first published in 1974 and republished in a shortened version in 1993, is the result of years of research and based on well over a hundred interviews and correspondences with Roth's friends and relatives; the work tries to cut through the web of half-truths and lies which the writer himself had been busy weaving. As Bronsen says in the introduction, he realised during his research that he was dealing with the 'unüber-windlichen Einbildungskraft eines Mythomanen ..., der seine Lebens-geschichte immer wieder umdichtete' (insurmountable power of imagination of a mythomaniac who again and again rewrote his life story).[17]

Roth's myth-making about his own origins underlines his problematic identity, having grown up as a fatherless Eastern Jew at the end of the Habsburg Empire where anti-Semitism was rife. 'The German political effort to consolidate the nascent Empire led many Jews there to regard anti-Semitism as a harmless, or at most an annoying, distraction. ... The political consolidation in Germany contrasted sharply with the fragmentation in the multi-national Habsburg realm. By the nineties, social cleavage was deep, marked by the Czech movement for Bohemian autonomy, Catholic loyalty to Rome, pan-Slavism, irredentism in Italian Austria, and German nationalism. Such conditions not only failed to inhibit the spread of anti-Semitism, but allowed [it] to become a characteristic or "normal" part of Austrian social and political life.'[18]

The experience of belonging to an embattled racial minority whose culture was considered old-fashioned and inferior must have been traumatic for the young man. As a student in Vienna he still signed his papers with his full name Moses Joseph Roth, but he dropped his first name when he began trying to get into print.[19] His hometown Brody at the furthest reaches of the Empire, a few miles from the Russian border (today in the Ukraine), was mythologised in many of Roth's works, but never given its real name in his autobiographical accounts; if he referred to it at all, he called it 'Schwaby' (a village near Brody) or 'Schwabendorf' in an attempt to germanise his roots.[20] The real Brody, which had been a Free Town until 1879 with flourishing trade, had declined since; of the 17,360 inhabitants at the turn of the century, 72% were Jews. Roth's grandfather, in whose house he lived with his mother, was still orthodox; in contrast to Roth's many accounts of the harsh poverty he had suffered during his childhood, it seems that he grew up in modest but far from impoverished circumstances. There are few accounts left by him about his mother, apart from referring to her as a 'Russian-Polish Jewess'[21]; the daughter of Roth's lover, Andrea Manga Bell, remembers the story he told her as a child in which he 'sei als Rabe zur Welt gekommen und seine unbarmherzige Vogelmutter habe ihn aus dem Nest geworfen' (was born as a raven and his cruel bird mother threw him out of the nest).[22] The theme of the cruel 'Rabenmutter' is taken up in other stories about his birth where he claims that they had been too poor for a cradle, and that he had almost died of cold after being left exposed at a window-sill. The images of early deprivation conflict starkly with the reality of his childhood which was spent closely protected by his mother within his maternal family, in emotional dependence on her, while resenting the financial dependence on his uncles.

Together with the many different versions about his father – 'Ich bin der Sohn eines österreichischen Eisenbahnbeamten ...' / 'Mein Vater war der "Kapsel-Roth", der bekannte Wiener Munitionsfabrikant' / 'Der Mann, der meine Mutter heiratete, war nicht mein Vater, denn ich stamme von einem Edelmann ab' / 'Ich bin der natürliche Sohn eines polnischen Grafen'[23] (I am the son of an Austrian railway employee ...' / 'My father was 'Capsule-Roth', the well-known Vienna ammunition producer' / 'The man who married my mother was not my father, for I am the offspring of a nobleman' / 'I am the natural son of a Polish count'), his self-dramatisation reflects the existential insecurity which came from his feelings of inadequacy in relation to his gender and his racial identity. He felt 'deserted' by his father, and overwhelmed by his memories of closeness and affinity to his mother, and his 'flight without end' (*Flucht ohne Ende* was the title of a novel published in 1927) was a flight from the mother as well as from his Jewishness. His account of leaving the unnamed hometown and his family to become a student in Vienna, which survives in short autobiographical sketches written in 1919, paints a picture of a young man, ruthless, cunning and cruel to women and animals alike: with his self-portraits, he constructed 'abenteuerliche Wunschbilder, in denen seine Feinfühligkeit verschwiegen und durch rohe Gewalttaten kompensiert wurde' (wild wishful phantasies in which his sensitivity was denied and compensated by brutal acts of cruelty).[24] His desire to be a 'real' hegemonic man, thus *rejecting the feminine as well as the Jewish element in himself*, is the source of his literary misogyny; it seems also to be the source of his highly problematic relationship to his young and beautiful wife – she became schizophrenic after a few years of marriage and spent the rest of her life in mental institutions, dying soon after Roth as one of the victims of Nazi euthanasia – as well as to his numerous lovers. He seems to have been very attractive to women, yet his relationships with them were characterised by possessiveness and extreme jealousy, guilt, resentment and desertion. Towards the end of his life, he confessed to a male friend: 'Wenn man eine Frau verraten hat, hat man nie wieder Glück auf Erden. Angefangen hat es damit, daß meine Mutter mich verfluchte' (If one has betrayed a woman, one will never have fortune again in this world. It started when my mother cursed me).[25]

It seems clear that the 'curse of the mother' was a projection and an expression of Roth's feelings of guilt towards her. According to Moses Wasser, who was a lodger in the Roth household when he and Joseph were schoolboys, 'Roths Mutter war auffallend stolz auf ihren Sohn und sah ihren Lebenszweck darin, für ihn in der bestmöglichen Weise zu sorgen' (Roth's mother was conspicuously proud of her son, and she saw her life's purpose in caring for him in the best way possible).[26] In his attempt to secure his independence from her in order to establish his own identity, he despised himself but had to project this very feeling on the person who made him the centre of her life: 'Alle Mütter sind dumm' (All mothers are stupid), he is supposed to have said among his cousins.[27] In relation to his mother, but also to Andrea Manga Bell – his lover from 1929 to 1936 – and women in general, he was afraid of being infantilised and domesticated; thus, in a letter to Stefan Zweig, he writes about his feelings towards Manga Bell:

> Es steckt in dieser Frau – wie übrigens in allen – der fatale und sehr natürliche Drang, mich einzuengen, familiär und zum Haustier zu machen. ... Ich muß souverän sein, wie ein Sultan im Harem. Ich bezahle nicht mit Beischlaf und auch nicht mit Erhaltung sogenannter Dienste.[28]

> [This woman has the unfortunate and very natural urge – as indeed all women have – to confine me, to turn me into a family man and a domestic animal. ... I must be sovereign like a Sultan in his harem. I do not pay with sex nor with accepting so-called services.]

He felt threatened in his self-image as a male creative artist, and believed that control and subordination of the female was a precondition of his male autonomy.

In discussing Roth's literary clichés of the mother, Marchand mentions in a footnote the fact that fathers are almost absent in the earlier writing: 'Problematisch wird das Vater-Sohn-Verhältnis erst mit Roths Rückwendung zum österreichischen Mythos' (The father-son relationship does not become problematic until Roth turns back to the Austrian myth).[29] *Radetzkymarch*, which marks the turn towards Imperial Austria, is Roth's explicit invention of his own position in a patriarchal order, a construct of masculinity born out of his experience of powerlessness, and an expression of his psychological needs to differentiate himself from women and to denigrate the feminine in himself.

The Experience of Male Powerlessness and Misogyny

If women's studies has theorised the oppression of women and described masculinity as the 'drive for domination, power and conquest', then men's studies as part of gender studies begins now to take this up as well, but it seeks to differentiate between 'men as a group' who are in power in relation to women on the one hand, and men as exerting power over other men. Thus, Michael S. Kimmel investigates, for instance, the function of homophobia in an increasingly competitive society of 'marketplace manhood' where the quest for hegemony is all-pervasive but where only the few can carry away the prize. In this competitive culture, men's personal experience of powerlessness – or merely the fear of potential powerlessness – forces them again and again to delimit themselves from 'the other' as woman or homosexual man: thus, male 'identity is based on homosocial competition', and '[m]asculinity becomes a defence against the perceived threat of humiliation in the eyes of other men'.[30] The construction of patriarchal genealogy in Roth's *Radetzkymarsch* involves the creation of the super-ego or 'father'; as Kimmel says: 'Masculinity is a *homosocial* enactment. We test ourselves, perform heroic feats, take enormous risks, all because we want other men to grant us our manhood.'[31]

Radetzkymarsch, which can be seen as a 'homosocial enactment' where relations between the sexes are ultimately severed, is also an identification with the oppressor in the *racial* sense, as the implicit ideal here is German cultural hegemony, in spite of Roth's explicit political support for a supra-national Habsburg Empire during the last years of his life. And yet Roth's 'arch-Austrian' novel can also be explained as 'arch-Jewish', particularly if we follow Harry Brod's exposition of Jewish masculinity as non-hegemonic, and this would explain more clearly the identification with the oppressor. Thus, Brod, drawing on work by Barbara Breitmann and Jacob Neusner, investigates Jewish misogyny in the context of the 'rabbinic tradition's construction of the properly virtuous personality structure and set of emotional traits for Jewish men'. In summing up Breitmann's analysis, Brod writes:

> Breitmann ... uses psychoanalytic categories to argue that the self-abnegation called for by a people suffering under oppression for generations requires some psychic compensation. She argues that the rabbis found such compensation in two turns made in Jewish theology and culture: the rabbis' elevation of their own wisdom to near-divine status and a projection of their rage on to Jewish women. Thus Jewish sexism emerges as a simultaneous deflection and internalisation by Jewish men of the dominant Gentile culture's anti-Semitism.[32]

This argument seems to apply neatly to the function of misogyny as a precondition of the erection of patriarchal rule in Roth's novel: the true enemy, namely hegemonic man, is internalised at a time of the Nazis' 'irresistible' rise to power.

In conclusion, it can be said that the insights from men's studies used here should not obscure the fundamental power imbalance between men and women which is the main subject of feminist theory; gender studies in general should, nevertheless, take such insights seriously with the aim to encourage a better understanding of *masculinities* as *ideologies* – whether expressed in literary or other political-cultural manifestations – and thus contribute to a clearer realisation of the fact that power discrepancies between men and men in hierarchical social structures and the internalisation of hegemonic norms by nonhegemonic men *and* women contribute to the preservation of patriarchy and thus to the continuing oppression of the majority of women.

Notes

1. David Bronsen, *Joseph Roth. Eine Biographie* (Cologne, 1993), p. 13.
2. Hermann Kesten, 'Einleitung', in Joseph Roth, *Werke in drei Bänden* (Cologne and Berlin, 1956), pp. vii–xxvi (pp. vii, xi).
3. Quotation from Helmut Famira-Parcsetich, *Die Erzählsituation in den Romanen Joseph Roths*, (Berne, 1971), p. 125. Emphasis added. Cf. Jeff Hearn and David L. Collinson, 'Theorizing Unities and Differences between Men and between Masculinities', in Harry Brod and Michael Kaufman (eds), *Theorizing Masculinities* (London, 1994), pp. 97–118 (esp. pp. 104–5).
4. Reich-Ranicki in *Die Zeit*, 7 December 1973, quoted in Günther Pflug (ed.), *Joseph Roth 1894–1939, Eine Ausstellung der Deutschen Bibliothek Frankfurt am Main* (Frankfurt, 1979), p. 524.
5. Cf. Harry Brod, 'Some Thoughts on Some Histories of Some Masculinities: Jews and Other Others', in Brod and Kaufman (eds), *Theorizing Masculinities*, pp. 82–96 (esp. pp. 90ff.).
6. Bronsen, *Joseph Roth*, p. 342.
7. Joseph Roth, *Der Neue Tag. Unbekannte politische Arbeiten 1919 bis 1927* (Cologne and Berlin, 1970), p. 222.
8. See Martha Wörsching, 'Die rückwärtsgewandte Utopie – Sozialpsychologische Anmerkungen zu Joseph Roths Roman "Radetzkymarsch"', in Heinz Ludwig Arnold (ed.), *Joseph Roth – Sonderband, Text + Kritik* (Munich, 1974/1982), pp. 90–100.
9. *Radetzkymarsch*, in Joseph Roth, *Werke*, ed. Klaus Westermann and Fritz Hackert, vol. 5 (Cologne, 1991), pp. 167–8. Future references to this novel are given in brackets in the text.
10. R. W. Connell, 'Psychoanalysis on Masculinity', in Brod and Kaufman (eds), *Theorizing Masculinities*, pp. 11–38 (p. 24).
11. Kesten, 'Einleitung', p. xxi.
12. See Hugo Dittberner, 'Über Joseph Roth', in Arnold (ed.), *Joseph Roth – Sonderband*, pp. 10–31 (p. 28).
13. Quoted in Reinhard Baumgart, *Auferstehung und Tod des Joseph Roth* (Munich, 1991), p. 69.
14. Ibid., p. 57.
15. David Bronsen, 'Zum "Erdbeeren"–Fragment – Joseph Roths geplanter Roman über die galizische Heimat', in Arnold (ed.), *Joseph Roth – Sonderband*, pp. 122–31 (p. 122).
16. Baumgart, *Auferstehung*, p. 61.
17. Bronsen, *Joseph Roth*, pp. 14–15.
18. Dennis Klein, 'Assimilation and the Demise of Liberal Political Tradition in Vienna: 1860–1914', in David Bronsen (ed.), *Jews and Germans from 1860 to 1933: The Problematic Symbiosis* (Heidelberg, 1979), pp. 234–61 (p. 244).
19. Bronsen, *Joseph Roth*, p. 21. The following biographical information is also taken from the early pages of Bronsen's biography.
20. Ibid., p. 22.
21. Ibid., p. 23.
22. Ibid., p. 25.
23. Ibid., p. 24.

24. Bronsen, 'Zum "Erdbeeren"–Fragment', p. 123.
25. Bronsen, *Joseph Roth*, p. 263.
26. Bronsen, 'Die Ambitionen des jungen Joseph Roth', in Arnold (ed.), *Joseph Roth – Sonderband*, pp. 32–9 (p. 37).
27. Miguel Grübel, a cousin of Roth's, quoted in Bronsen, *Joseph Roth*, p. 41.
28. Roth, *Briefe 1911–1939* (Cologne and Berlin, 1970), p. 422.
29. Wolf R. Marchand, *Joseph Roth und völkisch-nationalistische Wertbegriffe* (Bonn, 1974), p. 279, footnote 8.
30. Michael S. Kimmel, 'Masculinity as Homophobia: Fear, Shame, and Silence in the Construction of Gender Identity', in Brod and Kaufman (eds), *Theorizing Masculinities*, pp. 119–41 (pp. 122, 135).
31. Ibid., p. 129.
32. Brod, 'Some Thoughts', in Brod and Kaufman (eds), *Theorizing Masculinities*, pp. 90–2. See Barbara Breitmann, 'Lifting up the Shadow of Anti-Semitism: Jewish Masculinity in a New Light', in Harry Brod (ed.), *A mensch among men: Explorations in Jewish Masculinity* (Freedom, CA, 1988), pp. 101–17.

Homage or Parody?

Elias Canetti and Otto Weininger

Simon Tyler

Weininger's principal work, *Geschlecht und Charakter* (*Sex and Character*), received enormous interest in Austrian literary circles when it was first published in 1903, an interest heightened by the fact that Weininger committed suicide shortly after its publication in the house where Beethoven had died. This suicide is but one disturbing element in the conception and reception of this vehemently misogynist and anti-Semitic work, which Gerald Stieg has claimed to be a psychological and metaphysical prelude to National Socialism and its variants.[1] The extraordinary popularity of this work is indicated by the fact that it went through twenty-eight editions between 1903 and 1932. As Nike Wagner has shown, Karl Kraus, the man who most inspired the young Canetti, introducing him to the richness of Viennese culture, drew extensively on the writings of Weininger; and indeed, Kraus contributed greatly to Weininger's fame, although he did not agree with his anti-feminist conclusions.[2] Canetti himself acknowledges how popular discussions of Weininger's philosophy were in those circles in which he mixed during his studies at the University of Vienna throughout the 1920s: 'Other boys whom I met in this circle indulged in the arrogance of higher literature: if not Karl Kraus, then Otto Weininger or Schopenhauer. Pessimistic or misogynous utterances were especially popular ...' and 'Otto Weininger's *Sex and Character,* though published twenty years earlier, cropped up in every discussion.'[3] Alfons M. Bischoff informs us that Canetti attended the lectures given by Hermann Swoboda, who had been a close friend of Weininger and who published an evaluation of his work, *Otto Weiningers Tod*, in 1911.[4] It is therefore clear from external evidence alone that Canetti must have had a thorough knowledge of this infamous best-selling author.

That Canetti was influenced by Weininger has already been suggested by some critics. Jacques Le Rider has alluded to the possibility of such influence, and two articles have indicated some traces of it in *Auto-da-fé*, but these articles fail to account for the positive similarities between Canetti, Weininger and Kien.[5] The religious and racial aspects of Weininger's work go beyond the scope of this essay: a comparison between Weininger's views on the Jewish character and Canetti's characterisation of Fischerle deserves separate treatment.[6] This article will compare Weininger's notion of the masculine genius and of the female with the sexual imagery, characterology and world-view presented in *Auto-da-fé* and Canetti's later works in order to show that these parallels are even closer than has been suspected. I shall also attempt to account for this influence, to set it in the context of Viennese culture and to analyse its significance for an interpretation of his presentation of women.

The masculine genius

Although critics have tended to emphasise the importance of Weininger's ideas on Jews and women, his typology of the male as genius forms a large section of his writings and was considered by the young author to be an integral part of his whole philosophy. Just as Weininger prefers to circumscribe the female as an absolute negative type (W) rather than to describe actual women, so he constructs a positive type (M) as a masculine ideal. He posits a theory of universal bisexuality: every individual is constituted by a combination of both masculine and feminine characteristics. However, he claims that all men are more likely than women to display those traits characteristic of that absolute, metaphysical ideal represented by M: the masculine genius. The necessary features of this type include an extraordinary memory, clear, logical thinking and precocity.[7] Of these three qualities, memory is primary, 'the sure, most general, and most easily proved mark of a genius' *(Sex and Character,* pp. 114–15); logical thinking is the necessary precondition for memory, and precocity can retrospectively be attributed to the man whose first memory refers to an event very early on in his childhood. Hence Weininger claims that the desire and the ability to write an autobiography are signs of genius (p. 122). M, a supremely intellectual being, derives his ethics from Kant's categorical imperative and not from pragmatic, utilitarian or emotional considerations. The link Weininger thus establishes between the intellect and morality is taken to the extreme: he considers lying immoral in all circumstances because it is a betrayal of the intellect (as does Kant),[8] and even forgetfulness is considered a sin (p. 150) since '[c]onsciousness and consciousness alone is in itself moral; all unconsciousness is immoral, and all immorality is unconscious' (p. 182). As M, through logical reasoning, is an ethical being, he has a soul that harbours the desire for immortality ('Unsterblichkeitsbedürfnis'), a desire that his spiritual achievements be preserved (p. 127). The masculine genius must be able to comprehend the external world rationally by a process of assimilation while retaining the distinct unity of the self – a notion based on Leibnizian monadogy, according to which man is a discrete microcosm capable of grasping the whole of the macrocosm (pp. 169–72). He is further characterised physiognomically by sharp, distinct features, representing decisiveness and perspicacity (pp. 100–1).

The character in Canetti's works who comes nearest to this ideal is of course Peter Kien. He has a phenomenal memory, 'no less than a heaven-sent gift'.[9] His thought–patterns are always extremely clear and logical, even when he hallucinates *(Auto-da-fé*, pp. 306–7). Like Weininger, Peter was an early developer. The opening of *Auto-da-fé* presents Peter's young *alter ego,* Franz Metzger, whose enthusiasm for books and learning reminds Peter of his own youthful eagerness, comically, yet also uncannily, recalled in the episode describing the night Peter spent with a crowd of ghosts in a bookshop (pp. 13–14).

Kien was called Kant in one manuscript version of the novel, but his name was changed at Hermann Broch's request.[10] Like Kant, he claims to base his morality on the intellect, but this emphasis on the intellect is taken to extremes. For Kien, morality does not entail empathy for other individuals or social responsibility but an attempt to maximise the efficiency of his academic activities. His relationship with others – Therese and Benedikt Pfaff in the first half of the novel, and Fischerle in the second half – is founded on his own need to isolate himself from the rest of society, and in each case, books, the symbol of the intellect, are placed above human considerations. Benedikt is bribed to ensure that undesirables are removed from the house before they reach Peter's library on the top floor. Fischerle is paid to help unload books from Peter's head and, later, to rescue books from the clutches of the monsters in the Theresianum. Peter only marries Therese in order to have a supposed book-lover at hand to care for the library: 'I shall marry her! She is the heaven-sent instrument for preserving my library' (p. 47). Here, Kien is satirised by his own implied use of the dehumanising word 'instrument' to describe the woman he is about to marry, thereby transgressing Kant's ethical principle requiring that other human beings be treated as ends in themselves rather than means. Kien's resemblance to Kant and his adherence to Kantian tenets are thus shown to be superficial; he merely supports opinions that serve to justify his own asocial nature and selfish purposes.

Kien wishes to achieve immortality, not only by his publications, each of which serves as the inspiration for many other scholars' research, but also by his absurdly materialistic bequest of his 'skull with all its contents' (p. 20) to science. Peter is further described as if he is a microcosm: the windowless library on the top floor represents his own self, cut off from the world, yet its 25,000 volumes are themselves another window on the world (p. 67). And, finally, Peter is characterised by his sharp features and distinct gestures: he is tall and thin, bony and angular.

Even Peter Kien's sado-masochism can be seen, according to Weininger's world-view, not as a negative trait, but as another sign of his genius. Weininger dogmatically claims that all men of genius suffer from the strongest sexual perversions, either sadism or, more usually, masochism.[11] Kien's sadism is revealed in his vicious treatment of Franz Metzger when this nine-year-old boy returns to visit Kien's library, in his fantasising about Therese's death and in his strangling of Pfaff's canaries. His masochism is even more pronounced: when his self-transformation into stone fails to impress, he accepts Therese's physical abuse as a just punishment (p. 152), and his actions at the end of the chapter 'The Mussel Shell',[12] when he flees

Therese's clutches by locking himself in the toilet, correspond to Weininger's assertion that sadomasochism in the genius is the sign of a healthy aversion to the repulsive bestiality of any sexual contact.

This brief survey of Peter's character not only demonstrates the undeniable parallels with Weininger's ideal type, but also highlights, by the tenor of the instances I have cited, that Peter is a comic figure. Canetti's absurd exaggeration of Peter's memory capacity; the fact that even his dreams and hallucinations conform to the Cartesian criteria of clarity and distinction and are devoid of emotion; the uncanny eagerness the young Peter shows for books, (whereas Franz Metzger displays a healthy desire for knowledge, Peter's youthful obsession already showed signs of fantastical hallucinations); the ridiculous and vain project of bequeathing his brain to science in order to achieve immortality; his instrumentalisation of human relationships by paying others to help him maintain his condescending social isolation; his pathetic sadism and his self-deceptive masochism – all these traits indicate that Canetti is satirising the main protagonist of his novel. Canetti's satirical style requires detailed analysis beyond the scope of this essay, but his use of the ironic semi-distancing of free indirect style needs to be mentioned, as it is a technique which Canetti has commented on in several interviews and essays. The speech patterns of the 'acoustic mask' ('akustische Maske'), usually repetitive, tautologous and clichéd, reveal a character's dogmatic, obsessive and egocentric unconscious thoughts.[13] Even though Kien's thought-patterns are far more structured than those of the other characters, they still form a mask. That Kien's memory is a 'heaven-sent gift' is not an objective statement, but an example of free indirect speech as self-revealing irony; Kien's implied use of this term to describe himself is a sign of arrogance. Like his memorisation of pi, Kien's accumulation of books is an arid pursuit and the spiritual wisdom of Chinese culture is lost on him. The phrase 'skull with all its contents' indicates that Kien's own conception of knowledge is material, not spiritual – or rather physiological, as Canetti is perhaps parodying Paul Julius Möbius' revival of Gall's phrenology in *Über den physiologischen Schwachsinn des Weibes* of 1900 where brain size is linked with intelligence.

Yet this does not necessarily mean that Canetti is also satirising Weininger through Kien, implicitly condemning the whole of Weininger's philosophy to laughter. Elfriede Pöder's claim (echoed by Michel-François Demet and Gerald Stieg) that *Auto-da-fé* constitutes the definitive derisive satire of Weininger's concept of the male genius needs to be reviewed.[14] Kien is a complex figure, displaying both male and female traits: he is a satirical character not only because of the extremism of his ideas, but also because of his inability to remain true to the ascetic, masculine principles he has set himself. Kien proclaims a Kantian aversion to all lies and a love of the truth (p. 13), yet his unpleasant experience of the external world leads him to adopt, at first unconsciously, then consciously, a highly selective position towards his environment, one which carefully filters out anything which does not conform to his preconceptions: 'It is his right to apply that blindness, which protects him from the excesses of the senses to every disturbing element in his life. ...

Esse percipi, to be is to be perceived. What I do not perceive, does not exist. ... Whence, with cogent logic, it was proved that Kien was in no wise deceiving himself' (p. 71). Kien exploits Berkeley's philosophy of perception, according to which reality consists solely of what is perceived, by adopting an absurdly parodistic version: he deliberately fails to perceive those aspects of the material world he does not wish to acknowledge, thus denying their reality.[15] He unconsciously reconstructs certain events that have revealed his own failings: when he does not realise that he is being asked where the Mutstrasse is until the questioner starts hitting him, he later convinces himself that he did not want to humiliate the questioner by telling him that he was already standing in the required street; when he does not recognise who is in his bed, he prefers to believe that it is his wife's murderer rather than the fearsome Therese herself; when his plan to overcome his wife's brutality by turning himself into stone fails, he persuades himself that he was only trying to fool her and to encourage her to throw him out of his own house. Kien repeatedly disparages the masses: 'barbarians' and 'illiterates' are terms he frequently uses to contrast them to his own ideal of 'culture'. Despite this, twice in the novel he becomes aware of his isolation and decides to venture among common people, to be absorbed in the crowd (pp. 122–4 and p. 173), but his belief that he has finally managed to understand another human being (Fischerle) and his plan 'to become learned in men' (p. 219) only lead to his being swindled. He even briefly adopts a philosophy of love and pity for Therese (p. 123), yet this is soon replaced by an overriding hatred for her when she again insists on his writing a will in her favour. All these examples of self-deception are satirical, admittedly, but they also suggest a deeper pathos: Kien's blindness exposes him to exploitation by others, which ultimately leads to his madness and suicide. Kien's fate, in some respects, could be seen as tragic, like Weininger's.

There are various passages in Canetti's essays, 'Aufzeichnungen' ('jottings') and autobiography that suggest that his own conception of the ideal writer comes very close to that of Weininger. What Canetti principally satirises in the character of Kien is his specialisation; although, ironically, as Canetti explains in his conversation with Joachim Schickel, Chinese philosophy (especially that of Confucius and Chuang Tzu) rejects any form of specialisation.[16] This specialisation is a failing that Weininger, like Canetti, repeatedly attacks: 'There is no such thing as a special genius, a genius for mathematics, or for music, or even for chess, but only a universal genius' (*Sex and Character*, p. 112). Indeed, Weininger explicitly attacks the specialisation of the philologist's memory (p. 115). The sort of memory Weininger considers characteristic of the genius is not that of Kien, not a memory which has been crammed with bookish study, but that of men of genius, which 'is of what they have experienced, not of what they have learned' (p. 115). A similar idea is found in one of Canetti's satirical jottings, which implicitly characterises Kien: 'What he has read serves to catch his experiences; and without reading, he doesn't experience.'[17] Canetti satirises a form of misanthropic isolationism; Weininger insists that M should become acquainted with other men.

Besides satirising specialisation in the character of Kien, Canetti overcomes its dangers in his own work by covering the diverse fields of anthropology, literary criticism, psychology, politics, cultural history and philosophy, claiming: 'My whole life is nothing but a desperate attempt to overcome the division of labour and think about everything myself, so that it comes together in a head and thus becomes one again.'[18] Similarly, Weininger stresses the dual nature of *Sex and Character,* a work combining science and idealist philosophy, emulating Nietzsche's synthesis of Schopenhauerian moral philosophy and Darwinian biology, and advocates that the ideal man alternate between the pursuit of science and that of art *(Sex and Character,* p. 108).

As I have already explained, Weininger stresses that only a true genius is capable of the desire and the ability to write an autobiography because of its demands on one's memory. Canetti has been accused by some critics (especially Eigler)[19] of glossing over the difficulties of remembering, naïvely presenting reconstruction as an immediate account of lived experience. His response was to emphasise his trust in his own extraordinary memory: 'Often it is those who think they know what one is supposed to remember who expect you to emphasise and linger on your doubt, as if the one who spells out his doubts were more truthful for that. In reality he is just weaker and preempts the doubts of others with his own.'[20] As Jacques Le Rider has shown, the emphasis on the subjectivity of memoirs and autobiographies in Vienna at the start of this century is linked to the modernist crisis of the individual and his pessimistic awareness of the failings of language in a non-rational, decadent world lacking absolute values.[21] However, Weininger wards off the possibility of this disintegration by basing a strong, stable self on an intensified cognition of one's own ego, an 'Ich-Ereignis' *(Sex and Character,* pp. 246–66); and Canetti's autobiography wards off the same danger by the power of the reminiscing subject. Weininger's emphasis on the desire for immortality complements Canetti's own campaign as the 'Todfeind' ('enemy of death'), the writer who, proud of his own personal identity, refuses to accept death in any of its forms.

Weininger also emphasises the importance of gratitude, of piety towards one's ancestors (pp. 178–9) and, like Canetti,[22] he attaches great importance to a person's name as a link to the history of one's family (p. 133). He considers the artist, the philosopher or the founder of a religion superior to men of action, who are necessarily compromised by considerations of power and materialism (p. 139) – an idea reflected throughout *Crowds and Power.* Like Kien and Weininger, Canetti shows revulsion towards man's base instincts, and he not only seems to find sexual instincts distasteful, but all bodily processes, including eating, in accordance with Weininger's analogies between the oral, laryngal and anal regions'.[23] One of his jottings asks rhetorically: Wouldn't everything be better if we had a different aperture for food and used our mouths only for words?'[24] and in his autobiography he writes of his 'emerging sensitivity on all questions of eating and getting eaten' after visiting a slaughter-house on a school trip.[25] This sensitive, anti-instinctual attitude is particularly clear in Canetti's condemnation of the excesses of decadent Berlin in the fourth part of *The Torch in My Ear:* 'The Throng of Names'.

Canetti's oft-repeated ideal of 'Verwandlung' ('metamorphosis'), which receives especial elucidation in the essay 'The Writer's Profession',[26] bears a resemblance to Weininger's idealised conception of the perceptive processes of the genius. Weininger states that:

> To understand a man is really to be the man. ... and a man is the closer to being a genius the more men he has in his personality, and the more really and strongly he has these others within him *(Sex and Character,* pp. 105–6).

And Canetti:

> Man must learn to *be* many men consciously and to keep them all together. This latter and far more difficult task will give him the character he imperils with his plurality *(The Human Province,* p. 76).

If we take Weininger's above statement together with his insistence on a stable self *(Sex and Character,* p. 133), the resemblance between their views is striking: both hope to enrich their own inner life by the internalisation of other human beings' characteristics. Furthermore, both Weininger and Canetti have developed a theory of human characterology that relies on man's ability to metamorphose into an animal: Weininger writes that there are few men who do not have one or more animal faces.[27] Canetti had his own 'early childhood typology ... based on animals', and in an interview he claimed that man is the sum of all the animals into which he has transformed himself throughout history.[28] The physical nature of this form of understanding, underlined by the anthropological, biological and zoological origins Canetti ascribes to modern forms of human interaction (especially in the chapter 'Presentiment and Transformation among the Bushmen' in *Crowds and Power,* pp. 337–42), is foreshadowed in Weininger's physiognomy, and both consider metamorphosis as an ideal: Canetti calls himself the 'keeper of metamorphoses' and Weininger writes: 'The number of different aspects that the face of a man has assumed may be taken almost as a physiognomical measure of his talent.'[29] Despite both authors' insistence on rationality, the rationality they advocate is no arid pedantry: Canetti's jottings are whimsical and bizarre like much that is to be found in Weininger, especially the sections 'Aphoristisch Gebliebenes' and 'Metaphysik' in *Über die letzten Dinge.*

Because of these parallels between Canetti's and Weininger's view of the genius, the claim that *Auto-da-fé* is an incisive satire of Weininger cannot be upheld. Kien is an ambivalent figure: many of his characteristics are not so much reminiscent of Weininger as of Canetti. The love of books (especially as physical objects) and the interest in oriental religion and philosophy are particularly striking features that both Kien and Canetti share. However, although there may be points of comparison between Peter and Canetti, there are even more parallels between George Kien's philosophy and Canetti's: both advocate 'metamorphosis', are opponents of Freud,[30] and emphasise the importance of paying attention to the non-linguistic, musical aspects (the 'acoustic mask') of one's interlocutor *(Auto-da-fé*, p. 417). Yet George is not perfect: he confesses to making a mistake in his judgement of Therese and Pfaff, whose malice he failed to appreciate because of his overly sympathetic view of other human beings, a view that excludes rational value-judgements (pp. 463–4). Canetti recognises that man is a many-peopled microcosm, but he also insists that this microcosm be kept under control; George's anarchic vision of humanity as a termites' nest is not Canetti's ideal. George and Peter should be considered complementary opposites, which is suggested by the fact that they both fail to appreciate novels, each for an opposite reason: Peter because novels disrupt the unity of the reading subject, thus undermining the basis of logical thought (p. 42), and George because novels are overly structured and rational (p. 398). So if *Auto-da-fé* does contain a positive model of genius it is that proposed by George: a combination of the characteristics of both Peter and George, of the former's intellectual rigour and the latter's expertise in human understanding; as George explains to Peter: 'Both together, a memory for feelings and a memory for facts – for that is what yours is – would make possible the universal man' (p. 436).

Weininger's masculine genius conforms closely to Canetti's ideal, proposed in the novel by George; it is an ideal which stresses the importance of logic and memory, but also of empathetic understanding, it is an ideal combining intellectual rigour with flexibility. It is the ideal of the anti-traditionalist, yet also anti-decadent Kraus, opposing both rigid dogma and disintegration. Peter is parodied for his one-sided display of the qualities of the genius, but his devotion to his studies is also a positive quality, admired by George. George himself acknowledges that he lacks 'character', and that he learns from his brother (p. 427). But what he learns only confirms that trait which both brothers already share: misogyny.

The unstable female

According to Weininger's characterology, the female (W) is the opposite of the masculine ideal of the genius (M). She is a completely sexual being; if she ever seems otherwise, this is due to a man's influence *(Sex and Character*, p. 89). Whereas M thinks precisely and logically, W thinks in 'henids', characteristic of a stage of thinking in which emotional colouring and logical conceptualisation have not yet been distinguished (p. 100). As W cannot think logically (Weininger writes that 'she may be regarded as "logically insane"' [p. 149]), it is in her nature to be mendacious, not so much out of malice as because of an inability to distinguish truth and falsehood (p. 264). She lacks the will-power to form her own judgements, and therefore she attaches undue value to mere material possessions or diverting pursuits (pp. 201ff.). Her inability to understand the logic of Kant's categorical imperative entails that she is amoral and does not possess a soul (p. 186). Her physical features and gestures are characterised by indistinctness and curves, rather than resoluteness and lines.

Whereas Peter is an ambivalent embodiment of Weininger's masculine genius, Therese can be shown to conform to all aspects of his typology of women. Weininger establishes two contrasting pairs of female types. On the one hand: the mother and the prostitute, on the other: the hysterical woman and the shrew. The mother is defined by her desire to have children and her embeddedness in nature. As it is repeatedly stressed that Therese does not like children, a reader with a knowledge of Weininger would naturally classify her as a prostitute (which for Weininger is a psychological and physiological type, independent of social position, and not a profession). At the start of the novel, Therese conforms to the type of the hysterical woman. Despite Therese's claims to the contrary, her reiterated appeals to 'decency', she is shown to have a strong repressed sexual drive: this is revealed by the two occasions on which she faints, both of which are imbued with an intense eroticism *(Auto-da-fé*, p. 74 and p. 124), and by her obsessive condemnation of contemporary sexual mores: 'Every factory girl has to have a new blouse. I ask you, and what do they do with all their fancy stuff? Go off bathing and take it all off again. With boys, too. Whoever heard of such a thing in my time' (pp. 36–7). Her obsessive reading of personal advertisements in the newspaper (p. 64) confirms her latent correspondence with Weininger's fundamental typological trait for women: match-making, described by Weininger as 'the only positively general female characteristic' *(Sex and Character*, p. 259) because it reveals how W's sexuality destroys her personal individuality so as to encompass an obsession with sex in general. However, for W the bridal night is a turning-point (p. 91), and it proves to be so for Therese. Although Therese's bridal night ends in disaster, it is the point at which Therese is transformed from the outwardly respectable hysterical woman into the openly sexual shrew, another character type. Her failure to seduce Kien spurs her on to find another sexual partner. Just as, according to Weininger, a woman's vanity, revealed in her narcissistic use of a mirror, indicates a desire to be seduced (p. 201), so Therese, as she admires herself in a mirror, conducts an imagined erotic conversation with the shop-assistant Mr Brute ('Herr Grob') in anticipation of her desired love-affair *(Auto-da-fé*, pp. 270–2). However, Therese does not succeed in persuading Brute to kill Kien and become her lover; instead she manages to seduce Benedikt Pfaff. Therese's seduction of this retired policeman conforms precisely to the model Weininger suggests: 'It is a noticeable fact that a policeman usually finds his sexual complement in the housemaid' *(Sex and Character*, p. 272, note).

Therese not only conforms to Weininger's concept of female pansexuality but also to that of 'logical insanity', or 'Kartoffellogik' ('potato logic') as Dieter Dissinger has described it.[31] Whereas Kien's insanity derives from logical extremism, his obstinate refusal to accept any phenomenon that does not easily fit within his preconceived world-view, Therese's repetitive speech patterns, her 'acoustic mask', reveal an incoherence deriving from her emotional obsessions: sex, money and power. Among the words and phrases she overuses – along with 'Excuse me', 'Potatoes already cost double', 'a real man' – is the word 'beautiful' ('schön'),[32] the overuse of which word is explicitly condemned by Weininger as a sign of female shamelessness.[33] Therese's speech also reveals her own mendacity; having just failed to seduce Brute by inviting him to a meal, she indignantly persuades herself that she is still a respectable woman and that it is all Peter's fault: 'In the streets all the men stared at her. Whose fault was it anyway? It was all her husband's fault!' *(Auto-da-fé*, pp. 101–2). The fact that Therese just as frequently lies to herself as to others proves that her mendacity is of the sort Weininger attributes to W, a mendacity deriving from logical confusion and heightened emotionality, rather than criminal intent (*Sex and Character*, p. 273). Therese shows no sign of remorse for her crimes, no realisation of the consequences of her suggestions: she indignantly asserts the rightfulness of her having deceived her mother into believing that she slept with the latter's boyfriend; she calmly proposes that Brute murder her husband – she would not do it herself as she is 'decent'. Therese insists that her husband draft a will, but has no intention of drafting one herself – a sign, according to Weininger, of her lack of the male desire for immortality (p. 135). Canetti's description of Therese's physical appearance and movements also accords with the female characteristics laid down by Weininger: in opposition to Kien's sharply outlined features and gestures, Therese is characterised by her gliding gait, and a curvaceousness that she aims to conceal beneath her blouse and starched skirt, her armour against the external world.

Therese is not the only female character in *Auto-da-fé* who conforms to Weininger's characterisation. Fischerle's wife, humorously known as the Capitalist, is devoted to her husband and her regular client. She shows the same submissiveness as the gorilla's mistress (the 'secretary') and the Fishwife, whose catch-phrase 'He's all I've got in the world!' *(Auto-da-fé*, p. 223) tallies with Weininger's proposition that women's value judgements are always dependent on men. That this subservience can lead to crime is demonstrated by George's wife, who poisons her first husband, the director of the mental asylum, so that George may take over. Anna, Pfaff's physically abused daughter, is driven by romantic yearning for Franz, who works as a grocer's assistant. Her dreams, in which he appears as a knight on horseback, could be interpreted as a sign of her pliability to male domination, a transference of her need to be dominated by her father onto the character of Franz, or, on the other hand, as her exploitation of another man in order to escape from her family home. Her hidden sadistic tendencies are revealed by her strange fantasising:

> He [Franz] holds out the match to her and the cigarette burns. I'll burn you, she says, he's frightened. She points it at him, she touches him. Oh, he cries, my hand, that hurts! She calls: 'For love', and runs away (p. 372).

This may at first appear a distorted interpretation of what most readers will consider a wholly sympathetic character, but Dieter Dissinger views Anna in just such a negative light, without even referring to Weininger (*Vereinzelung und Massenwahn*, p. 96). However this may be in the case of Anna, Canetti satirises all his other female characters by presenting them as representatives of W: their lack of intelligence and moral awareness, their self-deception and their submissiveness make them appear comically absurd. Canetti presents his characters as Weiningerian types inasmuch as he refrains from presenting any account of individual psychological or social history. We receive no more explanation why the female characters are so egoistic and sexually obsessive than why Peter is so obsessed with sinology.

Not only do all Canetti's female characters show some correspondence with Weininger's typology, but his male characters, although they fall short of the ideal of the male genius, are all more or less misogynist. In the case of Fischerle and Pfaff this misogyny takes the form of crude slogans: Fischerle exclaims: 'A woman who isn't a whore, there's no such thing!' *(Auto-da-fé*, p. 285), and Pfaff declares: 'Women ought to be beaten to death. The whole lot of them. ... They're all criminals.' (p. 111). Kien's misogyny displays distinct similarities to the more intellectual misogyny of Weininger. He emphasises the sexuality of mothers: 'If a mother could be content to be nothing but a mother; but where would you find one who would be satisfied with that particular part alone? Each is a specialist first and foremost as a woman, and would make demands which an honest man of learning would not even dream of fulfilling' (pp. 12–13). He considers a woman's modesty as a cover for lasciviousness, using the punning phrase 'shamefacedness of the shameless' to characterise Therese (p. 453); similarly, Weininger writes: 'Women can give an impression of being modest because there is nothing in her to contrast with her sexuality' (*Sex and Character*, p. 200). Peter interprets figures of women in history and mythology (Cleopatra, Helen of Troy, Aphrodite, Calypso, Nausicaa, Penelope, Hera, Eve, Eudoxia, Messalina) in such a way as to reveal the immorality, or amorality, hidden under the gloss of male idealisation, supporting his arguments with the names of famous misogynists (Aquinas, Thomas More, Juvenal, Confucius, Buddha). This erudite misogyny is directly paralleled throughout Weininger's work; indeed the whole chapter 'Warywise Odysseus', devoted to Peter's lengthy tirade against women, resembles Weininger's list of authorities to support his claim that W does not possess a soul (pp. 186–8).

Although we must bear in mind that George is consciously attempting to cure his brother's psychosis in their discussion by pretending to agree with his rantings, there are passages in the novel indicating that he is as misogynist as his brother. George says to Peter: '... you don't even guess how much I owe you: my character as far as I have any, my love of learning, my way of life, my rescue from all those women ...' *(Auto-da-fé*, p. 427), and he reaches the conclusion: 'I believe in learning more firmly every day, and every day less firmly in the indispensability of love!' (p. 433). This praise of his brother is undoubtedly tongue-in-cheek, but George does admire certain aspects of Peter's work and acknowledges what he has learnt from him: 'From it George learnt that there was a cure for the woman, more certain than poison ...' (p. 494). We learn that George's period of womanising did not contribute to his love of women, and that he finds his wife boring in contrast to true 'characters': his patients at the asylum (p. 413). His ideal woman is one who has been transformed by the domination of a man, or rather, of a 'gorilla' (p. 436).

If as I have suggested, the positive ideal Canetti proposes in *Auto-da-fé is* that of a combination of the intellectual rigour of Peter and the empathetic understanding of George, this ideal does not seem to exclude misogyny. Peter Kien may be an eccentric misogynist, lacking self-awareness and mulishly blotting out aspects of the external world which displease him, but he is not as unambiguously antipathetic as Therese, who is deceitful, greedy, aggressive and manipulative. George conscientiously goes about his work at the mental asylum, developing his theory of psychotherapy based on empathetic under-standing and a genuine concern for the mentally ill (in contrast to his assistants and predecessors who are scornful of their patients); on the other hand, his wife is aggressively ambitious and has no qualms about murdering her first husband in order to further her second husband's career. As Therese and George's wife are presented as a potential and an actual murderess, within the fictional world of the novel the Kiens' misogyny appears justified. It is true that the violence exerted within Pfaff's household demonstrates how family ties can be perverted in order to reinforce male domination, yet Therese's treatment of her mother and her brutality towards Peter, as well as George's wife's murder of her former husband, suggest that women can be just as much a source of violence as men.

Canetti's own explanations of his characterology in *Auto-da-fé* run counter to the suggestion that his characterisation might be a parody of Weiningerian philosophy. As he explains in 'The First Book: *Auto-da-fé*' (*The Conscience of Words*, p. 123–33), Therese is based upon a real woman, Canetti's own housekeeper in the Hagenberggasse in Hacking from 1927 to 1933 (p. 124). This shows that Canetti does not consider Therese as the projection of a misogynist's distorted mind, but as a character reflecting reality, despite the exaggeration that satire entails.

That Canetti conceived of the relationship between the sexes as one of animosity is demonstrated in the chapter 'The Double Crowd: Men and Women. The Living and the Dead' in *Crowds and Power* and by the fact that Canetti claims not to have believed in love until he saw a performance of Kleist's *Penthesilea*, a play characterised by its portrayal of a murderous sex war (*The Torch in My Ear*, p. 48). Canetti's cynicism about love is suggested in some of the jottings: 'The dungeon that love has actually prepared will turn visible only gradually' (*The Human Province*, p. 76), and other jottings are curiously misogynist in a wistful way:

> As soon as the word 'love' occurs, a woman believes anything. Men reserve the same gullibility for fighting (*The Human Province*, p. 55).

> The stupidest women: those who come and report everything right away; to the nearest ear; it hasn't even fully happened yet (*The Human Province*, p. 131).

Canetti explicitly compares Therese with Tolstoy's wife (*The Conscience of Words*, p. 103) and with Goya's second wife (*The Secret Heart of the Clock*, p. 135), and implicitly with Felice Bauer.[34] Similarly, Canetti paints a devastatingly satirical portrait of Alma Mahler-Werfel, formerly married to a great composer, now just to a third-rate author, and of Fritz Wotruba's wife.[35] All these women, according to Canetti, shared a lack of appreciation for the work of their talented husband or fiancé and only hindered them in the expression of their genius.

Canetti's three plays also conform in their characterisation to Weininger's typology. In *Wedding*, Leni is wholly subservient to her husband Professor Thut. Anita, despite appearances, confirms Weininger's claim that there is no genuine female modesty. Gretchen, like Therese, has to remind Max of his duties as a man in order to get what she wants. However, in this play, all the characters display the decadent characteristics associated, by Weininger, with femininity (or Jewishness): lasciviousness and materialism. This play, like Kraus' *Die demolirte Literatur*, can be interpreted as an attack on a decadently feminine society.

In *Comedy of Vanity*, the feminine characteristic of vanity is presented in an ambiguous way. On the one hand, the fact that the female characters show a stronger need to use mirrors can be considered to reinforce the Weiningerian view that women lack self-esteem; yet, in a totalitarian society in which mirrors have been banned, vanity has become a form of resistance, contrasting with the hypocrisy of Fritz Schakerl's fascistic committee meetings. However, it is a woman, Therese Kreiss, who is most susceptible to the hysteria of the mass photograph-burnings; and one of the least sympathetic characters in the play, Emilie Fant, was, Canetti says, based upon Alma Mahler-Werfel.[36]

In *The Numbered*, the three main characters, who rationally discuss the positive and negative aspects of a society in which everyone knows when he will die, are all male. Whereas the two Colleagues and the two Young Men inquire into the effects of their society's laws, the two Ladies show an interest in match-making, and the two Old Women are only too willing to exchange their official lockets for Fifty's gold ones.

However, Canetti's later works show a slighter tendency to portray women in such a negative way. In *The Voices of Marrakesh* women are shown as victims of social circumstance, not as types: in the chapter 'The woman at the grille', Canetti sympathetically describes the imprisonment of a woman, and in 'Sheherazade' he recounts the story of Ginette, enslaved in an unhappy marriage. In *Earwitness*, although the Granite-cultivator resembles Therese, the Tempted Woman Anna Pfaff, and the Paper Drunkard Kien, many of the women appear in direct contradiction to Weiningerian typology: the Narrow-smeller and the Allusive Woman are entirely ascetic, not sexual; the Man-splendid Woman, the Archeocrat and the Horse-dark Woman are proud of their independence; the Syllable-pure Woman speaks eloquently and with precision. Often it is the male characters who display those traits Weininger ascribes to women: the Misspeaker is characterised by his confused thinking, the Bequeathed Man by his submissiveness.

Yet despite this less stereotypical portrayal of women in his late fiction, Canetti's autobiography still shows signs of a Weiningerian view of women, as Friederike Eigler has pointed out.[37] Frau Weinreb has lost all sense of self-worth since the death of her husband, whose photographs she licks in fetishistic adoration (*The Torch in My Ear*, pp. 181–2); Kokoschka's portrait of Alma Mahler-Werfel is described as 'portrait of the composer's murderess' (*The Play of the Eyes*, p. 52); Canetti's cousin Laurica is portrayed as only interested in her search for a husband, and as having such a bad memory that she cannot remember Elias's having tried to murder her with an axe (*The Torch in My Ear*, pp. 94–8). The portrayal of the principal woman in the autobiography, Canetti's mother, is highly ambivalent, and would merit a detailed study. Let it here suffice to note that, just as Weininger debunks the idealisation of motherhood by stressing the sexual aspect of breast-feeding,[38] so Canetti emphasises the mother's desire to exercise power over her child: 'The mother's power over a young child is absolute, not only because its life depends on her, but also because she herself feels a very strong urge to exercise this power all the time' (*Crowds and Power*, p. 221).

It is, therefore, unlikely that Canetti wished to satirise Weininger in his works. If Canetti satirised a form of philosophy in his works, then it is an inflexible dogmatism – a dogmatism, however, just as typical, in Canetti's view, of Aristotle, Kant or Kraus as of Weininger. If Canelli borrowed ideas, images and terms from Weininger, then his world-view and that of Weininger must overlap. The point of intersection is a particular view of women. It should not unduly surprise us that this novel contains misogynist elements. Canetti is known not only to have read Weininger, but also Strindberg, whose laudatory obituary of Weininger, 'Idolatrie, Gynolatrie', Kraus published in the *Fackel*.[39] Some motives in the novel are suggestive of Strindberg's early anti-feminist plays, which we know Canetti's mother read eagerly, but which were initially forbidden reading for the young Elias. Laura's attempt forcibly to remove her husband from the family home in *The Father* (a play Weininger praises for its supposed thematisation of his theory of telegony or 'germinal infection' [*Sex and Character*, p. 233]) resembles Therese's actions towards Peter, and in this play, as well as in the novel, a writing-desk plays an important symbolic role, representative of Kien's and the Captain's academic pursuits. Alfred Kubin's fantasy-novel, *Die andere Seite* (The Other Side), presents femininity as a decadent threat to civilisation; and it is Kubin whom Canetti chose to illustrate the cover of the first edition of *Auto-da-fé*. Despite the opposition to Kraus that Canetti describes in 'Karl Kraus: The School of Resistance' (*The Conscience of Words*, pp. 29–39), his attitude towards women still moves within the triangle Strindberg, Weininger, Kraus.

The disintegration of the self and of value-systems, which Canetti and Weininger hoped to arrest, is a far-reaching topic that is often thematised in Austrian literature of the early twentieth century. It is associated in Canetti's work with the conflict between the crowd and the individual, and in Weininger's with the opposition between Machian monist empiriocriticism and Neo-Kantian dualist idealism. In the battle between those acknowledging

147

a feminisation of culture ('Jung Wien', Altenberg, Otto Gross) and those who fear the crisis of identity and loss of values such an encroachment of the feminine might cause (Schoenberg, Loos, Kraus, Wittgenstein), Canetti has ranked himself among the latter.

Notes

1. Gerald Stieg, 'Otto Weiningers "Blendung": Weininger, Karl Kraus und der Brenner-Kreis' in *Otto Weininger: Werk und Wirkung*, ed. Jacques Le Rider and Norbert Leser (Vienna, 1984), p. 60.
2. Nike Wagner, *Geist und Geschlecht: Karl Kraus und die Erotik der Wiener Moderne* (Frankfurt, 1982).
3. Canetti, *The Torch in My Ear*, tr. Joachim Neugroschel (London, 1988), p. 77 and p. 118.
4. Alfons M. Bischoff, *Elias Canetti: Stationen zum Werk* (Frankfurt, 1973), p. 19.
5. Jacques Le Rider, *Der Fall Otto Weininger: Wurzeln des Antifeminismus und Antisemitismus* (Vienna and Munich, 1985), Elfriede Pöder, 'Spurensicherung. Otto Weininger in der "Blendung"' in *Elias Canetti: Blendung als Lebensform*, ed. Friedbert Aspetsberger and Gerald Stieg (Konigstein/Ts., 1985), pp. 57–72, and Gerald Stieg, 'Otto Weiningers "Blendung". Weininger, Karl Kraus und der Brenner-Kreis'. See also: Johannes G. Pankau, 'Korper und Geist. Das Geschlechtsverhältnis in Elias Canettis *Die Blendung*', in *Colloquia Germanica*, 23 (1990), 146–70.
6. But see: Ritchie Robertson, '"Jewish self-hatred?" The cases of Schnitzler and Canetti', in *Austrians and Jews in the Twentieth Century*, ed. Robert S. Wistrich (London, 1992), pp. 82–96.
7. See the chapters: 'Talent and Memory' (pp. 114–41) and 'Logic, Ethics and the Ego' (pp. 153–62) in Otto Weininger, *Sex and Character: Authorised Translation from the Sixth German Edition* (London and New York, 1906).
8. Cf. Kant: 'Levity, nay, even good-nature, may be its cause [i.e. of a lie], or some good end may be aimed at by it. However, the giving way to such a thing is by its bare form a crime perpetrated by man against his own person, and a meanness, making a man contemptible in his own eyes' (*The Metaphysics of Ethics*, by Immanuel Kant, tr. J. W. Semple, 3rd ed. (Edinburgh, 1871), pp. 244–5).
9. Canetti, *Auto-da-fé*, tr. C. V. Wedgwood (London, 1946), p. 210.
10. Canetti, *The Conscience of Words*, tr. Joachim Neugroschel (London, 1986), p. 232.
11. Otto Weininger, *Geschlecht und Charakter* (Vienna and Leipzig, 1903), p. 385, n. 1. This footnote is not found in the English translation.
12. The German word 'Muschel' points to the latent sexuality of this chapter. As well as meaning 'mussel', it is also a vulgar word for 'female genitals' and a colloquial Austrian term for 'toilet pan'.
13. The phrase 'akustische Maske' was used for the first time in 'Interview mit Elias Canetti: Leergegessene Bonbonnieren', in *Wiener Sonntag*, 19 April 1937.
14. Michel-François Demet, 'Blutphantasien bei Otto Weininger' in *Otto Weininger: Werk und Wirkung*, ed. Jacques Le Rider and Norber Leser (Vienna, 1984), p. 53, Gerald Stieg, 'Otto Weiningers "Blendung"', p. 61 and Elfriede Pöder, 'Spurensicherung', p. 69.
15. See David Darby, '"Esse percipi", "Sein ist Wahrgenommenwerden": perception and perspective in Berkeley and Canetti', *Neophilologus*, 75 (1991), 425–32.
16. Canetti, *Die gespaltene Zukunft: Aufsätze und Gespräche* (Munich, 1972), pp. 104–31.
17. Canetti, *The Human Province*, tr. Joachim Neugroschel (London, 1985), p. 93.

18. Ibid., p. 34.
19. Friederike Eigler, *Das autobiographische Werk von Elias Canetti* (Tübingen, 1988), pp. 63–6.
20. Canetti, *The Secret Heart of the Clock*, tr. Joel Agee (London, 1991).
21. Jacques Le Rider, *Modernity and Crises of Identity: Culture and Society in Fin-de-Siècle Vienna*, tr. Rosemary Morris (Cambridge, 1993), p. 35 and p. 40.
22. See 'Gesprach mit Joachim Schickel' in *Die gespaltene Zukunft*, pp. 104–31.
23. Weininger, *Über die letzten Dinge*, 9th edn (Vienna and Leipzig, 1930).
24. Canetti, *The Human Province*, p. 106.
25. Canetti, *The Tongue Set Free*, tr. Joachim Neugroschel (London, 1988), p. 228.
26. Canetti, *The Conscience of Words*, pp. 156–66.
27. Weininger, *Über die letzten Dinge*, p. 123.
28. Canetti, *The Tongue Set Free*, p. 150 and *Die gespaltene Zukunft*, p. 97.
29. Canetti, *The Conscience of Words*, p. 161 and Weininger, *Sex and Character*, p. 108.
30. 'He prods me to deal the decisive blow against Freud. Can I do that, since I *am* this decisive blow?' (*The Secret Heart of the Clock*, p. 53) The assistants in the asylum are satirised for their Freudian analysis of George (*Auto-da-fé*, pp. 411–12).
31. Dieter Dissinger, *Vereinzelung und Massenwahn* (Bonn, 1971), p. 107.
32. He was so beautiful, she was so beautiful, everything was beautiful ...' (*Auto-da-fé*, p. 273). 'She was looking forward to his beautiful punishment' (ibid., p. 298).
33. Weininger, *Geschlecht und Charakter*, p. 339. Passage not found in the English translation.
34. Canetti, *Kafka's Other Trial – The Letters to Felice*, tr. Christopher Middleton (London, 1974).
35. Canetti, *The Play of the Eyes*, tr. Ralph Manheim (London, 1990), pp. 50–5.
36. Manfred Durzak, 'Die Welt ist nicht mehr so darzustellen wie in früheren Romanen', in *Gespräche über den Roman: Formbestimmungen und Analysen*, ed. Manfred Durzak (Frankfurt, 1976), pp. 96–7.
37. Friederike Eigler, *Das autobiographische Werk von Elias Canetti*, p. 189.
38. Weininger, *Geschlecht und Charakter*, p. 291. Passage not found in the English translation.
39. *Die Fackel*, 144 (1903), p. 3.

'What matters who's speaking?

Identity, Experience and Problems with Feminism in Ingeborg Bachmann's *Malina*

Stephanie Bird

Ingeborg Bachmann's text *Malina* is too often interpreted as expressing a binary opposition between male and female. Criticism of this kind has usually stemmed from the desire to appropriate Bachmann as a feminist writer, a desire which results in readings which emphasise the oppression of the female narrator by the male figures. The position of the narrator as female is privileged and her suffering forms the basis for feminist identification. Her emotional stance, her difficulty in articulating her subjectivity and her debilitating relationships with her egoistic lover Ivan, her cruelly analytic alter ego Malina, and the sadistic father-figure all testify to the impossibility for 'woman' to exist in patriarchy. This view does not allow for the possibility that the narrator collaborates in her own destruction. On the contrary, as a writer, the narrator is seen as representing female creativity, which is threatened and finally eradicated by the three men. In one manifestation of this trend, the fairy-tale of the Princess of Kagran is upheld as a feminist utopia.[1] There is no doubt that Bachmann's work lends itself to readings based on the acceptance of binary oppositions, and many are subtle, fruitful and thought-provoking, finding theoretical justification in French post-structuralist feminist theories.[2] These theories, although they differ from each other in emphasis and in their positioning of woman within the symbolic order, do fundamentally accept oppositional structures of male/female. Deconstructionist feminist theory, on the other hand, is concerned to challenge not only polarities but any defining epithet. It is this theoretical debate which informs my analysis of *Malina*. The problem which concerns me is that binary oppositions are too readily accepted by feminist critics and that they are upheld even in the face of textual evidence which points to ambiguity or tension in those oppositions.

Two recent criticisms have in different ways highlighted the difficulties of interpretations which accept oppositions at face value and privilege the female element. In her review of the feminist reception of Bachmann, Sara Lennox is critical of the way in which the author has been appropriated by 'eighties feminism'.[3] She calls for new feminist readings which take into account Bachmann's historical context and which do not attempt to perpetuate 'wishful thinking' about Bachmann's politics. Erika Swales, sceptical of the legacy of French feminist thought, shows how Bachmann's story *Ein Wildermuth* relativises the polarities which it depicts, and thus self-consciously questions the validity of such oppositions. In relation to *Malina* she asks the crucial question whether it too is a text which consciously reflects upon its central male/female opposition.

By concentrating on *Malina,* I wish to show that Bachmann's primary concern in the text is not the privileging of the female perspective over that of the male, but is rather a study of the effects of different responses to historical experience and how these different modes of responding are central to definitions of the female subject.[4] The female narrator and Malina represent alternative ways of responding to experience, and both reveal strengths and weaknesses in that response. Bachmann is exploring the tension between an approach to history which insists upon the centrality of the subject and its perceptions, and one which emphatically denies experience as an adequate foundation for meaning: a tension which is also of central importance to feminist discourse. I will argue that there is ambiguity in the text and that tension is not resolved, but that it is precisely in that irresolution that utopian momentum is to be perceived.

The First Person Narrator

The trouble with first person narrators is that their perspective dominates, identification and sympathy are facilitated, and it can be difficult to maintain critical distance. The desire to read *Malina* as a feminist text has often meant that rigorous scrutiny of the reliability of the narrator has been neglected as a result of identification with her as the female element. As Swales argues, 'insofern *Malina* der Text einer subjektiven Gedankenbühne ist, stellt er a priori den Stellenwert seiner Aussagen in Frage',[5] (in that *Malina* is the text of a subjective mental theatre, it casts doubt a priori on the status of its statements). Yet failure to question the narrator's perceptions must affect the critical assessment of the status of the binary opposition of male/female. It affects whether the narrator must be viewed as the inevitably oppressed half of that polarity, thus effectively letting it stand unchallenged, or whether she is revealed as complicit in the performance of the polarity, thus undermining notions of its fixity.

I would argue that there is ample evidence in the text for maintaining distance from the perceptions of the narrator. Crucially, it is already in the prologue that it becomes clear that her recollections are not always accurate; at one point she states 'es war auf der Glanbrücke. Es war nicht die Seepromenade' (22) (It was on the Glan bridge. It was not the lakeside promenade) and two paragraphs later: 'Es war nicht auf der Glanbrücke, nicht auf der Seepromenade, es war auch nicht auf dem Atlantik in der Nacht' (23) (It was not on the Glan bridge, not on the sea-promenade, it was also not on the Atlantic by night). Her memories are often governed by what she would like to have happened: 'Im Café Musil habe ich vielleicht doch nicht das Stück Torte nach der Aufnahmsprüfung bekommen, aber ich möchte es bekommen haben und sehe mich mit einer kleinen Gabel eine Torte zerteilen' (21) (Perhaps I didn't have the piece of cake in Café Musil after the entrance exam after all, but I would like to have had it and see myself cutting up a cake with a small fork). It is clear that what is important for her is that memory is not limited to fact but is governed by emotional perception. The past, experience, is felt; its reality is not limited to the analysis and definition of science. The narrator describes her attraction to astrology in similar terms: 'weil ich mir die Zusammenhänge hoch oben über uns einbilden darf, wie ich will, weil mir keine Wissenschaft dabei auf die Finger sehen und draufklopfen kann' (23) (because I may imagine the relations high up above us as I like, and because no science looks over my shoulder and gives me a rap on the knuckles while I do).

The world as felt experience reaches its apotheosis in her relationship to Ivan, and again it is significant that in the structure of the novel this episode should come first. For in the narrator's deification of Ivan, her clichéd behaviour in relation to him, and her self-deception that 'für Ivan habe ich nichts zum Schein' (37), (I don't pretend to Ivan), the reader is presented with evidence that the narrator is gullible, naive and dominated by feelings which can clearly have a negative effect. That her relationship to Ivan reduces the narrator to conventional images of the desperate mistress has been commented upon amply by critics, but it rarely results in a questioning of her perspective as a whole. However, it is crucial to see this episode as an important indication of the narrator's inadequate modes of perception, not just in relation to Ivan, but in relation to what follows with Malina. The fact that the prologue's thematisation of the importance of emotion in reacting to experience is followed directly by an illustration of how the protagonist's feelings lead her into stereotypical patterns of behaviour is a textual invitation to be aware of the limitations of her viewpoint and not to privilege her perceptions in the book. For the text is concerned to explore two differing modes of responding to experience, not simply by setting up a simple opposition, but by systematically exposing the devastating implications of remaining trapped within opposition.

Experience

'Und wenn ich zum Beispiel in diesem Buch "Malina" kein Wort über den Vietnamkrieg sage, kein Wort über soundso viele katastrophale Zustände unserer Gesellschaft, dann weiß ich aber auf eine andere Weise etwas zu sagen – oder ich hoffe, daß ich es zu sagen weiß'.[6] (And if, for example, I don't say anything about the Vietnam War in this book 'Malina', or anything about the umpteen catastrophic conditions in our society, I do, though, know how to say something in another way – or I hope that I know how.) Bachmann's novel is certainly no naturalistic exposition of global catastrophe, but a history of abuse and how it can be lived with is her central theme, and one which cannot be treated by recounting events: 'Denn ich glaub' nicht, daß man, indem man zum hundertsten Mal wiederholt, was an Schrecklichem heute in der Welt geschieht, es geschieht ja immerzu Schreckliches, daß man das mit den Platitüden sagen kann, die jeder zu sagen versteht. In den Träumen weiß ich aber, wie ich es zu sagen hab'.[7] (Because I don't believe that by repeating for the hundredth time the terrible things that happen in the world today, and terrible things are happening constantly, that one can express them in platitudes that anyone knows how to say. But in the dreams I know how I have to express them.) This book is very much about history and experience and its effect on the individual; more specifically, about its effect on the female subject, how she is able to respond and how this response defines notions of subjectivity. The narrator reacts to experience emotionally, investing events with feeling and also with the desire to feel absolutely. She does not relativise through analysis and forms judgements based on the immediacy of the feeling which events provoke. In contrast, Malina remains emotionally distant and insists upon constant questioning of facts, causes, the meaning which might lie behind the appearance of an event. He insists on constant enquiry, she on the immediacy of the felt instant.

Far from removing *Malina* from the arena of feminist debate by seeing it as a text primarily concerned with interpretations of experience, I would argue that it in fact pinpoints one of the most crucial and controversial issues of the feminist discourse. Feminism depends upon women's feeling of being oppressed and on founding an identity politics based on the generalised concept of woman. Yet certain strands of feminist philosophy refuse to accept experience as an adequate basis for identity, seeing it instead as a way of reinscribing existing structures of domination. Thus on the one hand women's historical experience of oppression and exclusion is used to justify the existence of a female subject in the face of post-structuralist denials of the subject and Foucault's question 'what matters who's speaking?'[8] Women, it is argued, do care, for it is only now that they are able to articulate the subjectivity which has hitherto been negated or denied, and assert that subjectivity as different, but as equally valid.

On the other hand, deconstructionist feminists question the whole concept of experience and female identity, arguing that women's historical experience tends to be approached as though it is inevitably positive and with the assumption that recounting it must be beneficial for women. They object that experience becomes in itself a new foundation and source of truth, and, repeating the pattern of all foundationalist myths, one in which primary premises and presumptions are not questioned. Consequently the discourses within which gender is constructed are not analysed. As Joan W. Scott argues: 'Experience is at once always already an intepretation *and* is in need of interpretation. What counts as experience is neither self-evident nor straightforward; it is always contested, always therefore political'.[9] Any attempt to unite women on the grounds of their common experience as 'women' is effectively to elevate experience to the position of a new truth and so to impede the analysis of what structures that experience in the first place. It also means that the term 'woman' is taken as self-evident and not itself challenged as part of an already existing discourse. Thus to use the term 'woman' is to reinscribe phallocentrism. As Spivak points out:

> The claim to deconstructive feminism (and deconstructive anti-sexism – the political claim of deconstructive feminists) cannot be sustained in the name of 'woman'. Like class consciousness, which justifies its own production so that classes can be destroyed, 'woman' as the name of writing must be erased in so far as it is a necessarily historical catachresis ... It should be a lesson to us that *if* we do not watch out for the historical determinations for the name of woman as catachresis in deconstruction, and merely seek to delegitimise the name of man, we legitimise what is diagnosed by Nietzsche and acted out by Foucault.[10]

These two approaches to experience and identity lead to considerable tensions and rifts within feminist debate. Deconstructionist feminists are seen as denying female subjectivity just as it is emerging historically, and the insistence on the term 'woman' based on generalised experiences of oppression in patriarchy is viewed by deconstructionists as an obstacle to real radicalism. In *Malina* these two approaches to experience are being explored; one in which the female subject is defined by the immediately felt effect of experience on the self, and one which persistently seeks to analyse what lies behind experience. However, this contrast is not a simplistic one. For each type of response is shown to entail positive and negative aspects, and neither is evaluated as better than the other.

The Narrative Self

For the narrator, the meaning of an experience lies in the immediacy of its emotional effect upon her, and she seeks to comprehend the hidden truths of experience in this perceived effect. Her absolute involvement in emotion is coupled with an active resistance to questioning or analysing this involvement. Yet although she herself is shown to privilege this form of perception above reflexivity, it is not privileged in the text as a whole, where the devastating and negative effects of her responses are exposed. It is these I shall concentrate on first.

The narrator elevates her feelings to the status of absolutes which she never challenges, nor does she reflect about her own perceptions, for this would detract from the immediacy which for her is life-enhancing. She constantly emphasises her existence in the present, for to exist in the here and now precludes a reflexive stance, a distance from which to start analysing. She admits to Malina, 'Es muß einfach alles gleichzeitig aufkommen und auf mich Eindruck machen' (307) (Everything simply has to arise at once and make an impression on me), and she suppresses knowledge in order to persist in a particular emotional reaction: 'nie wollte ich denken, wie es im Anfang war, nie, wie es vor einem Monat war ... Ehe gestern und morgen auftauchen, muß ich sie zum Schweigen bringen in mir. Es ist heute. Ich bin hier und heute'. (154–5) (I never wanted to think about what it was like at the start, never about what it was like a month ago ... Before yesterday and tomorrow appear I must silence them within me. It is today. I am here and today.) The narrator perceives the effect of Ivan upon her as life itself, so to relativise that experience or cast doubt upon it by questioning it would for her be life-threatening. This response to Ivan is typical of her perceptions generally, whereby she derives her identity from her emotional reaction to experience and is therefore fundamentally threatened by the concept of analytical thought and self-reflexivity. She must defend herself against anything that can threaten her perceptions, for to question them would be to question her subjectivity.

Consequently, the narrator considers absolute concepts and secrecy as intrinsic virtues. She conducts her affair with Ivan behind closed doors, not in order to hide the fact, 'sondern um ein Tabu wiederherzustellen' (30) (but in order to re-establish a taboo). She is so struck by the 'Briefgeheimnis' (confidentiality of mail) because a letter cannot truly convey the authenticity of the moment; the present becomes the past once the letter is received. She comments in the prologue, 'denn vernichten müßte man es sofort, was über Heute geschrieben wird, wie man die wirklichen Briefe zerreißt, zerknüllt, nicht beendet, nicht abschickt, weil sie von heute sind und weil sie in keinem Heute mehr ankommen werden' (8–9) (for one should destroy what has been written about today immediately, just as one tears up real letters, scrunches them up, doesn't finish them or send them off, because they are from today and because they will no longer arrive on a today). What remains of an unopened letter is a secret which eludes any type of definition and analysis. Allied to the narrator's emphasis on secrecy is her dismissal of thought and of thinkers, and Ivan is not alone in being attractive to her because he does not seek explanations. Her weakness for road labourers is based on her reduction of them to their physique, and her delight in the Roman car mechanic similarly idealises his manual labour and his apparent stupidity. How unlike Einstein, Faraday, Freud or Liebig this mechanic proves to be, 'denn das sind doch Männer ohne wirkliche Geheimnisse' (for they are men without real secrets). The narrator describes her visits to this mechanic as a pilgrimage, once again elevating her emotional response to him to a religious plane, a response which she neither wishes to explain nor to have understood: 'aber man will ja nicht verstanden werden. Wer will das schon!' (292) (but of course one doesn't want to be understood. Who wants to be!). Her idealisation of the male body is part of a broader rejection of thought which also forms part of her utopian visions: '*wir werden aufhören zu denken und zu leiden, es wird die Erlösung sein*' (145) (*We will stop thinking and suffering, it will be the deliverance*). Again this is explicit in relation to Ivan: 'was habe ich gelesen bisher, wozu dient mir das jetzt, wenn ich es nicht brauchen kann für Ivan' (81) (what have I read up until now, and what use is it to me now if I can't use it for Ivan). And when she is lying next to him, she is 'befreit von allem Gelesenen für eine Stunde' (82) (freed from all I have read for an hour).

155

The consequences of the narrator's refusal to reflect upon or question her absolute identification with feeling are shown to be destructive. Her behaviour is reduced to the enactment of clichés of woman. [She dresses to please Ivan, views herself in terms of film slogans, and yearns to please him with gestures of absolute love involving self-sacrifice or domestic functions] 'aber Ivan verlangt nicht, daß ich mich aus dem Fenster stürze, daß ich für ihn in die Donau springe, daß ich mich vor ein Auto werfe ... Er will auch nicht, daß ich ... seine beiden Zimmer aufräume und seine Wäsche wasche und bügle' (266) (but Ivan doesn't demand of me that I fling myself out of a window, that I jump into the Danube for him, that I throw myself under a car ... And he also doesn't want me to tidy up his two rooms or do his washing and ironing). Although the 'Prinzessin von Kagran' story has been seen in terms of the narrator's exploration of new language or of a lost matriarchal ideal, I would agree with Sigrid Schmid-Bortenschlager that figures like the Princess and the women with golden hair point to traditional ideal images of women as found in fairy tales and reproduced in trivial literature.[11] This would certainly concur with the narrator's tendency to mould herself to formulaic patterns of female behaviour in order to please.

For all that the narrator is so devastated by different levels of experience, personal and political, she is so absorbed in her feeling of devastation that she becomes dominated by narcissism, which results in constructive concern for victims becoming marginalised. When she meets the Bulgarian with Morbus Buerger, her reaction is one of overwhelming panic. Her horror certainly drives her to make the necessary arrangements for his travel to Itzehoe, but the victim of the disease becomes an object of revulsion from whom she must escape, the personification of the disease itself: 'der Morbus ist da' (117) (the morbus has arrived). Similarly, after sitting with someone with leprosy, she is desperate to rid herself of the knowledge of the disease. She wants to wash her hands 'nicht um die Ansteckung zu vermeiden, sondern das Wissen von Lepra' (119) (not in order to avoid infection, but to avoid knowledge of leprosy). She asks herself 'warum solche Leute meinen Weg kreuzen' (119) (why do such people cross my path), but in fact she finds contact difficult even with 'healthy' people: 'Warum habe ich bisher nie bemerkt, daß ich Leute fast nicht mehr ertragen kann?' (175) (Why have I never noticed before that I can barely tolerate people any more?).

The individual is all too often lost to the narrator because of the domination of her own feelings. The shouting of a child is so painful for her, 'eine marternde Belastung für mein Gehör' (a tormenting burden for my ears), that she is resentful of Malina's interest in it: 'Malina muß etwas anderes daraus hören und meint nicht, daß man sofort die Ärzte oder die Kinderfürsorge verständigen müsse' (262) (Malina has to make something else of the shouting and doesn't think that the doctors should be called immediately or the child welfare services informed). She says of Malina: 'Ich habe nie daran gedacht, daß Malina Bronchien haben könnte' (280) (It has never occurred to me that Malina could have bronchial tubes). Likewise, political events are secondary to the importance of emotion, and her politics, be they personal or political, are governed by what symbolises absolute emotion: Ivan. He is at once lover and symbol, everything is 'von der Marke Ivan' (27) (of the brand Ivan) in comparison to which 'Washington und Moskau und Berlin sind bloß vorlaute Orte, die versuchen, sich wichtig zu machen. In meinem Ungargassenland nimmt niemand sie ernst' (25)[12] (Washington and Moscow and Berlin are simply impertinent places, which try to make themselves important. In my Ungargasse land no-one takes them seriously). In him she finds escape from the outside world and can immerse herself in the apolitical world of the senses: 'In dieser animierten Welt einer Halbwilden lebe ich, zum ersten Mal von den Urteilen und den Vorurteilen meiner Umwelt befreit, zu keinem Urteil mehr über die Welt bereit, nur zu einer augenblicklichen Antwort, zu Geheul und Jammer, zu Glück und Freude, Hunger und Durst, denn ich habe zu lange nicht gelebt' (76) (For the first time in this animated world of being half savage I live freed from the judgements and prejudices of my environment, no longer eager to judge the world but eager only for momentary answers, for howling and wailing, for happiness and joy, hunger and thirst, because I have not lived for too long).

However, although the narrator may wish to view her withdrawal into the personal realm as positive, as living, it is nevertheless revealed as intrinsically debilitating and self-destructive. She is rendered helpless by the impact of events upon her and is dependent on Malina for both maintaining the household and retrieving her from moments of extreme despair and collapse. She can do nothing to help herself because her identity is so utterly defined by the emotions of the moment which dictate her response. The narrator, although she can in one way be seen as passive, is nevertheless complicit in her own destruction, precisely because she actively insists upon the supremacy of emotion. Nor is she blind to the destruction it involves, and there are occasions in the text where the protagonist prefigures her final death. Early in the book when she does not answer the telephone, she comments, 'es kann nur Ivan gewesen sein, und ich will nicht gestorben sein, noch nicht' (39) (it can only have been Ivan, and I don't want to have died, not yet), and shortly after: 'Ich lebe in Ivan. Ich überlebe nicht Ivan.' (43) (I live in Ivan. I will not survive Ivan). Frau Senta Novak's analysis is astute when she describes the opposition between Malina and the narrator as 'der Verstand und das Gefühl, die Produktivität und die Selbstzerstörung' (261) (understanding and feeling, productivity and self-destruction).

The narrator's complicity in destruction relates not only to self-destruction, but also to the question of enabling destruction to occur without offering effective opposition. There is a revealing exchange between the narrator and Malina in one of their dialogues in the central chapter, in which Malina asks her why she sought to protect her father from the police. Her reasons are based on feelings of the moment: 'Meine Absicht war es ... das Schlimmste im Moment zu verhindern. Malina:Warum hast du das getan? Ich: Ich weiß nicht. Ich habe es getan. Damals war es richtig für mich, es zu tun.' (217) (It was my intention to prevent the worst at that moment. Malina: Why did you do it? I reply: I don't know. I did it. Then it was right for me to do it.) This indicates that although the narrator figures in the dream sequences as a victim of the crimes of the father, she is not herself uninvolved in their perpetuation. Similarly, her emotional perception of past crimes means that although the narrator is able to recall the crimes in dream images, she at the same time represses the implications of those images when they become emotionally overwhelming. In this way her mode of response functions both to expose the horror of the crime but also to resist examining her relationship to the perpetrators. So when Malina questions her about the compromises needed in order to survive, the narrator is evasive: 'Malina: Wie einverstanden aber muß man sein? Ich: Ich habe zu sehr gelitten, ich weiß nichts mehr, ich gebe nichts zu, wie soll ich das wissen, ich weiß zu wenig ...' (233) (Malina: But to what extent must one be in agreement? I reply: I suffered too much, I no longer know anything, I won't admit anything, how should I know, I know too little ...). On another occasion she speaks of the four murderers, and again she gives the impression of refusing to recognise what she must know: 'Von dem vierten kann ich nicht reden, ich erinnere mich nicht an ihn, ich vergesse, ich erinnere mich nicht' (297) (I cannot speak of the fourth, I cannot remember him, I forget, I cannot remember). Although on quite a different scale to the events recalled in the dream sequences, the narrator's relationship with Ivan nevertheless depicts how it is possible for her to be implicated in perpetuating patterns of oppression as a direct result of her emotional involvement.

The negative aspects of the narrator's identification experience have been emphasised at length, for they are often overlooked in order to privilege her perspective. However, these negative aspects are inseparable from what can be seen as the empowering qualities of the narrator's identity as oppressed female subject. It is to these qualities that I shall now turn, albeit briefly.

Despite what has been described as her rejection of reflexive thought and her own admission that 'die Abstraktion ... ist vielleicht nicht meine Stärke' (92) (Abstract thought is not my strong point), it is the immediacy with which she experiences events which enables her to adopt a critical stance towards society. Her attachment to absolute values gives her a yardstick with which to judge complacency and battle against silence. Her interview with Mahlbauer is a prime example, in which she refuses to give the expected and acceptable answers and leaves Mahlbauer angry, embarrassed but marvellously exposed as 'ein Sklave (seines) Blatts' (102) (a slave of his paper). In the interview she makes explicit the importance of remembering the past in a country like Austria, precisely because nothing else happens there: 'von hier aus gesehen, wo nichts mehr geschieht, ... muß man die Vergangenheit ganz ableiden ... man muß die Dinge ableiden, die anderen haben ja keine Zeit dazu, in ihren Ländern, in denen sie tätig sind und planen und handeln, in ihren Ländern sitzen sie, die wahren Unzeitgemäßen, denn sie sind sprachlos, es sind die Sprachlosen, die zu allen Zeiten regieren' (98) (Seen from here, where nothing happens any more ... one must suffer things away, the others don't have the time to do it in their countries, in which they are active, and plan and act, they sit in their countries, the truly outmoded people, for they are speechless, it is the speechless people who rule at all times).

158

Relating to experience emotionally enables her to react with indignation to injustice, to recognise hypocrisy and to challenge the detachment and cynicism of contemporary society. Much comes under criticism: the high society of which she herself is part, the deceitfulness with which the media report events, consumerism as an extension of the black market, commodification through advertising and the silence surrounding the first post-war years: 'diese Zeit ist aber aus ihren Annalen getilgt worden, es gibt keine Leute mehr, die noch darüber sprechen. Verboten ist es nicht direkt, aber man spricht trotzdem nicht darüber' (289) (but this period has been erased from its annals, there are no longer people who speak of it. It is not exactly forbidden, but nevertheless it is not spoken of). Her conclusion is that 'die Gesellschaft ist der allergrößte Mordschauplatz. In der leichtesten Art sind in ihr seit jeher die Keime zu den unglaublichsten Verbrechen gelegt worden, die den Gerichten dieser Welt für immer unbekannt bleiben' (290) (Society is the biggest murder scene of all. The seeds of the most unbelievable crimes have always been quite easily sown in it, crimes which will remain unknown to the courts of this world for ever). This quotation serves as a neat example of the combination of the negative and positive aspects of the narrator's responses; on the one hand she is empowered to stand back and criticise the hypocrisy of society, and the destructive and primitive relationships formed within it; on the other hand the comment is a universalising condemnation behind which the narrator is able to ignore her own participation. Finally, in relation to the past, it is the narrator's emotional perception of history that enables her to recount the horrors of war and murder in a manner which is unmediated and powerful, which can convey cruelty and fear, and which, through the refusal to accept a distanced position, reveals the devastating effects of events on the psyche.

It may appear contradictory to stress the inadequacies of the narrator's mode of perception, its destructive aspects, narcissistic domination and involvement in perpetuating structures of oppression, while concurrently affirming the critical stance with which the narrator is empowered. But it is precisely this double aspect which the text is concerned to reveal and refuses to simplify. Her emotional response to experience is both positive and negative, it at once empowers her and continues to deform her. And in relation to Malina, whose response to experience is that of the questioning analyst, a similar ambivalence is depicted, one that is destructive and constructive.

Malina

Malina responds to experience in the manner outlined by Scott, refusing to accept it as self-evident and constantly demanding that it be interpreted. For him, experience needs to be contested, as do the concepts with which experience is articulated, and herein lies the threat to the narrative self. The negative effects of the unremitting refusal to accept a subject's experience as a basis for identity are taken to a logical extreme in this text when the narrator perceives herself as murdered by Malina. He denies her identity by denying her experience and the emotional importance to the narrator of that experience. Hence the constant theme throughout the book that Malina is distant, does not like listening to her stories and is concerned only with analysis. As the narrator comments, 'Sein Zuhören beleidigt mich tief, weil er hinter allem, was gesprochen wird, das Unausgesprochene mitzuhören scheint, aber auch das zu oft Gesagte' (263) (His listening offends me deeply, because he seems to hear what remains unsaid, but also what is said too often behind all that is said). He actively ignores her experience and does not listen to her stories as she would like, whereas questions would always be appropriate: 'Was sich noch ereignet, was er meine kleinen Geschichten nennt, darf nie besprochen werden ... Fragen dürfte ich nach den unmöglichsten Sachen' (131–2) (What still happens, things which he describes as my little stories, may never be talked of ... I would be allowed to ask about the most impossible things). The narrator is adamant: 'Es ist Malina, der mich nicht ezrählen läßt' (279) (It is Malina who does not let me recount).

The narrator says of Malina that 'er (wird) immer Distanz halten, weil er ganz Distanz ist' (315) (he will always keep his distance because he is distance), and later describes him as 'unmenschlich' (336) (inhuman). I would argue that just as the narrator structures her identity upon the immediacy of experience, so Malina's identity is governed by the denial of emotional involvement and the privileging of analysis. His identity is thus shown to be threatened on the occasion when the narrator cites moments in the past when he has been close to death by crushing, drowning and electrocution. His reaction is emotional and violent and he attempts to deny the episodes. However, most crucial in his reaction is his denial that the narrator was present, for to acknowledge her presence in those moments would be tantamount to admitting the unavoidable emotional impact of those events. The ambiguity of the narrator about whether she was there or not, whether it was she who nearly drowned or Malina, is a device which emphasises the co-existence of the narrator and Malina as modes of responding to experience, a co-existence which in this case it is in Malina's interest to deny. His distance is thus revealed to involve active repression of emotional effects of experience on him; his identity depends on denying the immediacy of experience, just as the narrator's depends on denying self-reflexivity. The consequence is destruction and self-destruction.

The negative effect of Malina on the narrator has been amply examined in studies of *Malina*, but it is vital to balance this with the recognition that Malina's analytic mode is also given considerable positive value in the text. The narrator herself is aware of the importance of Malina's questions for attaining a greater comprehension of herself, saying 'er soll nach allem fragen' (181) (he should ask about everything), 'er soll mir meine Worte erklären' (200) (he should explain my words to me), and 'Malina sollte mir helfen, nach einem Grund für mein Hiersein zu suchen' (264) (Malina should help me search for a reason for my existence). The narrator depends on Malina to help her when she is overcome, and, as the central chapter reveals, is concerned to comprehend her suffering. However, although Malina is often hailed as the male ratio, aspects of his mode of analysing experience are far from antithetical to deconstructionist feminist discourse, which insists on challenging all concepts and values. Malina too challenges normative values, is critical of assumptions and rejects absolutes. 'Malina wendet sich allem mit einem gleichmäßigen Ernst zu, auch Aberglauben und Pseudowissenschaften findet er nicht lächerlicher als die Wissenschaften, von denen sich in jedem Jahrzehnt herausstellt, auf wieviel Aberglauben und Pseudowissenschaftlichkeit sie beruht haben' (261) (Malina approaches everything with equal seriousness, he doesn't even find superstition and pseudo-sciences more ridiculous than the sciences, which are themselves based on so much superstition and pseudo-scientific knowledge, as becomes clear each decade). He infuriates the protagonist by refusing to judge with the ideology-laden terms 'good' and 'bad': 'Ich glaube, daß Malina Änderung und Veränderung in jeder Hinsicht kalt lassen, weil er ja auch nirgends etwas Gutes oder Schlechtes sieht und schon gar nicht etwas Besseres. Für ihn ist offenbar die Welt, wie sie eben ist, wie er sie vorgefunden hat' (262) (I think that change and alteration leave Malina cold in every way, because he doesn't see good or bad anywhere, let alone something better. The world is for him obviously as it is, as he has found it).

In thus objecting to the amorality that such a stance can involve, the narrator resembles those feminist theorists who reject postmodernism because it denies the unified subject just when women are finding a voice. And indeed, Malina's approach does entail the denial of the female subject as represented by the narrator, as is most starkly portrayed by her disappearance into the wall. Malina no longer recognises her validity, her subjectivity, and this causes her death: 'Ich stehe auf und denke, wenn er nicht sofort etwas sagt, wenn er mich nicht aufhält, ist es Mord' (354) (I stand up and think, if he doesn't say something straight away, if he doesn't stop me, then it is murder). However, from the point of view of feminist deconstruction, the denial of a female subject is a necessary step to real radicalism and the dismantling of binary opposites, and in the figures of Malina the potential of this position is also represented. Thus Malina does not accept that a reversal of hierarchies is adequate for real change. When the narrator expresses the hope 'es wird nämlich so enden, daß ich über alles verfügen kann' (it will in fact end so that I can be in charge of everything), Malina responds, 'so kommst du nur von einem Wahn in einen anderen Wahn' (328) (that way you go from one delusion into another). From Malina's point of view, the destruction of the self can also be positive: 'Ich: Ich müßte mich ja selber beseitigen! Malina: Weil du dir nur nützen kannst, indem du dir schadest ... Es wird dir sehr nützen. Aber nicht dir, wie du denkst' (328) (I reply: I would have to get rid of myself! Malina: Because you can only be of use to yourself by damaging youself ... It will help you considerably. But not you yourself as you think). Malina emphasises the possibility of fighting differently: 'Du sollst jetzt weder vor- noch zurückgehen, sondern lernen, anders zu kämpfen'

(329) (You should now neither go forward nor back, but learn to fight differently). Whereas the narrator can only contemplate victory in relation to a symbol, Malina sees victory beyond both ideological sign and the insistence on the female subject: 'Ich: Siegen! Wer spricht denn hier noch von siegen, wenn das Zeichen verloren ist, in dem man siegen könnte. Malina: Es heißt immer noch: siegen. Es wird dir ohne einen einzigen Kunstgriff gelingen und ohne Gewalt. Du wirst aber auch nicht mit deinem Ich siegen' (330) (I: I win! Who is still talking of winning here, when the sign is lost in which one could win. Malina: It is still called winning. You will succeed without a single trick and without violence. But nor will you win with your Self).

Malina views the narrator's experience-related identity as a hurdle to change: 'Wenn man überlebt hat, ist Überleben dem Erkennen im Wege' (233) (If one has survived, survival obstructs understanding). Far from being complacent, he is concerned to disrupt the existing order and the unchallenged acceptance of concepts within it. In answer to the narrator about what can be done, he comments: 'Ruhe in die Unruhe bringen. Unruhe in die Ruhe' (327) (Bring peace to unrest. Unrest to peace). It is within this context that his challenge to the opposition of war and peace can be read, his assertion that there is only war and that individuals themselves are this war. For Malina there is a constant struggle against normalisation and the acceptance of dominant ideology, and the narrator's division of life into war and peace reveals individual internalisation of norms and the successful deception that there can be times at which the subject can afford to be complacent. As Malina says to the narrator: 'Du mußt nicht alles glauben, denk lieber selber nach' (192) (You don't have to believe everything, think about things yourself). On one level Malina is well integrated into society, unlike the narrator; he works at the Army Museum, an institution 'documenting the blood-stained histotry of male intellectual curiosity, which continues apace in the age of technology',[13] and, according to the narrator he mixes easily in Viennese society. Yet his conformity is external, and thus largely illusory. The narrator describes how he causes a rupture in Viennese society: 'Er webt nicht an dem großen Text mit, an der Textur des Verbreitbaren, das ganze Wiener Gewebe hat ein paar kleine Löcher, die nur durch Malina entstanden sind.' (315) (He doesn't help to weave the large text, the texture of that which can permissibly be circulated, the whole Viennese fabric has a few small holes that have come about solely through Malina).

The Utopia Problem

This article has hitherto been concerned to show that two different modes of responding to experience each have negative and positive features, and that the mode of response represented by the narrator is not privileged in the text. This carries important implications for the question of feminist utopias, for any reading of the book which seeks a utopian moment solely in relation to the narrator's perspective necessarily accepts and privileges the emotional and non-reflexive aspects of the narrator while ignoring the text's emphasis on these characteristics as *also* negative. Such a reading also accepts the male/female polarity at face value, and fails to consider that it is in fact the object of criticism.

However, I would suggest that the destructive conclusion of the novel comes about precisely because of the maintenance of the male/female opposition. The few utopian moments in the book are at those points where the narrator and Malina are shown to be in a relation of mutuality and exchange, even if only fleetingly, and can be found in 'Der dritte Mann'. In this chapter, Malina does indeed listen to and accept the importance of the narrator's perceptions of experience at their most devastating, and she is concerned for Malina to question that experience and its meaning. The moments are brief, but depend on this mutuality, and reinforce what the narrator later says to Malina, that 'was du und ich zusammenlegen können, das ist das Leben' (308) (What you and I can merge together, that is life). Thus through Malina's enquiry the narrator is enabled to speak of her perceptions more easily, without having to deny them: 'Wie leicht wird es, darüber zu reden, es wird schon viel leichter. Aber wie schwer ist es, damit zu leben' (243) (How easy it becomes to speak about it, it is already becoming much easier. But how difficult it is to live with it). Similarly, when Malina holds her, the narrator comments: 'wir kommen nicht voneinander los, denn seine Ruhe ist auf mich übergegangen' (246) (we do not let go of one another, for his calm has passed over to me). She has accepted his calm, but he has also accepted and acted upon the need for an emotional response to the narrator's suffering.

As has been emphasised, these moments are transitory. The subsequent destruction becomes inevitable as a consequence of the rigidity with which the narrator and Malina are fixed within the male/female polarity. But this polarity is not thereby being confirmed as inevitable and untransmutable. On the contrary, the opposition is thus exposed as spurious, as reductive, and not as a basis upon which change can be effected. Bachmann sets up the polarity in order to reveal its inadequacy and its potency as a tool of oppression. She is also pointing to the need for the interaction of both modes of responding to experience in the formation of identity. Neither mode is shown to be superior to the other. Yet here comes the final insoluble difficulty, a difficulty which the text does not shirk. Each mode of response does necessarily remain irreconcilable with the other; a female subject defined by the experience of oppression cannot at the same time question the very notion of the subject and refuse the universalising signifier 'woman'. The narrator and Malina co-exist in one woman, but an exchange between them can always only be momentary, for each must deny the other.

Yet Bachmann is not attempting to offer a utopia based on reconciliation; she is in this text acknowledging that conflict is part of the discourse surrounding the question of the female subject, while at the same time exposing the futility of fixed polarities. Furthermore, this conflict, if it is not reduced to fixed opposites by those themselves involved in it, can be a productive clash or tension, as suggested by those brief moments of exchange between the narrator and Malina. Momentum for change is produced not by the triumph of one way of conceiving the subject over another, but by the acceptance of conflict which would itself then undermine the destructive efficacy of fixed polarities. As Butler rather cryptically writes: 'I would argue that the rifts among women over the content of the term ("woman") ought to be safeguarded and prized, indeed, that this constant rifting ought to be affirmed as the ungrounded ground of feminist theory.'[14]

The final question which it is still important to address is why the book is written from the perspective of the female and in the first person, if her perspective is not to be read as privileged. I would suggest that the text itself thereby puts the reader into the very position of perceiving the two modes of responding to experience and of conceiving of the subject at once. On the one hand, the first person narrator elicits reader identification with the protagonist and her suffering; on the other hand, the reader is as a reader distanced from the text and concerned to comprehend it. Consequently the reader shares the same internal conflict which the text is depicting, and is left with a sense of tension and ambiguity aptly articulated by Swales when she admits: 'Ich muß es bei Fragen belassen, denn ich bin mir über meine eigene Einstellung zu diesem Text noch längst nicht im klaren'[15] (I must leave it at questions, because I am far from being clear about my own opinion about this text). Yet Bachmann's portrayal of unresolvable ambiguities is fundamental to the creative momentum in which the search for change and utopia lies.

Notes

1. Karen Achberger offers one such interpretation, arguing that the 'Princess of Kagran' fairy tale offers hope of women's sovereignty in the future, as it existed once in the past. She also sees in the emphasis on the colour gold in the narrator's imagined women (see *Malina* p. 140) the suggestion of queenship, hence the possibility of a future golden age for women. See her article 'Beyond Patriarchy: Ingeborg Bachmann and Fairytales' in *Modern Austrian Literature*, 18 (1985), 211–22.

2. Elizabeth Boa, for example, accepts the juxtaposition of male Malina and female protagonist at face value, and does not allow for deconstructive criticisms of the term 'woman'. Thus she comments on the conclusion of *Malina*: 'On the most pessimistic reading, *Ich*'s murder suggests that it is impossible to intervene in the public sphere, here symbolised in the act of writing 'I', without donning a male persona and impossible to write *as a woman* outside of the patriarchal definitions'. See her article 'Unnatural Causes: Modes of Death in Christa Wolf's *Nachdenken über Christa T*. and Ingeborg Bachmann's *Malina*' in *German Literature at a Time of Change 1989–1990*, ed. Arthur Williams, Stuart Parkes and Roland Smith (Berne, 1991), pp. 139–54 (p. 145).

   For another reading which makes use of the opposition between female protagonist and male alter ego Malina see Gudrun Kohn-Waechter's book, *Das Verschwinden in der Wand. Destruktive Moderne und Widerspruch eines weiblichen Ich in Ingeborg Bachmanns 'Malina'* (Stuttgart, 1992). In her imaginative and detailed analysis the opposition represents the confrontation between pre-modernist and modernist writing.

3. Sara Lennox, 'The Feminist Reception of Ingeborg Bachmann', *Women in German Yearbook*, 8 (1993), 73–111 (p. 104).

4. All references to *Malina* will be to the Suhrkamp Taschenbuch edition (Frankfurt, 1991) and will be given in parenthesis.

5. Erika Swales, 'Die Falle binärer Oppositionen', in *Kritische Wege der Landnahme*, ed. Robert Pichl and Alexander Stillmark (Vienna, 1994), pp. 67–79.

6. Ingeborg Bachmann, *Wir müssen wahre Sätze finden. Gespräche und Interviews*, ed. Christine Koschel and Inge von Weidenbaum (Munich, 1983), pp. 90–1.

7. Ibid., pp. 69–70.

8. Michel Foucault, 'What is an Author' in *Language, Counter-Memory, Practice. Selected Essays and Interviews*, ed. D. Bouchard (Ithaca, NY, 1977), p. 138.

9. Joan W. Scott, "Experience", in *Feminists Theorize the Political*, ed. Judith Butler and Joan W. Scott (London, 1992), pp. 22–40 (p. 37).

10. Gayatri Chakravorty Spivak, 'Feminism and deconstruction, again: negotiating with unacknowledged masculinism', in *Between Feminism and Psychoanalysis*, ed. Teresa Brennan (London, 1989), pp. 206–23 (p. 218).

11. See Sigrid Schmid-Bortenschlager, 'Spiegelszenen bei Bachmann: Ansätze einer psychoanalytischen Interpretation', *Modern Austrian Literature*, 18 (1985), 39–52.

12. The narrator's address is Ungargasse 6, Wien III, so the reference here is to her own flat, her own territory.

13. Boa, 'Unnatural Causes', p. 145.

14. Judith Butler, 'Contingent Foundations: Feminism and the Question of "Postmodernism"', in Butler and Scott, pp. 3–21 (p. 16).

15. Swales, 'Die Fallé', p. 76.

Austrophobia as it is

Charles Sealsfield, Thomas Bernhard
and the Art of Exaggeration

Andrea Reiter

Die Wut der Österreicher ist bekanntlich tief, jahrhundertelanges Ducken hat eine spezielle Staatsfeindlichkeit hervorgebracht, unter der Gemütlichkeit lauert stets die Lust auf eine Hetz.

Armin Thurnher, 'Das setzt dem Volk die Krone auf'[1]

At first sight, it would appear that the writers Thomas Bernhard and Charles Sealsfield had little more in common than having been born in Austria and spending much of their time criticising their native country. Their lives belong to entirely different eras – Sealsfield died in 1864, Bernhard was born in 1932. At a closer look, however, some striking parallels emerge.

It is by no means the purpose of this essay to extend the thesis of the Habsburg myth to Austrian contemporary literature, nor do I intend to search for intertextual relationships in the works of these authors. Rather, it is the form and function of their criticism of Austria in some of their writings which will provide the focus of this essay. I shall start with some parallels in their biographies, then go on to look more closely at Sealsfield's *Austria as it is* and Bernhard's *Auslöschung* ('Obliteration'). Inevitably, some known facts will be repeated; but I hope that they will thereby gain a new interpretative dimension.

Both Sealsfield and Bernhard came from an agrarian background. The former was born as Carl Postl in 1793 in Poppitz, a wine-growing community in Moravia; his father, a farmer and winegrower also held a public office in the wine business. While Bernhard's parents had already left the farming community they had been born into – his mother was a home help and his father a carpenter – he nevertheless was deeply influenced by his maternal grandfather, the writer Johann Freumbichler, a farmer's son who had escaped his native village of Henndorf with the intention of becoming a revolutionary in Switzerland. The extent to which the grandfather's experience influenced and shaped the grandson's life, especially regarding the latter's compulsive purchase of properties, has recently been shown by Hans Höller.[2]

Not only did Sealsfield and Bernhard come from similar backgrounds, they also resemble each other in having idealised themselves by shrouding their

166

identities in an aura of mystery. Their success in this regard is documented by a flood of books published upon their deaths in which the biographers view their subject from the perspective of a former friend.[3] Sealsfield cultivated the image of an influential diplomat serving alternately the French and American governments.[4] For a time he even worked for the Bonapartists, whose cause he supported in America in 1830, not least as a journalist for *Le Courier des Etats-Unis*. Previously – and presumably for desperate financial reasons – he had offered his services as a secret informer to Count Metternich and his government, which a little later he was to denounce so emphatically in *Austria as it is*, an act which earned him sarcastic criticism from posterity.[5]

Sealsfield led his life under an alias: only after his death was his true identity revealed, in his last will and testament. Even while in exile in Switzerland, his permanent residence after returning from the United States in 1831, he claimed to be an American; strictly speaking this was true, since he had possessed an American passport since the 1820s.[6] When his collected works were published between 1845 and 1847 Sealsfield – the 'große Unbekannte' ('great unknown') as his biographer Eduard Castle called him – gave up his anonymity. Yet he admitted to the authorship of *Austria as it is*, his first book, only shortly before his death to the Hungarian journalist and his first biographer Karl Kertbeny.[7]

While Bernhard had no need to hide behind an assumed name – not, at least, after his first success with the novel *Frost* (1963)[8] – he did manage to throw an aura of secrecy over his early childhood. In *Ein Kind* ('A Child'), chronologically the first volume of his autobiography, he recounts the story of a baby boy on a fishing boat in the port of Rotterdam. Eventually he adopts this story as his authentic biography, as the interview with Kurt Hofmann demonstrates:

> Dann ist meine Mutter als Hausgehilfin … in Rotterdam irgendwo hingegangen … und mich hat sie auf irgendeinen Fischkutter oder was im Hafen gegeben … da waren so Hängematten, immer wenn die Mutter gekommen ist, ist das Kind heruntergelassen worden, so war das. Bis zu einem Jahr ungefähr.

> [Then my mother went somewhere as a home help and left me on some barge in the harbour. There were hammocks; every time my mother came the child was lowered. This lasted till I was about a year old.]

Nine years after *Ein Kind* was published the French Bernhard scholar Louis Huguet was able to reconstruct the true facts of the first year of Bernhard's life, from which a much more prosaic picture emerges.[10]

Just as Bernhard always boasted an academic degree awarded for a thesis on Artaud and Brecht which could never be found, so he pursued links with the aristocracy. Not only is the action of his novels more often than not set in stately homes or on large estates, but Bernhard himself cultivated relationships with the nobility. Among his friends were the Lampersbergs, Count O'Donnell and the Reichsgräfin von Überacker, and the Üxkülls; the aristocratic circle in which he moved even included a descendant of Emperor Franz Joseph, Franz Josef Altenburg, who with his daughters Cäcilia and Amalia became immortalised in *Auslöschung*. Krista Fleischmann's interviewees in her latest book belong to a large extent to the Austrian aristocracy, even if the abolition of titles no longer makes this explicit.[11]

Sealsfield seems to have been similarly eager for contact with the aristocracy. In his time, however, the cultivation of good manners and the lifestyle of the upper classes, together with the ability to ride a horse, play the piano and speak foreign languages (in Sealsfield's case, English and French), was part of the programme of a social climber.[12] Yet Sealsfield's connections to the Bohemian aristocracy seems to have been of little use to him at the time when he would have most needed it. Or perhaps he had turned to the wrong person when in 1823 he approached Count Franz Saurau.[13] Despite this experience Sealsfield displays a great deal of affection for the nobility in *Austria as it is*. He defends them against Metternich and deplores their increasing exclusion from positions of political responsibility as an act of despotism.

A further resemblance can be detected in the unfolding of their literary careers. Both originally earned a living as journalists, an occupation that left its traces in their literary works. Both also choreographed their careers to a certain extent. It is known, for instance, that Bernhard asked the S. Fischer Verlag to return a prose manuscript that had already been accepted for publication so that *Frost* would be his first work to appear in print. 'Bernhard war von der Idee eingenommen,' Hans Höller writes, 'daß sein erster Prosa-Band unverwechselbar und überwältigend zu sein habe' ('Bernhard was possessed by the idea that his first prose volume should be unmistakable and overwhelming').[14] This betrays an astonishing confidence in his own talent, rare among young writers. Consistent with this are Bernhard's intentions with regard to the end of his writing career. Hilde Spiel documents Bernhard's thoughts as a passenger on a plane that nearly crashed: 'ich hab' nur darüber nachgedacht,' she quotes him, 'ja, wie ist denn das letzte Buch jetzt, das ich veröffentlicht hab'? Ist das ein Buch, mit dem man aus dem Leben gehen kann?' ('My only thought was about the latest book I published: is it fit to be a last book?')[15] This points to the centrality of Bernhard's oeuvre in his life, and moreover documents his uncanny ability to look at his life from an elevated position, such as that of literary history.

While Sealsfield apparently did not reach Bernhard's perfection as a self-stylist, the beginning of his writing career does – at least in retrospect – also seem well calculated. His first two works, *Die Vereinigten Staaten von Nordamerika, nach ihren politischen, religiösen und gesellschaftlichen Verhältnissen betrachtet* (Stuttgart and Tübingen, 1827) and *Austria as it is* (London, 1827) form the geographical vantage points which were to mark the political and ideological realm of his literary output. They point to the two hemispheres on whose first-hand knowledge the author's expertise would rest.

Fascination and repulsion characterises the relationship of both writers to the Church. One of the most striking parts of *Austria as it is* is a satirical picture of a Sunday mass at St Augustine's in Vienna. Without explicitly saying so, Sealsfield criticises from the position of one who has resigned his membership in a club: had he reflected about his impressions he could have said in Bernhard's words, 'ich bin aus der Kirche genau zu dem Zeitpunkt ausgetreten, in welchem ich mit der Kirche nichts mehr zu tun hatte geistig' ('I left the Church just at the moment when I had nothing more to do with the Church intellectually').[16] Like Bernhard, Sealsfield attacks the superficiality and hypocrisy of a church which no longer has anything to do with religious faith:

> Before the altar are the priest and his assistants, dressed in gaudy robes, with a number of priestlings, incensing, bowing, and dancing attendance, with an alertness which shows any thing but piety .... Four or five bells are incessantly ringing from the side-altars, where other priests hurry over their masses, surrounded by standing and kneeling devotees, who perform their Sunday duty of hearing a mass. The priest who is able to do it in the shortest time, about twelve minutes, is surrounded by the greatest crowd. (*Austria* 200)

Where they differ, however, is the means by which this criticism is expressed. While Bernhard chooses fiction and self-ironisation, Sealsfield claims documentary quality for his statement. Thus his narrator guards against giving the impression that he is taking an atheistic stand by contrasting 'heathen Austrian Catholicism' with British Protestantism. Criticism of the institution, moreover, does not prevent him from drawing on religious ideas in his later work, as is shown by the relationship between Nature and the human sphere in *Die Prärie am Jacinto*, a work characterised by a strange mixture of theology and politics.[17]

Bernhard's fiction never presents the church in an affirmative way; on the contrary, in his later works, notably in *Auslöschung*, the apparently seamless transition from National Socialism to Catholicism in Austria gives rise to emphatic outbursts against the 'Catholic-National-Socialist' state and its inhabitants:

> Und dann ... folgt unser nationalsozialistisch-katholisches Volk, dachte ich. Und unsere nationalsozialistisch-katholische Musikkapelle spielt dazu. Und die nationalsozialistischen Böller werden abgeschossen von der Friedhofsrampe und die katholischen Kirchenglocken läuten dazu. Und wenn wir Glück haben, dachte ich, scheint während der ganzen Zeremonie unsere nationalsozialistisch-katholische Sonne oder es regnet, wenn wir kein Glück haben, der nationalsozialistisch-katholische Regen. (*Auslöschung* 444f.)

The musical form of the passage,[18] a kind of theme and variations on 'nazionalsozialistisch-katholisch', makes a joke of the issue, while at the same time preserving an attitude of ambivalence towards the church. The form which his criticism takes almost neutralises its critical quality, or at any rate, makes it 'consumable'.

Bernhard's and Sealsfield's rebuking of politicians seems to be autobiographically motivated. Bernhard never forgot that he was not awarded the Traklpreis, which he had put in for as a young poet,[19] and later he could hardly conceal his disappointment about being rejected for the directorship of the Burgtheater. Moreover, as a seasoned writer he fought personal skirmishes against politicians: in 1985 against the then treasury secretary Franz Vranitzky and the education minister Herbert Moritz.[20] In his fiction such criticism assumes a life of its own in the verbal bombardments, condemning everybody and everything, that are so typical of the author.

The biographical motive of Sealsfield's critique of Metternich is also hurt pride. As already mentioned, the escaped monk tried unsuccessfully to better his dire financial situation by offering his services as a spy to the Austrian state chancellor, a fact which gave an early researcher of Sealsfield's works the idea that *Austria as it is* might have been conceived as an act of revenge (*Austria* LXX). Although financial reasons have now been conclusively identified as the most likely reason why he wrote the book, much personal animosity has certainly gone into the portrait of Metternich, the only figure to be assigned an entire chapter to himself. Characterising him as a cunning, intriguing and effeminate figure, Sealsfield likens Metternich to an 'immense spider' who 'has woven his net over the whole of Europe', a talented man but an 'indifferent lawyer, and an absolute idiot in financial matters' (*Austria* 153, 157).

As regards their production, the two books I am examining here could hardly differ more: one is a first publication, the other published towards the end of its author's life. Although the nucleus of *Auslöschung* was written in the early 1980s – about the same time as *Beton* ('Concrete', 1982) – and it has some similarity to the fragmentary novel *Der Italiener* ('The Italian', 1963; recast as a film script in 1971), Bernhard rewrote and extended it considerably for publication in 1986, taking on board several topical issues. Thus the novel betrays strong motivic and linguistic similarities with the above mentioned earlier texts,[21] yet a new political dimension emerges, according it a special place in Bernhard's work. In this sense *Auslöschung* is an *opus ultimum*: one could almost call it an 'Alterswerk' had its author not died so relatively young. As such it shows a certain amount of stylistic mannerism, which manifests itself in the perfection of 'musical' principles of composition. As an 'Alterswerk' it has, moreover, a self-critical narrator and some conciliatory motives. (Murau's friend Maria – a homage to Ingeborg Bachmann – is the only truly positive female figure in all of Bernhard's work, and one whose authority the narrator readily accepts.)

Sealsfield's text not only marks the start of his writing career but also belongs to a completely different literary tradition, 'as it is' in the title fuelling the contemporary reader's expectation of a revelation of the unheard-of (see *Austria* LI). The genre identified by this phrase seems to go back to a Count Joseph Hyppolyte de Santo-Domingo (*Austria* XXXVIIIf.), born in 1785 in France. Little is known about him except that he was widely travelled (in Italy and allegedly the United States), and is said to have been opposed to the

French Romantic movement and to have adored Napoleon. In 1824 he published the *Tablettes romaines* which earned him not only a court trial and three months' imprisonment but also sensational fame. The work, whose title was to become a synonym for political indiscretions, gossip and other revelations, was swiftly imitated by other writers who sometimes would publish their own product under the name of their model. The title was translated into German as *Wie es ist*, which is the German equivalent of 'as it is'. Conversely, *Austria as it is* was published in 1830 as *Tablettes Autrichiennes* in Brussels (see *Austria* XLI). A German version of part of the text appeared in 1834 in Leipzig under the title *Seufzer aus Österreich und seinen Provinzen* ('Groans from Austria and its Provinces'); the work was not published in German in its entirety until 1919.

Among the formal characteristics of the genre are its autobiographical framework and its presentation as a travel report. The abbreviation of names such as P...ss M...y is designed to underline the conspiratorial quality of this type of pamphlet. As in Sealsfield, this practice was prone to being overdone: even easily recognisable names were treated in this fashion (see *Austria* XXXVIII).

The reception of *Austria* intended by its author is based on the political character of its French model. Only in the opening chapter does the journey itself occupy a central position, taking the reader from Le Havre via Karlsruhe, Stuttgart, Darmstadt, Frankfurt and Leipzig to Dresden. The closer the tour gets to the Habsburg Empire and its capital, the more the narrator talks about its culture and government. Vienna is reached by the fourth chapter, and the remaining four concentrate solely on the political situation in Austria; its exponents who comprise the Emperor, the chancellor and the aristocracy; and the city of Vienna with her citizens, architecture and cultural life. The term 'travel novel' therefore applies mainly to its first half.

As for its political character, *Austria as it is* no doubt stands in the shadow of Sealsfield's later works, where he was able to find an appropriate literary form for their political content. In *Das Kajütenbuch*, for example, he describes the essence of American democracy by employing discussion and viewing issues from a number of angles[22]; by contrast the style of *Austria*, true to its character of a report, is mainly descriptive. Of the two narrative types which Walter Weiss has identified in *Das Kajütenbuch*, namely those of approximation and contrast, the latter is present only in a crude way in *Austria*. Approximation, however, is not described as process in the text but as a *fait accompli:* where it does manifest itself, such as where Great Britain is presented as a positive model, it has already been accomplished as the narrator identifies with that country.

While the political character of *Austria* is determined by its genre, *Auslöschung* must rather be described as a social novel with strong political overtones. These are easier to observe if the novel is compared with *Der Italiener*, which presents the central motif of the funeral spectacle. What is missing from *Der Italiener*, both as fragmentary novel and as film script, is precisely that political dimension which Bernhard added when he reworked

171

the theme. Even the presumed earlier version, a manuscript purportedly written in 1981–82 in Yugoslavia, could not have had this political dimension: the novel includes political events which did not take place in Austria until the mid-80s, such as the controversy about Kurt Waldheim's election for president and the takeover of the Carinthian Bärental (a formerly 'aryanised' property) by the notorious leader of the FPÖ, Jörg Haider.[23]

Auslöschung not only stands out from Bernhard's oeuvre because of its political character, it is also the text in which, more explicitly than elsewhere, he spells out his poetology. He introduces the figure of the 'Übertreibungskünstler' – this was quickly picked up by scholars working on Bernhard[24] – and explains it both in narratological and in psychological terms. On the one hand, Murau/Bernhard says, we have to exaggerate to bring the message across ('nur die Übertreibung macht anschaulich' (*Auslöschung* 128)), on the other he claims that he was literally dependent on his art of exaggeration and talks about it in terms of 'eine Kunst der Überbrückung ..., der Existenzüberbrückung' (*Auslöschung* 611). What he means by this is shown in the following:

> Mit diesem Übertreibungsfanatismus habe ich mich schon immer befriedigt, habe ich zu Gambetti gesagt. Er ist manchmal die einzige Möglichkeit, wenn ich diesen Übertreibungsfanatismus nämlich zur Übertreibungskunst gemacht habe, mich aus der Armseligkeit meiner Verfassung zu retten, aus meinem Geistesüberdruß ... (*Auslöschung* 611).

On the stylistic level this fanaticism of exaggeration expresses itself as excessive use of the superlative, which has been interpreted as 'grammatical-aesthetic equivalent of Bernhard's radical opposition to an evolutionary view of the world'.[25]

In an early interview, Bernhard claimed: 'In meinen Büchern ist alles *künstlich*'[26]; in later writings he did not generally reflect on his poetology. This is what makes the remarks in *Auslöschung* concerning the art of exaggeration all the more interesting. Exaggeration, however, is by no means a new feature of Bernhard's writing, indeed it has been recognised, especially by Schmidt-Dengler, as one of its hallmarks. Judging by Bernhard's invectives against politicians and his letters to the editors of newspapers, exaggeration almost seems to be part of his mode of thinking and not merely a stylistic mannerism. This would explain the striking similarity between, say, his novels and his non-fictional writings.

While Bernhard thus makes exaggeration his narrative principle, the relatively frequent use of superlative constructions gives Sealsfield's text a strong emotional tone. He does employ hyperbole in a strategic way when describing the landscape of his childhood or characterising Franz II or Metternich and their despotic style of government. The superlative thus expresses the narrator's bias. The black-and-white imagery and the simplification of the political situation in the Austria of the 1820s may have contributed to the early impact of the book. As far as the form is concerned, exaggeration is responsible for stereotyped phrases such as: 'There is not a less popular government in Europe' (*Austria* 189), 'The approach to Vienna, from this side, is truly grand' (109) or 'Never has there been a man more detested and dreaded than Metternich' (114). These lines, moreover, all occur at the beginnings of chapters. It is particularly surprising to find such phrases, and so many of them, in a text that advertises itself as presenting authentic reality. As Primus-Heinz Kucher observes in a recent study, 'Eine präzisere Rückbindung an die Wirklichkeit hat Sealsfield ... unterlassen' ('Sealsfield refrained from making a closer connection with reality').[27] We may add that it is the book's superlativistic style which is largely responsible for this. As with Bernhard's, the hyperbole is not peculiar to the text we are discussing here but is manifest also in his later texts, thus unifying Sealsfield's oeuvre not only on a thematic level but also on a stylistic one.

Another characteristic which unites the works of these two writers is the use of expressions that are typical of the German language as spoken in Austria, especially as it is used in the Roman Catholic religion. Thus the repetition of phrases, so typical of Bernhard, has been likened to the invocation of the saints as practised in the Catholic liturgy and interpreted as litanies, 'als säkularisierte Form der bannenden Beschwörung von Dingen und Sachverhalten' ('as a secularised form of the magical conjuration of objects and situations').[28] With Sealsfield's work it was Walter von Molo who pointed to the Catholic-Austrian quality of his language.[29] Although the Catholic clergy figures prominently in *Austria as it is* Sealsfield has not quite developed the idiom to which Molo referred. Only in his later works does he develop a kind of artificial language for his characters which consists of a mixture of different idioms, one of them being that of the church liturgy.[30] The use of Catholic forms by both writers is all the more interesting as both fiercely criticise the institution behind them. Yet by taking over its rhetoric they do not intend to ridicule it. It is quite obvious that Bernhard, in particular, imitates the idiosyncrasy of a system of discourse with the intention of creating a new one to fit his own themes and their messages.

In the introduction to *Austria as it is* the author, although keeping his anonymity, states that he himself had encountered the experiences which the book relays upon returning to his native country after a five-year absence. This proof of authenticity of the text, however, is not itself trustworthy, as subsequent research has shown. Sealsfield did come back to Germany in 1826 – this is proved by his correspondence with Metternich – but he never got as far as Austria (*Austria* XLV). Only in 1828 did he return, by which time *Austria as it is* had already been published the previous December (*Austria* V). The impressions that Sealsfield uses in his book mostly go back to the time before his escape in 1823, and thus are authentic but not of the most recent date. What Sealsfield presents in the text is anything but a personal report. While there is a first-person-plural narrator (a travelling companion, who is said to have saved him from the censors at the Austrian border, is mentioned on one occasion (*Austria* 26f.)), the personality of the narrator remains obscure. Only the following indirect reference is made: '... an observing traveller, not entirely excluded from the higher circles, will soon find out that

Austria is nearer a crisis than perhaps any other country' (*Austria* 156). It is evident that the identity of the reporter is kept vague in order to protect the anonymity of the author. Sealsfield seems keen, moreover, to give the impression of the utmost objectivity. This fits in with the claim made by the text's title to present the situation in Austria 'as it is' and not as it was perceived by an individual. That this notion is a fiction and that Sealsfield's report is as subjective as it is emotional can be seen from the inflationary use of the superlative.

While Sealsfield thus, in accordance with the genre he chose for his text, avoids any reference to the narrator, Bernhard does the complete opposite in his novel. Of the narrator in *Auslöschung* we read a great deal, and some of it is autobiographical. What Murau does not tell the reader about himself we can pick up in Uncle Georg, a character to whom he likens his own personality. Murau is not afraid of saying 'I', indeed he characterises his report as decidedly subjective: he intended to describe Wolfsegg, which is paradigmatic for Austria, exactly as he saw it, backing this up with the following poetological statement: 'Jeder kann nur beschreiben, was *er* sieht, wie es *ihm* erscheint, nicht anders' (*Auslöschung* 197). Nowhere is a comparable degree of self-reflection reached in Sealsfield. It is also Murau who decides to wipe out Wolfsegg for entirely subjective reasons, as he does not hesitate to admit: 'Wir hassen ja nur, wenn und weil wir im Unrecht sind' (*Auslöschung* 105). The act of utter and final destruction is thus relativised, and with it the hyperbolic style. The so-called 'All- und Existenzsätze' are revealed as founded in the individual and his whims.[31]

While for both authors the love-hate relationship with their home country acts as an important motivation to write, something they share with other Austrian writers such as Karl Kraus, it is this same love-hate which makes for the differences between them. Bernhard knew how to channel his rage into literary forms such as that of the 'Erregung',[32] that is to say, he instrument-alised it aesthetically. It is to his credit as a writer that he succeeded in doing so at an early stage in his career, for example in the form of the litany. Sealsfield, on the other hand, cannot abstract from his own sentiments; *Austria as it is* shows his deep emotional involvement. His invectives against the Austrian state and its government are guided exclusively, it would seem, by personal circumstances. First the political reaction under Metternich took his teacher, then the secret police at the border wanted to strip him of his foreign-language books. Had he stayed in Austria he could not have hoped to leave the Church legally and least of all to become a 'free', i.e. untroubled, writer. Bitterly, and more than somewhat ironically, he concludes: 'Even distinguished writers ... are here paid not so much to write as not to write' (*Austria* 215). On the other hand remarks like this also betray a certain self-justification: he seems to be saying, 'I did well in getting away while it was still possible.' Bernhard's narrator anticipates interpretations like this and makes them explicit while in Sealsfield's text they remain between the lines: this is the difference between the two writers.

The similarity of function in their criticism of Austria – in Sealsfield still governed by the genre, in Bernhard developed into an aesthetic form divorced from rules about genre – is likewise treacherous. Sealsfield's provocations, aided by the suppressed distribution, sensationalised *Austria as it is* and enhanced its sale. For an as yet unknown writer there was no better chance to get hold of some money quickly. This would account for the enthusiastic reviews, which have since been followed by a largely negative reception. Such a view, however, does not do the text justice. Recent research has at least hinted at the importance of *Austria as it is* within the work of Charles Sealsfield as a whole: it has been discovered how style and motives in his famous novels are already anticipated in this early text.[33]

Bernhard's notoriety was also enhanced by his frequent presence in the media. Above and beyond provocation as a condition of the market, Bernhard's invectives also have a specific literary quality which not only tames them but also ensures their consumability. Bernhard never claimed that his writings would change society; yet many, especially the earlier ones and most consistently *Auslöschung*, demonstrate this: what *Verstörung* ('Gargoyles') and *Korrektur* ('Correction') merely announce, namely the destruction of the family estate through the heir, Murau not only suggests in writing but actually puts into practice. The destructive tendency in Bernhard's novels is matched by its complete opposite in his biography, which is marked by the loving and knowledgeable conservation of the cultural heritage. Both the radical opposites and the passionate advocacy of each one in its context are more proof of the exaggeration which governs Bernhard's art and, indeed, life.

Sealsfield settled his accounts with the forces of reaction by severely criticising the 'immobility' of the Habsburg Empire and was not willing to sublimate it as renunciation of action, as did his contemporaries Franz Grillparzer on the stage and Adalbert Stifter in the novel. As a fugitive it was obviously easier for him to do so, since he did not have to make compromises with the regime. This is why it is all the more surprising that in 1848 he joined his literary colleagues in denouncing the revolutionary movements in Austria.[34] Whether this reflects financial considerations or the fear of Austria breaking apart, it is significant that, as in Bernhard's case, a radical writer turns out to be at heart conservative when challenged in real life.

Notes

1. *Die Zeit*, 3 February 1995, p. 79. (The fury of the Austrians is known to be profound. Centuries of cringing have created a specific hostility to the state. Underneath the geniality the eagerness for some fun is lurking.)
2. Hans Höller, *Thomas Bernhard*, Rowohlt Monographie 504 (Reinbek, 1993), esp. p. 95.
3. See Charles Sealsfield, *Austria as it is: or Sketches of Continental Courts. Österreich wie es ist, oder Skizzen von Fürstenhöfen des Kontinents*, transl. and ed. Victor Klarwill (Hildesheim/New York 1972), III, Introduction. – For Bernhard see e.g. Maria Fialik, *Der Charismatiker. Thomas Bernhard und die Freunde von einst* (Vienna, 1992); Krista Fleischmann, *Thomas Bernhard. Eine Erinnerung. Interviews zur Person* (Vienna, 1992); Gerda Maletta, *Seteais. Tage mit Thomas Bernhard*

(Weitra, 1993); Herbert Moritz, *Lehrjahre. Thomas Bernhard – Vom Journalisten zum Dichter* (Weitra, 1993).

4. See *Austria*: Introduction. – W. G. Sebald, *Unheimliche Heimat. Essays zur Osterreichischen Literatur* (Salzburg, 1991), p. 22, note 16.

5. See for example Gustav Winter, who talks in his 1907 essay of a 'kaum beneidenswerte Versatilität des Charakters' (*Austria* LXVIII).

6. See Sebald, *Unheimliche Heimat*, p. 21.

7. *Austria*, 'Nachwort' to the German translation, p. 207.

8. Höller mentions three early works published under two different pseudonyms, see p. 150.

9. Kurt Hofmann, *Aus Gesprächen mit Thomas Bernhard* (Vienna, 1988), p. 36.

10. See Holler, *Bernhard*, p. 28f., note 86.

11. *Thomas Bernhard. Eine Erinnerung. Interviews zur Person* (1992).

12. See Sebald, *Unheimliche Heimat*, p. 19.

13. The surprising identity of the name with that of Bernhard's protagonist in *Die Verstörung* must surely be coincidental.

14. Höller, *Bernhard*, p. 69.

15. Fleischmann, *Bernhard*, p. 150. (My only thought was my latest book: is it fit to be a last book?)

16. Thomas Bernhard, *Auslöschung. Ein Zerfall* (Frankfurt, 1986), p. 633 (future references in the text marked 'Auslöschung').

17. See Walter Weiss, 'Der Zusammenhang zwischen Amerika-Thematik und Erzählkunst bei Charles Sealsfield (Karl Postl). Ein Beitrag zur Dichtung und Politik im 19. Jahrhundert', *Literaturwissenschaftliches Jahrbuch der Görresgesellschaft*, N.F. 8 (1967), 95–117 (107f.). Cf. Claudio Magris, *Der habsburgische Mythos in der österreichischen Literatur* (Salzburg, 1966), p. 62.

18. See Andrea Reiter, 'Thomas Bernhard's "Musical Prose"', *Literature on the Threshold: the German Novel in the 1980s*, ed. Arthur Williams (New York/ Oxford, 1990), pp. 187–207.

19. Krista Fleischmann and Wolfgang Koch, 'Monologe auf Mallorca, Thomas Bernhard – eine Herausforderung', ORF-*Nachlese* 4/1981, p. 2–8.

20. See Jens Dittmar (ed.), *Thomas Bernhard. Werkgeschichte* (Frankfurt, 1990) p. 295ff.

21. See Andrea Reiter, '"Die Bachmann hab' ich sehr gern mögen, die war halt eine gescheite Frau. Eine seltsame Verbindung, nicht?": Women in Thomas Bernhard's Prose Writings', Ricarda Schmidt and Moray McGowan (eds.), *From High Priests to Desecrators. Contemporary Austrian Writers* (Sheffield, 1993), p. 155–73. See also Ulrich Weinzierl, 'Bernhard als Erzieher. Thomas Bernhards *Auslöschung*', *German Quarterly*, 63 (1990), pp. 455–61 (459).

22. See Weiss, 'Der Zusammenhang', p. 110.

23. See Weinzierl, 'Bernhard als Erzieher', p. 459.

24. See Wendelin Schmidt-Dengler, *Der Übertreibungskünstler. Studien zu Thomas Bernhard* (Vienna, 1986).

25. Karlheinz Rossbacher, 'Thomas Bernhard: *Das Kalkwerk*', Paul Michael Lützeler (ed.), *Deutsche Romane des 20. Jahrhunderts: Neue Interpretationen* (Königstein, 1983), p. 372–87 (379).

26. This interview with the title 'Drei Tage' was published with 'Der Italiener' in: *Der Italiener*, p. 82.

27. Charles Sealsfield – Karl Postl, *Austria as it is: or Sketches of continental courts by an Eye-witness*, London 1828. *Österreich, wie es ist oder Skizzen von Fürstenhöfen des Kontinents*, Wien 1919, ed. Primus-Heinz Kucher, Literatur in der Geschichte, Geschichte in der Literatur vol. 28 (Vienna, 1994), p. 377.

28. Rossbacher, 'Bernhard: *Das Kalkwerk*', p. 381.

29. Walter von Molo, 'Sealsfield-Postl', *März*, 11 (1917), quot. Franz Schüppen, 'Charles Sealsfield', Jost Hermand and Manfred Windfuhr (eds.) *Zur Literatur der Restaurationsepoche 1815–1848. Forschungsreferate und Aufsätze* (Stuttgart, 1970), pp. 285–346 (298).

30. See Friedrich Sengle, 'Karl Postl, Pseud. Charles Sealsfield (1793–1864)', in his *Biedermeierzeit. Deutsche Literatur im Spannungsfeld zwischen Restauration und Revolution 1815–1848* (Stuttgart, 1980), III: Die Dichter, pp. 752–814 (797f).

31. See Schmidt-Dengler: '"Der Tod als Naturwissenschaft neben dem Leben, Leben." Zu Bernhards Sprache der Ausschließlichkeit', *Der Übertreibungskünstler*, pp. 7–12.

32. See Thomas Bernhard, *Heldenplatz* (Frankfurt, 1988), p. 91, quot. Höller, *Bernhard*, p. 17. Cf. André Müller, *Im Gespräch mit Thomas Bernhard* (Weitra, 1992), p. 80.

33. See Charles Sealsfield, ed. Kucher, p. 351.

34. See Sebald, *Unheimliche Heimat*, p. 26.

Part Two
Review Articles

Recent Studies of Musil

Duncan Large

Gudrun Brokoph-Mauch (ed.), *Robert Musil, Essayismus und Ironie* (Tübingen: Francke, 1992), viii + 212 pp., DM 96.

Christian Rogowski, *Implied Dramaturgy: Robert Musil and the Crisis of Modern Drama*, Studies in Austrian Literature, Culture and Thought (Riverside, CA: Ariadne Press, 1993), xiii + 313 pp., $37.50.

Kathleen O'Connor, *Robert Musil and the Tradition of the German Novelle*, Studies in Austrian Literature, Culture and Thought (Riverside, CA: Ariadne Press, 1992), 181 pp., $28.00.

Heinrich Puppe, *Muße und Müßiggang in Robert Musils Roman 'Der Mann ohne Eigenschaften'*, Beiträge zur Robert-Musil-Forschung und zur neueren österreichischen Literatur, 1 (St. Ingbert: Röhrig, 1991), 202 pp., DM 30.

Gudrun Brokoph-Mauch's *Robert Musil, Essayismus und Ironie* comprises seventeen papers from a conference held at St Lawrence University, New York State, in 1988, and like her earlier *Beiträge zur Musil-Kritik* (New York, Berne, Frankfurt, 1983) this important collection provides a snapshot of trends in mid-Atlantic Musil criticism. The volume is more successful than most in sustaining its focus on the interrelated themes, and when they are arguably the two most important characteristics of Musil's mature style this is indeed welcome.

The papers in the first section consider essayism, irony and 'Möglichkeitssinn' ('the sense of possibilities') as more general principles of Musil's poetics. Geoffrey Howes opens the collection with a thought-provoking piece which relates Musil's formal and thematic concerns by considering the essay as 'Ein Genre ohne Eigenschaften' ('A Genre without Qualities'), comparing Musil with Montaigne and Sterne. Michael Jakob continues in this comparative vein, arguing that the perspectivism of *Der Mann ohne Eigenschaften* (*The Man without Qualities*) is a more comprehensive instantiation of 'Möglichkeitssinn' than earlier philosophical explorations of the theme (Socrates, Nietzsche) and other contemporary literary treatments of it (Gide, Valéry, Broch). Friedrich Wallner offers a dense but stimulating account in which he refreshingly brackets Musil's much-quoted binary of the 'ratioid' and the 'nonratioid', focussing instead on what he terms the 'indirect rationality' of Musil's ironic writing and arguing that it serves a therapeutic purpose which it shares with philosophy in the wake of Mach's elimination of the ego.

As one would expect, a number of contributions concentrate on the status and function of irony in *Der Mann ohne Eigenschaften*, although there are marked differences in both analysis and evaluation. For Martin Swales the first book of Musil's novel is particularly adept at anchoring its hero in a recognisable socio-political context, making him more of a representative figure than the eponymous hero of *Die Verwirrungen des Zöglings Törleß* (*The Confusions of Young Törless*) and giving Musil's ironic barbs a greater purchase. But whereas Swales reads the second book of Musil's monumental novel as lacking in the incisive irony of the first and thereby diminished, Philip Beard defends the second book against such accusations and maintains (to my mind less convincingly) that the rhapsodic portrayal of the relationship between Ulrich and his sister Agathe in the chapter 'Beginn einer Reihe wundersamer Erlebnisse' ('Start of a Series of Wondrous Experiences') is in fact the culmination of the novel. In turn Joseph Strelka argues, *contra* Swales and Beard, that the relatively 'gentle irony' of the first book actually takes on a harder edge in the second, becoming more radical and destructive. Strelka outlines a useful typology of the various forms of Musil's irony, although in making his initial claim that the function of irony in Musil has not yet been sufficiently addressed he curiously overlooks Beda Allemann's substantial discussion in his *Ironie und Dichtung* (Pfullingen, 1956). Thankfully Marie-Louise Roth gives Allemann his due, and she herself demonstrates the value of well-executed genetic criticism, making a persuasive case for her opening contention that 'Die Musilsche Ironie ist nicht primär' ('Musil's irony is not primary', 123) by analysing the increasingly ironic tone discernible in the successive stages of the sketch 'Kann ein Pferd lachen?' ('Can a Horse Laugh?').

Roth's developmental approach is shared by Annette Daigger and Peter Henninger in two more excellent papers. Daigger shows how the forthright and impassioned political activism of the essays which Musil published either side of the First World War, reflecting his adherence to the cause of the Social Democratic Party, modulates in the 1920s into the more 'characteristically' detached tone of 'geistig-politisch' ('intellectually political') scepticism. Henninger then uses examples from Musil's correspondence to demonstrate the discrepancy between his own and his public's appreciation of his works, examining in particular his love/hate relationship with his journalism and suggesting that *Der Mann ohne Eigenschaften* was so much more positively received than Musil's earlier works precisely because of his 'discovery of the formula' for effective writing over the period 1920–1930, a hybrid style which infuses lyricism with an arch self-consciousness perfected over his years of pot-boiling 'Publizistik'.

The final section of this volume is devoted to a series of further comparative studies: Peter Kampits argues that Musil's whole endeavour was to find ways of expressing what Wittgenstein's *Tractatus* so celebratedly claimed to need passing over in silence; Jürgen Thöming contributes an engagingly quirky piece on Musil, Brecht and the translation of Elizabethan poetry; Donald Daviau finds much in common between Musil and Bahr, especially in their reception of Mach, and vehemently disputes Claudia Monti's essay on the same topic (*Musil-Forum*, 1984). A good pair of complementary papers by Dietmar Goltschnigg and Gudrun Brokoph-Mauch herself considers the often fraught relationship between Musil and Broch (treating their essays and correspondence respectively), and Josef Strutz pursues a comparison with Altenberg, mounting a spirited defence of the latter's modernity.

All told, the great majority of the essays here implicitly bear out Roth's central argument that what is considered to be Musil's distinctive ironic tone was in fact acquired over the course of his writing career. Anne Servranckx's paper rather bucks the trend by dwelling on the relatively early unpublished fragment 'Lieber Pan-!' (1911/12), which already bears many of the hallmarks of Musil's later work, but the focus of the collection is, understandably enough, on that later works, and on the essays and *Der Mann ohne Eigenschaften* in particular. Wilhelm Braun's piece on the importance of the figure of Stader in *Die Schwärmer* (*The Visionaries*) is the only contribution to discuss Musil's drama, and none of the papers addresses the two collections of shorter prose fiction which Musil published before embarking on his last great unfinished novel, *Vereinigungen* (*Unions*, 1911) and *Drei Frauen* (*Three Women*, 1924).

The two books by Christian Rogowski and Kathleen O'Connor redress this imbalance, for they are the first in English devoted, respectively, to Musil's dramas and his Novellen. Their projects are similar in that both aim at once to advocate the merits of Musil's unjustly underrated contributions to these genres and to further an understanding of the genres themselves. Rogowski's, though, is undoubtedly the weightier of the two studies, and indeed his *Implied Dramaturgy: Robert Musil and the Crisis of Modern Drama* is one of the most substantial and well-researched pieces of Musil criticism to appear in any language in recent years – it is certainly the most comprehensive introduction to Musil's plays to date.

Musil published only two plays: *Die Schwärmer* appeared in 1921 but was initially considered 'unperformable' and did not reach the stage until 1929, when it opened disastrously and had to be withdrawn after a handful of performances; *Vinzenz und die Freundin bedeutender Männer* (*Vinzenz and the Girlfriend of Important Men*) fared somewhat better and was first produced with moderate success in 1923 before being published the following year. Both plays were quickly forgotten and were not performed again during Musil's lifetime – he himself was quite disparaging about *Vinzenz* – and even after the War, when *Der Mann ohne Eigenschaften* began to attract an increasing amount of critical attention, Musil's plays found few champions.

Yet as Rogowski convincingly demonstrates by considering Musil's many other abandoned projects for further plays, and especially his long journalistic involvement as a theatre critic, the theatre *mattered* profoundly to him throughout the major part of his career.

Adapting Wolfgang Iser's notion of the 'implied reader', Rogowski coins the term 'implied dramaturgy' to mean 'the way a play addresses its audience' (p. 16), and he focusses specifically on the unspoken narrative elements in the printed texts which contribute to the differences in effect between the plays on the page and on the stage. His overall thesis is that the plays were too subtly parodic of the dramatic conventions of their period to find an audience at the time, and that it was only after the 'crisis of modern drama' (Szondi) had played itself out that Musil could be recognised in retrospect as a precursor of many of the more 'advanced' dramatic techniques of the 1950s and '60s – a recognition, indeed, which to a certain extent he had gained by the early 1980s, post-Brecht, post-Beckett, post-Pinter et al. Rogowski's opening section establishes his theoretical framework (a combination of Szondi and Jauss) and sets the scene for his analyses of Musil's innovations by charting the 'crisis of representability' in European theatre from Chekhov, Ibsen and Hauptmann to Pirandello. The second section outlines Musil's own theoretical dissatisfactions, in his journalism and essays, with the theatrical traditions of both Naturalism and Expressionism, and with the Viennese performance practices of his time. Musil's dramaturgy is carefully situated between the legacy of Alfred Kerr and the more liberating collectivist potential he perceived in the Moscow Arts Theatre. On the one hand Rogowski acknowledges the conservatism of Musil's insistence on the primacy of the dramatic text ('das dichterische Wort'); on the other he argues persuasively that Musil's theoretical emphasis on 'Klärung' ('clarification') is, in its own way, as subversive of Aristotelian catharsis as Brecht's epic theatre, and that Musil's critique of the commodification of drama in contemporary Vienna anticipates the theoretical insights of the Frankfurt School.

The third and fourth sections are devoted to exemplary and exhaustive close readings of the two published plays, preceded in each case by a detailed discussion of the play's genesis, its performance and reception history, and the question of generic attribution. For Rogowski the minimal descriptions provided by the plays' subtitles ('Schauspiel' and 'Posse') each constitute a 'horizon of expectations' which the rest of the play then systematically counteracts. He shows an easy familiarity with the theatrical traditions within (and more usually against) which Musil is writing, and he is particularly alert to the plays' intertextual allusions, which he tracks down even on the level of typography (p. 161, n. 11). He defends the plays against all the criticisms which have commonly been levelled at them (the banality of their plots, the artificiality of their dialogue, their forced 'theatricality' in general), and instead celebrates their self-referential sophistication: the 'accumulation of overdetermined traditional plot elements' (p. 122) in *Die Schwärmer*, the 'Dramaturgy of Surprise' and 'Structural Dadaism' of *Vinzenz*, the resistance to closure of both. Against the odds, Rogowski's study of the 'implied dramaturgy' which both plays so consistently foreground vindicates his assertion of their originality and modernity, even if Musil himself ultimately became disaffected with his own dramatic efforts and turned to the novel as a genre more amenable to bearing the weight of his epistemic demands.

The argument of Kathleen O'Connor's *Robert Musil and the Tradition of the German Novelle* is broadly similar to Rogowski's: taking as her point of departure Musil's comment, in an essay of 1912, that what is at stake in the Novelle is 'das Problematische des Erzählens' ('the problematics of narration'), she argues that his shorter fictions draw even greater attention to their own artificiality, becoming increasingly 'writerly' in the (periodically) Barthesian terms of her analysis. Like Rogowski, O'Connor opens with a theoretical introduction drawing on reception aesthetics and situating Musil against the backdrop of a modernist 'crisis', in this case the more general crisis of language. But O'Connor's study of the Novellen lacks the kind of telling comparison with other examples of the genre which makes Rogowski's book so valuable, and it is significant that in her first chapter she should choose to summarise 'The Historical Development of the *Theory* of the German Novelle' rather than discuss in detail any actual instances of the practice of Musil's precursors.

This historical overview itself raises more questions than it answers, for the term 'Novelle' is treated in isolation from any of the other kinds of shorter prose fiction in German, such as the 'Märchen' ('fairy-tale'), so that its generic specificity is blurred, and when O'Connor does attempt to demarcate the Novelle from its more fantastic cousins she goes outside the German tradition altogether, invoking Poe (pp. 17, 21). Since the question of genre is so central to her study, it seems odd that O'Connor can so unproblematically consider all six of Musil's short stories as 'Novellen', and fail to address the fact that only *Drei Frauen* were actually given that subtitle by their author, whereas the earlier *Vereinigungen* stories are simply described as 'Erzählungen' ('Narratives') and 'Die Amsel' ('The Blackbird') is given no generic ascription at all by Musil himself – unlike all the other sections of the *Nachlaß zu Lebzeiten* (*Posthumous Papers of a Living Man*) from which it derives.

In her second chapter, on Musil's intellectual history, O'Connor isolates as his most important influences Nietzsche, Mach, and phenomenological and *Gestalt* psychology, and thereafter she focusses fruitfully on the term *Gestalt* to argue that Musil's originality lies in his relational, decentred characterisations which resist totalisation. Theoretical misgivings aside, then, O'Connor's analyses of the stories themselves are often insightful: she maps the trajectory from *Vereinigungen* to *Drei Frauen* as a progression 'From Mimesis to Myth', before isolating the two latest stories for a discussion of 'Subjectivity in "Tonka" and "Die Amsel"' which is particularly effective in highlighting the collapse of narrative structures mediating between perspectives, the interpenetration and mutual relativisation of inner and outer. Unfortunately, however, the excessiveness of O'Connor's claim to be furthering our understanding of the Novelle as genre becomes apparent once more at the end of her study, when she speculates on what a modern post-Musilian Novelle *would* look like, and hints that Bachmann's stories *might* fit into this category, but forecloses without considering what directions the genre has actually taken since Musil's time.

Heinrich Puppe's study, finally, is the first in a welcome new series of monographs (in this case a doctoral dissertation) sponsored by the Arbeitsstelle für Robert-Musil-Forschung in Saarbrücken and complementing Fink's now well-established annual series of *Musil-Studien*. Compared to the 'essayism' and 'irony' of Brokoph-Mauch's collection, the pair of concepts with which Puppe seeks to illuminate *Der Mann ohne Eigenschaften*, 'leisure' and 'idleness', might seem rather less central concerns. And indeed they are, although Puppe opens with a salvo of quotations illustrating their presence in the novel and confirming their status as *explicanda*. In tracing the theoretical history of his twin terms, Puppe ranges widely from Aristotle's *Nicomachean Ethics* and the Ciceronian *otium/negotium* distinction through to Nietzsche, although surprisingly he omits to discuss the work of Nietzsche's which was originally to have been called *Müßiggang eines Psychologen* (*A Psychologist's Idleness*), before it received the title *Götzen-Dämmerung* (*Twilight of the Idols*).

What emerges from Puppe's historical survey, to be confirmed by his second, comparative chapter on Huysmans' *À rebours* (*Against Nature*), Schnitzler's *Der Weg ins Freie* (*The Road to the Open*) and Mann's *Der Zauberberg* (*The Magic Mountain*), is a promising characterisation of 'Muße' and 'Müßiggang' in terms of 'Rollenlosigkeit und verfeinerte Wahrnehmung' ('absence of roles and refined perception'). Although he initially claims that his two terms are synonymous, after dutiful preparatory chapters dealing with the role of leisure and idleness in *Törleß* and *Die Schwärmer*, then the secondary literature on *Der Mann ohne Eigenschaften*, he establishes a neat distinction, and 'Müßig-gang' becomes especially associated with the free-floating individual (Ulrich) or couple (Ulrich/Agathe) *walking* through the streets of the modern metropolis. Puppe theorises leisure as a freedom from the need to play a role in society, but although he flirts with a sociology of literature he is unwilling to pursue a more radical critique and there is a certain disappointing blandness about his conclusions. He notes, for example, that what allows Ulrich and Agathe their leisure is their independence from material need, but he does not pursue the point, and although he successfully distinguishes the figure of the 'Müßiggänger' from the bohemian, the artist, the aesthete, the dandy and the plain lazybones, there is a rather greater and largely unaddressed overlap with the figure of the '*flâneur*', and a consideration of (Benjamin's reading of) Baudelaire would certainly have been helpful.

In his conclusion Puppe returns to his clutch of comparisons in order to argue that 'Musil's re-evaluation of leisure and idleness' hinges on Ulrich and Agathe's 'reflexiv-großstädtischer Müßiggang' ('reflexive-metropolitan idleness'), but since this conclusion is reached without reference to its wider (Marxist, existentialist) implications, and without any consideration along the way either of the flip-side of his themes (the twin problematics of *akrasia* and *action*), or of their relation to Musil's own writing practice, one cannot but wish that, like Wittgenstein's 'idling engine', it were doing rather more work.

Keeping up with Kafka

Ritchie Robertson

Franz R. Kempf, *Everyone's Darling: Kafka and the Critics of his Short Fiction* (Columbia, SC: Camden House, 1994), 128 pp., £35.00/$61.00.

Stephen D. Dowden, *Kafka's Castle and the Critical Imagination* (Columbia, SC: Camden House, 1995), 161 pp., £36.00/$63.00.

Manfred Voigts (ed.), *Franz Kafka 'Vor dem Gesetz': Aufsätze und Materialien* (Würzburg: Königshausen & Neumann, 1994), 192 pp., DM 48.

Such is the proliferation of commentary on Kafka that two of the books reviewed here are works of tertiary criticism. These 'Forschungsberichte', by Franz Kempf and Stephen Dowden, are notably brisk, agile, and dexterous studies, more pleasurable to read than most examples of their genre. Kempf, who established himself as a Kafka critic with an excellent article on *Die Verwandlung* and Expressionism (*Seminar*, 26 [1990], 327–41), has now produced a survey of Kafka criticism from the beginnings to the 1990s, referring chiefly to the shorter fiction, which will help anyone seeking a first map of this wilderness. It is in places refreshingly acerbic, especially when satirizing the inanity of deconstruction. Kempf favours commentators, like Clayton Koelb and the neglected Michel Dentan, who emphasize Kafka's artistry instead of his presumed message. The key to his art, Kempf believes, is that every proposition advanced is simultaneously withdrawn in a perpetual act of sublation ('Aufhebung'). This reformulates the familiar thesis that Kafka's texts are open to an infinite variety of readings or concretisations.

Even restricting himself to the reception of Kafka's shorter fiction, however, Kempf has taken on a task too massive to be accomplished in scarcely more than a hundred pages of text. By documenting how obediently Kafka's texts respond to every new critical fashion, Kempf is unable to describe the continuing problems to which Kafka critics give varying answers. He risks giving the unfortunate impression that Kafka criticism is merely, in Kafka's own phrase, a 'stehender Sturmlauf' ('static assault'). The limited space at his disposal obliges him to ignore editorial, philological, and biographical problems. Klaus Wagenbach and Malcolm Pasley are absent from his index. In a very unsatisfactory section, he reproduces the titles of numerous studies that seek to restore Kafka's historical context, and complains, unjustly, that 'they allow reference rather than rhetoric to gain the upper hand' (p. 99); but he does give short appreciations of the work of Mark Anderson and Rolf Goebel, who historicise Kafka with reference, respectively, to the European fin de siècle and the discourse of Orientalism. Kempf's book is admirable for reviewing pithily and often wittily an immense number of monographs and articles; but he does not prevent the diversity of Kafka criticism from seeming a little futile.

By confining himself to the reception of *Das Schloß*, Stephen Dowden has attempted less but achieved more. His accessibly and forcefully written book (enlivened by words like 'hornswoggle' and 'boondoggle') is more than a 'Forschungsbericht': it is also a judicious, stimulating, and original contribution to the understanding of Kafka as well as Kafka's critics. He follows Heinz Politzer in maintaining that 'meaning in Kafka is not so much revealed as generated, contingent on the particular constellation of text, reader, and historical circumstance' (p. 59). Dowden practises a cultural criticism that emphasises how 'historical circumstance' pushes Kafka critics into foregrounding aspects of his work and suppressing others. Thus Cold War critics in East and West stressed Kafka's affinities with the classical German tradition (Wilhelm Emrich), drew on psychoanalysis to find in him an ahistorical pursuit of the 'pure self' (Walter Sokel), or used him as a stick with which to beat a threatening and ill-understood modernism (Georg Lukács), while more recent commentators, especially in Britain and America, have responded to the new concerns of ethnicity and multiculturalism to elaborate feminist and Jewish-oriented readings. I should declare an interest by saying that, as one of the commentators discussed under this heading, I was surprised to find my work historicised within a context of which I was quite unaware while writing; but I have no quarrel with Dowden's comments, and it is salutary to be made aware of the historicity of one's own writing.

The problem of a Jewish reading of Kafka is touched on in all three books under review. Kempf surmises that German scholars find this 'a difficult, if not taboo, subject' (p. 91), and it is certainly worth remarking that in the important collection of essays on twentieth-century German-Jewish writers, *Im Zeichen Hiobs*, edited by Gunter E. Grimm and Hans-Peter Bayerdörfer (Königstein, 1985), the majority of contributors are either non-Germans or Germans who have long lived overseas, and that the article on Kafka is written by an Australian, Helen Milfull. In America, on the other hand, Kafka has been claimed by Harold Bloom as the most influential interpreter of modern Judaism. Dowden, who considers this claim at some length, finds it tempting but unprovable, and it would be difficult to dispute his own view that attempts to establish Kafka's own knowledge of Jewish tradition end in uncertainty. It is hard, for example, to ascertain what Kafka knew about the Kabbalah, especially as any knowledge he possessed must have come partly from unrecorded conversations with his friend Georg Langer, and yet the resemblances between Kabbalistic imagery and that of *Der Proceß* pointed out by the Hebraist Karl E. Grözinger in *Kafka und die Kabbala* (Frankfurt, 1992) are too striking to be easily dismissed. Kafka also read widely in the classics of Christianity – not only Kierkegaard, but also St Augustine and Pascal; and all three of his novels contain churches. He also showed an interest in the religious conceptions of the Greeks and of non-European peoples described by anthropologists. It seems that we should credit him with an eclectic (rather than syncretic) preoccupation with religion. In his later works especially, he sought to inquire into the very foundations of a religious approach to experience, and therefore could not draw on the expressive power of any traditional religious imagery.

This is the assumption behind the last and most rewarding chapter of Dowden's book, 'The Impossibility of Crows', where he addresses those aspects of *Das Schloß* that lie beyond mimetic representation. On this reading, the Castle represents not the divine but the inaccessibility of the divine, and 'the novel is about the human spirit in the postreligious era of the European mind' (p. 128). Hence its setting is frozen, paralysed, and ugly: art is no longer available as a secular substitute for transcendence or as a bridge between the earthly and the divine. The villagers are subject to an obsolete and abusive authority which they themselves sustain by internalising its domination. Moments of sublimity, however, occur in sexual experience, in simple human contact, and in the occasional imagery of light. This chapter is among the best things ever written about *Das Schloß*: so good, in fact, that it threatens to undermine the project of Dowden's book. For his account of *Das Schloß* persuades through his imaginative and careful reading of the text and his awareness of important concerns that were also Kafka's, irrespective of whatever historical circumstances may have made his insight possible.

Dowden shows by example that one can assimilate a vast quantity of commentary on Kafka and still return to the text with a fresh eye. This lesson is confirmed by the collection of essays on 'Vor dem Gesetz' edited by Manfred Voigts (along with a reproduction of the manuscript and some possible source-material), which demonstrates that the study of Kafka can make progress if critical rigour is combined with historical scholarship. The fine essay by Richard Sheppard examines previous criticism of 'Vor dem Gesetz', identifying recurrent issues and thus making his short 'Forschungsbericht' an intelligible narrative. Sheppard then suggests an ingenious and plausible explanation for the story's place in *Der Proceß*, 'as an attempt by the authorities to show K. not a mirror-image of his *actual situation* before the Law, but a mirror-image of his *perception of that situation*' (p. 28; Sheppard's italics). Sheppard has his own obsessions: he wants beards (like those of the doorkeeper and the judges) to represent 'natural, unfettered, spontaneous growth' (p. 25), forgetting that in Kafka's semiotic world beards signified age and authority; but his essay (like his book *On Kafka's Castle* [London, 1973]) is an exemplary study that restores one's confidence in the possibilities of Kafka research.

Most of the other contributions deal with the Judaic elements in 'Vor dem

Gesetz'. Here several problems arise. First: source study always suggests that Kafka's images are overdetermined. The series of doors leading to the Law are indeed strongly reminiscent of the gates leading to the Law, and guarded by accusers and advocates, in the Kabbalah, as Karl E. Grözinger points out in his essay here; but they also recall the Midrashic legend of Moses' ascent into heaven, adduced by Ulf Abraham in an essay first published in 1985 and reprinted here in revised form; and, as Rolf Goebel remarks in an extract from his forthcoming study of Kafka's Orientalism, they may have been partially suggested by a description of the Imperial Palace at Peking that also left its mark on 'Eine kaiserliche Botschaft'. It seems we can never find *the* source that would explain everything.

Second: how did Kafka acquire his Judaic knowledge? Abraham valuably lists several sources from which he could have learnt the legend of Moses in heaven; Grözinger leaves this problem vague, but does emphasise the evident importance for Kafka of the Day of Atonement with its imagery of trial which helped to inspire *Das Urteil* and probably also *In der Strafkolonie*.

Third: how did Kafka use his borrowed images? How much of their original context is relevant? What if any personal belief do his religious allusions imply? The legend's 'man from the country' is now generally understood to suggest an 'Am ha-aretz', or countryman unlearned in the Torah; but does this mean someone hostile to the Torah, which Manfred Voigts says was the meaning in the Talmudic period, or simply an uneducated man, which, according to the Hebraist Grözinger, was the term's usual meaning in nineteenth-century Eastern Europe? Gerhard Meisel, in an insufferably affected over-interpretation of doors in Kafka's work, insists on giving all religious allusions the most grandiose explication, irrespective of context; Ulf Abraham shows far more sensitivity to the tentative, riddling manner in which Kafka introduces them. As for the question of belief: Mark Anderson, discussing Judaic and Christian overtones in Kafka's clothing symbolism, is inclined to read 'Vor dem Gesetz' as a heretical attack on religious authority; Abraham, quoting Kafka's criticisms of Jewish ritual, denies that he is a religious writer at all; whereas Grözinger concludes that a writer who attacks or questions religion is still within a religious universe. No contributor, however, asks why the legend is recounted by a Christian priest in a cathedral.

Part Three
Reviews

Reviews

John Stoye, *Marsigli's Europe 1680–1730: The Life and Times of Luigi Ferdinando Marsigli, Soldier and Virtuoso* (New Haven and London: Yale University Press, 1994), xii + 356 pp., £29.95.

Apart from the pretentious main title, this is a good book, carefully researched and engagingly written. Luigi Ferdinando Marsigli was a Bolognese nobleman of relatively independent financial means who spent three decades in the Habsburg service. Starting off as a mere musketeer in 1683, he made a name for himself as a military surveyor, engineer, and negotiator during the reconquest of Hungary from the Turks. Having risen to the rank of infantry general in 1693, he was court-martialed ten years later for his role in surrendering the key imperial fortress of Breisach to the French. More than half the book deals with Marsigli's experiences in the Hungarian borderlands, where he surveyed march routes and river forges, built bridges and fortifications, assisted in the peace negotiations at Carlowitz, and then (as Leopold's boundary commissioner) established the precise course of the monarchy's southern frontier. The narrative adds somewhat to our portrait of Leopold, who appears characteristically slow but judicious, and to our understanding of the current Bosnian-Croatian frontier that Marsigli negotiated three centuries ago. It also provides a telling glimpse of Habsburg court politics that aided this distant relative of Piccolomini and Montecuccoli, but left him vulnerable after the death of his last aristocratic patron in 1699.

This book, however, is really about the frenetic activity and intellectual curiosity of an independent polymath. Marsigli impressed his superiors with his maps, geographical narratives, and analyses of the Ottoman military system. But here was also a man who purposely took roundabout routes to his next assignment, so that he could explore a different part of the earth's surface; once he had reached his destination, he devoted what spare time he had to studying and writing about the area's natural and archaeological legacy. He analysed everything, whether it was the Roman ruins of the middle Danube, fossils, plants, rocks and minerals, atmospheric pressure, the depths, currents and salinity of various bodies of water, and the marine life that they nurtured. A real-life Candide, Marsigli was everywhere and met everyone, including Louis XIV, Leopold I, Joseph I and various popes, as well as fellow scientists like Halley, Newton, and Boerhaave. When he was not serving the Habsburgs, he was a Venetian agent in Rome and Constantinople, a Christian slave in Bosnia, Clement XI's field commander in the last war ever fought between pope and German emperor. Even when he was not serving anybody, Marsigli had a knack for being in the middle of something bigger than himself. Thus he chose to study the Mediterranean waters off Toulon just in time to be accosted by a British warship participating in Prince Eugene's abortive assault on the city. In retirement he single-handedly established Bologna's celebrated Institute of Sciences.

The author does not shrink from exposing his subject's limitations. Time and again he demonstrates that Marsigli was surely a 'quarrelsome and tactless' (p. 168) fellow, whose pettiness often led him to choose conflict over conciliation. Less judicious is his suggestion that this 'virtuoso' was a dilettante, whose contributions 'were modest, if measured against the energy and idiosyncrasy that filled his days' (p. 309). This fascinating profile is assisted by splendid maps and illustrations, many of them from Marsigli's own hand. There are, however, many typographical errors, as well as some mistakes in fact, spelling, and grammar.

CHARLES INGRAO

T. C. W. Blanning, *Joseph II*, Profiles in Power (Harlow: Longman, 1994), x + 228 pp., £10.99 (paper).

Franz A. J. Szabo, *Kaunitz and Enlightened Absolutism 1753–1780* (Cambridge: Cambridge University Press, 1994), xviii + 380 pp., £22.95 (paper).

In recent years the scholarship devoted to the study of the Habsburg Monarchy in the eighteenth century has been of a remarkably high standard in terms both of the archival finds that have been revealed, the fertility of the ideas with which these discoveries have been interpreted, and the literary skill with which this large and complex polity has been made more accessible, interesting, and historically relevant to the understanding of the present day politics of Central and Eastern Europe. Gone indeed are the days when prospective research students were warned away from the Vienna archives as a multilingual morass into which the unwary would sink struggling before disappearing without trace: the works of Beales, Dickson, Evans, Ingrao and – not least – the two authors under discussion, have shown memorably what can be achieved here with a command of the essential languages, a secure sense of the broad European context within which the Habsburgs were operating, and the nuanced and inclusive understanding of the relevance of diplomatic and political history to social and economic history which is a virtual precondition of understanding the workings of this unique agglomeration of territories.

If the demands on the historian are large, so too are the interpretative questions at stake, of which two perhaps demand particular note here. The first issue – and one on which Blanning and Szabo are at variance – is whether the dynasty was embarked on a state-building process, and if so what method was most appropriate to the task. For Blanning, it was not possible for the Monarchy to become a true state because the various constituent territories were united only by their common relationship to the monarch and would never grow closer: this outcome would prevail irrespective of whether the approach adopted was the imposition of bureaucratic centralisation from above as Joseph II urged, or the cautious piecemeal pragmatism advocated by Kaunitz and to an extent implemented by him in Italy and other areas where he had a relatively free executive hand – a process which Szabo discusses in compelling detail. For Szabo, this attempt to build a state in a sense by stealth was intimately tied to the primacy of domestic policy in the calculations of the effective ruling *troika* of Maria Theresa, Joseph and Kaunitz. This second and

193

related issue is taken up by Blanning, for whom foreign policy priorities, especially the loss of Silesia and the *renversement des alliances*, are paramount in determining the domestic agenda. As crucial aspects of this process he identifies a 'dual withdrawal from Empire' (from the *Reich* to the Monarchy itself, and from the outer territories to the *Erbländer*) coupled to a reform programme in which a unified *Staatsrat* strove on broadly Cameralist principles to foster economic well-being and thus – by extension – the raising of government income. Ultimately, however, this dispute over the priority of foreign or domestic considerations in policy making is perhaps beyond final resolution when one is discussing a political entity whose hybrid structure ensured that the two would always be hopelessly commingled.

Both these books are model examples of a slightly paradoxical use of the genre of biography where the focus is on synthesis and suggestive general reflection, with the life itself providing a convenient organising prism through which an overarching interpretation of an empire may be refracted. As the first part of a two-volume study, Szabo's work is more expansive and far more detailed than Blanning's in its coverage of how Habsburg administration actually functioned. But while the importance of his study of the operations of the *Staatsrat* will be immediately apparent, it will not be until the publication of the second volume covering the last twelve years of Kaunitz's involvement in government that his larger claims surrounding the chancellor's contribution to enlightened despotism can be properly assessed. While it is surprising that Szabo does not refer more frequently to the work of Derek Beales (all the more so when on so many points their views and conclusions are similar), nevertheless, when finished, this book will certainly stand as the definitive biography, displacing the incomplete treatments by von Arneth and Klingenstein.

Blanning's shorter profile is written with the author's usual verbal panache and unerring magpie-eye for significant evidence and issues. In this sense it is an ideal book to place in the hands of students, who should be enthused by the expert combination of narrative flow and incisive analytical excursus. But there is also considerable archival work and brisk reinterpretation here for scholars to absorb and argue with. It is very refreshing to find a book amongst the literature in English that includes significant space for discussion of religious and cultural matters as well as high politics. Occasionally there is a whiff of lecture-room polemic about some of the recurrent arguments: for example, Blanning perhaps presses too far his otherwise laudable attempt to reintegrate England and Hanover into interpretations of later eighteenth-century European diplomatic perspectives. The humiliations inflicted on the Austrians by British negotiators at the end of the War of Austrian Succession remained part of the collective memory of both the Co-Regents and Kaunitz, and it must be unrealistic to castigate them for a failure to perceive the transparent virtues of alliance with England instead of with a France whom others could more easily view as increasingly unreliable and decayed in international influence.

While both these writers demonstrate how much can be achieved in

Habsburg historiography by a biographical approach, there remains the drawback that a biographer inevitably and often unintentionally prioritises the viewpoint of his subject. In this case, trying to interpret the real balance of power between Kaunitz, Joseph II and Maria Theresa and the other political players becomes sometimes like watching an unwritten play by Alan Ayckbourn with the title *The Habsburg Conquests*, which privileges in sequence the divergent perceptions of reality held by its protagonists. But perhaps that radical uncertainty is itself true to the pattern of decision-making in the curious pluralist diversity of the Habsburg polity itself.

T. J. HOCHSTRASSER

Charles Sealsfield – Karl Postl, *Austria as it is: or Sketches of continental courts, by an Eye-witness. London 1828 – Österreich, wie es ist oder Skizzen von Fürstenhöfen des Kontinents. Wien 1919*, edited by Primus-Heinz Kucher, Literatur in der Geschichte – Geschichte in der Literatur, vol. 28 (Vienna, Cologne, Weimar: Böhlau), 413 pp., 686 Sch./DM 98.

Charles Sealsfield's polemical indictment of Metternich's Austria is one of the most frequently quoted memoirs of the period. It inveighs against a despotic and hated government ('there is not a less popular government in Europe'), ruling from a capital city characterised by 'gross sensuality in the people' and 'dissoluteness among the high nobility', and suppressing liberty of expression ('a more fettered being than an Austrian author surely never existed') – in sum, a government 'which grasps with the iron claws of its emblem – the double eagle – the whole empire, and keeps it in its baneful embrace'.

The work was almost certainly written in German (probably on a visit to Germany), but no manuscripts have survived. It was first published in English in 1828, and quickly translated into French; the first German edition was an adaptation which appeared anonymously in 1834 under the title *Seufzer aus Oestreich und seinen Provinzen*. This, as Primus-Heinz Kucher shows, was probably written by Anton Johann Gross-Hoffinger (a well-known cultural journalist in Vienna who would become a prominent political commentator in the Vormärz period) and contains new material on northern Italy, based on *L'Italie sous la domination autrichienne* by Henri [Enrico] Misley; Kucher reprints the chapters concerned.

It was not until 1919 that a new German translation of Sealsfield's text by Victor Klarwill appeared, in an annotated and illustrated edition published by Schroll. In 1972 Karl J. R. Arndt published as Volume 3 of his edition of Sealsfield's complete works a facsimile reprint of the 1828 English text and of Klarwill's version, plus (also in facsimile) four early pieces of Sealsfield scholarship dating from the period 1895–1907. Only now, however, do we have an edition that locates the work in its cultural context, tracing both its publishing history and its reception. Kucher gives both the 1828 text and Klarwill's translation, adding extended annotation to the latter and indicating in the text where it deviates from the English. The texts are transcriptions of the first editions, but not facsimile reprints. How to present the 1828 text must have been a hard editorial decision, and I am not convinced that a literal transcription complete with the errors and misprints of the original was the best solution: spellings like 'Grillpatzer' ('an amiable young man') may have the charm of quaintness, but the disadvantages are that the pagination is different, and that inevitably the reset text contains further new misprints. The documentation of the reception, however, is invaluable. Kucher reprints not only nineteenth-century reviews in English and French but also all known documents relating to contemporary censorship in Austria; other material includes documentation of plans by Albert Ehrenstein (also in exile) to publish a Sealsfield edition in the 1940s. The book is rounded off by a substantial critical introduction, complete with a full apparatus of references to published scholarship, in which Kucher presents *Austria as it* is not as an evidential 'document' but in the context of contemporary travel literature, to which generically it belongs.

W. E. YATES

Eva Wagner, *An Analysis of Franz Grillparzer's Dramas: Fate, Guilt and Tragedy*, Studies in German Language and Literature 10 (Lampeter: Edwin Mellen, 1992), 253 pp., £39.95.

The main thrust of this book is that the contradictory interpretations of tragic experience we find in the history of *literary* tragedy are themselves evidence of the insoluble problem of undeserved suffering; and that the variety of rationalisations we find in Grillparzer's dramas, as well as the conflicting interpretations they have met with, are a mark of the truly tragic. Indeed, it is characteristic of the greatest tragedy not to explain away the problem, but to express it; from this comes a measure of the most tragic plays of Grillparzer, which are in the author's view *Das goldene Vliess, Des Meeres und der Liebe Wellen* and *Ein Bruderzwist in Habsburg*, precisely because there is no single idea that can explain them.

The book is in three sections, the first dealing with the definition of the tragic as outlined above, and illustrated by an historical review of the tragedy from the Greeks through to Shakespeare and Goethe; the last a conclusion which is not afraid to be polemical in addressing the varied reception accorded to Grillparzer's work; but the main interest lies in the substantial main section dealing with the dramatist's ten plays, which is terse, lucid and stimulating and fully engaged (both in the text and the notes which are conveniently at the end of each chapter) with the very extensive critical literature.

In such succinct discussions it is not surprising that there is room to disagree: not all summary judgements are avoided – for example, Bancbanus (p. 115) and Rudolf II (pp. 162, 196) are credited with more power, and therefore more guilt, than in reality they, or any one man, can possess, which is part of the tragedy of power and politics Grillparzer sees so clearly; Rudolf II is surely not the main source of the tragedy. Plays that appear to offer some kind of tragic reconciliation, such as the *Treuer Diener*, or expiation, as in *Sappho*, are thought on that account to be less than fully tragic, the author's preference being for the 'open-ended' tragedy where either no answers or contradictory ones are shown.

A problem here is that several of the explanations put forward in the plays are clearly rationalisations attributable to the settings, or religious ambience of the time (rather than to Grillparzer himself): are concepts like Fate, Chance, the Gods, etc on all fours with the 'real' factors involved, the human passions of love, ambition etc? Seen this way, there seems little reason not to regard *Sappho* as amongst the most tragic plays. Though there is much said in the book on rationalisation, this point is perhaps not as fully addressed as might be (cf. 'those, who – rather incongruously flying in the face of overwhelming evidence to the contrary – deny that there are metaphysical forces in Grillparzer's dramas', p. 208). Similarly, not all critical views are equally plausible; the author herself does not shrink from occasionally stamping some critical opinions as 'wrong'.

However, that may be, the book is a readable and often pithy account of possibly the most impressive corpus of tragedy in German literature (besides Schiller), and brings together an immense amount of information in its scholarly apparatus with a challenging argument. The bibliography is enormous and is clearly not just there (as is sometimes the case) for show.

The following misprints were noted: cathasis, p. 5; Prometheus (for Pentheus in *The Bacchae*), p.11; civlisation, p. 20; supercede, p. 38; plain (for plane) p. 111; cogence, p. 157.

RAYMOND LUCAS

Jeanne Benay, *Friedrich Kaiser (1814–1874) et le théâtre populaire en Autriche au XIXe siècle*, Contacts, Série I: Theatrica, 14, 2 vols (Berne, etc.: Peter Lang, 1993), xxiii + 957 pp., 138 SwF./DM 153.

With these two stately volumes Jeanne Benay completes the task that she began in 1989 with her edition of the extant letters by and to Friedrich Kaiser, and continued two years later with the complete bibliography of his plays. It is very largely to her credit that this interesting figure on the mid-nineteenth-century Viennese scene is now more than a mere name, and her academic trilogy seems bound to be definitive for years to come. If she were to edit a few of his comedies for publication, she would increase still further our gratitude; the plays might then even enjoy a modest theatrical revival, rather than require an explanatory footnote in Nestroy's *Der Talisman* (where Kaiser's kind of 'sad farce', the 'Lebensbild', is mocked) and his *Freiheit in Krähwinkel* (where the equivocal and opportunistic stance of the man himself is the object of ridicule).

The new monograph is thorough, even leisurely, in its approach. There are four main sections, concentrating on biography and Kaiser's literary and theatrical career; the Viennese theatre as he found it, was influenced by it, and affected it; the themes and techniques of the 'Lebens- und Charakterbild'; and the aesthetics and characteristics of this genre, Kaiser's principal innovation. There is also a tabulation of the play-titles in their original German, with the French translations that are used throughout the book (at the very least there should also have been an A to Z of the French titles, with their proper German titles attached). A lengthy bibliography (more than sixty pages) is impressive testimony to Professor Benay's wide and discriminating reading, though it could have been more clearly laid out; and there is a useful index of proper names.

The second section is in many ways the most useful for the general reader, containing as it does a wealth of chapters on administration, the Press, theatrical agencies, contracts, and censorship. It is possible to disagree here or there over points of detail – it is regrettable, for instance, that the author is content to use terms like 'Volksstück' in an uncritical, now thoroughly outmoded way. And for anyone other than a French monolinguist it will prove a cause of vexation that all play-titles are cited in the text in French translation, thus inhibiting the scholarly value of the entire project – a problem that did not occur with Benay's earlier volumes of Kaiser's correspondence and the bibliography of his dramatic output, nor with the other major French contribution to study of the Viennese Volkstheater, Roger Bauer's *La réalité, royaume de dieu* (1965). On the credit side, author and publisher have provided generous and well laid-out footnotes, which include French translations of foreign-language quotations in the main text.

Professor Benay's industry is remarkable, and no one with an interest in Viennese theatre history can fail to profit from a careful study of these two volumes, which are serviceably produced from typescript (but refuse to lie open).

PETER BRANSCOMBE

Ferrel V. Rose, *The Guises of Modesty: Marie von Ebner-Eschenbach's Female Artists* (Columbia, SC: Camden House, 1994), 213 pp., £33.50/$58.00.

Like Annette von Droste-Hülshoff, Ebner-Eschenbach is accepted into the so-called canon of literature on the basis of a small number of works. Feminist writers see this and her consequent reputation as a conservative, conciliatory writer as a distortion, and focus instead on works that articulate specifically female experiences. In this book Ferrel V. Rose examines the figures of artists for traces of Ebner-Eschenbach's consciousness of her inferior position as an Austrian woman, compelled to censor her work in order to appease male critics and an aristocratic family that feared the effect of her writing on its reputation. Rose suggests that Ebner-Eschenbach disguises, underplays and compromises with her own talent and ambition. By insisting that criticism should be impartial, Ebner-Eschenbach is obliged to shape her writing to the expectations of male readers, and while she develops a pragmatic understanding that in order to be published, she must deny herself freedom and independence, she thereby loses the opportunity to develop an individual style. According to Rose, her satirical criticism of the socialisation of women and her debate about the difficulties of combining the life of an artist with the traditional, domestic duties of a woman indicate not conciliation, but a combination of anger and anxiety.

After discussing Ebner-Eschenbach's early attempts at drama and the influence of a tradition dominated by male authors, Rose analyses a series of texts that focus on the problematic socialisation of women: the fictional travel letters, *Aus Franzensbad*; *Lotti, die Uhrmacherin*, dealing with the irreconcilable differences between art and life; the satirical pair of stories *Zwei Comtessen*; later satires such as *Die Visite, Prinzessin Leiladin, Gouvernantenbrief*; and the autobiographical *Meine Kinderjahre. She* identifies strategies like satire as acts of self-effacement, literary allusion or playing with genres as evidence of anxiety about how the works of a woman will be received, and shows how these add up to a form of emancipation that does not wholeheartedly undermine patriarchy. She also discusses Ebner-Eschenbach's use of familiar 'feminine' themes and forms, her aphorisms – many of which, as Rose says, treat the division between the sexes – and her relations with other women writers, especially Louise von François and Betty Paoli.

The problem with this approach is that, while the author sets out to correct the distortion created by selective reading, and while she points out the dangers of a biographical approach, her own selection of texts comes perilously close to blurring the distinctions between art and life. Her analyses of narrative strategies and forms do not entirely counteract this biographical slant, for they vary in quality and sometimes rely on strange generalisations, e.g. about women's writing and ideology, about women's travel writing, about the habits of male reviewers. The analysis improves as the book proceeds and the late chapter on autobiographical writings is truly illuminating. There is also a problem of presentation. Only a few titles are given in German, while every quotation from Ebner-Eschenbach's works is given in translation only. If this is merely irritating where known and accessible works are concerned, it is a disservice to the author and to scholarship to quote the unpublished papers to which Rose had access in this way.

PATRICIA HOWE

Ulrike Peters, *Richard Beer-Hofmann. Zum jüdischen Selbstverständnis im Wiener Judentum um die Jahrhundertwende*, Judentum und Umwelt 46 (Frankfurt: Peter Lang, 1993), 403 pp., DM 98.

Stefan Scherer, *Richard Beer-Hofmann und die Wiener Moderne*, Conditio Judaica 6 (Tübingen: Niemeyer, 1994), IX + 557 pp., DM 212.

The vogue of Viennese Modernism of the past two decades has largely bypassed Richard Beer-Hofmann, considered by Schnitzler the most important writer of Young Vienna. The two books under review attempt to put an end to Beer-Hofmann's marginalisation. Scherer's comprehensive and exhaustive study, destined to become a standard work in Austrian studies, does so very effectively. Peters' more limited approach yields less significant results.

Both Scherer and Peters explore Beer-Hofmann's entire oeuvre, but whereas Scherer is primarily interested in showing Beer-Hofmann's central importance in Viennese modernism and in the evolution of modernist fiction, Peters' book, written as a dissertation in comparative religious studies, almost exclusively addresses the issue of Beer-Hofmann's Jewish identity and his significance as a Jewish writer. The latter issue is not ignored by Scherer; he deals with it in his analyses of individual works, particularly of Beer-Hofmann's fragmentary biblical cycle of plays, *Die Historie von König David*, and in a subchapter on Beer-Hofmann's attitude to the 'Jewish question'. Both he and Peters agree that Beer-Hofmann's consciousness of and identification with his Jewish heritage was largely devoid of religious orthodoxy and the political implications of the Zionist movement, but whereas Peters stresses the religious component of Beer-Hofmann's Jewish identity, Scherer emphasises that Beer-Hofmann's avowal of his Jewishness rests primarily in the Jewish cultural tradition and the spiritual Zionism of Achad Haam and Martin Buber.

Peters' study should be of interest to readers who are primarily concerned with religious themes in Beer-Hofmann's works; students of Beer-Hofmann, Viennese modernism and the turn-of-the-century culture in general are better served by Scherer's book. Given Peters' focus and her expressedly stated exclusion of broader literary and cultural issues, it is hardly surprising that those familiar with Viennese modernism will find little in her book which is not already well known. Somewhat annoying is the perpetuation of certain clichés which have been refuted in recent scholarship. An all too typical example of this uncritical adoption of previously held views is the following statement: 'Bestimmend für die Atmosphäre in der oberen Wiener Mittel-schicht waren Dekadenzhaltung, Untergangsstimmung, Ästhetizismus und eine unverbindlichoberflächliche Lebensführung ohne Ernstnehmen diverser Probleme' (p. 209) (The atmosphere in the Viennese upper-middle class was marked by a decadent attitude, a mood of decline, aestheticism, and a relaxed, superficial life-style which refused to take various problems seriously).

Equally disturbing are contradictions within her argument. Peters asserts, for example, that the decadence and dandyism of the early Beer-Hofmann are indications of his assimilation (p. 68), in itself a questionable premise, only to declare unequivocally a few pages later that dandyism is 'eine Form der Selbstbehauptung des gesellschaftlichen Außenseiters' (p. 84: a form of self-affirmation by the social outsider). Beer-Hofmann's texts, quoted at length or summarised, serve primarily as materials to prove the thesis that Beer-Hofmann was the 'einzige Vertreter einer jüdischen Rückbesinnung religiöser Art im assimilierten Judentum im Wiener Fin de siècle' (p. 7: the sole representative of a religious return to Judaism amid the assimilated Jewry of the Viennese fin de siècle). In an appendix Peters publishes notes from Beer-Hofmann's 'Nachlaß' which reflect his fascination with the 'Jewish question' and the Jewish faith.

Scherer's interest in Beer-Hofmann originated in his 'Ungenügen an den vorliegenden Interpretationen des Romans *Der Tod Georgs*' (p. 6: dissatisfaction with the available interpretations of the novel *The Death of Georg*), and his study is centred on a detailed and substantive 140-page-long analysis of Beer-Hofmann's seminal work. The analysis is bracketed by a chronologically oriented and interpretive survey of Beer-Hofmann's oeuvre and a discussion of his place in the literary culture of the turn-of-the-century. Although Scherer occasionally characterises Beer-Hofmann's biblical dramas as his 'Hauptwerk' (pp. 120, 127) the thrust of his book makes it abundantly clear that for him Beer-Hofmann's significance as a modernist writer lies in *Der Tod Georgs*.

In his text-oriented, extensive and intensive reading of *Der Tod Georgs* that pays particular attention to the narrative strategies employed, Scherer argues convincingly that BeerHofmann's novel should be situated from a literary-historical point of view at the threshold of the modern German novel. Embedded as this appraisal is in a penetrating analysis of some of the major issues of the turn of the century (language scepticism, psychoanalysis, empiriocriticism, monism) and in a comparison of Beer-Hofmann's thematic and artistic concerns with those of Hofmannsthal, Schnitzler, Bahr, and Andrian among others, Scherer also succeeds in persuading the reader that *Der Tod Georgs* should be read as a text which is paradigmatic of Viennese modernism. In short, Scherer's admirable study fills a gap in our appreciation of one of the most important figures in Viennese modernism and should be read not only by those who are interested in Beer-Hofmann but also by anybody caught up in the vogue of Viennese modernism.

JENS RIECKMANN

Jürgen Nautz, Richard Vahrenkamp im Auftrag der Universität Gesamthochschule Kassel (eds), *Die Wiener Jahrhundertwende: Einflüsse, Umwelt, Wirkungen*, Studien zu Politik und Verwaltung, vol. 46 (Vienna, Cologne, Graz: Böhlau, 1993), 969 pp., DM 140/980 Sch.

This large illustrated volume collects 53 of the papers given in July 1991 at an interdisciplinary 'Symposium Wiener Moderne' at the University of Kassel. Even without all of the papers – notable exclusions are Klaus Theweleit's biographical sketch of Freud (from his *Objektwahl*) and Emil Brix's incisive exposition of the 'unmodern' factors formative of the turn of the century – the richness of a volume of this range on this theme is guaranteed. A theoretical section is followed by six others: philosophy and science, language and literature, art and architecture, music, society and politics, and 'the turn of the century elsewhere'. These conventional subdivisions may be taken as an admission that, despite the interdisciplinary competence of individuals, multidisciplinary consensus on defining such a phenomenon in a new way will remain elusive. 'Art and architecture', with papers on Max Klinger's *Beethoven* (Georg Bussmann), Klimt's *Beethoven Frieze* (Karl Schawelka) and a differentiated interpretation of Klimt's 'pictures of women' (Monika Wagner), is the section where contributors complement each other most successfully.

The editors' introduction is well supported by two surveys of research – Kurt Fischer's review of recent publications and Wolfgang Mantl's localising of modernity and his then rather hurried glance at the various 'fictions' and 'compensations' for the 'crises' which followed. Under the spell of Jacques Le Rider's *Modernity and Crises of Identity* (1993), the editors (and others) seek affinities between postmodernist plurality and negativity and Viennese modernism. But the logic which construes the city as *Gesamtkunstwerk* leads them via Norbert Leser's 'ambivalence' theory to emphasise – less controversially – the simultaneity of differing allegiances and political polarities in this supposedly depoliticised culture.

They allude to the formative tension between the battle with tradition and the 'synchronic' openness to European art (p. 41). Under the heading 'subjectivity' they link the 'empiricists' Mach and Freud with both *Jung-Wien* and Carl Menger's 'individualistic' economics. Two counter-currents to these, for which they borrow the label of convenience 'generation of 1905' (from H. S. Hughes, via David Luft), are the 'critics of universalism' and of ornament (Kraus, Loos, Wittgenstein, Schönberg) and the Expressionists (Kokoschka, Schiele). But just as this dynamic is linked to the functions of the Akademischer Verband für Literatur und Musik, other social-historical explanations are not far behind. Feminist perspectives and focus on ethnic identity problems abound, giving a necessary antidote to the 'Habsburg myth' tradition, but they bring new problems.

Inevitably the themes of death and reflection recur, for example in H. J. Schaefer's remarks on Mahler's visions of death and Elisabeth Bronfen's close interpretation of *Fräulein Else*, which studiously avoids other *Jung-Wien* references. When talking of the 'death' of the author Bronfen means 'author', too, metaphorically, as Else's '*qua* split body' (!) becomes, in death, the medium of semiotic inscription – a harmless enough theoretical paraphrase, perhaps, but without the immediacy of Schnitzler's text. Hannelore Bublitz, on 'repressed death' (!), characterises modernism *per se* as a dualism which reifies reality as 'dead' objects – an over-simplification, and a case of orbiting around other theoretical discourse, rather than exploring the cultural products which might be at issue. Perhaps taking Habermas' equation of modernism with modernity and rationality (p. 63) as the starting-point is too constricting, whereas the major problem and continued attraction of Viennese modernism is the disjunction in it between the Enlightenment tradition and new sources of creative tension (and conflict), for which Johannes Weiss uses Max Weber's concept of a 'polytheism' of value systems (p. 57). Reflecting on the fascination for such polarities and the paradoxes of self-negating insight in the wake of a crisis of reason, Weiss nevertheless warns against the postmodern tendency to treat such polarities as the insubstantial stuff of intellectual games. However, reification of the subject of discourse is precisely what characterises the hackneyed feminist phrases of, say, Brigitte Bruns ('the political occupation of the body', p. 330), in her problematising of the role of sex in Freud's private and professional relationships. Franz Eder, too, while recalling that 'repressions' in the history of culture have been reproduced by the historians' 'energy' model (p. 165), slips into this self-indulgent mode (with 'the self-affirmation of the bourgeois body' and 'the measures to maintain it', p. 171), in what is otherwise a competent résumé of the manifestations of a 'sexualised' Viennese modernism.

One of Viennese modernism's achievements was the creation of new forms or new logic from the crisis of traditional rationality, and this is explored by musicologist Adolf Nowak and in Hans Sluga's paper on Wittgenstein and architecture. Both this and Elisabeth Leinfellner-Rupertsberger on Mauthner (on nationality and language) add to our understanding of these language philosophers, but it is significant that the critique of language is now so contextualised. Hofmannsthal's *Chandos Letter*, once the obligatory source for a 'crisis of language', is nowhere mentioned, but we hear of the Habsburgs' 'hostility to language' (Achleitner, p. 577). Symptomatic of this tendency is Sigurd Scheichl's paper on Karl Kraus's image of society, where it takes an aside to point to language as Kraus's satirical touchstone. Most other mentions of Kraus in the book – possibly encouraged by Le Rider's ideological reductionism – appear like the belated revenge of 'phraseology' against the satire whose literary quality they ignore.

Werner Leinfellner situates language philosophy at the centre of the Vienna School's system of knowledge – but the interest is purely systematic, on the influences of that centre on a plethora of other disciplines. While Erhard Oeser compares Mach's and Boltzmann's epistemology, the systems model recurs in Ludwig Bress's (50-page) survey of Schumpeter and the Austrian School of National Economy and in Wolfdietrich Schmied-Kowarzik's informative account of the Philosophy Faculty at Vienna and its internal politics (especially in relation to Brentano and Jodl). His quotation from Trotzki on the Viennese coffee-houses (p. 201) indeed suggests other approaches to such systems than intellectual genealogy. Ritchie Robertson, for example, construes a singular ideological antithesis, of Freud and Pater Wilhelm Schmidt, the Roman Catholic ethnologist against whose theory of monotheism the *Moses* essay was (*inter alia*) directed, conceived as it was under the ideological pressures of Dollfuss's 'Christian' *Ständestaat*. A dynamic model is entailed in David Good's thesis of decentralised power in the hands of Austria's 'local elites' (p. 730), which is complemented by Lothar Höbelt's survey of 'conservative elites'. Edward Timms refines his (plausible) abstraction from Vienna's cultural ferment in the year 1910, a Venn diagram of intersecting 'circles', in a new version. Here he supplements them by hypothetical secondary layers, such as a 'cash-flow diagram' of patrons, another of origins, and another of the 'erotic subculture', which themselves echo questions either implicit in the Schorske model (culture as a surrogate, p. 114) or foregrounded by Eder and by Lisa Fischer's metaphorical (!) 'web' of questions about what constitutes cultural activity. However, a more far-reaching revision is Timms' comparison with the increasingly politicised late 'twenties, where the circles are being subsumed by polarised camps.

This increasing complexity is itself symptomatic of the challenge and yet difficulty of interdisciplinary research into Viennese culture at this end of century. To vary an aphorism by Kraus: the closer one looks at it, the more distant the look it returns. In the absence of a sovereign history, such asides as Höbelt's about the triangle of Austrian venues from which Franz Joseph's declaration of war emerged in 1914 suggest not just a symbolic topography but a critical potential to be found in unsystematic insights or coincidences, many pages apart, between dead metaphors of 'discourse' and social-historical 'realities'. Thus the difference between the sexual subculture's 'canalisation of bourgeois propriety' (Eder, p. 161) and the plight of Vienna's homeless *misérables* who resorted to the sewer shafts (Schwendter, p. 689) is that it is the latter subculture which proves to us that, as with 'repression', which is so often cited by theories of discourse, the system (social hygiene) which 'solves' one problem either makes it more intractable or creates another. In fact Emil Kläger's eye-witness reportage in 1908 brought that underworld literally to 'light', in slide lectures (which Schwendter does not mention). In one of the outstanding contributions of the volume, on the early Schnitzler's use of oil-lamp and other 'light' motifs, Konstanze Fliedl makes a whole series of connections in a differentiated argument about modernism's breakthrough in using and catalysing changes of perception: tracing the tensions between literature and the visual arts, genre pictures of interiors and *pleinairisme*, and criticism of family structures in the transition from naturalism to the *Jugendstil*. Another delight – which appears fragmentary outside her monograph – is Jutta Rossellit's recapitulation of Beer-Hofmann's and Hofmannsthal's verbal self-indulgence over food. Steven Beller builds on his previous work in a succinct résumé of the position of the Jewish intelligentsia.

The editors are aware of the subsequent international influence, particularly of Viennese art, music and philosophy. A very inclusive definition both of 'Viennese' and of 'turn of the century' gives the volume a potential for situating Vienna within European culture in general. This is attempted with some success in the contributions on Eastern Europe, but Wolfgang J. Mommsen routinely inspects modernism in the German Empire and misses the opportunity to relate German and Viennese modernism and to interact with other contributions on German-Austrian identity. Austro-German tensions are better focused in case studies, as in Reinhard Kapp's account of the conductor and opera director Mahler's struggle with the repertoire and public taste, a context where Kassel's claim to Mahler is not a mere formality, as it is elsewhere (p. 619).

To edit a volume of these proportions flawlessly is no doubt an insurmountable task, and the editors have done well to present so many of the papers intact, along with a useful select bibliography. Even so, some bibliographical details are missing ('Ogris', p. 679; 'Kuhlhoff', p. 874), punctuation is often rather inconsistent (Bronfen, Broucek), so is the use (or not) of different typefaces for quotations and book titles, and the headers 'Rudolf Schwendter' above Rolf Schwendter's tour below Vienna's poverty line may subvert his proletarian sympathies. It is a pity that Bussmann's paper on Max Klinger is not illustrated, and that there is no index of illustrations in the book. Grammatical errors include 'alle, die *daß* mühselig sind' (p. 540), '*der* Aufklärungspathos' (p. 714), '*unter die* konservativen Eliten zählten ...' (p. 784); misprints include 'Hygicia' (for 'Hygieia' in the title of a Klimt plate), 'Rienzie' (p. 654), 'Pesth' (p. 671), 'selbstständige' (p. 714), 'tschechoslawischen' (p. 755), 'dezitierten' (p. 763), 'Devirent' (p. 773), 'Graham Green' (p. 787), 'Herrmann Muthesius' (p. 869). Finally, the editors have in places been defeated by their authors' ignorance: Kürnberger's feuilleton 'Das Asiatische in Oesterreich' appeared not in '1891' (Maderthaner, p. 761) but in 1870; Klimt's allegory, according to Constantin Floros, is of 'Vera nuditas' (p. 615); Wolfgang Mommsen wishes us to believe that in Germany 'only' Herwarth Walden's *Der Sturm* actively promoted Expressionism (p. 874), that 'Herbert' (instead of Otto) Brahm revolutionised the Berlin stage, and describes Wedekind's tragedy of adolescent sexuality as 'sein Lustspiel *Frühlings Erwachen*, mit ihrer scharfen Kritik am Kommerzialismus der bürgerlichen Alltagswelt' (p. 880); a Freudian misprint crowns Isabella Ackerl's trivial paper on Viennese salons, appropriating the German poet Richard 'Demel' (p. 702) thus as a Viennese *patissier*.

While the editors announce re-evaluations of what, in Vienna, was progressive, traditionalist, or reactionary, of what was reality or dream (p. 24), the overall gain is rather of individual insights and general knowledge than of any new consensus in defining Viennese modernism. Despite the varied methodologies, the volume reflects neither a vigorous debate between the participants – an exception is Schwendter's jibe at David Good (p. 684) – nor a clear, decisive departure from the achievements of the 1980s, which it synthesises and recapitulates in such impressive breadth.

GILBERT J. CARR

Paul Stefanek, *Vom Ritual zum Theater. Gesammelte Aufsätze und Rezensionen* (Vienna: Edition Praesens, 1992), 468 pp., 495 Sch.

In these nineteen collected essays by Paul Stefanek, who died young in 1988 having built an international reputation as a scholar and as a university teacher in Austria, Great Britain and the United States, three figures of twentieth-century theatre dominate: Max Reinhardt, Robert Musil and Hugo von Hofmannsthal. No Reinhardt scholar can overlook with impunity the detailed detective work in periodicals, newspapers and longer studies behind the first three essays on Reinhardt's explosive impact on the British stage. Occasionally serious intent misses the sharp humorous edge of some adverse comments by British critics, but the account of Reinhardt's huge productions predating the Cecil B. de Mille heyday of Hollywood films is both informative and entertaining. The analysis of Musil's critical essays on theatre is a model of academic enquiry, where more questions than might seem possible are asked and clear distinctions made between the theatre practices of Artaud, Brecht and Musil. This is supported by illuminating studies of Musil's farce *Vinzenz* and of the so-called 'Lesedrama' as revived in modern productions. Stefanek's well-documented attempt to define the parameters of 'Stationendramen' is at first sight impressive. Yet many might wish to extend the outer self-reflective form to the inner vacuousness of Schnitzler's *Reigen,* or to the deliberate dialectics of Toller's *Masse Mensch* and to Brecht's categorical open-ended *Der gute Mensch von Sezuan.* Stefanek's argumentation deliberately restricts formal definition, thus making a typically vague literary label useful but also closing off reconsideration of many potential examples. The central essay 'Vom Ritual zum Theater' that extends the arguments of Stefanek's Habilitation doctorate is a scholarly account of research on the ritual of primitive societies as a background to the development of modern theatre. Consciousness of illusion and awareness of aesthetic distance form the dividing factor – or, as he points out, primitive man without knowing it was intimately involved with acting out theatre. The essays on Hofmannsthal, especially on *Der Schwierige,* reinstate accepted research findings (with particular reference to the mechanics of comedy) and relate the problems of language to the background of war, using Kraus's *Die letzten Tage der Menschheit* and Schnitzler's *Komödie der Verführung* as effective foils.

These essays and the nine reviews (whose hallmarks include asking challenging questions and providing clear assessments of each book's scholarly value) form a fitting tribute to a major contributor to theatre studies. In particular, his long appreciation of Erika Fischer-Lichte's *Semiotik des Theaters* (Tübingen, 1983) not only sums up the argument in her three volumes, but also points out its implications for an understanding of the mechanics of theatre performance and its reception. Stefanek's wide-ranging interests allowed him to draw meaningful comparisons between writers of the generation of Hofmannsthal and Musil and of those of today such as Handke, Jandl or Strauss where the primacy of performance over the dramatic text as an object solely of literary study is all-important. As Brigitte Marschall explains in the Foreword, Paul Stefanek's combination of 'Ekstase' and 'Arbeit' produced an endless process of self-enquiry reflected in the range and detailed knowledge of these essays.

BRIAN KEITH-SMITH

Ulrike Lang, *Mordshetz und Pahöl. Austriazismen als Stilmittel bei Karl Kraus,* Innsbrucker Beiträge zur Kulturwissenschaft: Germanistische Reihe 48 (Innsbruck: Institut für Germanistik 1992), 178 pp., 288 Sch./DM 48.

The stated aim of this book is to investigate Kraus's use of Austriacisms in three of his collected works: *Literatur und Lüge* (1987), *Sittlichkeit und Kriminalität* (1987), *Untergang der Welt durch schwarze Magie* (1989). The term 'Austriacisms' is broadly defined to include linguistic features which are found in the Southern German area. It is a fascinating subject and the title of the book aptly captures the crux of the issue; *Mordshetz* and *Pahöl* can be translated into 'Hochdeutsch' as *Riesenspaß* and *Wirbel* respectively, but to do so is to lose the essential flavour conveyed by the Austrian terms. Though the descriptive meaning is the same, the connotative meaning is quite different. Lang attempts to tackle this difference by setting up a model of stylistic meanings, considering not only those connotations which are intrinsic to the lexeme (e.g. *Rotzbuben*), but also how stylistically neutral words can become marked within a specific context.

The title of the book is, unfortunately, the best thing about it. Despite devoting a third of the work to discussing models of stylistic meaning, Lang's analysis is seriously weakened by the absence of a social component in her own model.

Firstly, the distinction between 'Dialekt' and 'Umgangssprache' is not adequately drawn. Secondly, the fact that the use of dialect in Austria correlates with social class – a correlation which was even greater in Kraus's day – is ignored, and with it an undeniable element of social élitism in Kraus's satire. This leads to an extraordinarily contorted analysis of the stylistic effect of employing socially marked features. Indeed, so anxious is she to avoid any mention of social class that she adopts the kind of approach which gives political correctness a bad name. Lang makes no mention of the low social status of dialect speakers, nor of the fact that Kraus clearly associates an inability to speak *Hochsprache* with stupidity or at least a lack of formal education. In consequence, Lang's analysis of the use of dialect in the following passage involves drawing a complex and unconvincing parallel between speaking dialect and being opposed to architectural functionalism:

> Eines Tages ... riß es an der Klingel. ... es war ... ein Mann, der ganz echauffiert mir zurief: 'Schaun S' zum Fenster außi!' Ich erwiderte, daß es in meinem Hof Gottseidank nichts zu sehen gebe, worauf er unwillig versetzte: 'Was, Sie wohnen gar nicht auf die Straßen?' Ich: 'Nein, was ist denn geschehn?' Er: 'Die Parteien, die was auf die Straßen wohnen, sollen außischaun!' 'Ja, warum denn?' ''s Haus wird photographiert!'

Lang claims that the use of *Hochsprache* corresponds to the idea of the functional object undistorted by decorations ('dem Gedanken vom funktionalen, nicht durch Verzierungen verunstalteten Objekt', p. 77). This is an odd conclusion to reach, not least because educated language is usually regarded as being the more ornamental and aesthetically pleasing variety. Yet the immediately obvious interpretation is that the man who is so excited about the house being photographed is a fool, and the fact that he speaks dialect merely confirms this, in contrast with Kraus, who not only remains coolly unexcited in the midst of this absurd hullabaloo, but expresses his superior attitude in cool, superior language.

Having analysed the stylistic effect of a handful of Austriacisms, Lang concludes that where Kraus uses dialect forms in an otherwise exclusively literary passage, the sudden shift in style serves as an 'Ironiesignal'; where he quotes Austriacisms in direct speech, he emphasises linguistic contrasts and brings a greater liveliness to the scene. Most usefully, she suggests that Kraus frequently uses stylistically marked Austriacisms as a form of *erlebte Rede*, presenting the point of view of the Viennese public. Since Kraus holds the

Viennese public in contempt, this use of such words serves to indicate the contempt he feels for the person or issue he is satirising. Lang's conclusions are thus not profoundly enlightening, and the crucial question of the different stylistic functions of socially marked dialectal Austriacisms and socially unmarked Austriacisms from *Umgangssprache* is never addressed.

VICTORIA MARTIN

Jennifer E. Michaels, *Franz Werfel and the Critics*, Literary Criticism in Perspective (Columbia, SC: Camden House, 1994), 178 pp., £35.00.

The series *Literary Criticism in Perspective* edited by James Hardin (South Carolina) and published by Camden House is a welcome aid to literary scholarship and the present volume by Jennifer E. Michaels on *Franz Werfel and the Critics* is no exception.

Divided into five chapters, it deals with Werfel's poetry, dramas and prose as well as with 'Geography and Culture' and his 'Religious and Political Thinking'. This study of the critical literature on Werfel arrives at a time of a resurgence of interest in the work of this controversial writer which started during the mid-eighties. The chronological list of critical works discussed gives a clear indication of this. There are no signs of the interest abating. Since the conclusion of the author's list, a collection of papers from the American Symposium at the State University of New York has been published under the title *Unser Fahrplan geht von Stern zu Stern*, edited by J. P. Strelka and Robert Weigel (Berne, 1992). And we can look forward no doubt to the publication of the papers given at a recent Symposium in France (organised by the Werfel scholar Michel Reffet).

Jennifer E. Michaels illuminates very well the history of Werfel criticism from the early adulatory days, showing that even later critics have found it almost impossible to avoid a strongly personal and subjective view. It is interesting to read her account of the contradictory evaluations of, for example, Werfel's poetry, especially when it comes to its aesthetic qualities, or the relative merits of his later in comparison to his earlier poetry. One is not surprised to read the widely diverging views about such works as the drama *Bocksgesang* or even about the symbolism of *Jacobowsky und der Oberst*. It is, however, fascinating to learn how Werfel himself changed his mind about the interpretation of such an apparently straightforward story as *Der Tod des Kleinbürgers* and how this is reflected in contradictory interpretations by the critics, one seeing the protagonist as an heroic figure (victory of spirit over body), the other considering him a representation of the 'philistine mentality of the petite bourgeoisie' detested and ridiculed by Werfel.

The author makes us aware how the emphasis in Werfel criticism has been largely on his ideas. She points out areas where there are gaps in the critical response to his work: the need for an edition of his letters, for example, or a new and comprehensive study of his dramas and an even greater need for a thorough study of his poetry.

It is very clear from this study that Werfel's strange mixture of styles, his apparent conservatism in form and ideology, his divided allegiance between Judaism and Christianity, just like his mixture of mysticism and irony, are still puzzling his readers. The book is always penetrating and clearly written. It is generally a very useful work of criticism and will be an indispensable tool for anyone interested in the study of Franz Werfel.

LOTHAR HUBER

Darius Gray Ornston (ed.), *Translating Freud* (New Haven and London: Yale University Press, 1992), 272 pp., £22.50.

The Complete Correspondence of Sigmund Freud and Ernest Jones 1908–1939, edited by R. Andrew Paskauskas with an Introduction by Riccardo Steiner (Cambridge, MA. and London: The Belknap Press of Harvard University Press, 1993), 880pp., £29.95.

Over the past fifteen years or so, a complex set of interrelated studies has developed for which we have so far lacked a word. It includes not only psychoanalysis but linguistics, biography, hermeneutics, history – of science, of late nineteenth-century Austro-Hungarian society, of the Jewish diaspora after 1933, together with the skills of literary criticism, good editing and – not least – diplomacy. Professor Jean Laplanche, bold as ever with new coinages, has supplied it: Freudology. For though in its modern modifications psycho-analysis is still a flourishing mode of therapy and way of understanding ourselves in the world, in its origins it has become historical, in its develop-ment it has become an institution, and in its dissemination it has passed through the filters of new languages, new mind-sets and new purposes. Nothing requires such a range of disciplines for its study nor registers these shifts more clearly than the passage of Freud's collected writings (1893–1939) through the language-grid of James Strachey's English translation, the great *Standard Edition of the Complete Psychological Works of Sigmund Freud* (1953–66).

This has come increasingly under scrutiny from intellectual historians, literary scholars and analysts themselves, who have learned not to read translations as transparent: the very strengths of Strachey's edition, its clarity and consistency, are an imposition upon a set of ideas which in their founder's hands were evolving and dynamic rather than fixed and finished. The Standard Edition's more questionable characteristics – the technical-scientist nature of some of its neologisms, its conceptualisation of the mind in terms of structure rather than of organisation, its sheer massive presence in the world's lingua franca – have to do with political developments within and without psychoanalysis as an institution: with Ernest Jones's pioneering eagerness 'to keep our movement strongly scientific, for that will greatly increase its "respectability"' (to Freud, 10.12.1908), and with his efforts to make London as much a centre of official psychoanalysis as Vienna – something which events after the Anschluss of 1938 accelerated in ways beyond any institu-tional ambition.

Among the contributors to this volume, Darius Ornston, as a professor of psychiatry, came to the problem of the Standard Edition's stylistic and ideological colouring from his dissatisfaction with its rendering of specific Freudian concepts and verbal clusters; Patrick Mahoney, a professor of English and a practising analyst, from his sense of the importance of the indeterminacy and procedural nature of Freud's thinking – and syntax; Jean Laplanche and his colleagues Andre Bourguignon and Pierre Cotet, a Germanist, from their work on the entirely new French translation, the *Oeuvres Complètes*.

Ornston, who contributes four of the nine essays in this collection, is a courteous critic who respects Strachey's integrity, and aims not so much to replace the Standard Edition as to improve it, with a finer sense of historical relativities, multiple criteria and possible alternatives. There are indeed obstacles to a new version. Alex Holder gives an account of the first: the absence of an authoritative source-text. There is as yet no historical-critical edition of Freud's *really* complete work in *German*. Ornston himself enumerates the problems of scattered copyrights, papers destroyed, texts silently corrected, over-protective archives and what he dryly calls 'the long and intact tradition of closed sources and controlled leaks in psychoanalytic studies' (p. 213). Indeed the book ends with a short Appendix compiled by Ornston and Mahoney of indexes and lists of necessary research materials, the first page of which lists what is available, the second what is desirable – but is not.

But, as the title indicates, the Standard Edition is by no means this book's only issue. It foregrounds more general theoretical problems of translating: of authority, interpretation, strangeness, the increasingly qualified nature of 'faithfulness'. But its strength is that these general issues are attached with tremendous intelligence and scholarship to a particular instance who presents distinctive problems of specific conceptualisation and style. *Translating Freud* is about translating *Freud* – who *matters*.

The debate has tended to polarise between two positions: one which recognises that the processes of editing and translating are unavoidably all of a piece with interpreting, that the purpose they serve is the need of the time; and on the other hand one which aims at an informed equivalence. The first has been put more strongly elsewhere, notably by Alex Hoffer.[1] It is represented here, though in more muted form, by Helmut Junker, who argues Freud's historicity – and that of his translators – and the need for many Freuds. Mahony suggests a translation with footnotes where the words repressed in translating's unavoidable selecting may be restored. Inga Villarreal, comparing the two Freuds in Spanish by Lopez-Ballesteros from the 1930s and by Etscheverry in the 1940s, shows how much they were affected by the spirit of their respective times. 'But', she adds, 'I think the late twentieth-century psychoanalytic zeitgeist favours more literal translation' (p. 133). This brings us close to the second position. This is given pride of place in a long and powerfully-argued article by Jean Laplanche and his colleagues, who set out from their own aims as makers of a new rendering unburdened by the presence of a strong predecessor. As they argue it, they are staking a highly-charged political and theoretical claim: they aim at 'rigorous faithfulness' to convey 'the text, the whole text and nothing but the text' (p. 143), including its indeterminacies and ambiguities, but in the form of a new text composed within the constraints and possibilities of the French (potentially Freud's French) language, a new idiolect as distinctive – as 'alien' – in its terms as Freud's was in his. It is a tremendously ambitious undertaking, close in kind to Goethe's category of those rare translations which function in their host culture not instead of the original text but in their stead. Its ambition is to override the relativities and the obstacles which give the other contributors pause.

There is no doubt that this collection offers a discussion at a high level of scholarship, analysis and engagement on a key issue for the history and the sense of present identity of psychoanalysis. But it is a late issue raised by historical hindsight. The thirty-year-long correspondence between Freud and Ernest Jones, on the other hand, is a wonderfully rich record of a professional and personal relationship from the early history of the movement itself as lived and represented to each other by its founder and his first British disciple. Their view of how 'the cause' was to develop was a matter of moving forward in the dark of time, not of reflecting on their own historicity: of Freud's continued exploration and creativity and Jones' political shrewdness and institutional inventiveness. It is remarkable how early in their relationship the eager young neurologist saw the importance of translation as *the* means of spreading the Word, and how clearly he perceived the difficulties, institutional as much as linguistic, to be overcome. Freud tended to take the whole thing more lightly: from the start he urged Jones not to be diverted from his real work by it, and even after the achievements of Jones's team in producing the *Collected Papers* of 1924 and 1925, admitted to Jones, then in the middle of complicated negotiations with American publishers, that 'the whole topic of English and American translations is, so to speak, on the periphery of my interest' (15 February 1927).

But Jones' energies were spent in making the peripheral central. His letters report the making of the new conceptual vocabulary which, now that it is old, sends Ornston back to re-read the German texts. A very early letter of Freud's of 20 November 1908, for example, offers a possible multivalent rendering of 'Besetzung' as 'interest' long before it became a bone of contention.[2] Jones sends Freud a copy of 'our Glossary' for comment; he had already sent him James Strachey as a patient; he gradually brings together a team of competent translators – though he had to call on Freud's diplomacy to mend his stormy relations with Joan Riviere; he supervises the Stracheys' work – often to James's irritation with the interfering ways of that 'little beast';[3] he finds a long-term English publisher (Leonard Woolf's Hogarth Press); staves off pirated editions (the first compiled by Freud's American nephew Edward Bernays); sees the texts through the press. And all this as well as the Congresses, as well as the creation of the famous 'Committee' and of the national and International Associations, as well as negotiating a path of his own between the defections and disruptions from Jung to Ferenczi, as well as his practical care for Freud in the aftermath of the First World War and the prelude to the Second, as well as his own writing and the analyses in the consulting-room. (And outside it: some of the personal comments on patients sound horrendously indiscreet and enjoyable.) Freud's tribute to Jones's efforts is as true as it is both gracious and ironical:

> So, is it really twenty years since you joined the cause? You have really made the cause quite your own, for you have achieved everything that could be made of it: a society, a journal, and an institute. What you have meant to it may be left to historians to ascertain (20 November 1926).

That is precisely what these two books in their different ways are about.

JOYCE CRICK

1. A. Hoffer, 'Can there be translation without interpretation?' *Int. Rev. Psychoanal.*, 16 (1989), 207–12.
2. For a defence of Strachey's choice of 'cathexis', see the editors' Epilogue to *Bloomsbury/Freud. The Letters of James and Alix Strachey*, edited by Perry Meisel and Walter Kendrick (New York, 1985), p. 319.
3. James to Alix Strachey, 9 October 1924, objecting to Jones' preference for rendering 'das Es' by 'the Id', *Bloomsbury/Freud*, p. 83.

Allyson Fiddler, *Rewriting Reality: An Introduction to Elfriede Jelinek* (Oxford and Providence, RI: Berg, 1994), xiii + 184 pp., £34.95.

This is the first monograph dedicated to Jelinek in English, and will doubtless prove an essential undergraduate introduction to this most outspoken and yet paradoxically elusive of writers: an Austrian with Marxist affiliations and an Yves Saint-Laurent wardrobe, a critic of the 'culture industry' who is addicted to TV soaps, a feminist who sets out to write pornography, a *Heimatdichter* who has been effectively banished from the Austrian stage. The study covers Jelinek's major works from the experimental novel *wir sind lockvögel baby!* (1970) to the controversial piece of anti-pornography *Lust* (1989), with useful pointers to some of the drama and lesser-known sketches and essays. As well as providing a clear exposition of the major thematic concerns of Jelinek's texts, Fiddler also sets out to situate them in their theoretical and historical context, with elegant accounts of feminist theory, Austrian literary tradition, and social and political history. The great strength of the study, however, is that it does not get side-tracked by the spectacular contradictions of the biography (ones which Jelinek of course nurtures to best effect), but concentrates on Jelinek the writer. The particular focus is her fraught relationship with a 'realist' tradition, and her development of what Fiddler would call 'supra-realism'.

A useful starting point is a comment by the narrator in the 1972 text, *Michael. Ein Jugendbuch für die Infantilgesellschaft*: 'in WIRKLICHKEIT geht es nicht so krass zu. in wirklichkeit ist es schlimmer'. Jelinek's aim is to destroy the notion of unmediated or objective 'REALITY' and to expose those patterns of oppression, particularly of class or of gender, which covertly inform and construct our understanding of the 'natural' or 'real'. This has little to do with GDR socialist realism, however; and comrades in Austria have been known to lament the decadence, pessimism, and apparent cynicism of Jelinek's texts. For in abandoning a traditionally mimetic representation in favour of a kind of specific and 'concentrated' reality, Jelinek in fact serves us up with an unmitigated catalogue of ugliness, brutality, perversion and ignorance.

This exaggerated emphasis is intended to debunk the 'myths' generated by patriarchal capitalist society: the 'culture industry', 'work, class and the everyday', 'nature and *Heimat*', and 'sex and subjectivity' (to borrow the thematic categories which shape Fiddler's account). This kind of literary method must involve a sophisticated balancing act if a writer is to avoid the danger of re-inscribing all those 'myths' s/he is aiming to expose, or (equally risky) of becoming locked into an unproductive 'anti-stance': *Michael* as 'anti-*Bildungsroman*', *Oh Wildnis, oh Schutz vor ihr* as 'anti-*Heimatroman*' and *Lust* as 'anti-pornography', etc. At her best Jelinek pulls it off with spectacular success. She mimics and parodies all kinds of discourses – from Kafka to quiz shows, from Mills and Boon to Bataille; these are then satirized by means of an archly intrusive meta-commentary, which is itself simultaneously undermined and dispersed. Elsewhere, however, she is less effective, and the method suddenly seems crude or simply too relentlessly the same.

Jelinek stands or falls on the sophistication and control of her linguistic sense; and one of the disadvantages of the thematic organisation of Fiddler's study is that analysis of Jelinek's method and language sometimes becomes secondary. It might be useful, for example, to get to grips with what Alexander von Bormann has called 'metonymisation of allegory' in Jelinek's early texts; to get closer to the source of Jelinek's grim humour; to trace the over-laid and unstable narrative perspectives; or even to face head-on the revulsion – and the perverse pleasure – which some of these texts inspire. Equally the author might have made more of Jelinek's work as a corrective to the overtly confessional mode which has dominated 'women's writing' since the 1970s, and has become a cherished fall-back position for for those attempting to define a 'feminine' or even a 'feminist aesthetic'.

But Fiddler will doubtless continue to expand on some of these issues in other contexts. This is the first in a new series of volumes to be published by Berg, which aims to introduce 'New Directions in European Writing' to an undergraduate audience. It is a stimulating and exciting beginning.

KAREN LEEDER

Joseph P. Strelka, *Zwischen Wirklichkeit und Traum: Das Wesen des Österreichischen in der Literatur*, Edition Orpheus 9 (Tübingen: Francke, 1994), 332 pp., DM 84.

In these essays Joseph Strelka returns to a theme he first adumbrated nearly thirty years ago in *Brücke zu vielen Ufern. Wesen und Eigenart der österreichischen Literatur* (1966). In the meantime much water has flowed under the bridge, but the book fails to reflect this as thoroughly as it might have. The 1970s and 1980s saw many contributions to the debate on the 'Austrian' tradition, not to mention earlier classics like Magris's *Der habsburgische Mythos in der österreichischen Literatur* and Walter Weiss's riposte in the *Deutsche Vierteljahresschrift* (1969). Both demand more than the passing mention accorded to them here. On the other hand, it is instructive to be reminded of Oskar Benda's pioneering study *Die österreichische Kulturidee* (1936), according to Strelka the first serious and scholarly attempt to pinpoint the peculiarly Austrian quality.

Summed up rather crudely, Strelka regards this quality or 'Eigenart' as being determined by its admixture of Germanic and 'foreign' elements, and an acute awareness of the shifting line between dream and reality. Following Benda, he attempts to summarise 'Die kulturmorphologische Struktur der österreichischen Literaturtradition' (pp. 3–18), concluding that the development of Austrian literature has four determining phases. First comes the feudal period, culminating in Walther von der Vogelweide's great lament for time past and his blurring of dream and reality. Then we have the Renaissance, with the emergence of a specific 'Humanitas austriaca', and Josephinism, 'eine vielfach mißverstandene und sehr österreichische Erscheinung' (p. 12). Finally there is the period after the collapse of the monarchy, encompassing the First and Second Republics 'sowie das dazwischenliegende kurze Zeitstück von Nationalsozialismus und Exil' (p. 14).

I suspect there will be some readers unable to accept such a framework. If there is a relationship between the Austrian 'idea' in literature and the existence of an Austrian 'identity' (as surely there must be), then the post-1918 period in particular demands a more differentiated approach than this. It is symptomatic of Strelka's difficulty with the complex identities of the modern era (which of course included the proscription of the very word 'Austria' between 1938 and 1945) that of eighteen essays on individual authors and works, the most modern contribution is on Celan, and before that Broch's *Bergroman*. Other essays range from the Renaissance to Joseph Roth, via Grillparzer, Sealsfield, Saar and the unjustifiably neglected Otto Stoessl.

Although I hesitate to criticise this work on the grounds of what it fails to do, the topic surely demands room for Doderer's attempts after 1945 to define/construct an Austrian identity through the medium of the novel, and for Thomas Bernhard's swingeing demolition of 'Austrianness' in *Auslöschung* (1986). Whatever one's reactions to him, Bernhard is too central to the debate on Austrian identity in life and literature to be ignored. From an earlier period the same could be said of Karl Kraus. He, however, only figures in an otherwise level-headed chapter on 'Jung Wien' which suddenly and meretriciously attacks present-day feminists who have lost sight of 'die Entwicklung weiblicher Eigenart und Größe' in order to promote 'die Quota weiblicher Traktorenfahrer und Luftwaffenoffiziere'. This paragraph then parades a touchingly anachronistic fear of a 'new wave' of literature-loathing left-wing radicals, comparable with Ottokar Stauf von der March 'lediglich mit geänderten ideologischen Vorzeichen' (p. 191).

Perplexing in a different way is the essay entitled 'Der Offizier in der österreichischen Literatur. Drei Hauptaspekte und ihre breite Skala' which delivers a stream of examples from such pens as Karl Emmerich, Robert Bayer, Karl von Torresani, Viktor Freiherr von Reisner and Rudolf Jeremias Kreutz but can only manage a lame résumé of Schnitzler's immortal cad Leutnant Gustl. Here, of course, is a figure singularly unwilling to separate reality from fantasy, in a work whose technical innovativeness must be seen as an integral element of what is specifically Austrian in the stream of modern German letters. There is also something recognisably Austrian in Gustl's relentless misogyny and anti-Semitism, but these are aspects of the culture with which the book mostly prefers not to grapple. It is this missing dimension, this absence of disquiet with very real issues in 'das Wesen des Österreichischen' in both literature and in life, which ultimately means that the book promises more than it delivers.

ANDREW BARKER

Notes on Contributors

MARK M. ANDERSON is Professor of German at Columbia University and author of *Kafka's Clothes* (Oxford University Press, 1992).

ANDREW BARKER is Senior Lecturer in German at Edinburgh University. He is author of *Telegrams from the Soul: Peter Altenberg and the Culture of Fin-de-Siècle Vienna* (Camden House, 1996) and co-author, with Leo A. Lensing, of *Peter Altenberg: Rezept die Welt zu sehen* (Braumüller, 1995).

STEPHANIE BIRD is a Lecturer in German at University College London.

PETER BRANSCOMBE is Emeritus Professor of Austrian Studies at the University of St Andrews. His most recent book is *Mozart: Die Zauberflöte* in the Cambridge Opera Handbooks series (1991), and he is one of the editors of the new critical edition of Nestroy.

GILBERT J. CARR is Lecturer in Germanic Studies at Trinity College, Dublin, and the author of numerous articles on Kraus and his contemporaries.

JOYCE CRICK has recently retired as Senior Lecturer in German at University College London. She has published studies of Thomas Mann, Christa Wolf, and literary translation.

IAN FOSTER is a Lecturer in German at Salford University and author of *The Habsburg Army in Austrian Fiction* (Lang, 1992).

T. J. HOCHSTRASSER is a Lecturer in the Department of International History at the London School of Economics and has published several articles on eighteenth-century European political thought.

PATRICIA M. HOWE is Senior Lecturer in German at Queen Mary and Westfield College London and author of studies of Fontane, Saar, Droste-Hülshoff and others.

LOTHER HUBER is Lecturer in German at Birkbeck College London. He edited *Franz Werfel: An Austrian Writer Reassessed* (Berg, 1989).

CHARLES INGRAO is Professor of History at Purdue University. His most recent books are *The Hessian Mercenary State* (Cambridge University Press, 1987) and *The Habsburg Monarchy 1618–1815* (Cambridge University Press, 1994).

BRIAN KEITH-SMITH is Senior Lecturer in German at Bristol University. He has published numerous articles on Hofmannsthal, Werfel, Expressionism, and post-war Austrian literature, and edited *German Women Writers 1900–1933* (Edwin Mellen, 1993).

DUNCAN LARGE is a Lecturer in German at University College of Swansea. He has published several articles on Musil and is currently working on a longer study.

KAREN LEEDER is Fellow in German at New College, Oxford, and author of *Breaking Boundaries: A New Generation of Poets in the GDR* (Oxford University Press, 1996).

RAYMOND LUCAS is Fellow in German at Brasenose College, Oxford; his main interests include Kleist, Nietzsche, and Thomas Mann.

VICTORIA MARTIN is a Fellow of St Anne's College, Oxford, and University Lecturer in German Linguistics; she has a particular interest in the German language as spoken in Austria.

R. C. OCKENDEN is Fellow in German at Wadham College, Oxford. He has published many articles on Goethe and Stefan George and is working on a book on Theodor Storm.

ANDREA REITER, Research Fellow at the University of Southampton, has a doctorate from Salzburg and has published articles on Kafka, Bernhard, Aichinger, Austrian antimodernity, and concentration-camp memoirs. Her book on the latter subject, *'Auf daß sie entsteigen der Dunkelheit'. Die literarische Bewältigung von KZ-Erfahrung,* was published by Löcker Verlag in 1995.

JENS RIECKMANN is Professor of German at the University of California, Irvine. His publications include *Aufbruch in die Moderne. Die Anfänge des Jungen Wien* (1985) and studies of Thomas and Heinrich Mann, Hofmannsthal, Bahr, narrative theory, and related topics. He is currently working on a book on Hofmannsthal and George and a critical biography of the young Hofmannsthal.

RITCHIE ROBERTSON is Fellow and Tutor in German at St John's College, Oxford, and author of *Kafka: Judaism, Politics, and Literature* (Oxford University Press, 1985; German translation published by Metzler, 1988).

JEFFREY L. SAMMONS is Professor of German at Yale University. His many books include *Heinrich Heine: A Modern Biography* (Princeton, 1979) and *Wilhelm Raabe and the Fiction of the Alternative Community* (Princeton, 1987).

SIMON TYLER did research on Canetti at Oxford and now works for a legal firm in London.

MARTHA WÖRSCHING is a Lecturer in German at Loughborough University. She has published articles on Joseph Roth and on the German media.

W. E. YATES is Professor of German at Exeter University. His books include *Grillparzer* and *Nestroy* (both published by Cambridge University Press in 1972) and *Schnitzler, Hofmannsthal, and the Austrian Theatre* (Yale, 1992), and he is one of the editors of the new critical edition of Nestroy.

Austrian Studies

Acknowledgements: The Editors gratefully acknowledge the support of the Austrian Institute in London. Thanks are also due to the colleagues listed below for their willingness to serve on the Advisory Board.

Advisory Board: Andrew Barker (Edinburgh), Peter Branscombe (St Andrews), Amy D. Colin (Pittsburgh), R. J. W. Evans (Oxford), Sander L. Gilman (Cornell), Murray G. Hall (Vienna), Leo A. Lensing (Wesleyan), Jacques Le Rider (Paris), Eda Sagarra (Dublin), W. G. Sebald (East Anglia), Joseph Peter Strelka (New York), Robert Wistrich (Jerusalem), W. E. Yates (Exeter).

Books for review should be sent to Ritchie Robertson, St John's College, Oxford OXI 3JP, England.

Manuscripts for publication should be submitted in duplicate to Edward Timms, Arts Building, University of Sussex, Brighton BNI 9QN, England.

Guidelines: Articles should be written in English and should not exceed 7,500 words. They should be typed double-spaced, using endnotes (not a numbered bibliography) to identify the source of quotations. Quotations should normally be given in the original language, followed by an English translation. A detailed style sheet is available from either of the Editors, on request.

Austrian Studies may be ordered through any bookshop. Since it is an annual publication, it may also be obtained by subscription direct from the publishers, Edinburgh University Press, 22 George Square, Edinburgh EH8 9LF, Scotland.

11